# POWER ON THE INSIDE

# POWER
## ON THE
# INSIDE

## A GLOBAL HISTORY OF
## PRISON GANGS

## MITCHEL P. ROTH

REAKTION BOOKS

Published by Reaktion Books Ltd
Unit 32, Waterside
44–48 Wharf Road
London N1 7UX, UK
www.reaktionbooks.co.uk

First published 2020
Copyright © Mitchel P. Roth 2020

Printed and bound in Great Britain
by TJ Books Limited, Padstow, Cornwall

A catalogue record for this book is available from the British Library

ISBN 978 1 78914 323 2

# CONTENTS

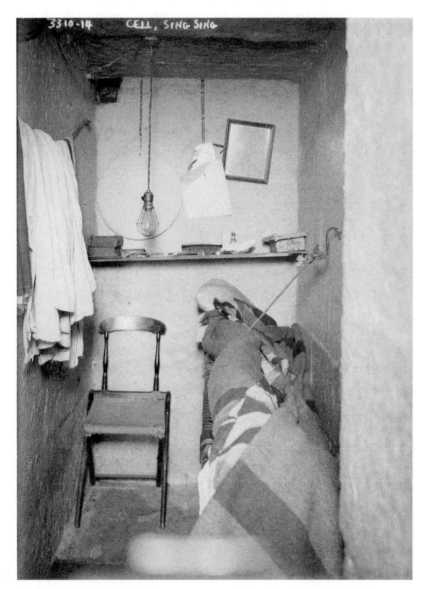

Sing Sing prison cell, New York, *c.* 1914.

# PROLOGUE

*Power on the Inside: A Global History of Prison Gangs* is the first attempt to examine the prison-gang phenomenon throughout the world from a historical perspective. Most countries with overcrowded penal facilities and understaffing are susceptible to the development of this prison sub-culture. The best-known and chronicled prison gangs are the subject of this book. Every continent except for Antarctica has birthed some form of prison-gang subculture, ranging from the Americas, Oceania and South Africa to Russia and Europe. In some cases, the history of a particular prison gang is rather murky, being that all gangs, inside and out of prison, have their creation sagas – sometimes more than one. These will be explored in due course.

Economists, sociologists, political scientists and criminologists have all offered their takes on the evolution of prison gangs. Too often their accounts are lacking actual historical research, which entails going a bit further back in time to better understand the historical continuum and evolution of a specific prison gang. The United States is a perfect case in point. It is home to the most-chronicled prison gangs in the world; the overwhelming majority of books and articles on the subject name the Gypsy Jokers in 1950 as the country's first prison gang.[1] Although there is no substantive evidence to back this claim up, since 1985 every prison-gang scholar has cited this as America's first prison gang. As will be shown in Chapter Eight, if this group ever existed at all as a gang, it was probably as an outlaw motorcycle gang outside prison walls. But even if 1950 has been the accepted starting point for the origin of the country's prison gangs, this claim would still be incorrect.

'Prison gangs' have been identified by journalists and penologists in American prisons at least as far back as the 1930s. But in order to chronicle and verify their existence and early mentions it takes research among the dusty files and microfilm of big-city newspapers located in hotbeds of mass incarceration. So, there is much more verifiable information available on the gangs in New York State's Sing Sing prison in the early 1930s than on Washington State's enigmatic 'Gypsy Jokers', accepted by so many prison-gang researchers.

As early as 1931, a Sing Sing warden recalled '132 gangs represented' in his prison.[2] He admitted that he 'had to watch them within the walls of the institution as carefully as the police watch the activity of their associates outside'. Unfortunately, the warden doesn't specifically mention any of the gangs. But several years later, for one of the first times, prison gangs were identified according to their ethnic exclusivity. They were not recognized by any catchy moniker, but it was clear that Irish and Italian gangs were accused of 'ruling Welfare Island' (now Roosevelt Island). One *New York Times* headline from 1934 noted 'Prison Gang Chiefs Served by Valets', identifying Joe Rao and Ed Clearly as the leaders of the Italian and Irish inmates respectively.[3]

Further demonstrating the existence of prison gangs in the 1930s were accounts of how they 'controlled the most important rackets in prison', and how various 'Welfare Island' factions converted the prison hospital into private quarters. Like the Neapolitan Camorra gangsters of the previous century, convicts at Welfare Island could identify gang bosses and shot-callers by their sartorial elegance, perhaps 'a sharp crease on the trousers', polished shoes or smoking Cuban cigars.

In 1943, observed historian Joseph F. Spillane, 'nearly every postwar account of times served in the Coxsackie [reformatory] mentions the prevalence and power of youth gangs' made up of juvenile miscreants at the early stages of their criminal careers. These reform-school gangs in upstate New York, including the Socialist Dukes and the Comanches, were, according to Spillane, the 'first gangs named in prison files'.[4] It has long been de rigueur for prison-gang experts searching for the origin of California's prison gangs, such as the Mexican Mafia, to trace them to the Deuel Reformatory, near Tracy, in the 1950s. But Spillane has demonstrated that the Dukes and Comanches pre-date the creation of the Mexican Mafia in California by almost a decade. The point of the above revelations is that the historical study of prison gangs is still in its infancy, and that the avalanche of American manuscripts on prison gangs has not furthered the historical discourse on the subject prior to the 1960s.

The term 'prison gang' summons up a variety of sinister images in the twenty-first century – from tattoo-covered bodies (and even faces) to ingeniously constructed knives and other weapons of war and to the segregation of inmates by race and ethnicity. Prison gangs operate in a shadowy, clandestine world mostly off-limits to researchers. Moreover, anyone admitted to the inner sanctum of most modern-day prison gangs risks life and limb for revealing their activities.

Prison administrators are rarely forthcoming about gangs in prisons in the Western world, let alone the developing one. In order to research and write about prison gangs around the world, the author, who is a historian and criminologist, has relied on journalistic, historic and eth-nographic research, as well as open-source documents, interviews with corrections officials and memoirs by former and present gang members.

Although there is a large catalogue of popular and academic books focusing on urban street gangs, outlaw motorcycle gangs and other organized criminality, and books dedicated to the specific histories of a handful of prison gangs (mostly in the United States), there is no single book offering a wide-ranging historical overview of the world's prison gangs.

Compared to the development of the penitentiary during the eighteenth-century Enlightenment in America and Europe, prison gangs are a relatively recent phenomenon. Some of the earliest depic-tions of prison-gang activity date back to at least nineteenth-century Neapolitan prisons (see Chapter Two), where prison extortionists formed a secret society and gained a foothold beyond the reaches of Naples' Vicaria prison. Indeed, the modern-day Italian Camorra traces its origins back to its prison progenitor. Not as well known, South African prisons have been home to the Number prison gangs for more than a century. And in the first decades of the twentieth century, a thieves' society developed in Russia's prisons and Gulag system.

Best known for breathtaking landscapes and pastoral settings, New Zealand and Australia, the largest countries of Oceania, have surpris-ingly complex and colourful prison-gang histories. Little is known about prisons in Asian countries such as China, Vietnam, North Korea and Myanmar, but there is a wealth of material on gangs in India, Bali, Singapore, Thailand and the Philippines.

Europe, where many countries prefer alternative sentencing and do not suffer the highest levels of overcrowding, is home to only a few identifiable prison gangs or gang subcultures, such as the Brödraskapet in Sweden, Muslim gangs in the United Kingdom and the Polish prison subculture known as grypsing. In Irish prisons, paramilitary gangs, including IRA factions, have been separated since the 1970s. More recently, the Kinahans, which by some accounts have a level of organization not seen behind bars in the UK, have been controlling entire landings of Mountjoy prison. As recently as 2018, at least fourteen major prison gangs were identified in Irish prisons.

Exploring the history of prison gangs in the United States contrasts sharply with the absence of prison gangs in European penal institutions. One survey in 2004 asked corrections officers around the United States to list the top three gangs at their institutions. When all was said and done, 71 different gangs were listed. With so many gangs in so many institutions it has been almost impossible for an American gang to 'establish hegemony within a prison unit', much less a prison system.[5] Much of the recent discourse on prison gangs has been predicated on 'the thesis of American exceptionalism'. Researchers have noted that this 'rests more on ignorance of possible comparisons than on a comprehensive examination of comparable phenomena elsewhere'.[6] Much of this is due to the availability of so much data on American (street and) prison gangs.

Today, except for the United Kingdom, European prison populations are falling, at the same time that American incarceration rates are levelling off, while Latin America is experiencing an unprecedented rise in its prison populations. Much of the recent surge is being driven by punitive drug-prohibition policies that have overwhelmed prisons with detainees waiting to go on trial for drug-related offences. Over the past decade, Latin America has followed in the footsteps of America and its love affair with punitive incarceration regimes and drug-prohibition policies. Prison gangs in Brazil, Venezuela, Central America and Mexico dominate the discussion and offer intriguing lessons in penal history.

It seems that every year brings more and more interdisciplinary studies of prison gangs that will only make the historical record more complete. While *Power on the Inside* builds on the research and contributions of so many scholars, I hope this global history of prison gangs can perhaps serve as a template for studies yet to come.

# 1

# PRISON-GANG SUBCULTURES

As the historical chronicle that follows demonstrates, a new generation of younger prison inmates is challenging the bedrock of traditional prison-gang cultures. For most of their history, prison gangs have been more a cypher than a clearly understood phenomenon. The gangs have controlled the conversation by attempting to conceal their misdeeds and practices and eliminating any defectors who would reveal them. Also stifling a better understanding of prison-gang subcultures are the difficulties faced by investigators attempting to conduct meaningful research behind bars. The very nature of prison makes data hard to come by. Plagued by overcrowding, disorder, complicated bureaucracies and resistance from inmates, prisons present a formidable barrier to better understanding modern prison gangs and subcultures.

Prison circumstances vary enormously between national prison systems. Likewise, conditions can vary significantly within a single prison system. As will be seen in the coming chapters, a number of variables can determine the evolution of prison subcultures, including cultural values and population demographics, levels of prison funding, how often gang members are transferred between prisons, various policies of formal and informal segregation, prison designs and staff-prisoner relations.

Another difficulty to overcome when looking at prison gangs from a global perspective is the fact that there is still no international consensus over the definition of 'prison gang'. Like the debate over definitions for terrorist groups, organized crime groups and hate groups, prison gangs appear in too many incarnations across the globe to be confined to any one generalized definition. In recent years, the research of David Skarbek and others who have explored the self-governance of prisoners in overcrowded and under-resourced prison systems has dominated the definitional discussion. Skarbek's 2014 book, *The Social Order of the Underworld*, examines the complicated organizational systems that make prison gangs so intimidating, but mostly focuses on the California prison system, which currently contains the second largest inmate population in the nation. Skarbek's research on prison governance has been influential, to say the least. Ultimately, more and more researchers are concluding that in many respects 'the prisons run more smoothly because of them [prison gangs]'.[1]

## Defining Prison Gangs

Several definitions of prison gangs, mostly by American academics, have been given prominence over the past thirty years, beginning in 1989 when Michael Lyman introduced one of the more widely accepted definitions of the prison gang as 'an organization which operates within the prison system as a self-perpetuating criminally oriented entity, consisting of a select group of inmates who have established an organized chain of command and are governed by an established code of conduct'.[2] Not surprisingly, this definition has become somewhat outdated as the term 'prison gang' has expanded to include prison-based gangs with distinctive outside counterparts.

In the 1990s, penal organizations such as the American Correctional Association (ACA) adopted more inclusive monikers, such as Security Threat Groups (STGs),[3] whose definition has been expanded over the past twenty years.[4] Some regions of the United States prefer the term 'Disruptive Group'. Like the definition of an STG, this is 'any group of three or more members of the same street gang, or prison gang, or the same extremist political or ideological group where such extremist ideology is potentially a security problem in the correctional setting'.

More recently, scholars such as Benjamin Lessing have challenged the outdated classification of 'prison gang', suggesting that a 'more accurate term would be "prison-based criminal organizations"'. Moreover, the term 'prison gang' does not really do justice to a prison subculture phenomenon that varies considerably, 'each with different strategies, membership profiles, degrees of institutionalization, and historical trajectories'.[5] Lessing instead suggests that a basic description of a 'prison gang' should more closely respond to 'all self-identifying associations of inmate groups that exhibit some form of collective behavior'.[6]

In recent years, the sociologist John M. Hagedorn has offered a different perspective, suggesting that the term 'institutionalized gang' might be more appropriate,[7] while the Federal Bureau of Investigation (FBI) views a prison gang as any gang that operates behind bars.[8] It is not uncommon for state prison systems, such as the Arizona Department of Corrections, to emphasize certain criteria and disregard others.[9]

### Informal Prison Governance: Are All Prison Gangs Bad?

Prison-gang formation has long been regarded as detrimental to rehabilitation efforts and the smooth operation of prisons. In recent years, this idea has been revisited by a number of scholars, who make strong arguments that prison gangs actually have become 'functionally important to both inmates and prison administration despite their serious rule violations'. In the Philippines, several criminologists have demonstrated how gangs, or *pangkats*, provide Manila's New Bilibid Prison (NBP) with a system of governance, prison order and network of social support in what is generously described as an overcrowded and deprived environment.[10]

A 2014 article by Jones and Narag, entitled 'Why Prison Gangs Aren't All Bad', made a case for how some prison gangs – due to a lack of resources, particularly in developing countries – 'are left to be run by ruthless gangs'.[11] After conducting interviews with more than one hundred gang leaders, inmates and prison officials over a four-year period, the authors found that the Philippine *pangkat* system, first conceived in the 1940s, 'kept [inmates] busy with legitimate activities', allowing them the opportunity to 'do their own time productively' and dispelling the notion that prison-gang subcultures are 'exclusively about crime'.

It is common for modern prison-gang researchers, including some studying prison gangs in the Philippines, to subscribe to the 'self-governance' theory. Some have concluded that, in Jones and Narag's words, there are numerous 'positive aspects of gang life . . . often overlooked yet crucial for inmate survival'. In their study of Manila's NBP, the authors reiterated what others have observed in prisons around the world: that in overcrowded prisons where the inmate-staff ratio 'exceeds safe levels', the task of maintaining order and providing prisoners with a safe environment 'becomes complex and problematic'. It is at this point that prison administrators are forced 'to not only compromise organizational integrity, but also relinquish aspects of their management

New Bilibid Prison, the Philippines, 2017.

function to inmate leaders'. At NBP the inmate to guard ratio (1:80) has increased to such an extent that

> it has become unofficial practice to operate under a system of shared governance. By default, and not design, gang leaders help maintain internal control and safeguard inmates as best they can. Even though prison stability is fragile, gang leaders help prison guards restore stability once disorder occurs.[12]

In overcrowded and poorly funded institutions, belonging to a gang offers some of the best chances of survival, by providing protection and access to commodities necessary for subsistence. It is common for convicts to be abandoned by their families and any social support system they might have had on the outside once they are behind bars. At NBP, gang members refer to each other as brothers and fathers (big brothers). Thus, a *pangkat* member might call a leader *tatay*, or father, or even refer to him as an older brother, or *kuya*. This is 'a Filipino cultural dynamic that orders the social standing of inmates'.[13]

Another study of 'self-governing' prisons examined prison gangs in Kyrgyzstan, Northern Ireland and Brazil.[14] According to this comparative survey, conditions varied depending on the type of prison system, culture, resources, staff-convict interactions, prison architecture, overcrowding and formal/informal policies of prison segregation.[15] Testing the self-governance model on a range of regions – United States, Bolivia, United Kingdom and Sweden – Skarbek asserted that in situations where the demand for governance is met by prison authorities, centralized prison gangs are less likely to materialize. This perhaps explains why prison gangs are not much of an issue in most European countries, with much smaller prison populations and more alternatives to imprisonment available.[16] In some Australian prisons there is even a fifteen-hour period when the prison is unofficially turned over to the gangs until the guards return for their first shift the following morning.

## Convict Code

Prisoners lived according to a 'convict code' long before the emergence of prison gangs. Prisons were much less demographically diverse, and the prisoner-guard ratio was more congruent prior to the 1950s and '60s, especially in the United States. During this era, unwritten rules dictated daily relations and behaviour behind bars. The foundations for the 'informal governance' concept[17] built on the theories of earlier investigators who asserted that convicts introduced a 'social equilibrium' around 'unwritten rules'. New inmates were expected to be quickly brought up to speed on these rules under tutelage from veteran convicts. According to the inmate or convict code, inmates were expected to follow a set of informal rules that penologists have long recognized as governing prisoners' behaviour and relationships.[18] Having lost their free-world status and likely to brood over the loss of whatever feelings of self-worth they once had, not surprisingly, this, combined with a lack of privacy and forced contact with others, meant that prisoners were more likely to drift into groups or cliques than those in normal society.[19]

The study of prison gangs focuses almost exclusively on men's prisons. There are a number of reasons for this, which are beyond the scope of this book. However, an interview with a female California inmate revealed that 'women don't form gangs . . . we're not into it.' Another inmate sagely put it, 'We are not like the men, because we learn to live with each other. We communicate. It's not a racial thing here.'[20] Most research on prisoner governance in female prisons focuses on prisoners cohering along the lines of a family unit.

As American prison populations grew in the 1950s, so too did the ethnic and racial diversity of convicts. It was in this era that a new type of inmate was making his presence felt. Many of these young men, especially in California, were first-time offenders and products of violent reform schools. This is best exemplified by the birth of the Mexican Mafia in the Deuel facility in 1956, before it spread throughout the Californian prison system. These newcomers were more belligerent, 'less predictable' and less likely to respect the old-time prisoners. As a result, norms that once ensured a semblance of order began to go by the wayside, as authorities lost the control that exemplified the heyday of the convict code, and by 1970 'there was no longer a single overarching convict culture'.[21]

By most accounts the convict code was a variation of the 'thieves' code', which emphasized, 'Thou shalt not snitch.'[22] While there was no systematic code, it usually included acknowledged provisions, which now often sound like clichés, such as 'don't interfere with other inmates', 'do your own time', 'don't rat on or fight with other inmates', 'don't exploit weaker inmates', 'share scarce resources', 'work together to survive', 'be tough and take any punishment coming your way', 'pay your debts and bets', 'never trust guards' and 'don't steal from other inmates.'[23]

The code might include learning to recognize territorial boundaries within the prison, which were often based on rank and ethnicity. Moreover, at a time when American prisons were less ethnically and racially diverse and prison populations low, inmates shared an understanding that behind bars they were all in this together and viewed prison keepers, rather than each other, as the enemy.

By the mid-1960s, at least in the United States, observers noticed that a surge in prisoner population, combined with desegregation, led to the obsolescence of the former convict code. Hence, inmates could no longer depend on this phenomenon to protect and coordinate their daily lives inside. The expansion of the inmate population in the 1960s paralleled the changing demographics of American prisons, where small groups developed along lines of ethnicity, race and pre-incarceration gang alliances. A new generation of inmates unfamiliar with the machinations of the convict code increasingly challenged the status quo in prisons across the United States. During the era of the convict code, penal institutions were 'historically stable environments'. This changed dramatically in the 1960s as prison demographics underwent a radical transformation. As the decade concluded, inmate solidarity was no longer predicated on the accepted tenets of the convict code of old.

The altered environment of 1960s prisons has been chalked up to a number of factors. According to one former convict, the introduction of more and more 'state-raised youth' meant a new type of young inmate, 'thoroughly institutionalized' and more than ready to engage in violence in order to increase his prestige, status and power. It didn't take long for like-minded inmates to band together into gangs that could use their numbers to steal, intimidate, extort and take advantage of weaker non-gang-aligned inmates. Compared to the followers of the old convict code, these criminals were no longer concerned with doing their own time or 'remaining stoic in an oppressive setting'. Rather, they saw prison as an opportunity to develop a reputation and maintain power over other inmates through violence and intimidation.[24]

Prior to the appearance of prison gangs in New Zealand in the 1970s, if one belonged to a gang in the free world, one's commitment to that gang ended there, and was considered secondary to being a part of the inmate population as a whole. According to one former prisoner-turned-criminologist, 'it was meant to be all for one and one for all. There were no gangs in the prisons.' But in the 1970s, as an older generation of convicts that lived according to the traditional convict code were released, more gang members began to fill the prisons, and for the first time gang members announced their presence by wearing various insignia. It was at this time that the New Zealand prison culture first began to be organized along gang lines.

There is a continuing debate among researchers and prison inmates as to what convict code exists today. One inmate stated that there is no convict code and that 'prisoners simply import their own norms and values into prison.' According to the inmate, 'convicts bring with them a moral and ethical code of conduct that they learned and developed from their individual street experiences.' He cites the Mafia bringing in its Mafia code and drug addicts importing 'a junkie's code of conduct'.[25] In the United States, there is no standard code of behaviour observed by all inmates. However, the major groups all have either written, or at least unwritten but well-understood, by-laws, constitutions and other standards that members are expected to live up to.

## Propagation and Segregation Policies

The expansion of prison gangs from one prison to another in a prison system frequently occurs when members, often at odds with another group in an institution, are transferred to another facility in the hope of restoring a semblance of peace and order at the original institution. This has been done in Africa, Asia, Latin America, the United States and elsewhere to little effect. If anything, this poorly conceived policy has helped strengthen prison gangs by putting all the members of a gang in the same institutions, offering them what one observer has described as 'localized hegemony'. It is accepted by penal experts that if you want to 'propagate' a gang through a system of institutions, the best way is by transferring groups of specific gang members. Prison-gang expansion is also facilitated by the release and reincarceration of gang members. As one researcher put it, gangs have not just expanded their reach, but also their numerical power through 'mergers' and 'franchising' between previously 'unaffiliated groups'.[26]

## Informal Governance

Examples of prison gangs as a form of 'informal governance' can be found in overcrowded and understaffed prisons in Asian countries, South Africa and the Americas. The placid and low-crime country of Canada seems an unlikely location for finding examples of this phenomenon. Recently, however, the Canadian prison system has been facing increasingly diverse forms of gangs behind prison walls. The flourishing of street gangs, biker gangs and indigenous gangs meant that this diversity made Canadian prisons more difficult to run. More than 2,600 prisoners belonging to indigenous, Asian, outlaw motorcycle and street gangs, as well as sundry members of cults and extremist, terrorist, white supremacist or hate groups, were branded as members of security threat groups. According to a spokesperson for the Correctional Service Canada, 'The security threat group population has become increasingly fluid, which has made the identification of groups, members, associates and the compatibilities of each, increasingly difficult to identify definitively.' These observations led one Canadian researcher to note,

> In some cases, gangs can actually help prison units run smoothly . . . If an entire prison unit is in the hands of a particular gang, and

there are no other gangs in that unit they have disagreements with, and they all believe the same rules should be followed, you don't usually see fights and disagreements.[27]

This is the notion of 'informal governance' in a nutshell.

Few outsiders would argue that prison gangs are a good thing. However, from an inmate and correctional perspective this is not necessarily true. According to one California inmate,

Look, there are a lot of problems caused by gangs, no doubt. The thing is, they solve problems too. You want a structure and you want someone to organize the businesses so the gangs have their rules. You don't run up a drug debt, you don't start a fight in the yards and stuff.[28]

## Prison Subcultures

Informal and formal prison subcultures often feature a peculiar argot, a distinctive set of norms, attitudes, beliefs, values, statuses and roles that give prisoners a perspective that clashes with free-world norms. In many instances they have imported their norms and values from the streets into prison. In the United States, there has been relative uniformity of rules that gang members are expected to live by. However, there are variations within prisons and even within prison gangs elsewhere. For example, the Number gangs of South African prisons are divided into three different factions, the 26s, 27s and 28s, each with its own laws, tattoos, salutes, flags, hand signals and types of justice. Tattoos, next to race, are especially important in multiracial prisons, where most of the men dress the same way. But, ultimately, one's race provides other inmates with the quickest information when confronting one another, since it cannot be concealed.

Prison gangs usually employ clandestine communication skills, whether it be jargon or simple body movements. For example, a convict's Number-gang (26, 27 or 28) affiliation can be revealed through body language, the way he sits and waits in a chair, or which knee is held up in the air. Much of any prison gang's lexicon has roots in the free world. Black prison gangs in the u.s. have experimented with using Swahili to communicate. In South Africa, any new Number-gang member is expected to learn how to communicate with the others in a

Tattoos from a gang member of the 28s.

multilinguistic patois, or to 'Sabela', a tedious but necessary process in a prison system where at least eleven different languages are spoken. In South African prisons *fanigalore*, a mixture of the four most commonly spoken languages, Afrikaans, English, Xhosa and Zulu, dates back to the communications system used by white mine owners and their workers in the nineteenth century. Similarly, hardened Russian criminals in the Soviet Gulag system who prosaically self-identified as 'thieves with a code of honour', or *vory-v-zakone*, also developed an argot rich 'in maxims and proverbs'. Their slang, called *fenya*, involved placing extra syllables between syllables of regular words.[29]

## Initiation

The sociologist Diego Gambetta suggests that prisons act as 'screening devices' that allow hardened cons to distinguish pretenders from the real deal. Every new prisoner enters a demi-monde, where one's past is often a predictor for future actions. One popular mantra goes something like this: 'The longer the sentence, the better the credentials'. This refers to the fact that the most severe crimes demand the longest sentences, hence offer violent criminals a street credibility, if you will, that your typical non-violent offender lacks. Such distinction means that the length of sentence offers an 'objective' measure of respect for certain inmates. Some prison gangs view one's prison record as 'a sign of distinction'. Prison subcultures, such as the Russian thieves with a code of honour, or *vory*, at one time 'made having been in a prison camp a formal requirement of membership'.[30]

From the moment prisoners enter prison they are subjects of great interest to fellow inmates, who quickly size up prospective gang members or potential victims. It is common for prison gangs to have some form of initiation process that tests a prospect's criminal capacity. Major American prison gangs, such as the Aryan Brotherhood, Mexican Mafia and La Nuestra Familia, live by a strict 'blood in, blood out' rule – meaning one needs to shed blood to get into the gang and membership is a lifetime commitment. To become a soldier in the Number gang, one must stab (but never kill) a pre-selected target. In so-called blooding the prospect is told, 'just flesh, no organs'. Once the stabbing has been accomplished, members will pass on the information with the Zulu phrase, 'the number is complete'.[31]

### Non-gang Members: The Unaffiliated

Not every inmate in a prison dominated by prison gangs joins a gang. For one reason or another some inmates are not allowed to join even if they want to, or simply do not want to join – there are many inmates who just want to do their own time and eschew the gang life. In most cases this means they are constantly on guard with no group to protect them. In other cases, they cannot share in the resources that gangs tend to accumulate. In the Philippines, where *pangkats* represent the gang system, unaffiliated members are known as *querna*, or *Brigada ng Querna*. Not only must they provide for their own needs, they can never leave their cells unarmed. On the other hand, since they do not have any obvious enemies, they do not require inmate bodyguards as the *pangkat* does. Moreover, the *querna* are said to avoid joining if there is access to social support services as well as from a 'desire to maintain their pre-prison identity'.[32]

Like those in the Philippines, South African prisoners who remain unaffiliated with a prison gang are also categorized – as *franses*. In this country's prisons a new inmate has a choice: join a gang and become a soldier, or *ndota*, or become a *franse* and be considered a non-entity. Non-members are treated much like cell-servants, tasked with cleaning cells and the clothing of gang members. It is the *franse* who is most often the target of gang violence and intimidation. Any time he receives a parcel from the free world he is expected to hand it over to gang members, who decide how it will be distributed.[33]

## Latin American Prison-gang Diversity

Prison overcrowding in Latin America is a 'regional phenomenon'. Together with rampant violence and poor conditions, it has ensured the development of organized crime entities in and out of prisons. The Brazilian prison system gave birth to two of the most powerful inside/outside gangs in the region: São Paulo's First Capital Command (PCC) and Rio de Janeiro's Red Command (*Comando Vermelho*). One recent survey identified six different types of prison gang in Latin America. There are some that operate exclusively in jails (inside prison gangs), more formidable inside/outside prison gangs, insurgent prison gangs, drug-trafficking prison gangs, Central American Mara prison gangs and military prison gangs.[34] At least ten gangs, or 'councils', are said to run Bolivia's prisons, and, like their earliest counterparts (Neapolitan Camorra), extort money from prisoners.

In Venezuela and El Salvador, by most accounts, gangs virtually run the prisons. In El Salvador, the Mara Salvatrucha (MS-13) and Barrio 18 gangs dominate all others. MS-13, not usually discussed in terms of structure and hierarchy, has been associated with its domination of El Salvador's Zacatecoluca Prison (aka 'Zacatraz'). Venezuela's prisons are home to the Pran system, directed by prison shot-callers known as 'prans'. Besides running the prisons' black market, they direct kidnapping and extortion schemes on the outside. Like Ecuadorian and other prison

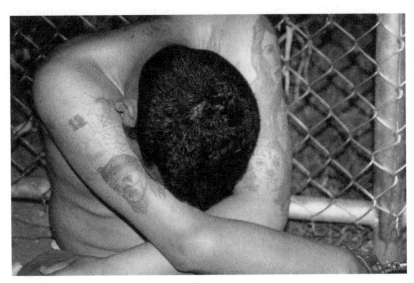

MS-13 gang member suspect with distinctive tattoos.

gangs, one of their biggest moneymakers is taxing inmates. Inmates are expected to pay fees for conjugal visits, the right to sell drugs and so forth. Their criminal structures in the free world are called *trenes* or trains.

## The Diversity of Asian Prison Gangs

Asian prison gangs vary considerably. In the Philippines, the term *pangkats* is preferred to 'gangs', which members feel is pejorative, and allied groups can be found under various linguistic banners. For example, those following the Sigue Sigue banner speak Tagalog, while non-Tagalog speakers belong to the oxo (Original Ex-convict Organization) gangs. In Bali, Indonesia, street gangs are well represented behind bars and in the tourist industry. It is common to see their trademark *trishula* tattoos on their hands, as members at gang-owned restaurants serve unsuspecting tourists. In Thailand, prisoners refer to inmate groupings as 'Homes'. Each Home is named after a shared home-town neighbourhood or former street-gang membership, and has its own set of values. With Homes ranging numerically between five and one hundred members, the largest gang typically wields the most power. The oros, named after a famous Thai gangster, wear related tattoos on hands and fists. In Singapore, a country with far fewer prisoners than many Asian countries, the dynamics of ethnic minorities in prison means that there are low-status Malay and Indian gangs, the Omegas and Sara Jumbo respectively, and more powerful Chinese secret societies. The ethnically exclusive and Muslim Omega gang has members swear allegiance upon the Koran. The minority gangs are distinctive for offering automatic membership merely by being Indian or Malay. And India's diversity of castes means that its prisons have become huge melting pots as well.

## Indigenous and Importation Models

Over the years there has been debate as to whether prison gangs are extensions of street gangs or were developed by inmates independently inside prison, with little or no connection to street gangs. Most research on gang subcultures has concentrated on free-world street gangs, who have been prowling the urban landscape of America for more than two hundred years. One comparative study of street and prison gangs found that prison-gang members tended to be older and more sophisticated, at least as far as their criminal acumen and organization go. Prison-gang members have been considered more disciplined and structured with loyalty to the gang 'absolute', compared to the 'weak bonds' characteristic of street gangs. Moreover, 'the hierarchical structure of the prison gang facilitates the entrepreneurial orientation of these groups, who despite being in prison, still manage to control substantial drug and contraband exchanges' on both sides of the prison walls.[35]

More recently, in a study of Filipino *pangkats*, the authors argued that the

> importation theory ... needs to be reformulated ... inmates import their pre-prison characteristics inside the jails and prisons. However, in the Western developed context, racial and demographic traits are the salient factors. In the Philippines, due to pervasive social inequality, social status of the inmates is highly predictive of jail and prison life. The inmate's level of resources and connections are the key traits imported inside the facilities.[36]

Indeed, the coping mechanisms exhibited by Filipino inmates coming to grips with the thin margin of survival in most prisons share similarities with those adopted by deprived inmates in Latin America, Africa and other Asian countries.[37]

## Indigenous Gang Subculture: 'Pure Prison Gangs'

Some well-known prison gangs originated in prison before expanding their influence into the outside world – gangs and criminal prison subcultures that included the Camorra, the Mexican Mafia, La Nuestra Familia, Aryan Brotherhood, the Black Guerrilla Family, First Capital Command, the thieves-in-law or *vory-v-zakone*, and the Number gangs, all of which will be chronicled in the forthcoming chapters. Prison-gang researcher George Knox refers to these types of gangs as 'pure prison gangs', since they were not street gangs imported into prison. However, 'pure prison gangs' that evolve inside prisons remain in the minority.[38]

## Importation of Street-gang Culture

Most modern prison researchers subscribe to the theory that an importation model of prison-gang formation most accurately explains inmate subcultures. Importation emphasizes the role street-gang cultures play in shaping prison gangs.[39] Most modern prison gangs, particularly in the United States, are imported from the streets, as members are convicted and imprisoned. As a result, it is common for inmates to join a street gang before making the transition to a prison gang for the first time behind bars. No matter how prison gangs originate, they remain 'the dominant subculture in the entire American corrections system today'.

### Colonialism and Race: The Persistence of Racially Indigenous Prison Gangs

Seldom mentioned in studies of prison-gang subcultures is the impact of European colonialism on conditions that gave rise to prison gangs. Australia's aboriginal peoples, New Zealand's Maoris, South African Number gangs and Native American gangs in North America testify to some of the long-lasting repercussions of colonialism, imperialism, racism and the movement of people from reservations and agriculture to urban areas. In order to understand the evolution and persistence of indigenous gangs, again a historical approach is required. Except for studies on the New Zealand Maori prison gangs, such as the Mongrel Mob and Black Power, and the Number gangs in South Africa, little attention has been directed towards native prison gangs.

The South African Number gangs, for example, were influenced by colonial military discipline and adopted a quasi-military command structure in the aftermath of the Second Boer War (1899–1902). Moreover, much of the South African indigenous black population was systematically removed from their homelands either through war or removal strategies, effectively losing control of their destinies to interloping European colonists.

Australian aboriginal people make up only 3 per cent of the country's free-world population, but fill at least 25 per cent of prison cells, making them by the 1990s the 'most imprisoned ethnic group in the world'. Likewise, in New Zealand, the Maoris make up 15 per cent of the island's population but fill close to 50 per cent of prison cells.[40] Most outsiders would be baffled by the fact that New Zealand has more street- and prison-gang members than soldiers. Many of the gangs surfaced in the 1950s and '60s as Maoris left rural areas for the opportunities of urban ones, but struggled to adapt, like their indigenous counterparts elsewhere. The country's largest prison gang, the Mongrel

Mob, has adopted salutes and tattoos predicated on their disdain for the British Empire.

The U.S. has long been known for its racially based gangs, mostly of the Hispanic, African American and Caucasian variety. However, Native American prison gangs were discerned as early as 1982 in the Arizona prison system. America's reservation system has been an oppressive debacle for years, plagued by some of the highest per capita crime rates in the country. Most Native American gang members from the reservations or the streets of urban areas join the Native American Brotherhood once they land behind bars, notably in Arizona, Washington and Minnesota.

In 2001 the Warrior Society, a Native American gang, was certified as a security threat group in Arizona. Similar to other American racial prison gangs, they have adopted tattoos, written by-laws and even expect a lifetime commitment in some cases. Originally exclusively Navajo, Dine Nation expects members to respect each other and take care of debts. The Indian Brotherhood in the Oklahoma prison system even allows smaller Hispanic gangs to join up for protection.

## Political Prisoners and Prison-gang Formation

There have been instances where prison gangs were established after the mixing of common criminals with incarcerated political insurgents and guerrilla groups, particularly in Latin America. In Brazil, the first prison gang to be publicly known and recognized was Comando Vermelho (CV; Red Command), at Ilha Grande prison in Rio state. By most accounts, its creation in 1979 is largely attributed to the shared experiences of political prisoners and common criminals, and their willingness to work together to seek improvements in prison conditions. Former guerrilla fighters and political insurgents taught ordinary criminals how to organize, while promoting solidarity and the adoption of collective action to achieve goals.

A number of countries beset by ideological conflict have seen their opposing paramilitary groups continue their conflict in prisons. Efforts to segregate members of the United Self-Defence Forces of Colombia (AUC) in the early 2000s turned a section of Bogotá's La Modelo prison into an armed fortress from which attacks were launched against rivals. Military prison gangs, with their former security-force members, operate very differently from their non-military counterparts. Mexican Zetas, Guatemalan Kaibiles and other paramilitaries can be found in gangs throughout Central America. Moreover, at one time or another, Ireland's prison system has been plagued by clashes between Protestant and Catholic paramilitaries and their splinter factions.

Although America has the world's largest prison population, its prisons are comparative sanctuaries of safety and order. One curious aspect from a penological perspective is the persistence of conditions for breeding gangs that it shares with many developing countries. Except for the rare outbreak of carnage, such as the 1971 Attica Riot, which left 43 inmates and guards dead,[41] there are no parallels to the dozens and sometimes hundreds of deaths that take place yearly in violent gang-driven riots in Brazil, Honduras and other countries. One convincing explanation for the dearth of prison-gang-driven riots in the United States and in other countries is the fact that any type of lockdown – the usual response to prison strife – could put a damper on various illicit prison revenue streams. Prison gangs and their customers would have a hard time doing business or communicating in the prison yard while locked down 24/7 in their cells.[42] As will be seen, protecting lucrative revenue streams in prison always trumps differences in gang belief systems.

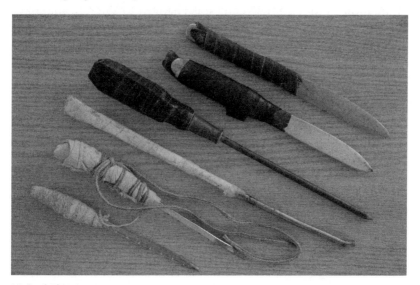

Makeshift prison weapons.

# 2

# THE CAMORRA

In June 1911 the American writer and lawyer Arthur Cheney Train (1875–1945) attended a criminal trial in Viterbo, Italy, hoping to better understand the intricacies of the Neapolitan Camorra, who had recently become such a concern to New York City's police and Italian community. While the crime being adjudicated took place in the vicinity of Naples, it was decided that it would be best to move the trial elsewhere in order to prevent the intimidation and the influence of the local *camorristi*. Its venue was changed to Viterbo, some 250 kilometres (155 mi.) from Naples and almost 80 kilometres (49 mi.) north of Rome.

The trial of Camorra boss Enrico Alfano and several dozen associates was held at Viterbo's ancient Church of San Francesco. The American lawyer eagerly followed the trial of Alfano and his co-conspirators for their alleged murder of rival boss Gennaro Cuocolo and his wife in 1906. The Cuocolos were suspected of being police informers. This well-documented trial lasted for a year and was avidly followed on both sides of the Atlantic. The trial was ultimately transformed from simply a murder trial into one targeting the entire Camorra. The middle-aged Alfano looked the part of the sinister crime boss, bearing the mark of *sfregio*, a deep scar across his cheek and 'a sign of camorrista punishment'.

Countering the contention by the *New York Times* that he was a 'president of the confederation', Alfano cleverly responded, 'I was neither its head nor its tail.'[1] Nonetheless, in July 1912 he was found guilty and sentenced to thirty years in prison. However, if there was any doubt about his status it was quickly dispelled once he entered Sassari prison on the island of Sardinia, as 'convicts did all they could to pay court and put [themselves] at his disposition as subjects would a sovereign.'[2] He was released in 1934.

Train apparently kept scrupulous notes at the trial and would later recount the testimony of Governor Abbate, a veteran chief prison warden at Pozzuoli near Naples. Abbate was certainly no fan of the Camorra, noting that,

> In the course of my thirty years' experience I have had the worst scum of the Neapolitan camorra pass through my hands. I have never met a gentleman nor an individual capable of speaking the truth among them . . . I always follow the system adopted in most other Italian prisons of putting all Cammorist [*sic*] prisoners together in a pack by themselves. When new inmates come, they spontaneously declare if they be Cammorists,[3] just as one might state his nationality or his religion . . . unless we follow this system a perfect inferno of terrorism ensues. The Cammorists seize the victuals, the clothes and underwear of non-Cammorist inmates, whom, in fact they despoil in every imaginable way . . . I come to learn the grades of Cammorist prisoners inasmuch as Cammorists, probationers, freshmen and the rank and file show studious obedience to their seniors and chiefs, whom they salute with the title of 'master.'[4]

Each of the three most prominent Italian criminal organizations, the Sicilian Mafia, the Calabrian 'Ndrangheta and the Neapolitan Camorra, has its own creation myth. However, the Camorra was the only one of the three founded in prison. Over time the Sicilian term, *mafia*, 'became an umbrella term' for the aforementioned organizations.[5] By some accounts, it was the prison-themed play *I mafiusi di Vicaria* (The Mafia of Vicaria Prison) that led to the adoption of the sinister moniker. According to one leading expert, this 'sentimental tale of an encounter between prison camorristi and a patriotic conspirator', prior to Italian unification, had 'eerie echoes of the real meetings between patriots and prisoners that played such a crucial role in the history of Italian gangland'.[6] Written in Sicilian dialect in 1863 by Giuseppe Rizzotto and Gaspare Mosca, the play glorified the daring of certain prisoners in Palermo's Vicaria penitentiary, better known as Ucciardone. The play was so successful, it was staged three hundred times in 1875 alone.[7] The first two acts are set in the Nuova Vicaria, the new prison built by Bourbon king Ferdinand II in 1837. The Mafia boss of the play was

Camorra trial, Viterbo, 1911.

Camorrists taken to court during the Camorra trial, Viterbo, 1911.

based on an actual incarcerated Mafia boss, Joachino Funciazza, who supposedly suggested writing the play, which explained the jargon and customs of its subjects. The play offered a number of details that would be familiar to anyone who studies prison gangs – initiation, codes of conduct, how nicknames are given, prison slang, sartorial embellishments, unwritten laws, the power of the gang boss, and the rough justice that enforced the code of silence, or *omertà* – all of which became Mafia features.[8]

The term *camorra* was brandished in Naples as a reference to bribes and extortion many years before it became shorthand for the society of criminals.[9] Between 1500 and the early nineteenth century, Naples was Europe's third largest city, a cosmopolitan metropolis boasting a population that hovered around 350,000 (in fact it 'often vied with Paris for the title of Europe's second largest city').[10] By the twentieth century, gang rule had been a fact of life in southern Italian prisons for close to a century. It flourished, in part, because of an official penal strategy introduced under the old regime and since adopted by understaffed prisons around the world, one that placed day-to-day carceral exigencies in the hands of inmates. According to the most accepted version of the Camorra origin saga, some time in the 1800s prison extortionists created a sworn secret society and over time gained a foothold beyond the confines of the prison walls, and thus the Italian Camorra was established in prison some time in the early nineteenth century.

During the nineteenth century, Italian officials tended to use the terms *mafiosi* and *camorristi* interchangeably. One researcher suggests that this was probably because officials in the era 'were unable to interpret many [criminal] phenomena other than in terms of the work of a secret society'.[11] In any case, both terms became synonymous with sinister organizations that operated in the shadows. The etymology of the term *camorra* remains rather vague, with some sources tracing its origins back to the fourteenth century and an Arabic dice game known as *kumar* and outlawed in the Koran. One source linked the origin of the term *camorra* to *chamarra*, a 'jacket of untrimmed sheep's skin so much worn by Spanish peasants'.[12] Others suggest that it derived from a combination of the words *capo della* and *morra*, a gambling game. According to one source the *capo della morra* was the individual who watched the gamblers. What makes this latter assertion convincing to some researchers is the fact that the Camorra did indeed exercise a monopoly on any form of gambling, including the levying of a tax upon every game of *morra* played. But for John Dickie, the connection to the gambling game is probably apocryphal, as *camorra* was used in Naples to refer to a bribe or extortion long before it was applied to a secret society.[13]

This simple game was favoured by older Neapolitan prisoners. According to the rules, 'one player holds up his doubled fist' and 'throws out one or more fingers'. Another player then guesses the number of fingers as they are displayed. If he cries out 'five' and the number is three or four, the other player wins. With little of value left at most new prisoners' disposal after the Camorra had got to them, the stakes were measured in wine. Not surprisingly, the wine was supplied by the Camorra.[14] In any case, the word *camorra* did not appear in Italian dictionaries until 1735, when it was used in reference to the gambling halls of Naples.[15]

Although the origins of the term remain speculative, the emergence of the Camorra can best be explained as the unintended consequences of widespread urban delinquency and gangsters running gambling and extortion rackets. Nonetheless, the consensus today is that it indeed originated in the jails of Naples, an apt setting for the fraternization of the growing delinquent and criminal subcultures. In Neapolitan prisons, members played both sides, keeping order in jail for administrators for a fee, while taxing prisoners for every facet of their prison existence. Like their modern-day American counterparts, such as the Mexican Mafia and the Aryan Brotherhood, once members were released they extended the reach of their criminal activities beyond the prison walls, in this case into Naples proper.[16]

Naturally, there are plenty of far-fetched Camorra origin stories that have gained a wider currency than they should, and have only confused the search for its historical roots. One of the most repeated was the assertion that the Camorra was a 'direct offshoot of the Garduna', a fifteenth-century Spanish secret society.[17] If these accounts are to be believed, then the Camorra did indeed come to Naples from Seville in the era of Spanish rule. Similarly to Camorra activities in Naples, at Seville, Garduna members purportedly raised funds outside prisons by extorting all gaming houses and drinking establishments. Arthur Train apparently bought the story of its Spanish origins lock, stock and barrel, writing in 1912 that 'La Garduna was the mother of the Camorra.' Moreover, he asserted that as early as 1417, it had rules, customs and officers identical to the nineteenth-century Camorra, and like the Camorra, it 'flourished in the jails', which were practically under its control.'[18]

As evidence of its Spanish origins, Train pointed to the writings of the author of *Don Quixote*, Miguel de Cervantes Saavedra, who in his work *Rinconete y Cortadillo* (1613) offered a portrait of a thieving brotherhood that 'divided its profits with police and clergy'. However, to a great extent this theory rests on the previously mentioned link to the Spanish word *chamarra*, a jacket of untrimmed sheep's skin favoured by Spanish peasants, and the appearance of a thieving brotherhood in the work of Cervantes.[19] But claims that the Garduna, or even the Camorra, existed in Italian prisons in the sixteenth century are not backed up with any real evidence. The overwhelming consensus among modern scholars is that the Camorra was born in Neapolitan prisons with little help from La Garduna or any other secret society.

According to one authority, the existence of a fifteenth-century secret society known as La Garduna can best be regarded as fiction, 'an intellectual con trick' if you will. Dickie makes perhaps the best argument against these oft-repeated theories. First, while the term *camorra* is indeed a Spanish word for 'quarrel or fight', the origins of the Spanish word are Italian anyway, 'putting us back in Naples'. As for the Cervantes connection, it should be remembered that his novel *Rinconete y Cortadillo* was fiction. While the 'criminal confraternity' might bear a passing resemblance to the Camorra, it in no way proves this relationship with the society two hundred years before its birth. There is no reference to the supposedly medieval sect prior to 1845, when it makes an appearance, seemingly out of the blue, in a very successful French pulp novel about the horrors of the Spanish Inquisition, translated into Italian in 1847. Dickie, a professor of Italian Studies at University College London, suggests that perhaps its author was inspired by some of the events and characters in Cervantes' *Rinconete*. His claims that 'There is absolutely no trace of the camorra before the nineteenth century' carry a much more authoritative weight than the theories expounded above.[20]

The first official reports of Camorra activity date back to 1820, when police records detailed a disciplinary meeting of the organization, indicating that it had made the transition from a local gang, earning its lucre from theft and extortion, to something more complex, some form of organization that now had a 'fixed structure and hierarchy'. This was also the same year that the 'first written statute of a camorra organization was discovered . . . indicating a stable organizational structure amongst the underworld'.[21]

The Kingdom of the Two Sicilies (Sicily and Naples) (1815–61) was the largest state of Italy prior to unification. During its halcyon days it boasted sixteen jails, most run by the Camorra, which had the ability to communicate with the outside world. For example, it took four members in prison to elect a temporary *capintrito*, but once he returned to society his prison rank would return to the common *camorrista*. On the outside, *capintrito* referred to town leaders or captains, but while behind bars the *capintrito* was in charge of weapons, had the power to impose penalties and required obeisance from other prisoners.

The *contaiulo*, or accountant, ran various moneymaking schemes and extortion rackets inside prisons, including the 'Our Lady's oil tax' scheme. Only non-society members were expected to pay this.[22] One early account reported on this 'masterful practice', where weaker prisoners were squeezed for anything of value to pay for 'subscriptions to keep the Madonna's lamp furnished with oil'.[23] This extortion scheme was chronicled by a number of political prisoners. Almost as soon as a new inmate appeared at Naples' Vicaria prison, he would be asked to contribute money for the lamp that hung in front of the Madonna in the entrance hall of the prison, for which inmates provided oil. In reality, the inmate was paying tribute to the prison bosses. The bosses served a dual purpose as a sort of de facto prison government and controller of prison markets for various goods inside. For example, if a new prisoner lacked bedding, food or luxuries, these could be bought from the bosses. When one political prisoner was reportedly suffering from some sort of malady and needed a bed, another inmate told him he would speak with 'the Camorrista of the room' to see what could be done. He managed to get him a bed in the corner of the room, but it is unclear what it ultimately cost the sick inmate.[24]

### 'God of the Bagno'

Some of the best early accounts of Camorra prison-gang activities can be found in the mid-nineteenth century. Not surprisingly, most of these reports came from the quills of well-educated political prisoners. In the 1850s, the political prisoner Antonio Nicolò began serving ten years inside various prisons in the Campania region (including Naples). He would later recount his encounters with the Camorra in the *bagno*, or penal colony, at Procida and other facilities in his book *Narrative of Ten Years Imprisonment in the Dungeons of Naples*.[25] In 1830 a former governor's residence was converted into a prison on the island of Procida, in the Gulf of Naples. Known today as Palazzo d'Avalos, the prison has been closed since 1988. During its heyday it served as a *bagno* for Italian political prisoners and common criminals. The term *bagno*, or *bagne*, was used in southern European countries (France, Spain, Italy) to denote penal colonies and regimes that featured hard labour, usually on public works projects such as fortresses, harbours and roads. First popularized in France, *bagnes* served as land-detention cells for galley slaves in earlier years, before being converted to a facility for holding serious offenders sentenced to anywhere from death to ten years' incarceration. One prison architectural historian described them as mammoth dormitories, capable of holding several thousand convicts in four large rooms.[26]

Soon after Nicolò arrived at Procida, he probably considered himself an urban sophisticate among knaves, finding most prisoners clothed, if that is the right word, in 'filthy worn out rags'. By comparison, it was relatively easy to pick out what seemed to be a different class of prisoner:

> here and there a cap might be seen with a silk tassel, a coat with a velvet collar, a green velvet waistcoat with silver buttons, or a pair of trowsers [*sic*] with a band of fine blue cloth, or black ribbon. Those who were thus clad carried themselves with a proud and martial air, tossed their heads, and appeared to exert some authority over their fellow-prisoners.

If he wasn't sure what to make of them, one prisoner told him, 'A Camorrista is the god of the Bagno.'[27]

As in other Neapolitan prisons, in the *bagno* the *camorristi* were a familiar presence, as they strutted about 'accompanied by their adepts and cut-throat hirelings. No one could change his place without their permission . . . Not a place of security remaining in which we could sleep at night without fear of their mercenary poignards; not a week elapsed without a murder.' Political prisoners felt so threatened that they petitioned an official to separate them from the gangsters. The official reproached the prisoners for asking for help, answering that the *camorristi* were 'only fifty in number, surely the 800 political prisoners can defend themselves against them.'[28]

Nicolò would soon learn that the members of the Camorra were 'a class of criminals celebrated for their crimes, both before imprisonment and while in the galleys'. He noticed their 'peculiar slang language', which allowed them to plan activities and share intelligence under the noses of the jailers. From an organizational perspective it was probably more important that they had an argot that would allow members to continue 'a most active correspondence with their fellows in other Bagni'. Like modern prison gangs, they had regular rules and a tribunal of their own, if it was necessary to discipline members or punish others. They had affiliated members who served as spies, and even their own executioners. What's more, they had a regular supplier of weapons and sometimes even 'their patrons among the commandants of the Bagni themselves'.[29]

Their clandestine communications allowed decrees to be sent from one place to another. This ensured that targeted victims could not escape their clutches. Camorra members were faced, like their counterparts in other institutions, with the challenge of access to only a limited number of hiding places to conceal homemade weapons, messages and contraband. The anus has long been used by inmates as a hiding spot for weapons and contraband. According to one researcher, a secret code book was confiscated from a prison *camorrista*, who had kept it hidden in his anus. If so, this is one of the first reports of the use of this strategy.[30]

Most Camorra members wore 'two long poignards', which in many cases were furnished by the officers of the *bagno*.[31] They also maintained a treasury, thanks to an initiatory fee demanded from potential members. Few went hungry, since the institution's distributors of bread, restaurant keepers, fruit vendors and others were all members of the society as well. They exacted entrance money from all prisoners, assigned them their places for a capricious fee and, in short, were 'complete masters of the lives and properties of their fellow prisoners'.[32]

At the Procida *bagno*, two *camorristi* factions were often at loggerheads. The Calabrese sought dominance, while the Provincials were more interested in mistreating political prisoners. At one point, the Provincials tried to win over the Calabrese; calling its leaders together, the Provincials 'reminded them that the government was equally their enemy and ours'. However, this competition seemed to end after two noted leaders of the Calabrese Camorra, who were already on good terms with several of the political prisoners, arrived at the *bagno* and seemed to bring order between the two factions.[33]

Peace might have been established between the Camorra factions, but for those unaffiliated, things went on as before:

Never a day passed that we did not give money to the head of the society to be divided among the rest; never a day passed without our receiving a visit individually from one of the set who began by humbly removing his cap, and finished by getting all that he could out of us; never a day passed that begging notes were not sent around to each of us, so that the sums which our families impoverished themselves to send to us were eaten up by prison officers and Camorristi.[34]

At one point the political prisoners decided to resist the Camorra. The society responded by holding an 'extraordinary council', where it condemned Nicolò and eleven other political prisoners to death. When Nicolò was alerted to his looming fate he knew from experience that it could not be appealed, meaning 'certain death when least expected' at the points of poignards.

A common strategy in prisons around the world, especially those that are understaffed and overcrowded, was to attempt to alleviate violence by physically separating potential victims, such as political prisoners, from their adversaries. However, at Procida, although separated from the gangsters, 'it frequently happened that [they] came in contact with common prisoners. The officers who distributed the bread and the soup were all friends of the Camorra, and had free access to our rooms; through them, then, the blow might easily be struck.' As a result the politicals avoided leaving their rooms. The administration, to use the word lightly, responded to the complaints by issuing a proclamation that prohibited common prisoners from being out of their cells when the political prisoners were in the courtyard.[35]

### Vicaria Prison: Extracting Gold from Fleas

Naples' Vicaria prison was the best-known bastion of the Camorra. The largest prison in the Kingdom prior to unification, it was in the slums of the eponymous Vicaria quarter, named after 'a medieval block that housed courtrooms and, in its basement, a notorious dungeon'. It originated as a site to concentrate the various law courts of Naples in one central location. Inmates were held in vast rooms and broad corridors where they were separated according to their criminal propensities, an early form of prisoner classification if you will. From the outside the building seemed sturdy enough, but 'in reality the walls were

The prisons of the Vicaria, at Naples: engraving from the *Illustrated London News*, 29 November 1856.

a membrane through which messages, food and weapons constantly slipped into and out of the surrounding slums.'[36]

One of the earliest references to a 'criminal society' in Vicaria prison dates back to the early seventeenth century. It does not explicitly state that it was the Camorra, but its activities indicated some sort of harbinger of what was to come. According to one account,

> thefts were so frequent that no sooner was some poor wretch imprisoned than he was immediately stripped of his clothes to be sold to the bystanders; they were so skillfully stripped that the hapless victims had no time to realize what was being done to them, and even if they had realized they would not have been able to report the theft for fear of retaliation, fearing even that they might be killed in the ambushes that were customary in those places. Very often the prisoners themselves went on committing their crimes within the prison, having by then formed a very profitable internal criminal society; life outside the prison would not have afforded them such convenient conditions as they found in their confinement, where everything was allowed with the connivance of the jailers.[37]

In the 1850s the inmates of Vicaria prison, like the Procida *bagno*, were clearly under the dominance of the Camorra gangs. The writer Marc Monnier (1827–1885) was well acquainted with the influence of the Camorra in Vicaria in the last years of the Bourbon regime.[38] He was of French and Swiss parentage, and his early education took place in Naples, followed by studies in Paris, Geneva, Heidelberg and Berlin, before he became a professor of comparative literature at Geneva. He recounted that,

> when a new arrival entered Castel Capuana, or Vicaria prison, and passed under the grand entrance, he reached two separate doors, both leading into the interior, and after the usual ceremonies of reception he fell into the hands of the Camorra. Its representative came up with outstretched hand and made the stereotyped application – money for oil to burn in the Madonna's lamp. This custom was universal; the lamps were to be met with everywhere, even in the lowest and vilest haunts. The sum raised in the Vicaria alone would have sufficed to illuminate the entire city – of course only a pretext for innumerable arbitrary assessments. The prisoner was at the mercy of the Camorra body and soul. He must buy permission to eat, or drink, or play cards, or smoke; the privilege of buying was taxed and also that of selling. He paid for justice; for the concession of rights and privileges to which he was entitled or which he had fairly earned. The ill-advised person who refused to be thus blackmailed risked being beaten to death.[39]

As noted above by Monnier, inmates weren't 'allowed to eat, drink, smoke or gamble without a camorrista's permission'. They were expected to 'contribute' a tenth of any money received and had to pay for essential and non-essential items. An inmate paid to get legal advice, which *camorristi* considered a privilege. 'He even paid when he was poorer and more naked than the walls of his cell, he was forced to deprive himself of everything. Those who refused to accept such impositions ran the risk of being clubbed to death.'[40]

When English Member of Parliament William Gladstone sojourned in Naples in 1850, seeking a milder climate to improve his daughter's health, local authorities made the unwise decision of allowing him to visit some of the local jails, where he was astonished to find the prisoners running the facilities. Gladstone later wrote several scathing letters reproaching the Bourbon king for allowing violent prisoners to manage the prisons. He noted, 'They are a self-governed community, the main authority being that of the gamorristi [*sic*], the men of most celebrity among them for audacious crime.'[41]

Among the more edifying early chroniclers of the *camorristi* in Neapolitan prisons was the political prisoner Sigismondo Castromediano (1811–1895), Duke of Morciano, Marquis of Caballino and lord of the seven baronies during the years before unification.[42] The duke had been sentenced to thirty years for plotting against the government. According to Camorra authority John Dickie, the duke's book, *Camorra*, published in 1862 'as a guide to the Neapolitan Honoured Society of the nineteenth century, has never been surpassed.'[43] Entering prison in 1851, the duke observed and recorded the development of the Camorra during his more than seven years inside. He reported how members levied taxes on virtually every aspect of the prison experience.

The Isle of Nisida in the Gulf of Naples, the site of an infamous Bourbon prison that gained notoriety in the 19th century when William Ewart Gladstone exposed its harsh conditions in his *Two Letters to the Earl of Aberdeen, on the State Prosecutions of the Neapolitan Government* (1851).

Castromediano reported witnessing one incident that exemplified how pragmatic the Camorra could be when it came to raising money. One member had just eaten a repast of 'a succulent soup and a nice hunk of roast' when he tossed a turnip in the face of a man 'whose meagre ration of bread and broth he had confiscated in lieu of a bribe. A slew of insults accompanied the thrown vegetable, including "Here you go, a turnip! That should be enough to keep you alive – at least for today. Tomorrow the Devil will take care of you."' Much like the American prison-gang member who offers favours freely, expecting future pay-back of some kind, the Camorra turned the needs and rights of fellow prisoners into favours that had to be paid one way or another. Thus, 'the camorra system was based on the power to grant those favours and to take them away.'[44]

In 1857, the Neapolitan economist Antonio Scialoja, a veteran of Bourbon jails, wrote a pamphlet chronicling his experiences among the prison demi-monde. He claimed there was a society of *camorristi* that was so powerful it could carry out death sentences in any prison in the Kingdom. Moreover, he validates the claims of other writers, noting that prisoners were forced to pay for everything, even for escaping the 'turpitudes [that is, rape]' of fellow detainees.[45]

As noted earlier, one of the most frequently recounted extortion schemes was payment for 'oil for the Madonna's lamp'. Although it was rarely lit, it remained an essential scheme in the Camorra playbook. Prior to Italian unification, most dungeons and prisons in the Kingdom had a tiny altar to the Madonna. As in many developing countries today, prisoners were expected to rent 'each patch of ground'. In prison slang, the above routine was dubbed *pizzo*, a term that is still used today to describe a bribe or protection payment. Not surprisingly, anyone reluctant to pay the *pizzo* could expect any of a range of punishments, including insults, beatings, razor attacks and even murder.[46]

### The Camorra Code of Conduct

The Camorra had a well-understood set of rules and behavioural guidelines, along with penalties for breaching them. Death, usually by poignard, was the sentence for anyone who brought an accusation against a member, revealed the place where poignards were concealed, 'by word or deed' offended a member or testified against him, made a complaint against one of the leaders, or was suspected of spying on them.[47]

The trial was helmed by the chief *camorrista*, or president, and the other members sat in judgement. Once an accuser stated his case it was left to the majority to make a final decision. If the sentence was death, the members placed their names in a 'ballot box', a lottery to decide who would execute the condemned. So that the victim was not alerted, sentences were always kept secret. If the criminal was from the lowest class, the execution was rarely committed by a *camorrista*. Instead, 'a wretched and separate hireling was engaged'. The techniques of the executioners varied, but one tried and true method was to get the target very drunk before leading him to his fate. Posted in the corner of a staircase or doorway, brandishing a poignard, the assailant was assured that once the task was completed he 'should be made a camorristi [*sic*] as a recompense'.[48]

In many cases, a witness or witnesses were available to swear that the deceased had started the altercation, in order to lessen any punishment. However, there were usually consequences. The killer could expect to be beaten and placed in solitary confinement. This was often followed by a two- to three-year sentence. By comparison, a political prisoner could expect a much more punitive sentence for simply being caught sending a clandestine letter.[49]

Gang members also extorted money from prison authorities in exchange for keeping order (anticipating the inmate trusties of the twentieth century, prisoners who worked as unpaid guards for prison administrators). By most accounts the *camorristi* left the few aristocratic and middle-class prisoners alone. While some gang members had achieved a modicum of wealth, as mentioned earlier, they usually maintained a certain level of deference to the high-born. For example, the Camorra claimed the authority to either allow inmates to carry knives or withhold permission. However, when anyone of rank or prominence entered prison, a leading Camorra member approached him, formally presented him with a stiletto knife and, with a low bow, commented, 'Will your excellency accept this? We authorize you to carry it.' This led one chronicler to assert that the prison *camorristi* 'were snobs', always paying their respects to persons of means, while tyrannizing the poor and destitute.[50]

## Prison Argot

Prison lingo is one of the most common elements of any penal subculture. The Camorra adopted and helped create a criminal vernacular that eventually became part of the lower-class lexicon. While many words have passed into common use, it is difficult to determine exactly how many are of Camorra origin. According to Arthur Train, those that were probably of Camorra origin include *freddare*, which referred 'to turning a man cold', a more neutral expression for killing. The word *agnello*, or lamb, meant victim. A robbery victim, or dead one, was referred to as *il morto*. Other examples of Camorra slang include *bocca*, or mouth, for pistol, and *tric-trac* for revolver. Train asserted that there were perhaps 5,000 words in the Camorra vocabulary, a large number of which came from Neapolitan slang.[51]

In his writings, Train referred to a 'secret diary' kept by a Camorra member during his thirty years in prison.[52] In it, Train noted, he chronicled Camorra rituals and culture. By the time he was released, this Camorra member was so tied into that milieu that he would regularly visit various criminal hangouts after he was freed. Almost like a preacher, he took to the streets, where he taught the mostly young, uneducated men and perhaps future Camorra acolytes, the *picciotto*, versing them in such things as the ceremonies and argot of the society.[53]

In Train's telling, it is unclear under what circumstances he learned about the diary, but in his book *Courts, Criminals and Camorra* (1912), he nonetheless details the Camorra hierarchy according to the secret diary. The *garzone di mala vita*, or apprentice, was considered the first grade, or lowest rank. The *garzone* served as a combination servant, errand boy and valet for the higher ranked, and in doing so earned himself the moniker 'honoured youth', or *giovine onorato*. The second grade was the position of novice, or *picciotto di sgarro*. In its earliest stages this position was considered difficult to attain since it required six to ten years of service. Once the novice reached the third and final stage, he was ready for the initiation ritual and prepared to operate as a *capo paranza*, a district leader or local gang boss. Train claimed that these ceremonies had been abolished on the outside at the time of his writing and only existed in prisons 'where the society retains its formality'.[54]

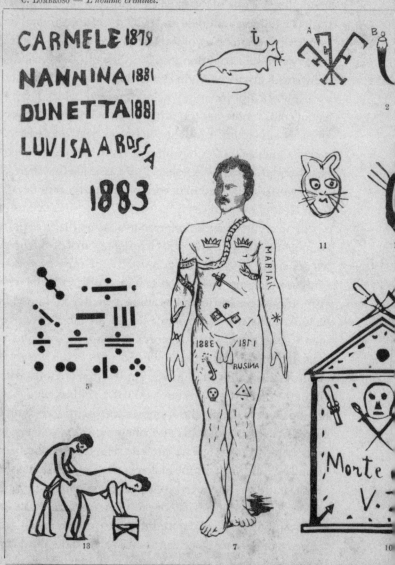

TATOUAGES DES (

Abele de Blasio, 'Tattoos of the Neapolitan Camorras' in the Cesare Lombroso atlas for *Criminal Man* (1895). Among the examples is Antonio G. (no. 7), depicted with a 1.25-metre-long (4 ft) snake biting his left breast, as

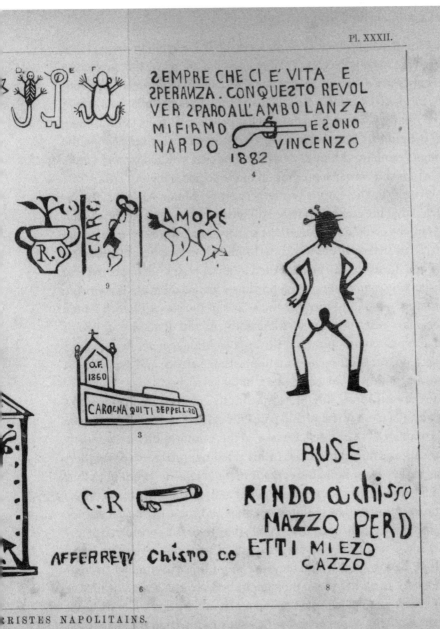

Pl. XXXII.

well as the names of his mistresses and the dates of his exploits against the police. The three-point triangle above his knee represents his rank in the Camorra.

## The Camorra in the Twentieth Century

The Camorra continued to reign supreme in Neapolitan prisons as it entered the twentieth century. Train cited one 1905 case that involved a duel between a dozen 'Camorrists and Mafiusi' at the Pozzuoli penitentiary, in which five men were killed and the rest 'torn about by muzzles of the infantry'. In another instance a prisoner named Lubrano was tried behind bars for revealing secrets. Following a formal session, the 'brothers' sentenced him to death, and he was stabbed by a *picciotto*, who as a result earned a promotion to the society's highest rank.[55]

Writing in the early twentieth century, Major Arthur Griffiths asserted that the *camorristi* were still used to enforce obedience 'when the wardens could not'. Indeed, the society had become so widespread in Italy that all the prisons were now brought into its sphere of influence. How well it worked can be discerned in the correspondence between a high-ranking *camorrista* and a subordinate lieutenant in another prison. This letter apparently 'dictated the affairs of the society, which issued orders, gave decisions, inflicted punishment and divided its funds'. If unable to pass communications through traditional methods, members fell back on transmitting information with the arrival and departure of prisoners, thanks to the connivance of the wardens.[56]

In the early 1900s, discipline was strictly enforced among the ranks and 'advancement was slow and painfully earned' until a long novitiate was completed.[57] Griffiths's version of the Camorra hierarchy mostly conforms to Train's chronicle. In his retelling, prospective members began at the lowest rank, the *garzone di mala vita*, or 'youth of vicious life'. At this stage they were 'kicked about and did dirty work', not unlike the prospects of outlaw motorcycle gangs and some prison gangs.

Rising next to the level of *picciotto*, they were still considered of low rank, and it might take several years of 'gangrenous service' to move up. In some cases this would require committing a murder when commanded to. In earlier years, they might be tested on a more primitive basis. There was once a rule that a coin should be thrown to the floor and the *picciotto* was expected to pick it up as his 'comrades stabbed at his fingers with the point of knives'.[58] If committing murder or risking knife wounds to pick up a coin wasn't enough, individuals could move up the ranks with a 'tremendous act of self-sacrifice', such as accepting blame for a crime committed by someone of higher rank. In some cases this might result in an innocent criminal spending ten to twenty years in the galleys. Ultimately, it depended on how badly someone wanted to become a full member. Many apparently considered this protracted probation 'worth it to secure the coveted position of the Camorrist'. Once in this position he was able 'to dictate to others and share spoils when divided', while relishing the 'adulation and respect from lower orders'.[59]

Once he had gained full membership, he would be eligible to become one of the 'supreme chiefs', and if elevated to *capomastro*, or grand master, he could rule with unlimited power. Among the most-reported rules of modern American prison gangs is the rule of 'blood in, blood out'. This is still true with gangs such as the Aryan Brotherhood and the Mexican Mafia. Likewise, a Camorrist can become too old for active membership, 'but could never wholly withdraw from the society'. His wisdom and institutional memory might be called on. He was helped out in old age, his widow pensioned and children provided for. By 1920, at least according to Griffiths, the Camorra still flourished in the south and especially in convict colonies established in various parts of the kingdom. At the time of his writing the society was considered active but not as numerically strong as in the past.[60]

### Raffaele Cutolo and the New Organized Camorra

Some time in the mid-1970s the Camorra was transformed under the leadership of Raffaele Cutolo. One observer suggests that the origins of the Nuova Camorra Organizzata, or New Organized Camorra (NCO), in some ways resembled those of the Camorra of the nineteenth century.[61] Known as *O professore*, the professor, Cutolo had spent a good portion of his time between 1963 and the mid-1970s in maximum-security facilities and psychiatric units. He was sentenced to life in prison at the age of twenty in 1963, for killing someone who dared offend his sister, but his sentence was reduced to 24 years on appeal. Cutolo carried himself like a 'man of respect', even adopting monikers such as 'State of Poggioreale's Leader', 'NCO Prince' and 'the Great'.[62] In the 1970s he demonstrated his control in prison by deciding which jail his gang members would be transferred to, and by using a prison governor's phone to make calls all over the world. In one instance he even got away with slapping a Naples jail governor for daring to have his cell inspected.[63]

While incarcerated, Cutolo built up his organization. He began by 'befriending young inmates unfamiliar with custodial institutions and offering them a sense of identity and worth', a common ploy of prison shot-callers. He insinuated himself into their lives to the extent that when they were released they would send Cutolo 'flowers', money in prison patois, which enabled him to expand his network.[64] One Cutolo chronicler suggested that he enhanced his clout among the *giovani onorati*, or distinguished youth, by purchasing food for the poor prisoners from the commissary. Many would later become his acolytes in the NCO. By most accounts he frightened other prisoners, burnishing his respect by often walking with a book in his hands – that is, when he wasn't absorbed in a book in his cell.[65]

Cutolo was convinced that the Camorra was indeed born behind bars. He remained a respected and feared presence, while at the same time helping inmates learn to read and write. Doing this allowed prisoners to write to family members and others perhaps for future favours. He retained the allegiance of his followers by having regular payments made to the families of incarcerated members. Giving impoverished

Raffaele Cutolo and his son Roberto, who was killed in 1990.

inmates food created many 'debts' or 'rain cheques', which he would cash at the opportune moment.[66] But there was always an ulterior motive. Cutolo believed it was essential to recruit new young members in prison, who would become the nucleus of future organizational growth. In the meantime, he continued to embrace alliances with other criminals and political representatives.

### The NCO and the Cirillo Affair

The NCO was able to demonstrate its clout outside prison in 1981, following the kidnapping of Christian Democrat councillor Ciro Cirillo by the Red Brigades. As it turned out, when Cutolo was behind bars at the high-security Ascoli Piceno's prison he had established a relationship with members of the Red Brigades (Brigate Rosse) terrorist group. By some accounts he entered an agreement with the group in which both groups would reciprocate favours when necessary. As a result he was able to intervene in the case, leading to Cirillo's release less than three months later.

It turned out that the powerful Christian Democratic Party was willing to use Cutolo as a go-between. Following an initial meeting, the Camorra boss agreed to use his 'influence within the jails to persuade the Red Brigades' to release Cirillo. More meetings, including one at the Ascoli Piceno jail where Cutolo was detained, took place. According to Tom Behan, this was 'an incredible venue considering the fact that notorious criminals who were wanted for serious crimes also took part in meetings inside the jail, and apparently were given carabinieri uniforms and passes' to complete the charade.[67]

One observer noted that the negotiations 'moved with astonishing speed' after the Italian secret services gained permission from the National Prison Office to speak with Cutolo the day after the kidnapping.[68] The initial meetings included senior NCO members, secret service agents and the Christian Democrat mayor. The NCO's motives in helping were not altogether altruistic. Apparently the driving force in its intervention was to end the massive police build-up in its municipal strongholds. The almost constant searching through homes and buildings, combined with numerous roadblocks, had brought NCO smuggling activities to a virtual standstill. These factors, probably more than anything else, explain Cutolo's interest in ending the crisis.

### The Twenty-first-century Camorra behind Bars

More recently, the Camorra has been charged with rigging a state exam for prison guards in order to get their own members inside the penal system. These accusations are believed to be the first to insinuate that the national exams had been tampered with. The exams had been set for four hundred prison-guard jobs, but 88 were said to have been caught wearing bracelets or carrying mobile-phone covers containing the test answers. Some who were caught brazenly carried radio transmitters and ear pieces via which they were told the answers to some test questions.[69]

In recent years the court system has been so successful at locking up veteran Camorra bosses that the 'task of holding Naples in thrall to the Camorra has fallen to ever-younger, more reckless affiliates'. Teenage gangsters are especially attractive to criminal organizations due to their protections under law. For instance, if they are younger than fourteen 'they cannot be held criminally liable for their misdeeds'. In 2017, the Carabinieri arrested a seventeen-year-old alleged 'baby boss'. One explanation for the continuing grip of the Camorra on the young is the fact that it can offer higher-paying jobs in a region where the employment rate for those aged 15–24 is under 12 per cent. With the incarceration of the influential Camorra bosses, 'a younger, more reckless generation of aspiring clan leaders' are now fighting it out to fill the vacuum in authority left by the older bosses.[70]

The Camorra and other Italian criminal societies continue to exercise influence in Italian prisons. As recently as 2016 the Italian state estimated that 7,000 gang members, including seven hundred senior members and Mafia bosses, were being held in Italian prisons.[71] However, in recent years the presence of the Camorra has been most felt outside prison walls. One leading Italian organized crime researcher suggests that the Camorra's 'investments are more geographically widespread' than in times past, encompassing a slew of businesses critical to the construction industry and the disposal of toxic waste.[72] Today, the Camorra has expanded its operations well beyond its confines in the vicinity of Naples into the industrialized north of Italy. While the society continues to adhere to its nineteenth-century roots, which emphasized kinship and familial ties, it has not been unaffected by changes in the broader modern world. As far back as 2001, the stereotype of the Mafia wife – 'loyal, deferential and tight lipped – began changing when the role of women in organized crime became more prominent'. This was perhaps best exemplified by the case of Camorra boss Luigi Giuliani, locked up in a Neapolitan prison. For a short time his wife took over some of his duties, until she was arrested for threatening to kill the widow of a rival crime boss, and other crimes. But, as one Neapolitan police spokesman put it, 'Family ties are very tight here, and women have always had a far more dominant role in the family here than in Sicily.'[73]

# 3

# 'THIEVES WITH A CODE OF HONOUR': LORDS OF THE RUSSIAN GULAG SYSTEM

Russia has long had one of the largest prison populations per capita in the world, a legacy of the former Soviet Union and the harsh Gulag system that was introduced during the earlier tsarist era, when Peter the Great (1672–1725) oversaw the creation of a vast network of Russian prison camps. By the early 1720s, prisoners were obliged to work on public works projects, building roads and fortresses and even ships in his namesake capital, St Petersburg. In 1722, Peter commenced specifically banishing criminals (with their entire families) to exile in the wilds of eastern Siberia, where they were forced to work in the silver mines. With the abolition of the death penalty in 1753, tsarist Russia began to transport all the formerly condemned to labour camps, or *katorgas*, for life (*katorga* is derived from the Greek word *kateirgon*, 'to force'). It was in these labour camps that hardened criminals banded together, spreading in time throughout the entire Gulag Archipelago.

Following the demise of the tsars, a new society of convicts emerged, bound together by a rigid code of conduct that prohibited them from seeking a legitimate job once freed, from paying taxes, serving in the military and cooperating with authorities. To some observers the emergence of the *vory-v-zakone*, or 'thieves with a code of honour', with its castes and ranks, mirrored the highly regimented tsarist society, 'in which officials from almost every occupation had their uniforms and place'. Put another way, the *vorovskoi mir*, or the 'world of thieves', introduced a 'network of exacting regulations that extended to the most minute matters and ultimately . . . a system of "collective beliefs" that is remarkably uniform among criminals with different ethnic roots.'[1]

The *vory* are unlike most of the prison gangs in the chapters that follow. They did not restrict membership according to race, ethnicity, culture or religion. Nor did they conform to the stereotypes of modern prison gangs in the way that most researchers understand them. One would be hard-pressed to find a *'vory* gang' or a *vor* (singular of *vory*) 'who was limited to just one group'. The thieves didn't just follow their own code of behaviour. In many ways they were the most influential authorities in the daily life of the prison camps. They might have lived by a thieves' code, but they were much more than that. They could determine life or death, solve problems and provide goods and services inside the camps. The *vory* can be best understood as similar to judges for hire, asked to resolve disputes for which they were paid in one form or another.[2]

However, like the development of the Italian Camorra in the previous chapter, a number of criminal subcultural traditions developed in the Russian prison-camp system that eventually became more formalized. In Russia, this criminal fraternity had developed by the late 1920s and it remained distinct from other groups of prisoners due to its rules, rituals and code of behaviour.

Russian criminal gangs flourished as far back as the fifteenth century, long before the introduction of the penitentiary or the GULAG system (Gulag is used elsewhere in the text).[3] By the seventeenth century some of the so-called thieves' traditions and slang that identified early denizens of the future gulag complex had emerged, but the foundations of Russia's criminal underworld and associated subculture only became discernible during the tsarist era, when thieves' and beggars' guilds controlled petty crime.[4]

There has been a long-running debate as to whether the *vory* existed prior to the Russian Revolution of 1917. Recent research suggests that references to the *vory-v-zakone* cannot be found during the tsarist era. According to one leading scholar, if one were to go searching for its origins, it could only be done by searching for it under different nomenclature. In any case, there is little doubt that it was well established in the Soviet prison labour camps by the 1930s.[5]

Since the majority of labour-camp prisoners prior to the Russian Revolution were illiterate peasants, criminals and labourers, what is known about life in the Siberian camps is preserved in the memoirs of political prisoners. It was not until the Soviet publication of Alexander Solzhenitsyn's 1962 novel, *One Day in the Life of Ivan Denisovich*, according to Gulag expert Anne Applebaum, that the 'only authentic piece of Gulag literature [was] published by an official Soviet publishing house'.[6]

Henry 'Hy' Sandham, 'Interior of a Kamera in the Kara Political Prison':
illustration in George Kennan, *Siberia and the Exile System* (1891).

## Prison Subculture during the Tsarist Era

During the late nineteenth century a number of behaviours that
marked the post-revolutionary prison criminal subculture emerged
in Russian labour camps. In the early 1860s, the Russian writer Fyodor
Dostoevsky (1821–1881) recounted some of his prison experiences in
*The House of the Dead*. He recalled that the 'bulk of the prison population were exiled convicts or *sylno-katorzhny* of the civilian division
(heavily punished convicts)'. Dostoevsky went on to report how these
criminals were 'entirely deprived of all rights of property, fragments
cut off from society, with branded faces to bear witness for ever that
they were outcasts'. Of the various inmate castes, a 'special section'
comprised 'the most terrible criminals, principally soldiers . . . They
considered themselves in for life, and did not know the length of their
sentence. According to law they had to perform double or treble tasks.
They were kept in the prison until some works involving very severe
hard labour were opened in Siberia.'[7]

According to one researcher, numerous sources cite *The House of the
Dead* as evidence that a prison-gang-like subculture was developing long

George Kennan, 'Group of Convicts', Siberia, c. 1885–6, photographic print.

before the revolution, with passages describing the vanity and boasting of certain convicts, as well as an overarching passion for card games. Indeed, certain convicts rose to prominence and earned a measure of heroic status by defying the authorities and enduring harsh physical punishment in return. There is also plenty of evidence demonstrating how new convicts were expected to pay tribute to more senior prisoners, which has been one of the 'near universal features of prison life'. However, what is missing from the historical record, except for individual examples of professional criminals directing some aspects of prison life, is any real evidence of an organization or society with strict rules and rituals and other characteristics that later exemplified the post-revolutionary-era *vory*. Moreover, one pioneering scholar asserted that 'neither the writings of Dostoevsky nor archives he has consulted refer to an organized group of convicts that systematically refused to work or collaborate with authorities, and, most importantly, that possessed an initiation ritual, strict rules of behaviour and criminal "courts" to enforce such rules across different prisons [prior to 1917]'.[8] Likewise, more recent research also demonstrated the fact that 'the pre-revolutionary underworld [mostly outside prison] was not yet dominated by substantial

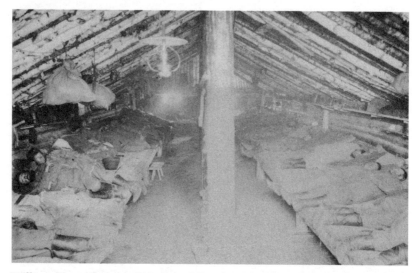

William Henry Jackson, 'Interior of Convict Barracks, Khabarovsk Area',
c. 1895, photographic print.

and durable criminal organizations, but consisted of myriad small gangs and groups.'[9]

Despite these assertions, there are examples of nebulous prison-gang-like activity, but none could match the scale and reach of the 1920s and '30s thieves. In 1882, for example, a Polish prisoner wrote:

When Dostoevsky [served 1849–59] arrived in prison, the gang, as we called it, did not like it. The criminals in prison had their own laws, and they lived according to these laws. They could even stab to death the other prisoners who violated these laws. Dostoevsky took a gift of tobacco from a soldier guard; it was a tobacco leaf. According to the rules of the criminal world, if somebody received tobacco as a gift, he should take half of it and divide the second half into several parts, and the other prisoners cast a lot to see who would get it. Dostoevsky refused to take it or to cast a lot. He divided the tobacco into two equal parts, and gave it to two sick prisoners. So, our local criminal chiefs of the gang were angry at him, and they decided to set him up on the next occasion . . . The guard soldiers took in Dostoevsky and Golovachev only. I do not know how they were punished, but the next day we heard a rumor that Dostoevsky had died. I knew that he was not used to torture, and besides, he was an ill man . . . We were all confident in his death, but we did not know the details . . . About a month and a half after this execution, people forgot about Dostoevsky, but I continued thinking of him, and his image was in my memories. One day he returned to the prison barracks from work, and I heard a familiar voice, 'Hello, Rozhnovsky.' I looked at him – it was Dostoevsky . . . it seemed to me that he was a ghost who came from the world of the dead. I wanted to say, 'Dostoevsky are you alive,' but I could not say a word, and we embraced each other. It turned out that when he was brought to the prison hospital, there was another very sick person who died the day after he arrived and a nurse wrote the wrong name on the register by mistake. When he recovered from his illness, everything cleared up, but our gang gave him the nickname 'a dead man.' Nobody called him by his real name afterwards.[10]

### Early Criminal Castes

Several Russian criminal 'castes' had been identified by the beginning of the twentieth century. At the top of the hierarchy were 'Ivans', the professional criminals of the underworld demi-monde. The main distinction of this group was their tendency 'to not "remember" their kinship', referring to the fact that by ignoring their societal and familial kinship they were to be considered social outcasts. As noted in the *vory* code, a thief was expected to shed any ties to family and society, 'a criterion for affiliation with a fraternity of criminals'.[11] This concept is made particularly clear by what happened when individuals were picked up and interrogated by police. Any questions about family ties were typically met with: 'I do not remember.' Of all the criminal castes, it was the so-called Ivans who most adhered to the ideology that a true thief must maintain a nomadic existence, living without family or house and without subjecting himself to any facet of state authority.[12]

The castes, in descending order, were Ivans, 'robbers of prison laborers'; the *Khrapy*, 'instigators of various caste groups'; *Players*, or 'card swindlers'; *Asmadei*, loansharks tied to the card swindlers; *Slaves*, or 'prisoners who had lost their lives to gambling'; *Sukharniki*, 'who performed work for others and served time for pay'; and *Shpanki*, or 'simple peasants'. However, 'these distinctions among criminals did not exist outside of prison'. Of these seven classes the first four were regarded as 'aristocratic', due to the fact that they had access to the most financial resources.[13]

### After the Revolution

By the time of the 1917 Russian Revolution, the *katorga* was considered a rare form of punishment and the total number of convicts was estimated at less than 30,000. Following the eradication of the tsars, the country's prison system deteriorated into a 'university within the underworld'. The hierarchy of criminals, in many respects, corresponded to the thieves' specializations, although physical strength, intelligence and charisma remained the ultimate determinant of one's place in the criminal hierarchy.

The ability to stand up for oneself became a means by which to evaluate a thief's authority. Consequently, any thief who had not served a stint in prison was barred from rising to higher positions within the criminal hierarchy. Moreover, the thief had to have the expertise and abilities necessary to resolve disputes without the use of physical violence. This was particularly significant 'considering the fact that murder was viewed as the ultimate sin'.[14] Prisons proved fertile ground for the recruitment of new members, as they do today. Here criminals were taught, trained and initiated into the thieves' world.

The familiar Gulag system was fine-tuned under Soviet leaders Vladimir Lenin and Joseph Stalin.[15] In 1917, Lenin announced that forthwith 'class enemies' should be treated as criminals, whether there was

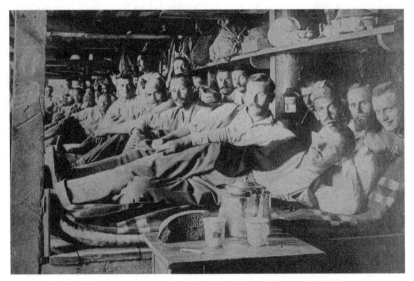

Prison camp, Irkutsk, *c.* 1915–20, glass photographic negative.

Prisoner miners, Vaygach expedition of the OGPU on Vaygach Island, 1933. From left to right: I. A. Gotsiridze, N. V. Kukuradze and I. A. Namidze.

evidence or not. It did not take long for the *katorgas* to be flooded with class enemies ranging from former nobles, merchants and businessmen to large landowners and government officials who had been accused of sabotage and corruption. As a result of this edict, political prisoners and criminal gangs were pitted against each other, not unlike the Neapolitan Camorra and the political prisoners who mixed behind bars.

In the years to come, the Gulag became a much more sinister presence in Russian life. The term's general usage gradually referred to 'the entire slave labor complex', including labour and punishment camps, as well as any camp holding criminal and political prisoners, Moscow's prisons, rural railway carriages and so forth. Indeed, 'hardly a single major population center in the former Soviet Union did not have its own local camp or camps, or a single industry that did not employ prisoners.'[16]

As Stalin's control over the secret police expanded after 1929, the Gulag population swelled from 200,000 (1932) to 1 million (1935) (if other penal colonies are also included). Before the death of Stalin in 1953, an estimated 18 million people passed through some aspect of the system, with another 6–7 million deported to exile villages in the faraway hinterlands.[17]

## Vory-v-zakone

By the late 1920s, Soviet prison camps had expanded to such an extent that legions of professional criminals had created their own society, adhering to a strict behavioural code that prohibited them from having anything to do with the Soviet state. If one were to be taken seriously as a thief-in-law, one was expected to sever all links with conventional society, to refuse to work, own a passport or collaborate with officials in any way (unless it involved exploiting them), and not to start a family. The system of *vory* rules was often more theoretical than real. According to one Russian expert, it was not uncommon for *vory* to break these rules when it suited them. Moreover, as times changed, so did the rules. Ultimately, the *vory* set up their rules to benefit themselves, and when they needed some adjusting, they did this as well. The very existence of the rules 'was as much about creating an image and mystique of power so as to make it easier to get *frayeri* [inmates who were easy prey, or 'suckers'] to comply'.[18]

In Soviet Russia's vast Gulag system, a pecking order existed among the criminal elements, in which professional 'big-time' criminals were considered dominant. At the top of the food chain were the hardcore criminals, variously referred to as *blatnoi, urki, urkagany* and *blatary*. One historian described them as 'the exclusive elite of the vory', the *vory-v-zakone*, or thieves-in-law, who lived according to a distinct set of rules and customs 'which preceded the Gulag, and which outlasted it'.[19] They clearly considered themselves a class apart and had little to do with petty criminal types. There was little love lost between these milieus, as the ordinary criminals hated them as well. While there was a distinction between professional criminals and *vory*, unless one knew what to look for, these prisoners would be indistinguishable.[20]

A *vor* had a variety of methods for determining another thief's status. In cases where a new inmate projected obvious signs of affiliation with the underworld subculture, thieves, perhaps in a cell or elsewhere in the labour camp, would invite him to a clandestine meeting to establish his bona fides and identification. One trick used to identify members was to 'spread on the floor of the entrance to a cell a new silk shirt or clean towel'. A new arrival or non-clan member would typically try and avoid it. On the other hand, a thief would step on the shirt or towel and 'quietly clean them' afterwards, revealing membership.[21]

Anyone who deviated from the thieves' unwritten rules was expected to appear before a secret tribunal. If found guilty, he would give up his status, a process known as 'earthing'. Passive homosexuality was forbidden. Breaking this rule transformed the gang member into an outcast who was considered less than human. He would be dubbed a 'rooster', which forced him to 'keep company' only with the camp's male prostitutes. Any thief raped by enemies was expected to kill the perpetrator(s) and then himself.[22]

Like other professional criminals behind bars, there is some evidence that thieves could demonstrate incredible ingenuity when it came to manufacturing drugs and alcohol (however, these were more likely to have been smuggled into the camps). One account written in the 1970s asserted that 'spirits could be made out of almost anything, including tooth powder and brake fluid'. Prison-camp stories were told of phenobarbital drugs, designed to control seizures, being combined with cocaine, morphine and opium to provide succour to drug addicts and epilepsy victims.

One of the more bizarre claims was that the *vory* permitted incredible 'freedom of action', including 'cannibalism'. Escape was never far from the minds of long-term prisoners, even if it usually meant certain death from starvation or exposure in the wilds of Siberia. The ever-pragmatic thief found a way around this by bringing an unsuspecting common criminal(s) with him on the prison break. The future victim had no clue that they were being brought along as 'meat' or 'walking cans'. Viewed as a 'walking larder', slang was created to describe such 'hapless prey – myaso, or meat'.[23] The plan was that in order to avoid starvation the *vory* could murder and consume his 'meat'. This act fell neatly into the *vory* ethos that allowed murder only in the case of emergency; however, like any type of *vory* murder, it was expected to be justified later on.[24]

Among the most strictly upheld principles of the *vory* was the prohibition against working for the state. The state took any refusal to work seriously and created draconian rules to enforce the order. The challenge was that if a thief refused orders to work three times, he could be executed. Not surprisingly, it was a common conceit that most *vory* would do anything to avoid having to reject the third order. In some cases, for example, rather than refuse to work for the third time, a thief might provoke a fight, wound or kill someone or injure themselves in order to end up in a punishment cell or hospital for several weeks rather than earn execution. Although *vory* refused to work, particularly on public works projects like building barracks and prisons, stretching barbed wire or any type of cleaning, they were typically punished, but by some accounts, 'authorities generally avoided direct conflict with them.'[25]

## The Thieves' World: Initiation and Hierarchy

The institution of the *vory-v-zakone* was 'a product of prison culture ... a feature that distinguishes them from Sicilian Mafiosa [*sic*]'.[26] What's more, the correctional labour camps acted as a pipeline for the further development of the customs and traditions of the thieves' world, further increasing their power and encouraging group cohesion.[27]

The *vory* was distinctive due to its lack of 'strict vertical hierarchy'. One authority described the world of the *vory* as 'egalitarian' or 'a fraternity of equals'.[28] Another Russian organized-crime researcher went a step further by enumerating the various tasks and ranks fulfilled by labour-camp *vory*. The *Sovetnik*, for example, was considered a 'trusted advisor', who was proficient at manipulating the prison system, playing all the angles to exploit vulnerable points in the camp and internal procedures in the furtherance of establishing channels to smuggle in alcohol, drugs and women. Not surprisingly, this was considered among the most important *vory* tasks.[29]

In order to help the *Sovetnik*, there was typically an assistant, or 'watcher (*smotriaschchyi*)', who was expected to vet new arrivals and help determine what role they might play in the labour camp. Under these two positions was the 'supply group', which was responsible for organizing and storing supplies or, when needed, coming up with monetary resources. Next in descending order was the 'security group', which was tasked with more challenging administrative tasks such as debt collection from protected members or gamblers who did not pay their losses, and punishing non-productive convicts. Ex-athletes were perfect in this position and were referred to as 'bulls' or 'torpedoes'. In modern parlance, they would be closer to a prison enforcer. At the bottom rung of the ladder were 'sixers (*shestiorka*)', named after the lowest-value card in traditional Russian card games. These individuals were glorified 'gofers', typically expected to perform the grunt work, such as cleaning and laundry.[30]

In order to be accepted into the thieves' world, an individual had to be recommended by at least two or three *vory*. Naturally the more support the better. By some accounts, the prospect had to swear an oath in front of his new brothers: 'being an inmate, I have chosen the thieves' path and swear before equals to be a worthy thief and never with the Chekists [early Soviet secret police].'[31] In the 1950s, according to Federico Varese, one initiation ceremony took place in a transit prison that contained ten cells for hardened criminals. Since they were locked in isolation cells, it was necessary 'to conduct the ceremony in writing, by pen and paper'. A note was passed from cell to cell, praising the prospect and supporting his admission into the thieves' world. One of the thieves wrote 'his behaviour and aspirations are totally in accordance with the vory's worldview.' Another applauded him for defying 'camp discipline for a long period of time and practically never being let out of his punishment cell'. A police officer later confiscated the paper and turned it in to the proper authorities.[32] By most accounts, being accepted into the thieves' world was akin to becoming a made member of a traditional Mafia family.

## Vory Culture

There are several features of *vory* culture that make it distinct from other prison-gang subcultures that value the accumulation of lucre and the shedding of blood. By contrast, the *vory*, rather than zealously accumulating assets, was expected to show contempt towards this sort of goal. Only short-term use of stolen cash or goods was allowed, rather than owning anything on a long-term basis. Compared to America's myriad gangs, which in the past followed the edict of 'blood in, blood out', or shedding blood to get in and to get out, a *vor* could leave the fraternity but could never betray old fellows. This strange code against murder effectively barred professional killers from joining. The only instances in which violent confrontations were permitted were situations involving self-defence and defending one's honour. Nonetheless, any time a thief took a life he had to explain the circumstances to his fellow gang members.[33]

The *vory* took gambling very seriously. Applebaum, for example, describes one card game between two high-ranking thieves. The game didn't end until one participant lost all his possessions. In this instance, instead of betting an arm or a leg, the winner demanded an awful humiliation, by ordering the barracks tattoo artist to ink 'an enormous penis on the man's face, pointing at his mouth'. Minutes after this was done, the loser used a red-hot poker to obliterate the tattoos on his face, leaving him scarred for life.[34] Varese relates another story, in which a criminal bet his left hand in a game of cards but could not bear to pay up after he lost, and tried to escape from the camp. He was quickly recaptured and sent to another camp, but 'his fate was sealed.' The criminals found out where he had been sent and arranged for his execution to be carried out in his new surroundings.[35] There was no escaping *vory* law in the labour-camp and prison system.

## Argot

According to one early student of modern Russian organized crime, 'the language of the criminal went largely unstudied until the last years of the Soviet Union since ideologically, professional criminality could not exist and, therefore, there was no reason to study its language.'[36] There is little consensus as to when *vory* slang developed or where it came from, but by most accounts Soviet prison- and labour-camp jargon dates back at least to the 1920s. Like other examples of prison argot, it 'expresses the unique and grim experience of its users, often and purposely difficult for outsiders to understand'. Moreover, it was developed among the hardcore inmates so that it could 'readily be incorporated into the speech of any Russian user'.[37]

According to Meyer Galler and Harlan E. Marquess, 'Russian speech in general, is rather rich in proverbs, maxims, and similar sayings,' often denoting 'such basic concerns as hunger, beatings, dealing with the established higher authorities ... concerns that occupied convicts'.[38] Moreover, 'In its earliest form, prison camp speech consisted of pre-revolutionary jargon of criminals. But new words and expressions, devised to reflect new conditions in the camps and in Soviet free life, were gradually added to the initial stock of words until eventually they came to outnumber the criminal component'.[39]

One leading researcher felt that

> striking evidence of the coherence and complexity of the underworld of the vor can be found in its two languages, the criminal cant known as *fenya* [fenyia] or *ofenya* [ofenia], and a visual one encoded in often complex tattoos which had criminal careers inscribed on bodies.[40]

The criminal slang was distinguished by the use of extra syllables, 'usually "fe" and "nya" inserted between syllables of regular words'. Galeotti offers the example of the term for prison, *tyurma*, which would be transformed into *tyurmanya* in fenyia.[41]

## Tattoos

Besides argot and other customs, what most distinguished the thieves from other prisoners was their distinctive use of tattoos that identified where each prisoner stood in the thieves' world. Tattoos proved integral to the criminal and prison experience. It was not uncommon to see a convict tattooed head to toe in order to 'display his dedication to a life of crime and specifically, a life behind bars'.[42] Tattoos revealed

*Eastern Promises* (2007, dir. David Cronenberg), starring Viggo Mortensen. The film was noted for its realistic depiction of Russian career criminals, including detailed portrayal of the tattoos that indicate their crimes and criminal status.

a convict's criminal history: what types of crimes he committed and his criminal speciality, how many times in prison, level of authority in the underworld, attitudes towards other prisoners, and if he had ever escaped. One expert suggests the use of tattoos increased after the Communist Party took over the country. It was one of the rare ways prisoners could 'express their political beliefs, demonstrate their positions in the complex prison hierarchy, and most importantly, proclaim their personalities, talents, and plans'.[43] Tattoos also indicated homosexuality or drug addiction.

Although the majority of tattoos were chosen by the inmates, sex offenders and other marginalized prisoners were forcibly tattooed with the image of a knife running across their shoulder blades and through their necks. In some cases, prison inmates were tattooed from head to toe, while a *vory* might have negligible tattooing complementing the identical eight-point stars tattooed on each side of the torso just below the collarbone, or on the knees – the mark of the *vory-v-zakone*.

During the Stalinist era it was de rigueur to tattoo images of Lenin and Stalin on one's chest, in the belief that no firing squad would dare shoot at the strategically placed convict tattoos of such revered icons. Other tattoos included illustrations of playing cards or suits to indicate if a convict was a gambler, a dollar sign for a safe-cracker, or a tree-branch tattoo to identify an independent thief who worked outside the purview of any specific gang. Any 'wannabe' *vor* wearing a tattoo that he was not entitled to could be killed or have the piece of skin sliced off.[44]

### *Vor* Fashion Sense

The gangsters of the Gulag came in many incarnations. A number of observers throughout the Soviet era commented on a specific type of labour-camp inmate who was identifiable by a particular sartorial style and accompanying behaviours. According to Applebaum, the highest-ranking *vor* spoke differently from other inmates. But perhaps more than their prison argot, they were recognizable for their 'bizarre fashion sense', which served the purpose of identifying them as a 'separate identifiable caste, which contributed further to the power of intimidation they exercised'. One observer in the 1940s described some *vory* wearing 'aluminum crosses around their necks, with no religious intent. It was kind of a symbol.' During the long, harsh winters, *vory* preferred 'peakless caps, folded down the tops of their felt boots, and wore a cross around the neck. The cross was usually smooth, but if an artist was around, he was forced to use a needle to paint it with the most diverse subjects: a heart, cards, a crucifixion, a naked woman.' Another prisoner in the 1940s described the 'distinctive walk of thieves'. According to the inmate, the gait featured 'small steps, legs slightly apart'. It was not uncommon for them to wear gold or silver crowns on their teeth which they affixed as a sort of fashion. One account from 1943 describes the typical *vor* wearing 'a dark-blue three-piece outfit, with trousers tucked into boxcalf boots. Blouse under the waistcoat, tucked out. Also a cap, pulled over the eyes.'[45] But *vor* camp fashions were often in flux. Twenty years earlier, thieves were instantly recognizable from their 'trade school caps', and in prior years the military officer's cap was considered all the rage.

## The Keepers and the Kept

The dearth of staff and guards plagued the camp system almost from its inception. 'As late as 1947', according to Galeotti, 'they were short 40,000 armed guards.'[46] Similar to other future prison gangs that are covered in the following chapters, the keepers and the kept sometimes entered into informal agreements from which both profited. By some accounts, prisoners had been recruited to collaborate with the state and tsarist police as far back as the seventeenth century.[47]

By the 1930s, the Soviet government recognized that indoctrination and education strategies to reform prisoners were failing. Initially the programme was directed towards the *vory*, who the administration felt were more reformable than political prisoners; however, once confronted with the fact that this was not happening, the prison system gave up on reforming them and shifted its strategy to using them to control and intimidate other prisoners, particularly 'counterrevolutionaries', whom 'the vory naturally loathed'. This schism between criminals and political prisoners dates back, as mentioned previously, to the nineteenth century, when, according to Dostoevsky, 'convicts in Siberia already hated political prisoners.'[48]

A concerted effort was made to 'openly deploy small groups of professional prisoners to control other inmates from about 1937 to the end of the war'. While it was conventional *vory* behaviour to refuse to work or cooperate with authorities, there was always the caveat that the latter was permissible as long as they did not exploit their position. So, during this period the highest-ranking thieves did not work but made sure others did.[49]

## The Bitches' War, 1947/8–53

Only with the Second World War, when hundreds of thousands of Soviet prisoners were released to fight for the motherland with promises of amnesty after the war was won, was there any decline in the penal population. After the German army invaded Russia in 1941, many inmates joined the military (by either their own volition or coercion). Over a three-year period, close to 1 million left labour camps for the Red Army, demonstrating that some gangsters still had a 'deeper loyalty to Mother Russia.'[50] However, by 1944, as the tide turned, the Russian government reneged on its initial promises of amnesty and parole and returned many of the *vory*-turned-soldiers to the camps, where they were lambasted and persecuted as collaborators by the traditionalist thieves.

Following the end of hostilities in 1945, violators of the *vory* code, who hoped to reintegrate into the thieves' world, were rejected en masse. At the same time as the perceived defectors were returning to the prison camps, they were joined by other criminals, deserters, repatriated Russian prisoners of war, civilians and even Nazi concentration-camp survivors. Many were battle-hardened survivors of the war on the

Prisoners of the Vorkuta Gulag (Vorkutlag), one of the major Soviet labour camps, Russia, Komi Republic, 1945.

Eastern Front. Among the new inmates were hundreds of thousands of Soviet soldiers and officers who had been German prisoners, survivors of the Russian army that fought alongside the Nazis to upend the Communist regime – ordinary citizens and criminals.

The *vory* who had violated the thieves' code by fighting for the state were branded bitches, or *sukis*, when they were reincarcerated in the camps. These new inmates were not cast in the same mould as earlier denizens of the Gulag, who had been less bellicose or inclined towards violence. Rather than the legions of mostly political dissidents, intellectuals, party officials and peasants who dominated the incoming hordes in the 1930s, the post-war years witnessed the arrival of individuals skilled in the use of violence and posing an immediate threat to any traditional underworld. As this new breed of prisoner began to fight back, they realized that the only way they could maintain their position was with support from the authorities – but for a thief to seek this alliance went against the *vory* code and represented an open break with the past.[51]

The war had done what the penal authorities could not: created a split among the *vory*. Those who violated the code and fought for the state were now ostracized as bitches, shorthand for defectors or turncoats. *Vory* expert Mark Galeotti identifies the biggest flaw in the *vory* convict code: 'the absolute ban on any form of cooperation with the state'. During the Stalin regime, featuring 'totalitarian dreams and massive state power', this tradition became unsustainable. So, in effect, Stalin's policies helped unify the *vory* and at the same time divided it, 'creating a new body of collaborators'.[52]

Tensions between the two *vory* factions resulted in the so-called Bitches' War. Those who were new to the Gulag system found themselves in 'a world divided between exploited politicals, collaborators, and career criminals', most of whom were inclined to side with the *sukis*.[53] The choice for the most part was made for the new prisoners by the traditionalists, who shunned and intimidated them. The uninitiated prisoners might side with the *sukis* and accept the idea of the thieves' code on some level, but would not let this status prevent them from working with the prison authorities and within the system.

The Gulag system welcomed new ethnic groups as the Soviet Union expanded its boundaries after the war. When Russia 'closed [its] fist on central Europe', it led to legions of Balts, Poles and others ending up in the vast labour-camp system. According to one account, a prisoner described his cell wall as being marked with not just the engraved names of a litany of prisoners, but symbols that marked the continuum of inmates over the decades, such as the swastika, a Star of David (SOS) and graffiti such as 'Poland Is Conquered.'[54] As in other overcrowded, poorly policed institutions with prison gangs, various ethnic groups tended to self-segregate for protection and national solidarity. The professional criminals, or *blatnye*, expected the new prisoners to be pushovers. However, their solidarity trumped the inclinations of the criminals. Those perceived as easy marks in the past were now supported by legions of compatriots ready to fight back. Mirroring the conflict between the *vory* cliques, there were several 'interethnic struggles' as well, between Chechens, Ukrainians and Russian labour gangs. One thief of Chechen descent recalled leaving the *vory* to side with other Chechens, commenting 'the code is important, but blood is everything.'[55]

The Bitches' War played right into the hands of the Soviet authorities. What started as 'a battle over supremacy over the camps and for the soul of the *vorovskoi mir*' had major ramifications for the *vory*'s hold on the Gulag system and ended up restructuring the world of the thieves; however, this would prove to be a battle 'the authorities encouraged but came to regret.'[56]

## Power Shift

One of the unintended consequences of the government-encouraged internecine conflict between the old guard and the *sukis* was that while the collaborators were quite willing to help run the Gulags, it would only be for their own benefit.[57] The Stalinist system was a constant feeder of inmates into the prison camps. Its biggest challenge was doing it cheaply. A continual shortfall of armed prison guards meant there was always a shortage of camp-keepers. Considering the harsh working conditions, it was hardly surprising. If anything, the inmate war demonstrated that the ways of the old guard traditionalists were no longer tenable and led to the changing of some of the old *vory* rules behind bars.

The traditional *vory* survived until the 1950s, when it was virtually destroyed by a new generation of criminals who had rejected the code and killed most of its members. One prominent researcher suggested that if one knew what to look for, it was possible to discern the handprint of the government, particularly due to the fact that the *suki*-on-traditionalist assaults occurred 'near enough at once across the camp system in 1948'.

A number of well-planned battles between inmates support the notion that the government was behind the destruction of much of the *vory* ethos. In one case, 150 *sukis* were supplied with shovels, axes and other tools that could easily function as deadly weapons. This group was then transferred to a mining camp run by perhaps one hundred professional criminals, all but ten of whom were killed during the ensuing battle. In the early 1950s tension between the two factions continued. But in contrast to the pre-Second World War era, now the 'working prisoners' had the ability to fight off the weakened *vory*.[58]

## Political Prisoners and the *Vory*

In the last decade of the Stalinist regime more and more political prisoners were sent to the labour camps. During this era, once prisoners were freed from a camp or prison they were restricted from working in a number of free-world occupations and sometimes barred from living in urban centres, often leading to behaviour that put them back in prison.

According to one political prisoner, Lev Razgon, who spent the years between 1938 and 1955 in prisons, camps and exile, some political prisoners found ways to get along with the thieves, especially after the Bitches' War.[59] In his telling, some of the most prominent crime bosses enjoyed using these prisoners as 'mascots or sidekicks'. In one case, Alexander Dolgun (1926–1986), an American who served time in the Gulag, won the respect of a crime boss in a transit camp by beating up a lower-ranking criminal.[60] Applebaum relates a similar story about a 'young political prisoner[,] Marlen Korallov', who so impressed a camp crime boss that he was 'allowed to sit near him in the barracks after winning a fight'. Such an incident could change a prisoner's status in the camp, and in this case led to him being 'regarded as protected and given much better sleeping arrangements'.[61]

## Criminal Collaborators after the Bitches' War

One leading Russian organized-crime researcher asserted that only 'a minority of truly criminal inmates' were utilized at any one time in helping authorities control 'millions of dissident intellectuals, out of favor Communists and political prisoners'. Perhaps 3 per cent of criminals controlled the rest of the prisons, otherwise. Without 'criminal cooperation being institutionalized', it would have been almost impossible to control hundreds of thousands of prisoners. An inmate could not become a supervisor without the approval and cooperation of authorities. In 2005 this practice was legalized, and 'now, prison authorities officially nominate one of the inmates as supervisor.'[62]

The end of the Bitches' War changed much of the equilibrium in the Soviet penal system. The *suki* had won with the apparent backing of the prison administration and the new thieves' code no longer proscribed collaboration with authorities. Any *vory* who continued to hold tight to the old code soon found themself sentenced to the much less salubrious environment of a Siberian prison, while those who made the transition and renounced the title of professional criminal could expect to be relocated to better facilities. By some accounts, this was the result of an unofficial decree by the Supreme Soviet, dated 4 June 1946, which stated that stricter punishment contributed to greater cooperation of professional criminals with authorities as well as creating more collaborators (*otkazniki*).[63]

### The *Vory* in the Post-Soviet Era

With fewer and fewer *vory* scattered in prisons across the Soviet Union, by the 1970s their presence was greatly diminished behind bars. By most accounts, without the Gulag system to inculcate traditions in a new generation of inmates and without the ability to operate openly, the subculture of the thieves' world began to dissipate. It has not gone unnoticed by Russian organized-crime experts that the collapse of the Soviet Union in the following decade also contributed to the discontinuation of several *vory* trademarks, in turn bringing a new disdain for all aspects of the prison experience. Where in the past it was considered a badge of honour or rite of passage, the modern *vor* considered it his duty to avoid prison at all costs. Other traditions, such as tattooing, fell out of favour as well. Also, in times past, *vors* were expected to abstain from owning an apartment or house and other material objects; the new thieves, however, can often be seen cruising major cities in luxury vehicles and even having suits tailor-made and shipped from Paris. By contrast, 'no thief of the old school was interested in getting rich.'[64]

In 1989, Russian authorities estimated there were 512 *vory-v-zakone* (about half in prisons). By 2005, this number had declined by more than half, to about two hundred. According to Joseph Serio and others, the drop can be explained in part by killings during the so-called Great Mob War of 1992–4, as well as natural causes; but what was probably more reasonable was that many had fled overseas, either to escape law enforcement or to establish new operations. Despite its decline in Russia, the *vory* code remained vital to organized crime groups in the former Soviet bloc, in countries such as Georgia.[65]

In 2018, Mark Galeotti offered a fitting send-off to the traditional *vory-v-zakone*, writing: 'their prison records, garish tattoos and clannish rituals increasingly became anachronisms' and '[their] name and the mythology would survive, but lose their strength and meaning.' While there are criminals who identify themselves as *vory*, it does not have the same meaning, making it a 'largely empty honorific, often one bestowed as a favour or bought as a vanity perk. These faux vory are known by the surviving traditionalists as *apelsiny*, "oranges".' Ultimately, most of the modern-day *vory* should be considered 'oranges', since they 'have not earned [the name] according to old traditions, nor do they recognize limitations on behaviour.'[66]

By most accounts, 'the clandestine society of the vory', a product of the Soviet Gulag system, did not 'fare too well in capitalist Russia.' For the most part, the traditional form of prison society is overshadowed today by more innovative and flexible bandits.[67] Moreover, unable to impose their will on emerging criminal groups and 'their street troops – entrepreneurial youth gangs', it appears that the *vory*'s traditional code and principles 'no longer corresponded to the changing realities of Russia.'[68] Today, it is impossible to resurrect the conditions of the Gulag era, when inmates had the time and freedom during almost permanent incarceration to create their thieves' world.

The heyday of the *vory* lasted only from the 1930s to the 1950s, but during its halcyon years, the *vory*-dominated labour-camp system was truly a 'formidable achievement for a criminal fraternity, considering the vastness of the country and the scope of its activities.' An estimated 18 million prisoners did time in the Gulag system between 1934 and 1952. The number of inmates at any one time was never the same. Inmates were constantly on the move, whether coming in, going out or transferring to other camps. This process of coming and going facilitated an almost constant communication between various camps, permitting this society of thieves to stretch from Russia's border with Western Europe to Arctic-facing Alaska. No other prison criminal subculture ever stretched as far geographically, and the almost constant movement of prisoners offered a sophisticated prison grapevine that will probably never be surpassed as far as distance and the number of criminals involved are concerned.

'Intra-Gulag transfers' facilitated the sharing of timely information, in coded messages in a system 'perfected by generations of criminals'. that was necessary to certify purported reputations, expose pretenders and inform members of new *vory* and of those hiding from them.[69] Distance was no protection for prisoners seeking anonymity in another correctional facility. In the words of Federico Varese, 'as the population of the Gulag grew in size it became an even more significant source of contact between criminals scattered across the Soviet Union'. Indeed, 'the camps became the best possible medium for the swift dissemination and maintenance of vory rituals and traditions.'[70]

By the mid-1950s the number of *vory* residing in Soviet prisons had dwindled into the low hundreds. Their role has been further diminished in the correctional facilities of capitalist Russia. Most *vory-v-zakone* and other criminals with police rap sheets have become marginalized in the communities where they were once lionized and exerted social and cultural influence. Individuals with criminal records, according to one police officer, do not enjoy the same prestige today as they did in the 1950s, 'when half the country went through the camps . . . the smart ones don't end up in jail. Mainly people get there for minor crimes.' Prison was no longer a sign of gangster credibility, but a 'repository for losers, petty hooligans and people who were not smart enough to find ways to avoid incarceration.'[71]

Nonetheless, the *vory* continue to wield influence in prisons in some former Soviet territories such as the Republic of Tatarstan, where one survey in the early 2000s found that most of the convicts in its penal colonies continued to follow the prison code, and that in the event of problems they could still turn to imprisoned gang leaders for mediation, rather than administrators.[72]

So, while the Russian prison gangsters lost their cultural relevance in the new Russia, this is not to claim that the subculture no longer exists or wields power in penal institutions. The apprehension that gripped society as the Soviet Union crumbled also impacted the thieves' world. Almost without warning, a criminal's long stint behind bars 'didn't count for much outside . . . Moreover, a new generation of gangster found it was sometimes necessary to cooperate with law enforcement.' Some even had families, in violation of the code. The older traditional prison modes of behaviour might have still carried some weight inside prison, but not outside prison walls.[73]

Similar to the modern incarnation of the South African Number gangs chronicled in the next chapter, the *vory* saw their power and traditions fade in the twenty-first century as a new generation of youth gangs and professional gangsters hit the streets and prison yards. While in former days, a member of the prison-gang demi-monde was expected to earn his reputation on the inside, in Russia, South Africa and other countries, street gangsters were more likely to be accepted into a prison gang and given rank and prestige before they were even inside prison, based on their street credibility. However, in the twenty-first century even a single day behind bars was unacceptable to the modern gangster. Likewise, even traditional symbols such as tattoos were being discarded.

### The Thieves' Code

A thief is bound by the code to:
- Forsake his relatives – mother, father, brothers, sisters, and so on.
- Not have a family of his own – no wife, no children; this does not, however, preclude him from having a lover.
- Never, under any circumstances, work, no matter how much difficulty this brings – live only on means gleaned from thievery.
- Help other thieves – both by moral and material support, utilizing the commune of thieves.
- Keep secret information about the whereabouts of accomplices (for example, dens, districts, hideouts, safe houses).
- In unavoidable situations (if a thief is under investigation), take the blame for someone else's crime; this buys the other person time or freedom.
- Demand a convocation of enquiry for the purpose of resolving disputes in the event a conflict between oneself and other thieves, or between thieves.
- If necessary, participate in such enquiries.
- Carry out the punishment of the offending thief as decided by the convocation.
- Not resist carrying out the decision of punishing the offending thief who is found guilty, with punishment determined by the convocation.
- Have good command of the thieves' jargon.

- Not gamble without being able to cover losses.
- Teach the trade to young beginners.
- Have, if possible, informants from the rank and file of thieves.
- Not lose your reasoning ability when using alcohol.
- Have nothing to do with the authorities, not participate in public activities, nor join any community organizations.
- Not take weapons from the hands of authorities; not serve in the military.
- Make good on promises given to other thieves.[74]

# 4

# SOUTH AFRICA'S NUMBER GANGS

The South African corrections system took shape during the expansion of British colonial rule in the nineteenth century. Indeed, as in other African countries, the 'colonial model of the prison was transferred practically untouched to the African elite' in the 1950s.[1] Although it was influenced by developments in Europe and the Americas, the Cape Colony was recognized for aiming imprisonment more towards offenders of pass laws than towards conventional criminality. In the late nineteenth century, settler communities introduced pass laws to control the movement of native Africans and regulate the labour force. Anyone could be arrested at any time for not carrying the appropriate documentation that permitted them to be in a specific place. Those sentenced to prison often ended up as convict labour for gold- and diamond-mining companies. One chronicler of the era went as far as to assert that the pass laws 'insured that the absconding laborer would be almost certainly confined to another large male institution – the urban prison'.[2] Thus, the evolution of the prison system has been closely linked to the progressive institutionalization of racial discrimination in the country.[3]

South Africa 'was the first country in Africa – and the only one with nineteenth century roots – to undergo a fully-fledged industrial revolution'.[4] In the wake of more than sixty years of colonialism and the onslaught of industrialization, hundreds of thousands of farmers and herders were forced to make the transition to common labourers, scratching out a living as farm and factory workers or miners. Some historians have gone as far as suggesting that these changes were 'at least as harsh and disruptive as those in early industrial Britain'. Moreover, just as the 'shadow of the workhouse and the "dark satanic mills" were an ever-present reality [in industrial Britain], so South Africa spawned its own distinctively labour-repressive institutions as its industrial revolution gained momentum in the early twentieth century.[5]

Prisons in the region have been described as uniformly grim, characterized by overcrowding, poor sanitation, limited health services and a paucity of correctional staff. While not all South Africa's prisons fall into this category, today those that do often have at least three men sharing a single cell and communal cells holding more than three dozen; others are teeming with double the number of inmates they were designed for. One inmate recounted being assigned to a 'large rectangular room lined with bunk beds and with ablutions at the front. Exactly 52 men were in each cell, with 100 cells just like this.'[6]

Many inmates spend up to 23 hours a day locked up in communal cells where the lights never go off. However, although prisoners are locked up, they are unsupervised for the most part, allowing gangs to operate unhindered for at least fifteen hours each day. Gang and non-gang members are subject to both the confinement regime of the

Mikhael Subotzky, *Cell 33 E2 Section (3), Pollsmoor Maximum Security Prison*, Cape Town, 2004.

prison and the strict rules of prison gangs, which determine who sleeps where and how much money, food and other items must be shared.[7]

A large number of inmates are on remand, a status equivalent to pre-trial custody, meaning they have not even been sentenced yet – a major contributor to overcrowding. This situation is driven by the proclivity of the South African police for hurriedly locking up suspects. Many cannot afford to pay bail or hire lawyers and can spend months and even years behind bars before going to trial, ensuring a never-ending supply of new gang recruits.

As a result of rampant overcrowding and the lack of trained staff, prison gangs have been able to fill the organizational void. In some of the more brutal West Cape prisons, new inmates are forced to join one of the gangs in order to survive. As one inmate put it, 'If I didn't join a gang very quickly, there's a chance I would have been raped in the first days.'[8]

With so little support, prison correctional officers, or 'warders' in regional parlance, focus most of their attention on keeping the inmate population 'contained' and permitting the gangs to operate. While it is not uncommon for inmates to have to sleep on floors while waiting to 'graduate' to a bunk bed, 'joining a gang meant [an inmate] had access to food, a bed and social interaction to pass the time.'[9]

## The Number Gangs: Origins

Of the country's 242 penal institutions, 42 are in the Western Cape. Estimates suggest that 80 per cent of the 30,000 inmates housed there are gang members. The best known of these are the three Number gangs: the 26s, 27s and 28s. Their history reaches back to the early nineteenth century, making them, by most accounts, the earliest incarnations of the prison-gang phenomenon.[10] Their structures are hierarchical, and discipline is strictly enforced with nothing less than absolute loyalty accepted. Their origins saga depends on who is telling it. Of the Numbers, the 26s and 28s are the most powerful. In between is the 27 gang, which is only intended to operate as a mediator or peacemaker between the other two gangs. Their influence has spread through most prisons in South Africa. While they are the most numerous and powerful, other prison gangs exist as well, and will be covered later in this chapter.

The discovery of diamonds and gold in South Africa in the second half of the nineteenth century led to tremendous societal transformation that resulted in the indigenous black population being systematically separated from its land and livestock through either wars or removal schemes. Ultimately, not only did they lose political control of their destinies to European colonizers, but they were forced to move from farms, cities and towns to areas where they could sell their labour, their 'only remaining asset'.[11]

The historical chronicle of the Number gangs begins some time in the late nineteenth or early twentieth century.[12] South Africa, particularly the Johannesburg area, has long been host to criminal gangs, often formed in all-male mining compounds on the Witwatersrand, better known as the Rand. Many of these miners and gang members would eventually pass through the prisons of South Africa, in no small part because of the pass law system, which guaranteed that a large proportion of black South African males would be exposed to the criminal justice system at one time or another. Among the most prominent gangs was the Ninevites, led by the legendary Zulu migrant Mzuzephi Mathebula (1867–1948), who would later enjoy mythic status as 'Nongoloza'. His followers consisted of mostly dispossessed young men who had been forced off their ancestral lands to work for wages and white bosses in various mining compounds.

## Mzuzephi/Jan Note/Nongoloza Mathebula

Nongoloza came into the world as Mzuzephi ('where did you find him?') in rural Natal in 1867.[13] He spent his youth herding cattle before joining the migrant labour pool in 1883. After losing a horse and unwilling or unable to compensate its owner, he cut all ties with friends and family and assumed the Afrikaans name Jan Note (pronounced 'Not' by his African associates). Some suggest his new name might even have been derived from the word *unotha*, which refers to 'cannabis of the best quality.'[14] But Jan Note would remain his moniker until he reinvented himself as Nongoloza.

Note had no trouble falling in with one of the myriad gangs of robbers that plied the roads around early Johannesburg. It appears he was a natural, and after serving what could best be described as his 'criminal apprenticeship', he went off and started his own gang. Building on lessons gleaned from his old crime boss, Note put together a gang of 'largely shapeless riff-raff drawn from fringes of the underworld' and was soon commanding a motley gang of hundreds of male and female vagrants, petty thieves and armed robbers.[15]

Now a gang boss, Note developed his group into a 'well-disciplined tightly structured society run on quasi military lines', which was soon dubbed 'the Regiment of the Hills'.[16] He found perhaps his greatest inspiration in the Old Testament Book of Nahum, probably after reading how 'the state of Nineveh had rebelled against the Lord,' and thus chose the name of his gang, the Ninevitesas, as homage.[17] It was at this point that Note ordered women to be sent away, apparently worried they were destroying his soldiers with sexually transmitted diseases. It was relatively easy at this point to convince his followers that women were 'the source of poison', and as 'King of Nineveh' he henceforth prohibited sexual contact with women. Similar to the adjustments sometimes made in male prisons, older gang members initiated younger males into the gang as 'boy wives' or 'wyfies'. With the promulgation of this decree the Ninevites as well as the all-male prisons and mining compounds became associated with homosexuality.[18]

The years 1890–99 can best be viewed as the formative years for the Ninevites. Note would later testify that it was during this period that the gang penetrated prisons for the first time, where it gathered recruits and taught convicts its organizational structure.[19] In 1899, as the Second Boer War between Britain and South Africa loomed on the horizon, the Ninevites were disbanded, although Note and a small band of robbers continued their thieving ways. Arrested several months later, the remnants of his gang were each sentenced to 25 lashes and five years in prison with hard labour. But short on troops and prison guards, the South African Republic (Transvaal) recognized that it did not have enough men to guard them securely and came to an agreement that the Ninevites would be released shortly after their lashings. However, just as a leopard cannot change his spots, Note and company went back to their thieving ways and in 1900 were sentenced to thirty lashes and seven more years for attempted murder. Incarcerated at Pretoria prison, it did not take long before the erstwhile gangsters were in 'open confrontation with a brutal system of administration'.[20]

It is instructive that many followers and other petty criminals had received some form of military discipline and training while serving under the British during the Second Boer War.[21] The colonial system at the time exercised a particular pull on Note's imagination – so much so that Note adopted a rank structure, complete with 'imaginary uniforms' based on the military force of the Natal Colony. This refers to the fact that a 28 member might hold the rank of sergeant, a middling position, but imagine himself actually 'wearing an old Boer uniform, complete with brass buttons and medals, even though he is just wearing plain prison clothes.' As one modern member of the 28s explained it:

> The ranks of our gangs and all we do is based on the military. The uniforms we wear today are all in our minds. I am a man of gold. Everything in me is gold. My rank is gold; my cap is gold; the buckles on my boots are gold; even my belt is gold. In other words I am a blood officer.[22]

According to the leading chronicler of the Numbers, after Note was captured he told his 'white captors . . . "I reorganized my gang of robbers. I laid them under what has since become known as Nineveh law. I read in the bible about the great state Nineveh which rebelled against the Lord, and I selected that name for my gangs as rebels against the government's laws."'[23] The Ninevites enjoyed a run of about twenty years in the first decades of the twentieth century. It wasn't long before they insinuated themselves into not just the gold-mining compounds but the Transvaal's fledgling prison system as well, where they soon took control.

Following the end of the Second Boer War, it became clear that the Ninevites were active in a number of prisons and, by 1906, operational on the outside as well. Between 1908 and 1910, Note created a new and highly organized Ninevite corps, making this period 'the most troubled and turbulent' in Pretoria Central Prison. For about four years Note united several gangs under his aegis.[24]

Behind bars in Johannesburg, Note was still able to recruit criminals and extend his reach over an organization that encompassed prisons, mining compounds and black townships.[25] The prison authorities found their only choice was to isolate him in Pretoria Central Prison. It was at this point that he adopted the name 'Nongoloza', a Zulu name that 'refers to an elevated person, one who gives out or hands down the laws'.[26] Although his criminal career would end in ignominy, he is widely regarded as the 'father' of the modern South African prison-gang structure. Nongoloza was responsible for inaugurating the gang's para-military structure, which included colonels, captains and sergeants in charge of rank-and-file soldiers. As one scholar put it, 'This is exactly the structure of modern gangs in correctional centres today.'[27]

In early 1912 Nongoloza's organization reached its apogee. With an army approaching 1,000 followers, the Ninevites had established 'a sophisticated system of communication, rigid discipline and well-defined criminal objectives'.[28] Moreover, the mythic Zulu bandit led his outlaw gang according to 'a simple but potent ideology of

Nelson Mandela's prison cell, Robben Island.

banditry-as-anti-colonial-resistance'. As the precursor to the Numbers gangs, the Ninevites should be considered among the earliest incarnations of the prison-gang subculture, with a hierarchy and disciplinary code that pre-date the South African Prisons Department.[29] Concomitantly, the South African Parliament addressed growing concerns about prison gangs.[30] The Department of Prisons 'held meetings with all prison heads and proposed that gang membership be declared a punishable offence' and arranged for gang leaders to be incarcerated on Robben Island.[31] Located 12 kilometres (7½ mi.) off the coast of Cape Town, it came to prominence as a penal facility for political prisoners such as Nelson Mandela, Walter Sisulu and others during the apartheid regime.

Ninevite Justice

The Ninevites took their internal justice system seriously. Discipline was mostly of the physical variety. However, lesser offences relating to matters of status, privilege and prison etiquette, or any member who developed a fully fledged homosexual relationship before attaining a particular rank, could be tried before the magistrate. Lenient punishments included having certain privileges withheld, such as access to sex, tobacco and food. For more serious offences, a superior 'court' was convened. Mimicking the traditional justice process on the outside, trials included judges, prosecutors, doctors and jurymen. Serious charges, usually relating to breaches of security, resulted in a range of violent penalties. Harsh and bloody punishments included having one's front teeth knocked out or being stabbed through the shoulder blade with sharpened nails, or even 'ballooning', in which victims were tossed higher and higher into the air with the aid of a blanket. At a prearranged signal to withdraw the blanket, the prisoner came crashing down to the concrete floor of the cell.

As if these violent punishments were not enough, others included having your ribs pummelled with fists. The number of punches ranged between three and ten and was determined by a *nyanga*'s prior consultation. This so-called doctor first examined the pulse of the victim in order to arrive at some notion of his strength. His conclusions could reduce a ten-punch total to half that if he thought the subject was not up to the beating. Like everything the Numbers did, there was an established protocol or ritual for following it through. Once the punishment was decided, the guilty party was ordered to stand up straight with his hands folded. Gang members were then signalled to begin pounding him from side to side. One administered the beating from the front, another from the rear, until they were ordered to stop.[32]

In cases that demanded the ultimate penalty, such as snitching, strangulations were performed by means of a handkerchief, rope or wet towel. One interesting facet of this punishment was that the executioners were primed to chew maize (mealies) and force it down the target's throat to make it seem as though he died from choking on maize rather than from the actual strangulation.[33]

## From the Ninevites to the Number Prison Gangs

Some time in 1912 Nongoloza sent a message to prison administrators pleading to make a deal to have his sentence reduced. He was able to come to an understanding with a white warder, who offered the prospect of remission if he renounced the Ninevite movement and began working for the state. Nongoloza agreed to the offer, writing to the Director of Prisons:

> The new law and the new prison administration have made me change my heart . . . I am quite prepared to go to Cinderella Prison or any other prison where the Ninevites say they get orders and to tell them that I give no order even if it costs me my life. I would tell them that I am no longer king and have nothing to do with Nineveh.

In 1913 Nongoloza was approaching fifty years old and had tired of the life he had chosen. No one could have predicted that he would agree to become a native warder in the Department of Prisons. He served in this position for about four years, and after a hiatus returned to the job in the 1920s. Although he had taken this divergent path, it did not mean the end of his army. Due to a continued convergence of pass laws, mining compounds and prisons, the Ninevite *raison d'être* remained intact and 'there continued a host culture more than capable of sustaining such movements.'[34] Released from prison in 1940, Nongoloza took to drink and died impoverished in 1948 at the age of 81. He was subsequently buried in a pauper's grave.

The end of the First World War signalled a recrudescence of Ninevite activity as more Africans turned to crime due to economic exigencies and the prison population skyrocketed. As a result, prisons became incubators for anti-colonial ideology and general contempt for the rule of law. By 1919 former followers of Nongoloza were 'increasingly confined to the prison system'.[35] Almost a century after Nongoloza first sought shelter in the hills, remnants of his army continue to function within the South African prison system as the much feared 28 gang.[36]

The 26s, 27s and 28s all have an elaborate quasi-military command structure, comprising up to thirty ranks each. Each rank has specific duties and is subject to strict internal discipline. Promotion usually involves a violent act against a non-member. The three Number gangs are distinguished according to their aims and established subculture. The 28s are the senior gang, distinct for their organized system of coerced sex partners, or 'wyfies'. The 26s handle money and the 27s protect and enforce the codes of the 26s and 28s and are symbolized by blood.

The Number gangs comprise an elaborate system of gangs through which inmate-on-inmate violence is mediated. They are spread across the South African prison system, so that when a gang member is transferred to another prison, or is released and then reincarcerated, he keeps his previous status in the new institution. There are several myths testifying to how the term 'Number' came about, but its etymological origins remain murky and a subject for debate. However, there is no argument against the fact that the Number gangs are among the more fearsome exemplars of the prison-gang subculture.

All the Number gangs have a rigid hierarchy and follow distinctive rituals. For example, Friday of each week is considered the 'day of rations', when possessions are distributed among gang members according to rank. On Saturday, the 'day of wrongs', gang members meet to pass sentence on rule-breakers. Sunday is the 'day of rights', when newly recruited members are welcomed into the gang, while others are promoted and 'victories' celebrated.

When gang members enter prisons, they have to be familiar with a clandestine way of identifying their previous gang affiliation. This is typically accomplished through body language. For example, if a man is sitting and waiting to be processed at an administration office, the way he sits would communicate his association with the appropriate gang. It is important to follow his movements as he changes position while sitting on a bench. While the hand gestures indicate gang affiliation, a 28 will typically have his left knee in the air and a 26 or 27 his right knee.[37]

From the moment an inmate steps into a South African prison he becomes a focus of great interest to gang members as a potential victim or recruit, and in some cases both. Each new inmate represents a fresh source of cherished commodities such as food, cigarettes and so forth, while others regard him as a sexual object. Researchers have described the main roles open to new prisoners in the South African inmate culture. Their choices are mostly limited to being a gangster or soldier; an unaffiliated prisoner, or *franse*; or a wyfie (the last an Afrikaans term referring to a 'female animal partner'). According to Marie Rosenkrantz Lindegaard and Sasha Gear, 'A wyfie is a male inmate who usually (but not always) has had a feminized identity imposed on him, and is in a sexual relationship, usually coerced, with another inmate who is often a gang member.'[38]

When an inmate is transferred from one prison to another or is a first-timer, he is shown to his cell. An individual known as the 'cell cleaner' will typically approach him and ask 'Who are you?' to determine his authenticity. If he is already a member of the 28s, he is expected to reply, 'I am a son of Nongoloza that works by night'. In the case of a 27, he would answer he is Kilikijan, 'That works by day'. New arrivals are put through a series of well-established tests to confirm that a purported member uses the correct metaphors and has mastery of the Numbers argot.

## Number Salutes and Tattoos

Each of the three gangs has developed its own salute. When they give it, they will say something to the effect of, 'this is my sign, my flag, my gun and my pen'. The 26s' characteristic salute comprises two raised thumbs, while the 27s use two thumbs up and index fingers pointing toward the horizon. The 28s, being the most powerful, use thumbs up, 'with the index and middle finger together and pointing forward'. The two sections of the 28s (gold and silver) use distinctive salutes. Those who choose the Silver or Sodomy Line hold their index and middle fingers together; those who are blooded members of the Gold Line hold the middle fingers apart.

A familiar aspect of most prison gangs, distinctive tattoos have been adopted by the Numbers as well. The 26s display their tattoos mostly on the right side of the body, a symbolic statement that they do not allow or practise same-sex relations. They also favour tattoos that focus on the dollar ($) sign, cash and coins, with each often pierced by a blade. Others include fists holding wads of cash or an open book with the number 26 on it. By contrast, the 27s tend to favour tattoos of crossed scimitars and a rising sun. All members have at least one tattoo that either notes that they are armed with some type of weapon or testifies to their violent inclinations.

The 28s have a more complex set of tattoos. Since they usually operate in the late afternoon or at night, their symbol is a setting sun strategically tattooed between the buttocks. If a member has a 'Moliva Boy' tattoo it alerts others that he entered the 28s through the Silver Line, which 'represents beauty/people being sexual things'. Moreover, it indicates that these members have an 'easy time as wyfies in prison'.[39] If he joined through the Gold Line, he will bear an image representing blood or death. It is not uncommon for members to have numerous tattoos over most of their body, indicating that perhaps they entered through the Silver Line but were promoted to Gold. This phenomenon offers further proof that, as with the Russian *vory* in the previous chapter and others to be examined in coming chapters, tattoos offer a window into the criminal lifespan of each gang member in an environment where communication between prisoners is both limited and imperative.

## The 28

The 28 is considered the 'blood line of the gangs' and is the largest prison gang in South Africa, due in no small part to the fact that there is little discrimination as to who is accepted. The 28s have two lines of membership: those who climb ranks by sodomizing other inmates and those who prefer to stab warders and face the consequences. Members of the 28 are frequently at odds with those of the 26.

Once an incoming 28 member establishes his credentials in his new prison, he is introduced to the *glas*, or 'binoculars'. Typically a senior gang member, the *glas*'s main mission is to conduct business in *die bos*, 'the bush', parts of the institution where the 28s are not active. It is the *glas* who confronts a prospective recruit with a riddle (Who are you?) and examines his response to determine which line of the gang he will fall under. The *glas* observes how the new member interacts with non-Numbers members, or *franses*, and is often a problem-solver. Once the gang member is with his appropriate group, he is expected

Lee-Ann Olwage, *The Dreamer*, 2017: photographic portrait of a former gang member of the 28s.

to go into great detail explaining the complicated hierarchy of ranks to his audience. What's more, he will omit his own position in order to identify his role in the Numbers food chain.[40]

According to a typical scenario, the *glas* will say, 'I am going to ask you a question. Think very carefully before answering.' He continues with a hypothetical, 'It is raining. You are standing under an umbrella. I say to you I am getting wet, I may get sick. What are you going to do?' If the inmate responds, 'I will come out in the rain with you,' it means he is prepared to live like him and they will live and die together.[41]

Once the *glas* is satisfied with the response, he will give the prospect a task. At one time, this meant the fatal or non-fatal stabbing of another inmate or warder. Members were supposed to inform the prospect that prior to the stabbing he would receive a knife, often with a very short blade, and direct him to stab his target below the shoulder, 'just flesh, no organs'. He was also warned to avoid injuring the spine. If he proved unable or too scared to commit the stabbing, a senior member had to do it on his behalf. But make no mistake about it, the prospect would be punished. Once the stabbing was completed, arrangements were in place to make the knife disappear. If by chance he killed the warder there was always the possibility the 28s might kill him in turn, depending on the circumstances of the incident.

Just before the assault, the knife was passed to the assigned recruit or member when he went to pick up his food tray outside the kitchen. He would soon learn that the length of blade – which determined whether the attack was to be fatal or not – was set by the nyangi, or 'doctor'.[42] Prior to the attack, the recruit was informed that he should be ready to be beaten severely by the warders after the stabbing. In order to prepare for the punishment, he was instructed to put a wad of paper in his mouth to help muffle his screams during the beat-down.

After the stabbing, or 'blooding', is out of the way, inmates who are observing the incident will yell '*Nangampela! Die nommer is vol!*', meaning 'the Number is complete.' The Zulu word translates to 'there it is indeed!'[43] With the blooding out of the way, the *glas* 'will circle him slowly scrutinizing skin for "dirty papers", or tattoos from other gangs. If the 'mark' of a rival gang is detected, the recruit is brutalized and the recruitment ceases. This ritual takes place on Saturday (the day of wrongs). The ceremony continues the following day, Sunday (the day of rights), when the recruit is ordered once more to stand in the middle of the room and continue what is a mostly metaphorical induction. He is surrounded by several others, and the first to approach him is the *nyangi*, who takes out an invisible gold pipe and slaps it on the recruit's right fist, after which he takes an unseen silver pipe and slaps the left wrist. The *nyangi* next checks the recruit's pulse and declares either 'this man's heart beats twice a year', consigning him to the Silver Line (wyfies) of the 28s, or 'three times a year', giving him entrée into the Gold Line (soldiers). Once this is done, a senior member places a handkerchief on the floor and slips a knife under it. The recruit is told:

> From today you are no longer a franse [non-member]. You are a 28, you will never swear to your brother. You will never hurt your brother. You will never do anything that reflects badly on the camp. If you leave the camp, you leave by your own blood.[44]

The next step in the promotion ritual is for the 'magistrate', or *landros*, to approach the inmate and take out four unseen stamps. If it is a white or green stamp it means he has been recruited to or promoted within the Silver Line. The *landros* then uses white or green pens to write the new member into the 28s record book. The recruit moves out of the circle and the ceremony is complete. One of the most curious aspects of this ceremony is the fact that there is no physical record book. In his book *White Paper, White Ink*, gang member Sipho Madini explains that his title refers to the fact that the 'proverbial' book should be considered the 'Pure White Book', written in closely guarded code and to all intents invisible because it is written on pure white pages – 'A book that no one can see or hold in their hands but which is passed down orally by Number gangs in prisons from generation to generation.' During the course of his incarceration and interaction with the 28s, Madini asked a gang member where the so-called Makhalu Book (Big Book) was located, the repository of the history of the gangs, codes, rules, structure and so forth. The 28 quickly set him straight, telling him:

> Don't you understand anything? It has never been written – it is in our heads and blood and on our tongues – that is why we spend so much time Sabela-ing and teaching new recruits the book . . . The book is now lost – has become corrupt – Even the gangs on the outside, most of those gangsters have never been to prison and they are using our language and our rituals.

Ultimately, whenever a reference is made to the book of the Number it should be understood as an oral history rather than a written one.[45]

## Learning to Sabela: The Forties

The next major step in the initiation process leads the Number recruit into a section of gang members referred to as the *mambozas* (the Forties). These, for the most part, are senior and inactive members who are too old or injured to actively participate in the more physical realm of the gang, or have had their positions filled by another. For example, there cannot be two active *nyangis*, so if one is transferred from another prison to one where there is already a doctor, the transfer is considered inactive and sleeps in the section with the Forties.

It is in the realm of the Forties that the initiate is taught how to Sabela, or speak prison jargon, which can be a long process. The Number gangs are made distinctive by their use of words, symbols and colours that differentiate gang members from each other. Their complicated communication codes are of paramount importance, specifying how gang members should approach each other and such promulgations as the 26s 'rule by day' and the 28s 'by night'.

This language, or Sabela, is the result of the diverse nature of South African prisons, in which at least eleven official languages are spoken: Afrikaans, English, Ndebele, North Sotho, Sotho, Swazi, Tswana, Tsonga, Venda, Xhosa and Zulu. For various cultures and tribal groups to communicate with each other, a mixture of Afrikaans, English, Xhosa and Zulu, the most commonly spoken languages in the country, are used. It is not unusual for inmates to be conversant in more than one of these languages. According to one inmate, one of the first things he noticed when he was incarcerated was that most prisoners will say the same thing two or three times in different languages: 'First they say it in the language they think you will understand best; Afrikaans for coloureds, Zulu for blacks and English if they can't speak Zulu'.[46] This mix of the four commonest languages listed above is known as *fanigalore*. It originated in the late nineteenth century as a way for white mine-owners to communicate with black miners, and for the miners to communicate with each other (a shortcut instead of learning all four languages).[47]

The new member must Sabela day and night with a teacher, or 'blackboard'. During his first sixty days as a Number, he will not be allowed visitors or to write letters and read books but must instead 'focus on the Number task at hand'. A slow learner can be harshly punished, perhaps stripped and thrown into an ice-cold shower until he 'finds the Number' or 'gets it right'. While most of these fundamental principles continue, in the modern 28s the man who trains you is now allowed to have sex with you. This change began after the war between the Silver and Gold Lines in the late 1980s, which will be covered later in the chapter.

## The Gold and Silver Lines

The 28s are divided into two parallel structures. The Gold, or *gazi* (blood), Line is made up of 'military' soldiers who fight the gang's battles, led by those considered descendants of Nongoloza. Gold Line members purportedly do not provide passive homosexual sex for other 28s. Sex is provided by the Silver Line, as explained below.

There is still some debate over the guidelines for *gazi optel*, 'to pick up blood'. According to one authority on professional killers, a Number might be asked to kill, or to 'pick up blood' of, another who violated the norms of gang society or committed some egregious act. Once the killing is completed the assassin has achieved a status comparable to the 'mafia conception of a man of honor' – a 'made man' in Mafia parlance. The murder cannot take place without an 'elaborate process'. For example, if a senior gang member is the target, it cannot be done without permission from the most senior members. Once the target has been eliminated the killer is said 'to round the Number'.[48]

There is enough evidence to suggest that 'hitmen' are sometimes recruited in prisons. One street-gang member unfamiliar with life behind bars, for example, met a former inmate who had stabbed someone to death during his prison stint. The former inmate told the street-gang member, 'they knew of the work [he] did in prison, so they asked [him] to continue.' Putting his skills out on the streets now, he was asked to continue to kill for money. He reportedly bragged, 'the money is good. I use a knife.'[49] It is worth noting that a killer is highly valued behind bars, and his gang for the most part owns him. In such a position he has no chance to leave behind his gang identity. By comparison, once asserting his skills on the streets, he will find it much easier to leave the job since he is not subjected to the same scrutiny as behind bars.[50]

### The Silver Line

Members of the Silver Line are the sex slaves of the Gold Line, although this has been disputed by Silver Line members, who assert that they are the brains of the gang. The origins of the term 'Silver Line' are said to go back to around 1899. According to several accounts, a Polish-American pimp named Joseph Silver ended up in South Africa by way of London.[51] His 'talent for organizing' was put to use in the so-called white slave trade. He had been busy recruiting and seducing vulnerable young women in London's East End right before alighting at the Rand. He trafficked women to several countries, including South Africa. However, it was not long before he was arrested there and sentenced to two years in prison. Shortly after his incarceration he raped a black prisoner, while other inmates watched through a surveillance slot. He then handed his victim a shilling. However, this did not keep the victim from reporting the assault and filing charges. Together with his reputation as a procurer, Silver's name earned 'a permanent place in [the lexicon] of South African Prison Gangs.'[52]

As mentioned previously, if a member has a tattoo of the words 'Moliva Boy' on his upper left shoulder, it indicates he entered the 28s through the Silver Line, and served as a sex slave during his probationary period. If he bears symbols of blood and death, it means he entered through the Gold Line. Some may have an assortment of tattoos because they might have entered through the Silver and moved up to Gold. The 28s often tattoo the number on their body, or may bear the quotation 'my heart beats 3 times per year', indicating Blood Line or Gold Line entry, or 'my heart beats 2 times per year' if they came in through the Silver Line.

During her interviews for *God's Gangsters?* (2010), Heather Parker Lewis discovered that members of the 28 gang 'will go to amazing lengths to hide the role of the designated women, the so-called wyfies, within the gang structure. This is likely because just about every one of the 28s has had to play this female role at some point in his prison history.' Moreover, 'They would possibly rather die, and will certainly lie, rather than disclose their sexual status.'[53]

Talk to any 28 and they are likely to tell you that no sexual activity takes place. If it does, by most accounts, the sexual contact 'is between the thighs only', according to traditional Zulu courting practices. That said, the rise in AIDS indicates that there is most probably complete penetration. In any case, the practice of full anal sex with wyfies was not permitted under Nongoloza until members achieved the appropriate rank.[54]

## The 26

The 26 was formed behind bars in the first decade of the twentieth century and is the 'only branch to have been formed inside'.[55] Members are mainly focused on making *kroon*, or money, for all the members, frequently from a wide range of criminal ventures, including extortion and smuggling schemes. They regard themselves as the 'clevers' of the three Number gangs.[56] For the 26, violence was considered secondary to the goal of accruing lucre, making it the least brutal of the three Number gangs. If a member gets out of hand or acts too aggressively, he is required to become a 27, otherwise there is nowhere for him to go. He would no longer be allowed to be part of the 26, which is based on the tenets that its members do not 'look for blood nor seek same sex relationships'.[57]

Unlike the 28s, the 26 has no private line for selecting wyfies, who are not permitted to join the gang. Its strict membership criteria imply that it will not accept anyone who has been raped, has informed on someone, or is marked by any physical defects. More recent evidence suggests that 'most raped men avoid having to stab to cleanse themselves and as a result they almost cease to exist, they are left in limbo until some other 26 has to prove himself by challenging him.' In the interim the outcast can still belong to the Number, but must sit apart from the circle as a form of retributive humiliation. Moreover, he is not permitted to 'sit on the haunches in the traditional manner but must sit on the floor on his rear end while issues of importance to the Numbers are discussed and debated', 'since he never knows when he will be stabbed. His time in limbo is not made much easier by knowing that he might become a wyfie in the 28s and 'lose all privileges', as well as being 'taunted with comments like "Give us a piece of your backside!"'[58]

In the event that a 26 has been severely injured, perhaps a head injury, he might be marked as having 'physical defects', casting him into a more tenuous position, but one that could be rectified by stabbing a warder to validate his continuing physical prowess.

It is common for members to seek jobs close to administrative offices in order to be privy to information that impacts the gangs.[59] Many observers suggest that the 26 is 'considered a soft option when it comes to violence'. A member of the 26s is also permitted to join the 27s 'for the purpose of communicating with camp 28 for the moment'. But if he wants to retain his status he 'must take blood'.[60]

Any wealth obtained by a 26 must be shared with 28s (if they are low on resources). The 26s are recognized for their ability to accumulate wealth for all members. If one were to ask the purpose of his gang, a 26 might respond that their duty was 'keeping the jail alive', due to his responsibility for accruing financial wealth, obtaining drugs, cigarettes and luxury items, and basically beating the system. Until 1998 it was still mandatory for a 26, in order to obtain rank, to stab or slice a *vuil franse* – someone who informed on the gang.[61]

One of the advantages of belonging to the 26 is that there are no wyfies in the gang. It has a complex hierarchy, comprising a Number One (top structure) and Number Two (secondary structures). An assembly known as the 12-point ring makes gang decisions according to jurisdictions. Every rank has specific assigned duties and offices, which include training lower-rank members in duties and Sabela language.[62]

The 26s have traditionally been viewed as subservient to the 28s, but this has not stopped them from rising up and taking control in some prisons. Researchers have observed that in recent years the balance of power has varied from prison to prison. For example, if a Number gang feels it has enough power to take over, it will declare a 'general election', which involves full-on gang warfare that can last as long as two years. Often the 27 will join battle on the side of the 26s. Once the war is over, one of the gangs will be declared the 'ruling party'. Two particularly notable wars took place at Bellville prison (1967–9) and Brandvlei prison (1974–6). In both instances the 26s were declared the ruling party.

The six laws of the 26s are:

1. You will not do what you want.
2. You will not lie to your brother or argue with him.
3. You will respect the honest work of police and wardens.
4. You will not sleep under the same blanket as your brother (no sex).
5. You will not physically harm a non-prison gang member the first time he offends you, and first give him two warnings before harming him.
6. You will die with your brother under the flag of the 26s.[63]

The 27s

A member of the 27s is focused on drawing blood, especially that of a warder – the best way to rise through the ranks. Assault and bloody conflict are never off the table. Although not official goals, smuggling and rape are not uncommon activities. The 27s are expected to keep the peace between the 26s and 28s. Since the 28s do not traditionally speak to the 26s, a 27 will be used to convey the messages and concerns of the 26. The 27s were always the least numerous of the three gangs. This can best be attributed to the fact that they had to take blood and then survive merciless beatings from the warders. Their actions left them in prison much longer, with some never leaving.[64]

The 27s can best be viewed as the protectors of law, responsible for correcting wrongdoings of gang members by means of assaults ('taking blood'). To join the 27, one has to stab an informer, and then protect and enforce the codes of the 27 and 26 gangs.[65] Most have tattoos of crossed scimitars and a rising sun, or others that indicate that they are either armed with a weapon or violent in nature.

### *Franses* (Non-gang Members)

The *franse* is an inmate who either rejects recruitment efforts or 'aspires to gang membership' but has not been formally initiated.[66] The bottom line is that a new inmate either chooses to pursue a role in the prison subculture or eventually has it forced upon him. Ultimately, in South African prisons a new inmate has this choice: join a gang and become a *ndota* (gang member or soldier) or become a *franse*, considered by gang members as 'a nobody'. Obviously, not all inmates belong to gangs, whether by choice or because of their unacceptability to the Number gangs. It is the *franses* who 'bear the brunt of gang violence and intimidation'.[67] When one receives a parcel from a visitor, he is expected to hand it over to the *ndotas* in his cell, who will decide how to distribute it. Likewise, if a *franse* wants to engage in some type of profitable transaction, such as selling merchandise, he must ask permission from *ndotas* in his cell. When *ndotas* sit to discuss gang business, each *franse* must sit with his face to the wall and remain silent. Non-members are treated much like the cell's servants, tasked with keeping it clean and washing members' clothing. Individuals become *franses* for several reasons. Some just do not want to join a gang, but they face a tenuous existence, always vulnerable to gang attacks.

### Independent and Dependent Franses

In some cases, non-members might be allowed to maintain a modicum of autonomy and might even gain some respectability by committing a highly publicized act on the outside – the more aggressive the better – that demonstrates some type of 'manly', brutal behaviour prior to prison. One independent *franse* recounted in a widely publicized interview:

> [the] English press was there . . . they took my picture [and] their front pages [were], 'Teacher gets twelve years, blah, blah, for cold-blooded murder' . . . And so when I landed in prison . . . they were already reading [about me], so they respected me from there. Inside it helped me.[68]

Once the independent *franse* earns his requisite identity in prison it is possible for him to take advantage of his own social network, accrue wealth and move freely around in the courtyard, without fear of harassment. What's more, his violent street credentials and willingness to stand up for himself inside enable him to survive behind bars without belonging to a gang.[69]

Below the independent *franse* is the category of dependent *franse*, a status that in some cases protects the unaffiliated. An individual, for example, might 'manage to resist pressures to join the gang' if 'heavily involved in Bible study groups'. However, they are more likely to stay isolated in their cells and perhaps find sanctuary in separate cells further away from the prison areas with more gang activity (such as single cells and the kitchen). These individuals rarely resort to violence unless it is a case of self-preservation. Their ability to communicate in a religious manner has reportedly resolved potential problems with the gangs. In contrast with the independent *franse* who has established his street bona fides, the dependent *franse* must rely on his association with and participation in other activities, such as religious groups, sports and rehabilitation efforts, to avoid being forced to join a gang.

Nonetheless, the position of any *franse* means that they are always vulnerable to certain demands and abuses. Vulnerable inmates are most likely to be described as 'good looking', unacquainted with prison life, physically unimposing or not prepared for violence, especially if they are behind bars for a 'sissy' (not weapon-assisted) crime, and already 'identifying as gay or transsexual'.[70]

*Franses* are always subject to coercion and vivid threats, particularly those who lack the wherewithal to be accepted into the Numbers. It is not uncommon for a *franse* to be threatened while being transferred in prison vans. If, for instance, he refuses to smuggle drugs into prison in his anus, he might have a parcel of dagga, or cannabis, forced into it. The so-called dagga poke is 'wrapped in plastic' and considered as valuable as gold on the inside. According to Lewis, 'a small amount that fits on top of 20 cent coins sells for 10 rand'. It is apparently common for gang members to either swallow a parcel or secrete it in the anus. In the event that the *franse* refuses to smuggle it in, gang members might take his pants off and 'use a bottle to kick the dagga up his arse'. Once this is accomplished, he will be watched as he enters the prison. If he is unable to get it out, a Number gangster will 'put a plastic packet over his hand and they wrench it out and the guy, well, there is lots of blood'.[71]

### The Valcross

There are two dependable conduits for communication between gangs. But the 'kitchen is the only place that connects every point of the prison with every other', and is considered 'the prison's telephone lines'.[72] The daily 'Valcross' meetings are another source of communication. Although the three Number gangs keep largely to themselves, there is a necessity for leaders of each to meet somewhere each day. This meeting, called the Valcross, involves two members from each gang, typically the *glas* and the *draad*, who meet at the end of the warder's day, which happens to be the beginning of the gangsters' day, which of course is the next fifteen hours of night.[73] It is during this shift that they agree on how things will be organized for the following night. During the meeting, the *draad* remains mute while the *glas* conducts gang business. He will then report his findings to the 28s. During the meeting the two 28s are not allowed to converse with the two 26s, but must communicate through the 27s. This is the time when a 28 can relate that his gang has recruited a new member. They will tell the 27s, who will pass it on to the 26s. This type of message is a 'hands off' warning to other gangs, or a thinly veiled threat that the recruit is spoken for.[74]

The inter-gang conference takes place in a cell that is outside the perimeters of all three Number gangs' territory. In the middle of the cell a 'courtyard' is set up, really 'four bunk beds curtained off to make a private space, which feels like an office or courtroom'.[75]

## Numbers Justice

In the 28s, when an indiscretion is committed there are always consequences. According to protocol, an inmate forum and 'highest judicial structure of the gang', known as the Twelve Points, must adjudicate the case, but first the judge must speak, typically arguing for conviction. A high-ranking 28 and 'most senior member of the silver line', known as the *mtshali*, might respond in favour of acquittal. The Twelve Points then debates both sides before the judge ends the discussion by offering a verdict and sentence. If the sentence is death, the *mtshali* will stand up and argue for mitigation and recommend that the sentence be commuted to a gang rape, or 'band'. A vote then takes place and all, except for the *mtshali* and an officer known as the general, cast their votes. If the vote is five to five, the *mtshali* can cast the deciding vote and potentially save a life, meaning that the vote is decided by up to eleven people, so there can be no tie. If the majority vote against acquittal, the *mtshali* will protest by not voting at all. One of the more curious aspects of the proceedings is the activity of the man of light, or *Goliat*-one. He will shed all his clothes and run naked around the Twelve Points, screaming all the while in the 'most haunting voice he can, pleading for mercy'. By doing this, the *Goliat*-one is attempting to take the 28s out of darkness (their decision to kill) and bring them back to the light. If this fails to change their minds, it is the final option, and the death sentence goes on as scheduled. The accused is present for the trial but is not informed of his fate right away. Once the penalty is passed, three soldiers are given the order to carry out the execution. The execution squad will usually either suffocate the gang member in his bed or cut his throat. The death penalty is referred to as 'number one'.[76]

The second worst punishment an individual can receive is a ritual known as 'slow puncture'. This was still being used in the early 2000s. It is a relatively new form of punishment, probably dating back to the late 1980s or early 1990s, when the HIV/AIDS crisis was at its peak. The disobedient individual sentenced to be punished in this way can expect to be raped by a gang member carrying the AIDS virus, an indication that the target is meant to die over time instead of immediately. In the 2000s South Africa had the highest number of individuals living with HIV in the world. Some estimates suggest that one out of nine citizens was affected. By some accounts, the victimized gang member might have a cut made in his anus in order to draw blood prior to being raped by an HIV-positive inmate.[77]

There are several other, less severe sanctions, including *klappe*, ten slaps to the face with an open hand. In the case of *beker*, the victim is smacked in the head with a tin cup attached to a sock. Other sanctions include gang rape and 'carry on', in which the gang member is lifted up by his arms and beaten with padlocks, sticks and cups. However, the murder of a non-gang member typically does not result in any physical punishment to the perpetrator(s).

### Prison Gangs, Apartheid and Political Prisoners

Under apartheid (1949–94), South Africans were classified, according to the 1950 Population Registration Act, into three racial groups: white; native (black African); and Indian and Coloured (mixed-race) people. A person's racial identification was everything, determining where they could live, jobs they could hold and whom they could marry. By most accounts, identification was often arbitrary, depending more on outside perception than on factual reality. Moreover, it had major ramifications for inmates and prison-gang subculture.

Robben Island, the site of the prison where Nelson Mandela spent many years during apartheid.

The term 'apartheid' entered the Afrikaner consciousness in the 1940s. But race-based discrimination went back much further, to the arrival of European colonizers centuries earlier. In 1948, the National Party came to power, championing the policy, and 'a more comprehensive separation commitment to racism began.'[78]

Between 1962 and 1991 most black male political prisoners 'who opposed the regime' were imprisoned on Robben Island. In the 1980s the government opted to send them to Numbers-controlled institutions such as Pollsmoor instead, as in the case of one political activist arrested in a 1987 demonstration and tossed into a section of the prison controlled by 26s and 27s. He viewed this as a 'brutal political strategy', but it was actually well-thought-out by administrators, who were sending out a clear notice: rather than being sent to Robben Island, a hotbed of revolutionary politics, transferring inmates to 'inland jails' run by gangs was akin to saying, 'the gangs will sort you out in prison.'[79]

One of the best first-hand accounts of the Number gangs through the eyes of a political prisoner was written by Moses Dlamini (b. 1947), who was sentenced to six years on Robben Island during the 1960s for his association with and support of a banned organization (three years on each count). Dlamini chronicled the conflict and relationships with the prison gangs on Robben Island at a time when Number members were

> handpicked by the enemy from the most notorious prisons of South Africa to come and demoralize and humiliate us with the assistance of the uncouth, uncivilized, raw Boer warders so that we would never again dare to challenge the system of apartheid colonialism.[80]

However, similar to the conflict that occurred between political prisoners and gangsters in Neapolitan Italy and the Russian Gulag system, there came a time in the mid-1960s when most of the gangsters were removed from the midst of the political prisoners after the latter had banded together and were able 'to neutralize, politicize, and even recruit them into the political organizations.'[81]

## Robben Island and the 5s and 6s

When Dlamini arrived on Robben Island, he quickly recognized that the Big 5 Gang was assisting the warders in the ill-treatment of political prisoners, having experienced a similar alliance at previous institutions. His autobiographical revelations offer a number of insights into the Big 5s and Big 6s operating in a prison unimpeded by warders or the Number gangs.

At one point, about a hundred Big 6 gang members were transferred to Robben Island from Bellville prison, having worn out their welcome by stabbing warders and Big 5s. The gangs clearly distinguished themselves from each other by using iconic symbolism from the Second World War. The 5s adopted the Nazi salute, whereas the 6s preferred Churchill's V for victory sign. Their tattoos set them apart as well. The 6s were covered with tattoos of women's bodies (what this had to do with Churchill or the war is unclear), while the 5s remained consistent, preferring the swastika.[82]

The political prisoner Dlamini was warned that war was about to break out between the two gangs. Subsequently, the 6s lost the war, and most were turned into wyfies by the 5s. The 6s soon joined the politicals on the sidelines as the 5s took charge. Christmas Day meant a day off work and an extra cup of black coffee for the Big 5. Freed from their cells for part of the day, they could roam freely and sing tribal dances and songs, while all the recently capitulated 6s and the politicals could do was watch from their cells.[83]

At lunch it was customary for the 5s to sit facing the direction of sunrise, while the 6s faced a symbolic waning sunset. Sixes could resign and convert to the 5s or remain independent, but had to endure eight punches to the face before leaving. After the punishment, the 6 would shake the hand of his assailant, while a Big 5 often stood by and applauded. Cases have been reported where 6s left that gang without a formal resignation (eight punches) and were later targeted for worse punishment by their former gang. If this conversion took place, the 6 might no longer be required to stab 5s and warders, but would be expected to give himself to his new gang as a wyfie.

Sixes had various reasons for leaving the gang; as one revealed to a warder, he 'was tired of always being given assignments of stabbing warders and other convicts' over the past decade or so. This interesting case demonstrates the conundrum of switching gang allegiances. He had belonged to the 5s earlier in his prison career, and was reluctant to trade in his 6 membership for a gang whose members were expected to inform on fellow inmates. He also recognized that if he stayed independent instead of rejoining the 5s, he could be turned into a wyfie. He reconciled his choices and concluded that he would let the prison system decide his future by committing an assault with the intent to murder, hoping that he would be charged for murder and hanged.[84]

Demonstrating the unpredictability of these prison gangs, there is at least one case where a gang leader was turned into a wyfie by a competing gang. In this instance, reported by Dlamini, the Big 6 president was abducted, placed in a cell with 5s and raped all night – 'he was now a wyfie.' He subsequently 'broke down and surrendered and promised to abandon the 6 and its presidency in return for becoming a wyfie and a soft job inside the yard'. As one contemporary political writer put it, 'the leader of the most powerful prison gang has now become the wyfie of his antagonists. It's mind-boggling.'[85]

Following the kidnapping of the president of the 6s, it was now time for his gang to select a new president. However, the gang's numbers had been shrinking to the point where it was decided to dissolve the gang. It was determined that the best move would be to become members of the 28s. Joining the 28s revealed how alliances come and go in the world of South African prison gangs. When combined, the Six, the 28s and a group called the Desperadoes made for a formidable gang (but one that was still no match for the Big 5s). However, it was at this juncture that cultural variances came into play. Homosexuality was banned in the 6 but predominated in the 28s.

A new cast of inmates was arriving all the time, mostly criminals but also political prisoners. Many would be politicized in prison, joining either the African National Congress (ANC) or the Pan-Africanist Congress (PAC). It wasn't long before the new political recruits recognized that they gained nothing by distancing themselves from the criminal gangs, and in fact faced far worse conditions. Many political prisoners disintegrated into other groups; some became Big 5s, 28s and Desperadoes. Those who did not join gangs remained political prisoners under the aegis of either Pro-PAC or Pro-ANC groups.[86]

At one time there was an attempt to turn political prisoners into wyfies, but this was met by a 'tougher than expected resistance', with many vowing to die first. However, those who did give in were rewarded with warmer clothing, shoes and socks, but they were ostracized by other politicals. One observer noted that those who gave in were 'easy to spot . . . Their cheeks are round and gleaming' thanks to the more nutritious food provided regularly and their assignments performing soft jobs with little oversight by prison warders.[87]

In the 1960s, the power of the vaunted Big 5s was diminished after the mistreatment of political prisoners by staff and gangs was widely reported and a subsequent Commission of Inquiry revealed the assaults by warders and their collusion with the Big 5s. As a result, warders could no longer assault inmates on work details or carry truncheons. Once these rules were put into effect, it quickly became clear that the 5s had lost their protectors, and they were soon fair game for other prison gangs. It wasn't long before 5s were tossed into cells with 28s and Desperadoes and beaten. Former members of the Big Six were seen making the Churchill victory salute, 'some ululating, waving the red flag of the former Big Six', as cells echoed with screams throughout the night. It should be noted here that many of the 6s had fought the Nazis under General Montgomery in North Africa in the 1940s and probably reserved a healthy dose of animus for the 5s, who identified with the Nazi swastika.

Curiously, the 6s often warned political prisoners of potential violence so that they could avoid it, as was the case one night when they warned of an impending murderous plan to waylay some 5s returning from dinner. Political prisoners were sometimes involved in the beatings of their former antagonists and even adopted the 'third-degree strategy' of the gangs by covering victims with blankets before beating them. (These tactics were supposedly borrowed from Special Branch practices, where, as a precaution, beatings were administered in such a way that the body and head were left unmarked.) Nonetheless, all the pent-up anger and humiliation they had formerly endured was now unleashed in brutal beatings.[88]

## Closing the Number Bloodlines, 1987

In 1987 the Number gangs faced a crisis as the 'line was erased dividing men from women'. In other words, once the Silver Line defeated the Gold Line, the 28s introduced a law that an individual 'must become a passive sexual partner to join the gang', eliminating the distinction between the *ndotas* and the *wyfies*, making both sexual partners indistinguishable from each other. The reasons for this are complicated and still debated by researchers. Number researcher Jonny Steinberg has interviewed dozens of *ndotas*, but each offered a different explanation. However, the decision to stop the traditional initiation stabbings proved 'nothing less than [a] cataclysmic' choice, being that it 'was the centerpiece in the initiation process'.[89] The only issue that is mostly agreed on is that it was the soldiers themselves who made the decision to 'stop taking blood'. One of Steinberg's interviewees was a 26, who claimed:

> It was the 27s who did it. You had to have been there and seen them to understand why. They had been too badly fucked up. Some were on crutches; others were so damaged on the inside that they couldn't eat properly. Others were just miserable inside their heads. They were a sorry bunch. They had to do it to keep their own dignity.[90]

One Silver Line 28 told Steinberg:

> The soldiers in the 28s just laid down their arms. Their work was too tough for them. They couldn't handle the carry-ons and one-ones . . . Too many of them were nursing their wounds. They destroyed the Number because they lost their courage.[91]

In 1987 the Silver and Gold Lines went to war. Some of those interviewed claim the Silver Line started the war over the fact that the Gold was no longer doing its job as soldiers. Another issue, revolving around food, seemed also to have been a precipitating event. It had long been the rule that Gold Line 28s, who were expected to look fit, were deprived of food – no meat, just bones, eggs always went to the Silver Line, and sugar, coffee and tea were prohibited, since Silvers were 'not allowed to get fat'. After the Gold Line stopped taking blood, its *ndotas* demanded an equal distribution of the food. In order to keep the status quo, Gold Line members tried to starve the Silvers by guarding the trays of food for three days. At this point the Silver Line declared war on the Gold. Ultimately, after several months of internecine conflict, the Silver prevailed and closed the Gold Line. Once the line between the Silvers and Golds was obliterated, 'The entire edifice of 28 myth . . . fell apart.' In the following decades, South African street gangs and the trafficking of new drugs, such as heroin and crack cocaine, linked the region into the global marketplace. As a result, the whole relationship between the streets and the prisons changed.[92]

## The End of Apartheid and the Prison System, 1994

Almost as soon as apartheid ended in 1994 and the African National Congress came to power, South Africa witnessed the 'worst jail disturbances in its history'. Between March and June, inmates in more than fifty prisons tried to burn them down. According to the Number gangs, they felt betrayed when 'the new ANC government refused to celebrate the inauguration of democracy by granting prisoners a general amnesty.'[93]

Beginning in 1994, the prison system was no longer run along strict military lines. Warders stopped patrolling corridors with dogs. But for common prisoners much went on as before, as the Numbers continued to rule the roost and rapes, fighting and cell-burning continued into the next century. According to Numbers lore, the gangs had been at the forefront of the fight against apartheid as well as for equality and better treatment behind bars. But, as with so many other spurious claims they have made, there is little support for their braggadocio. According to one leading Number expert, the notion that they were revolutionaries who won against apartheid in prison is ludicrous. Conditions behind bars did indeed improve, not because of the machinations of the prison gangs but due to the actions of political prisoners: 'It was political and not criminal prisoners who began using the courts to contest conditions.'[94] Put another way:

> It is nonsense to perpetuate the myth that Number gangs are romantic outlaws . . . History conclusively proves that the Number never, ever had any desire to assist the poor, never ever intended to lobby for better conditions, nor take a stand against the apartheid regime, it never supported a political movement . . . [its members] were not part of the struggle and were despised by political prisoners who were held in separate sections of the prison.[95]

## Street Gangs and Prison Gangs: A 'Subtle and Fascinating Relationship'

Prison is a fact of life for street-gang members in Cape Town and elsewhere. One young gang member claimed his uncle, who had been part of the formidable Mongrel street gang and had spent seven years inside, had warned him 'how you must behave [in prison]. Either you must wash dirty underwear or you must give bum.'[96] An interview with the youthful gangster indicated 'how ingrained the prisons were in the lives of people from a very young age'. Apparently, these street hood-lums talked among themselves and shared plans for surviving prison, although these were often unrealistic. The gang member was asked by another what he would do if he was asked to wash underwear. He naively replied that he would become a 7 (or 27) – 'You know, those who kill in there. It's easy.' Conversations between peers indicated that talking as much as they did about prison meant 'going there as a likely event, not a remote, far-fetched possibility'.[97]

Traditional Numbers members can't help but lament the decline of the old ways. As one member put it:

> I took the long road of blood and learning to get to this position, but now there are fokken newcomers who are gang leaders from the outside. The gangs they are part of are not Number gangs, just fokken street gangs. There is no Number outside the prison, but the Firm is calling itself the 28s and the American the 26s.

This member recognized that at the root of the current symbiosis between the Number and street gangs was the growing prominence of the lucrative and growing drug trade. According to one autobiography by a Numbers member:

> These guys know how to smuggle drugs and other luxuries into prison, and in exchange for these things, the corrupt Numbers captains let them buy their *nyungas*, these stars on our shoulders [tattooed on a gang member's to indicate rank]. These captains who sell the Number are also thinking about their futures ... If and when they leave this place, they will get jobs in the street gangs.[98]

One leading gang researcher suggested that 'The relationship between street gangs and prison gangs is a subtle and fascinating one,' one that continues to evolve.[99] More than forty years ago, many incarcerated 26s had been former Born Free Kids street-gang members. Similarly, among the incarcerated 28s were gangsters from the Cape Town Scorpions. However, in the 1970s this was 'as far as the connection went'. But by the late 1990s 'going to prison [was] a prerequisite for taking a leadership position in any street gang.' Moreover, 'There are many young men who have sought a prison sentence in order to prepare themselves for life on the streets.'[100]

In the last years of the 1990s a major territorial conflict between West Cape's two biggest street gangs, the Americans and the Firm, signalled 'the opening of the economy to the world drug market'.[101] Over the next several years many more street-gang members attached to drug-trafficking networks ended up in South African prisons. So too did their multi-millionaire gang bosses. No longer on the streets, where they could count on the protection of legions of street-gang members and their high-calibre weapons, once incarcerated they became vulnerable to the traditional prison gangs. As a result, the changing street scene became 'too volatile, too consuming to leave prison out of the picture', and as a result these drug kingpins 'needed jail to look more like the streets'.[102]

So, after more than a century, the Number gangs were faced with making major adjustments to their rules and rituals in order to have any chance of enjoying the fruits of the drug trade. With apartheid over, in the early 1990s the Americans began adopting some characteristics of the 26s, including rituals and recruitment structures. In the process of emulating the Number it did so 'in a cobbled, bastardized fashion'.[103] The Americans, also known as the Gentlemen, are closely connected to the 26 and 27 prison gangs and specialize in white-collar crime. They also have their hands in drug trafficking, robbery, theft and burglary. One of their smuggling tactics is to select certain jails as their territories for contraband trafficking. In certain instances, the illicit activities have been facilitated by officials working in the centres and often on the Americans' payroll. When these officials are arrested, they typically join the 26. The Americans also maintain a gang hierarchy like that of the 26. This gang represents almost 80 per cent of gang members operating in the Western Cape.[104]

Like the Americans, the Firm has adopted several features of the 28s, and in the early 2000s its members identified themselves as 28s. Its leaders have adopted military ranks such as generals and sergeants and even judges to adjudicate internal discipline. Mimicking the operational features of the 28s, the Firm is considered the 'decision making body for 28 gangs operating in the community', making decisions such as the boundaries in which the 28s can operate. The Firm is well represented at the Brandvei, Helderstroom and Caledon correctional centres and specializes in murder, drugs, prostitution, car theft, money-laundering and corruption.[105]

While the street and prison gangs have begun integrating at some levels, there remains a substantial difference between the two. Some street gangs have gone out of their way to reject the entire organizing principles of the Number, seeing it as a thing of the past. According to an interview with a member of the Clever Kids, a violent street gang in Manenberg, 'here we don't give a fuck about a Number! We will kill you if you are not a Clever Kid. You must *raak wys* [get wise] because, see, this is not prison, so these rules don't mean anything here.'[106]

The debate continues in South Africa and elsewhere as to whether street gangs influence prison gangs or vice versa. Steinberg asserts that the street gangs adopted part of the world of the prison gangs, 'its metaphors, its nomenclature, its logic – and imprinted it on the ghetto'. During the last decade of the twentieth century, 'street gangs began using prison as a metaphor to understand their relationship with those upon whom they preyed.' According to this theory, the street-gang members operated like the Numbers' *ndotas*, while the street merchants, bar owners and taxicab drivers whom they preyed upon were like the *franse*, or unaffiliated prisoners who had to 'rent the air they breathe' inside prisons.[107] Steinberg concluded that it is 'safe to say that prison and street gangs were not separate entities. Rather they animated one another in intricate ways, and had always done so.'[108]

Ultimately, the impact of drug trafficking and its kingpins inflicted chaos on traditional prison-gang culture, something that the 'successive white administrations had been unable to destroy'.[109] As the West Cape gangs morphed into increasingly sophisticated trafficking enterprises, they in turn spread the Numbers subculture 'all over Cape Town's ghettos', and in the process, correctional institutions have helped extend underground markets 'to every village in the country'.[110]

The breaking down of the tradition-based gang culture began in the opening years of the post-apartheid era as old loyalties unravelled and a new criminal economy undermined the Number system. The street gangsters who claimed to be Numbers had not been initiated within the prison-gang milieu and 'cared less about the old system than about making money on the outside'. Longtime Number gang members viewed these new converts as 'Mongrels . . . lacking the credentials of pure-bred Numberman [sic]'. The most recent incarnation of this evolving criminal enterprise is more dynamic, increasingly unpredictable and violent.[111] In 2013, one journalist noted the convergence of prison- and street-gang cultures, writing: 'Young people wearing hooded sweatshirts and trainers throng Manenberg's litter-strewn sidewalks, many of them sporting tattoos that brand them members of the so-called numbers gangs, the 26s, 27s, 28s, that operate in the country's prisons.'[112]

As a result of this cross-fertilization of gangs, the most dominant gangs in the South African prison system include the 26s, the 28s and the Air Force. Most recently, other gangs have claimed Number status as well. For instance, the Desperadoes, active mostly in the Cape, now identify as 29s. According to one academic, 'They have breached Nongoloza's age old number rule and are treated with hostility by others.'[113] However, the Air Force, which distances itself from any Number connection, has been influenced by the Numbers' argot and structure. As a result they have been referred to as 24s.

### Other South African Prison Gangs: The Air Force, Big 5 and Desperadoes

There are several number gangs that are not recognized by the original three. These include the aforementioned Air Force, or the 24s; the Big 5, or 25s; and the Desperadoes, or 29s. The Air Force, or Royal Air Force, operates with the main goal of escaping from prison. One explanation for the proclivity to escape is the fact that 'their goods' are hidden outside the walls and need to be protected at all costs. Members have often been referred to as 'men of the wind'.[114] One of the strategies that the Air Force uses to recruit is telling prospective members that they do not believe in sex. However, new recruits must undergo a classification process that determines whether they will be allotted a feminine or masculine rank. The individual tasked with making these choices is called the 'blacksmith'. This is accomplished by asking 'are you a young man or soldier?' If the recruit does not want to fulfil the requirement of shedding blood he will become a wyfie.[115]

The Big 5 operates in cahoots with the authorities to gain protection from other gangs. The Fives consist of non-gang and gang members who have left other gangs. It was common to see some with tattoos from the 26s, 27s, 28s and others.[116] It has its own rank structure, hierarchy and rules, and is concerned with smuggling and sodomy. In the Big 5 the 'medical doctor' determines who are soldiers and who are wyfies by checking the pulse. Big 5s have thigh sex; 28s anal. Neither gang has the same respect and stature as the three traditional number gangs, and their members are derided as 'dirty dogs'. It is common for gang members such as the Big 5 to use their positions as cleaners and orderlies to disguise smuggling activities.

The Desperadoes formed on Robben Island around 1964 as a counter-measure against the Big 5 gang. The main interests of the gang are violence, sodomy and doing 'nice time' – basically doing what they want whenever they want. They enjoy control over others and are always willing to help others escape.

Newer gangs such as the Big 5s and the Air Force are regarded as illegitimate. While membership is supposedly voluntary, being locked up in large cells with many other prisoners and gang members 23 hours a day tends to place great pressure on individuals to join, if for no other reason than protection. It all comes down to inmates competing for rare resources. Thus, if an inmate is not a member, he can expect gang members to take his personal belongings, deny him access to privileges, such as buying the right to a bed, or make him pay to be allowed to see visitors. At any time, the equilibrium between the gangs can be upset by an influx of new gang members from other parts of the prison system.

## Namibian Number Gangs

While the Number gangs originated in South Africa almost a century ago, they have spread to neighbouring countries as well. Namibia, bordering South Africa, has long been home to the 26, 28 and Air Force prison gangs, especially Windhoek Central Prison, where the 26 and 28 exist. They are apparently affiliated with counterparts in South Africa. Although a series of bloody riots in the early 2000s brought the gangs to the attention of Namibian society, they have never been given the same prominence as their brethren in South African jails.

In September 2002 violence caused havoc at Windhoek Central Prison, when eighty members of the 28 brutally retaliated against two members of the rival 26s and two other unaffiliated inmates. The bloodshed was said to be over the theft of N$70 from another inmate, who just happened to be a 'monitor' of the leader of the 28. The monitor has the 'unenviable burden of washing the leader's clothes, serving him with food and, more importantly in the context of this case, of keeping possession of the gang's contraband, including money.'[117] It might seem a paltry amount of money to an outsider, certainly not enough to kill over, but in prison (closed and captive prison communities) it is a significant sum. The theft's importance was multiplied by the fact that the rival 26s were the perpetrators. Members of the 28 armed themselves with 'sharpened spoons, wires, toothbrushes, plates, iron mugs, iron bars shaped like pangas and broomsticks', before attacking the four suspected thieves. Despite being viciously beaten and stabbed, they all survived. Later they unsuccessfully sued the Minister of Prisons and Correctional Services for damages, since there were only ten warders for almost five hundred inmates in the section where the attack took place. In 2008, the Namibian gang victims testified to the bloody conflicts being played out in the prison system. Their testimony opened a portal into the gang subculture of the country's largest prison.[118]

With a much smaller prison system, the Namibian Numbers are a weaker incarnation to be sure. However, they do exist in facilities such as Windhoek, Hardap, Walvis Bay, Oluno and elsewhere. Some years ago, an effort was made by the Namibian Ministry of Safety and Security to break up the gangs. It was quite effective. Nowadays, you still find the Number system, but it is much more clandestine. You also find other gangs behind the walls, based on ethnic groups or on shared interests. It is natural for an inmate to want to avoid isolation, especially since being on your own in a facility can be dangerous, and being part of a gang or a group can offer the inmate a sense of belonging and protection.[119]

## South African Number Gangs in the Twenty-first Century

Beginning in 2015, the Cape Town government embarked on a groundbreaking plan to 'crush the province's thriving prison gangs'. In a step towards better classification and proactivity, impending and existing gang members were to be profiled before entering prison. These efforts followed one of the nation's largest gang trials, held in the Western Cape High Court.[120] With seventeen gangsters convicted and heading to prison, it was incumbent on the authorities to determine where they should be housed. The trial revolved around the activities of 28 gang leader George 'Gewald' (Violence) Thomas. The intention was to send the convicted gangsters to prisons where they would be least likely to recruit and 'stir up violence'. Thomas was sentenced to seven life sentences and other lesser sentences that totalled 175 years for a series of murders and ordered assassinations while behind prison walls. These and other crimes were facilitated by the ubiquity of mobile phones, even inside solitary-confinement units. Among the murder victims were six state witnesses killed in the Bishop Lavis prison between 2006 and 2010. The sixteen other criminals were sentenced to terms ranging between ten and fifteen years.

The Numbers still have a grip on the national consciousness and popular culture. In recent years the Number gangs have been featured in several films, including *Four Corners* (2013) and *The Forgiven* (2017), the latter starring Forest Whitaker as Archbishop Desmond Tutu and Eric Bana as apartheid assassin Piet Blomfeld. One of the most note-worthy performances was given by a high-ranking 28 named Welcome Witbooi. Few would have predicted that this man, who had been a top student in high school, would rise to First Star General, the highest rank within the dominant 28, commanding 2,500 men and making more than R500,000 a month (more than U.S.$34,000) for the gangs while inside prison. Described as thoughtful and articulate, when he entered the gang he did it through blood. He commented, 'But the deeper I got the more I understood that when moving up to the highest rank, there was a way out.' Witbooi appeared in *The Forgiven* and served as an advisor on *Four Corners*. In the 2017 film, Witbooi plays the right-hand man of the Number gang leader. His realistic portrayal was based on having lived the life and activities shown in the film. The film-makers did their homework as well, accurately showing the tribulations of a new inmate. Once in prison he navigates the *stimela*, in which gangsters ask him who he is. If he answered with his name he got slapped; as mentioned previously, new inmates are expected to answer that they are either members of the 27 or 28 or non-gang members (*franses*).[121]

Fear Free Life

The recent emergence of the Fear Free Life (FFL) group at Johannesburg's Medium B Prison is only the latest manifestation of gang life behind bars. While the Number still reigns supreme, with the support of South African correctional service, a new group now challenges them in most prisons. Fear Free Life was founded in 2005 by a former leader of the 26s. Within five years it was recognized by the corrections department as an organization dedicated to helping with rehabilitation programmes. In return members were expected to sign a pledge promising to leave 'Gangsterism and drugs' behind. By most accounts they have the full support of warders, even going as far as helping them search inmates for contraband. On the surface this group might seem to be making a noble gesture. Their support by corrections officers has led other prison-gang members 'to believe they are powerless' against them. On several occasions, they have attacked other gang members and have even

*Four Corners* (2013, dir. Ian Gabriel). Set in present-day Cape Town, the film chronicles the story of Farakhan (Brendon Daniels), a general in the Number gang, who is released from Pollsmoor prison after thirteen years and finds himself in a world where street gangs control the ghetto.

been joined in assaults by prison staff. The advent of FFL has added a new and confusing element to what was already a confusing prison sub-culture. A violent battle between gang members and FFL members at one Johannesburg prison resulted in a three-week lockdown. It is too early to predict the future of the FFL, but inmates have expressed concerns that the group has morphed into a vigilante organization. Contrary to their claims that they do not beat other convicts or encourage violence, one Numbers leader disagreed strongly, stating 'they are the gangsters now'. In any case, charges are pending against several FFL members.[122]

Since the late 1990s, South Africa's violent crime rate has continued to rise, and so has the number of young men behind bars, mostly as a result of more remand inmates awaiting trial. The 'psychological state of helplessness and insecurity' felt by new inmates in any prison in the world can be alleviated by gang membership. As noted elsewhere, gangs mean more than just protection, but are also reliable sources for drugs, tobacco, use of mobile phones and other items considered luxuries in prison. As times change, many tried-and-true methods of gang recruitment continue. A new inmate can count on being approached by several gang members during his first week. The richer the inmate, the better. Rapes continue to take place as part of some gang rituals, and, unfortunately, there is still no adequate support for victims of sexual assault.

Recent interviews with warders and prisoners suggest that although South Africa made the transition from apartheid to democracy in 1994, it had little impact 'on the Number and the way the gangs control the prisons of the country'.[123] By most accounts the hierarchical organization of sex roles and relationships among the 28s is mostly unchanged since the 1980s. Not unlike other prison gangs around the world, traditional Number members lament the fact that the gangs have moved further and further from their roots. This has been reflected in the lack of respect accorded senior members by new and younger inmates. Over the past thirty years, the 27 gang has experienced a decline in membership. Since 1994, the Gold Line of the 28s has seen its activities reduced as well, so much so that it has even disappeared from some admission centres. As a result of the decline of the 27 camp, the 26s have lobbied for an alteration in Number protocol that would allow them to communicate directly with the 28s, rather than having to go through the 27s.[124]

It is not uncommon to find grievances among members of long-lasting criminal groups. Longtime Number members, especially at the lower levels, are convinced they have been used by the more elite members, who keep most of the money from outside drug sales. Others object to gang members coming into prison from the streets already accepted as a Number member with rank. One disgruntled member pointed out that in the past you had to go through an initiation to gain entry to the gang. However, if a street gang member sells drugs on the street and is arrested the next day, they can come in as a member with rank.[125]

Lest there be any doubt about the hold of the Number on South African prisons, consider the recent experience of one celebrity prisoner. No sooner had the notorious former Olympic athlete Oscar 'the Blade Runner' Pistorius been sentenced to time in a South African prison for the killing of his girlfriend, Reeva Steenkamp, than a target was placed on his back by the 26 Number gang. As he entered the inner sanctum of Pretoria Central Prison in July 2016, little did he suspect that Khalil Subjee, the General of the feared 26 gang, had already announced that the formerly inspiring Paralympic athlete would be 'taken out' or murdered. Anyone familiar with the country's Number gangs recognized that this was not an idle threat. Thanks to a prison 'call box', or telephone, Subjee, who was more than three decades into his sentence, sent word out that he would make the double-amputee's life hell, warning that 'his wealth would not buy him a lavish prison lifestyle – instead he would be taken out'. The General confided to a reporter that:

> Anyone who thinks they can come here and live like a king, will have a hit on the head. If he thinks he is going to come here and buy his way to get computers and cellphones and a lavish lifestyle, he must know that will never happen for as long as I am around.[126]

# 5

# OCEANIA'S PRISON GANGS: AUSTRALIA AND NEW ZEALAND

The legacy of British colonialism made a permanent imprint on the prison systems of Australia and New Zealand. While the same could be said about South Africa in the previous chapter, there was no official system of apartheid in the major countries of Oceania. Australia and New Zealand have the largest prison systems in the region. Both share a number of common origins, none more important than their English colonial heritage and the fact that an enormous number of indigenous people continue to be imprisoned in both countries. As far back as 1993, the Australian aboriginal population was 'the most imprisoned ethnic group in the world'. At the time, they represented almost 20 per cent of the prison population, but only 2 per cent of the entire population. By 2018 conditions had worsened, with aboriginals making up 3 per cent of the Australian population, but filling 25 per cent of Australia's prison cells. Young indigenous men have one of the highest suicide rates in the world, and indigenous children are ten times more likely to be in state care. Beyond the shared proclivities of Australia and New Zealand for locking up their marginalized population, distinctions between the two exist. One can look across the Tasman Sea to the Maori in New Zealand, who remain on the lowest rungs of the economic ladder but 'live longer and healthier lives than Aboriginals'. But Maoris still account for 15 per cent of the 5 million-strong population and fill more than half of New Zealand's jail cells, although they are less likely to go to prison than Australia's Aborigines.[1]

Australia: High-density Gangs

Most of the modern conflict between prison gangs in Australia has been tied to the internal drug trade. At some prisons, members of various

Inmates from Berrimah Prison, Darwin, in the musical documentary *Prison Songs* (2015, dir. Kelrick Martin). Aboriginal citizens make up 30 per cent of the Northern Territory's population, but in its largest prison over 80 per cent of the inmates are indigenous.

High-density Gangs (HDGs) that had operated on the outside have now entered the prison maelstrom. Many are members of outlaw motorcycle gangs (OMGs), or 'bikies' in Australian argot. With little gang affiliation inside prison, OMG members formerly lacked influence on the inside. To rectify this, a member of one OMG might temporarily join up with a Lebanese gang behind bars, for example, or another formidable prison gang. There was a time when members of rival OMGs might even join the same gang while behind bars, where they were expected to put aside their differences until they got out.[2]

Scenes in prison yards in Oceania often mirror their counterparts in other prisons around the world. If inmates are not separated into different yards because of policy, they will self-segregate by race, ethnicity and culture, so much so that there might be as many as ten different groupings in a yard with less than two hundred inmates in total. Of the various racial/ethnic gangs, the 'Asian gangs were the quietest' and often stood in a circle in the yard so that they 'would never have their backs turned to anyone for a moment'.[3]

It is not uncommon to witness individuals, most of whom were of European descent, walking the yard without any affiliation. But, as one gang member put it, he will probably have 'his shoes stolen in a second'.[4] At prisons such as Long Bay jail, near Sydney, the unprotected can expect to have all their possessions taken by gang members – that is, except for prison-issued items. The power inside Long Bay shifts from one day to another, depending on the number of inmates from one gang coming in or going out. The appearance of the HDGs paralleled a rise in violence in the early 2000s. More and more information on Australia's prison gangs is being accrued through gang intelligence gathered with the help of various legal listening devices. In New South Wales jails, for example, there 'were at least 100 listening devices'.[5] By 2016 it was accepted policy for very high-profile inmates in NSW to have a listening device planted somewhere in their cells.

### Australian Bikies

Long Bay jail reported its first smuggled mobile phones in 2001, as they had finally become small enough to smuggle easily into correctional facilities. The changing prison subculture is exemplified by the incarceration of more and more OMG members. In the past a hardened career criminal might take a new inmate under his wing and show them the ropes; now gangsters such as outlaw motorcycle gang members are more likely to use mobile phones to call a new inmate's parents and extort A$1,000 or more as a membership fee to prevent their son from being beaten.[6] Over the past few years, South Australia's prisons have become much more dangerous, in no small part due to the influx of OMG members. Between 2012 and 2017 there was a 73 per cent increase in biker inmates. This rate is a testament to amended legislation in South Australia that branded ten gangs as criminal organizations. The new law allowed police to ban bikers from meeting or wearing their gang colours in public and owning tattoo parlours, and even to mandate the crushing of their cherished motorbikes. With the authorities given more power to target OMGs in special operations, many gangs responded by closing their headquarters on the outside.

In Barwon Prison, in the town of Lara, Australia, the Hells Angels joined forces with the violent Prisoners of War (POW) prison gang led by Matthew 'the General' Johnson, allowing the Angels to exert 'unprecedented influence inside Victoria's highest-security jail'.[7] Johnson is among the most prominent and dangerous prisoners on the continent, having already battered to death a serial killer and prison informer in the high-security unit they shared. Earning 159 convictions over a twenty-year period, he was first sent to prison at fifteen, at a time when the POW gang was beginning to flex its strength on the streets. It was also a time when the Hells Angels, Comancheros, Mongols and Bandidos[8] were recruiting 'from various jail gang members to increase their influence inside prison and to have a fresh source of muscle when inmates are released.' As a result of a state campaign against bikies, there was more than enough support to create a 'bikies only' prison in Queensland in 2013.[9] Members were kept in their cells 23 hours a day. Other states planned to deport foreign gang members, who have rushed to Australia to join warring sides in an ongoing OMG conflict.[10]

One of the unwritten laws in Long Bay and other prisons was that any bikie with seniority 'was not to be touched'.[11] This rule was broken when a Hells Angel sergeant-at-arms was brutally assaulted. The attack was carried out by brothers Michael and Sam Ibrahim, who had dropped out of the Nomads OMG,[12] to form the Notorious OMG,[13] made up of Lebanese and Polynesian members.[14] Although not formally recognized by other bikie gangs, they flaunted their colours or gang insignia in jail.[15]

Until around 2003, prison gangs in Australia operated according to race. One observer described them as 'jail developed gangs based on culture and ethnic background'. The aboriginals would hang together and were often at war with Asians and Polynesians. But it was the Lebanese

Long Bay jail, near Sydney, 2007.

Members of the Bandido motorbike gang attend the funeral of their national president, Michael Kulakowski, in Mulgoa, 18 November 1997.

who were considered the most powerful, at least at Long Bay, 'Australia's hardest prison'.[16] But 'in 2003, the entire gang culture was turned on its head' after OMG groups 'rewrote their charters' and decided that any member who went to jail 'must stick to their own gang'.[17] Simply put, if you were in one gang on the outside you were forbidden from joining another gang in jail. This rule extended from bikies to gangs such as the Syrian Kings and Brothers 4 Life. In the past, for example, a Lebanese member of the Nomads OMG on the outside could enter jail and join a Lebanese gang that might include members from rival OMGs. They would mix in prison and forget their outside differences. With the change in rules the bikie wars entered prison, where the practice of 'leaving your colours at the gate' led to a more complicated gang scene. Moreover, the new strategy of recruiting OMG members in prison has also transformed the character of bikie culture.[18]

In 2017 a series of stabbings and beatings between the Bandidos and the Comancheros took place at Port Phillip Prison, Truganina, Victoria. The threat of violence remained high enough that regular visitors were warned to stay away. The facility has been plagued by other criminal activities as well. Home to notorious lifers Peter Dupas, Raymond 'Mr Stinky' Edmunds and Leslie Camillieri at the time of writing, it also hosts a Middle Eastern organized-crime boss considered a key player in the drug trade. Smuggling and corruption are rampant at Port Phillip, with reports of corrupt correctional officers, visitors bringing in contraband and others throwing snowballs (in rare cases of snow) filled with drugs over the prison walls. Between July 2016 and January 2017, the prison had the state of Victoria's highest proportion of inmates randomly testing positive for drugs. While 'hillbilly heroin', or buprenorphine, is most commonly detected, inmates have also tested positive for amphetamine, opiates and methadone.[19]

The metamorphosis of bikie gangs in prison in the first decades of the twenty-first century led to several new prison policies, including the incarceration of members and associates in four different classifications. The first category comprises those identified as recognized, or 'patched', members of gangs, sporting gang insignia whenever possible on their clothing. In the second group are their 'close associates', but not full members. In the third group are members who have left their gangs on 'bad terms and fear retaliation'. The last grouping contains members of OMGs who have been linked to various organized crime networks, including the Notorious, DLASTHR, the Bra Boys and the Muslim Brotherhood Movement, a more recent incarnation of radicalized Muslim inmate gangs. Bikie gangs demonstrate their solidarity with specific colours, in this case 'an emblem of a red hand grenade and two handguns'.[20]

## Bassam Hamzy: Brothers 4 Life/Muslim Gang

In 2013, an Australian journalist headlined an article with the rhetorical question, 'Is Australia's Most Dangerous Gangster Bassam Hamzy Still in Control?'[21] At the time, Hamzy was leading the Brothers 4 Life (BFL) syndicate from prison. His reach extended outside to Sydney's large Muslim community, ordering kidnappings, shootings, kneecappings and murder in NSW and in other states. Hamzy was 34 at the time and had been in jail for the past sixteen years. Thanks to the new ubiquity of smaller and smaller mobile phones, he was able to orchestrate his criminal network from Lithgow jail in New South Wales.

BFL can be identified by an insignia that shows two AK-47s and is said to be modelled on bikie colours. Many members have even tattooed Hamzy's name 'prominently on arms and legs'.[22] Hamzy made his reputation as one of the country's most dangerous gangsters on the mean streets of Kings Cross, Sydney. A drug addict in his teens, in 1998

The tattooed back of Michael Odisho, former Brothers 4 Life gang member.

at nineteen he killed another teen at a nightclub and was sentenced to 21 years for murder. Sent to a supermax prison, he converted to Islam and radicalized others as he put together his criminal organization. Authorities soon moved him into Lithgow jail and into segregation. In 2008 security cameras alerted guards that a mobile phone was being passed between cells on a line of dental floss. Once police started listening in, they discovered Hamzy's extensive criminal enterprise, as he made 450 calls, often to relatives, each day. Hamzy has been described as an Al-Qaeda devotee and is forbidden from speaking Arabic in Goulburn Prison, where he is incarcerated. In 2007 he was suspected of trying to engineer a jihadist jailbreak that never came to fruition.

The BFL leader has demonstrated considerable business acumen running his extensive drug network with the aid of mobile devices, as well as supervising an occasional kidnapping and directing the murder and torture of enemies from inside his Lithgow jail cell. By some accounts, he has made at least 19,000 phone calls. At the apogee of his activities it was estimated that he was directing the trafficking of amphetamines and cannabis to the tune of $250,000 a week by truck between Sydney and Melbourne.

Hamzy continued his criminal operations despite his classification as an 'Extreme High Risk Restricted' prisoner, the highest-security inmate classification. In 2013 he claimed to have made a deal with the

NSW Crime Commission that gave him permission to sell commercial quantities of drugs in jail in return for helping them recover stolen rocket launchers. It is believed that his gang has joined forces on the outside with the Bandidos bikie gang in a violent drug war.

Hamzy was suspected of being involved in a number of Muslim conversions at Goulburn. Authorities feared he was using religion to cloak the activities of Brothers 4 Life. Since the Lebanese Yard was next to the aboriginal Yard, the proximity of the aboriginals meant easy recruiting. A walkway only 'about 15 metres' wide (49¼ ft) for corrections officers separated the two groups, who were close enough that a conversation could be held between the two yards.[23] Ultimately the aboriginals became the main group targeted for conversion. Sharing a history of persecution with the Lebanese, it is easy to see why.[24]

The administration at Goulburn feared that the recruitment of aboriginal inmates to the Muslim faction could lead to an internal jihadist threat, and dubbed them the 'Supermax Jihadists'.[25] Others have labelled this form of prison conversion 'prislam'. After finding out that the extremist elements were using an Al-Qaeda training model with the possible intention of taking over the prison system, officials were forced to take unprecedented steps to intervene.

In 2007, of the 37 Goulburn supermax inmates (Muslims or converts), 12 were placed in the most secure facility. New protocol allowed 24-hour surveillance of Islamic inmates, especially when it was revealed that outside money was being used to influence inmates to convert. Further investigation found that inmates who converted were clandestinely paid up to $100 per week for services. In order to do this, money orders were used and placed into accounts belonging to trusted Hamzy associates who then made payments to converts across NSW. By some reports, Goulburn prison authorities were under the impression that Hamzy 'was buying loyal followers to create a prison gang that would obey his every demand'. Once this took place he would use them to take over the jail in order to escape and join up with his street gang.[26]

Almost a decade after the new protocol was adopted, fears had still not diminished over the perceived threat from 'Muslim radicals' in the prison system. By some accounts they had changed tactics from paying inmates to convert to utilizing intimidation and violence, leading one official to warn: 'the Islamic State has managed to gain a foothold in prisons across the nation.' In 2016 it was estimated that 8–9 per cent of convicts in Victoria and NSW (at least 35 correctional centres) identified as Muslim (compared to 2–3 per cent in the free world). A number of NSW prison officers have even gone as far as to call their turf 'their Gaza Strip'.[27]

At Kariong Detention Centre in New South Wales, for example, a number of inmates were beaten after refusing to convert. A plot was uncovered, regarding the beheading of those who declined conversion, but nothing like this has come to pass. In this particular case, the plan was to film the beheading on a mobile phone and post it to the Internet as ISIS propaganda. There have even been reports of inmates being stabbed for shaving off their beards before they attended parole hearings (seen as reneging on religious commitments). As noted earlier, some prisons have created yards exclusively for Muslims in order to protect non-believing inmates. It is this 'conversion by the fist' recruiting approach that administrators fear most.[28]

## Goulburn Prison: The Killing Fields

Dubbed 'the Killing Fields', Goulburn Correctional Centre is Australia's highest-security prison, as well as its most dangerous. Home to gangs such as Brothers 4 Life and Will to Kill, some observers have compared the institution, which opened in 1844, to the American Guantanamo Bay facility in Cuba. It is located in NSW, almost two hours' drive from Sydney. In 1998, it unofficially became the first Australian jail to racially segregate inmates. Although it was never intended as policy, it brought control to the yards, effectively ending the 'Killing Fields period'. According to one official, it was only meant to be a temporary fix 'to stop the Aboriginal fellas from starving'.[29] Here, prison gangs and other groups are separated into various yards. It has four large wings (ABCD), with the two largest, C and D, holding mainstream inmates. A and B hold those in protective custody. Each wing is divided by fences and razor wire into four yards containing thirty inmates each. Aboriginals were kept in one and positioned next to the Lebanese/ Middle Eastern cliques. Nearby was the yard for Caucasian Aussies and Asians, and the next for another group of Caucasian Aussies and Islanders. The policy has been to place Caucasian Aussies into a variety of locations. By most accounts, the Aussies were split up into two groups because 'they could not get along with each other.' New players on the gang scene included OMGs, Asians and ethnic Lebanese and Islander gangs. By some accounts they have allied with each other to put up a more united front against the most powerful gangs.[30]

Goulburn was not the only prison to experiment with the separation strategy, and some critics have gone so far as to compare it to an apartheid policy. With constant strife at Long Bay jail between Pacific Islanders and Lebanese gang members, bikies and others, in the early 2000s inmates were segregated by race. It might have toned down the violence, but, as one observer put it, if you were not in a gang you were 'in a bad position'. According to former inmates, if you were unattached to a gang 'you were fucked. And it was the poor Anglo-Saxons who were fucked. They were always in the minority – came in for stealing cars, didn't know anyone.' So unless a new inmate came in with a badass reputation, he would almost certainly be targeted immediately. Coercion was the rule. Some Anglos were forced into 'dirty jobs' that included anally smuggling drugs into prison.[31]

In 2002 it was first revealed publicly that different ethnic groups were being isolated in separate yards, a strategic move to more easily manage inmates and prevent violence. One spokesman referred to it with the unfortunate term 'ethnic clustering'.[32] As of 2018, Goulburn inmates were still separated by race. Officials claimed it worked well there, while the results of this policy have been somewhat mixed at other institutions.

Goulburn Correctional Centre, 2006.

## Mark 'Chopper' Read, the Overcoat and Prisoners of War Gangs

Seldom does a prison-gang-affiliated inmate attain the prominence of one Mark 'Chopper' Read. He originally carved out his bloody reputation on the mean streets of Melbourne, making the transition from robbing drug dealers to kidnapping and torturing denizens of the Australian under-world. Between the ages of 20 and 38 he became well acquainted with the Australian correctional system, having served only thirteen months of that time as a free man. He was brought up as a Seventh Day Adventist by stern Christian parents, who apparently failed to inculcate him with their belief system. His convictions would eventually include armed robbery, kidnapping, arson, impersonating a police officer, assault, attempted murder, and worse. While many of his fans attributed his nickname 'Chopper' to him asking another inmate to cut off Read's ears with a razor blade in the 1970s, he apparently had earned it by second grade, named after a cartoon character in the popular TV show *Yakky Doodle*. His behaviour might be partially explained by the fact that he was committed into psychiatric care at the ages of 15, 19 and 23.

Often at the centre of violent conflict behind bars, Read lost several feet of intestine after being stabbed by 'fellow inmates and longtime friends' Jimmy Loughnan and Ned Clonan. Read wrote numerous books behind bars, eventually selling more than half a million copies of his 'autobiographical' Chopper books and the children's 'Hooky the Cripple' book series. According to his co-authors, journalists Andrew Rule and John Silvester, these books were so poorly written that they should be regarded as 'the greatest crime committed against literature in the history of the written word'.[33]

Read was a driving force in prison, at one time leading a group of inmates known as the Overcoat Gang, so named for concealing homemade weapons under heavy prison-issue overcoats. The prison-manufactured grey coats had blue patches stitched over the heart of the wearer front and back, so that armed guards on prison towers could 'shoot to kill' more easily in a riot or escape attempt. The bulky coats offered some degree of protection from makeshift knives and were ideal for hiding weapons. Read often wore similar coats on the rare occasions he was out of jail in the 1970s and '80s because he could hide firearms in the pockets. As legend has it, the Overcoat Gang was born in Pentridge Prison's H Division in 1975 after a gunman and fellow inmate named John Palmer – affiliated with the Federated Ship Painters and Dockers

Poster for *Chopper* (2000, dir. Andrew Dominik), starring Eric Bana as Mark Read.

Union – accused Read of eating extra sausages issued for Christmas lunch. While operating under a veil of legitimacy, one historian suggests that 'the painters and dockers, with their bizarrely murderous culture and strange nicknames, provided a little colour in a generally dreary political and economic landscape.' Read denied the accusation by the gunman Palmer and killed him, igniting a long-running vendetta that became known as the 'Sausage War.'[34]

If Read is to be believed, he has been involved in nineteen murders and eleven attempted murders. Over time, as he tried to tone down his claims, he admitted to between four and seven murders. However, those in the know agreed that Chopper 'never would let truth get in the way of a good yarn.'[35] Released in 1998, he turned to more aesthetic pursuits, such as painting. He sold more than one hundred works for up to $6,500, but there is no way of determining whether they were purchased as murder memorabilia or for his artistic talents. Following in the steps of America's 'Son of Sam' laws, which prevent criminals from profiting from their crimes, amendments were passed in Australia that prevented him from earning money from his writing and his art. Instead, his share of royalties went to the Royal Children's Hospital in Melbourne.

In 2000 the Australian actor Eric Bana portrayed Read in the film *Chopper*.[36] In 2009 Read revealed that he had contracted hepatitis C after using a 'blood-stained' razor. Despite the knowledge that he would die if he did not have a liver transplant, at 55 years old he made it known that he would not accept one if offered. He died in palliative care in Melbourne on 9 October 2013, aged 58.

## New Zealand Prison Gangs

Known more for its phantasmagoric *Lord of the Rings* scenery than its gangsters, New Zealand is home to more than forty street and prison gangs. According to the *Economist*, New Zealand has 'more gang members than soldiers.'[37] One gangster went even further, recently boasting that NZ had 'one of the highest gang membership rates in the world', citing the fact that out of a country of 4.7 million, more than 5,000 were either members or prospects of different gangs. What cannot be disputed is that the country is 'one of the highest jailers in the world', with an 'alarmingly disproportionate quotient of indigenous people locked up'. While Maoris make up around 15 per cent of the population, they account for half of the more than 8,000 inmates. Rates for women are even higher, at 60 per cent.[38]

Prior to the early 1980s there were few gang members in NZ prisons. But by the end of the decade an estimated 15 per cent of the male sentenced prison population belonged to gangs. Officials attribute this to the proliferation of indigenous gangs such as the Mongrel Mob, Black Power and the King Cobras. An entire subculture revolves around gang membership, and according to one estimate by the National Police Association there are as many as 6,000 full members and another 66,000 gang associates, described as 'partners and other family members involved in gang behaviour'.[39] One survey placed the number of gang members in prison as increasing 350 per cent between 2011 (1,051) and April 2017 (3,711).[40]

Most of the country's gangs were created in the 1950s and '60s, after thousands of residents left rural areas looking for better lives in urban centres. Of course, not all found them. Many indigenous Maoris and other Pacific Islanders struggled in the new urban environment, often 'short of cash, sometimes dependent on alcohol and drugs'. Among them were numerous teenagers who found the family and protection they had left behind 'in the tattooed, leather-clad arms of gangs'.[41]

At mid-century, gang membership was originally dominated by younger *pakehas*, those of European descent. Today, the term is applied to those of non-Maori descent. In fact, during the 1950s there was not even a Maori gang in Wellington, and only about ten Maori members were identified as gang-affiliated. Originally, patches sewn on the back of their leather jackets and vests were a way for like-minded groups to recognize one another. The rise of emblem-wearing, 'patched' street-gang members, indicating their affiliation and status, in the 1960s and '70s coincided with the transition of the Hells Angels to an outlaw motorcycle gang. Around the same time, the Mongrel Mob (MM) became the prominent street gang. At first they were mostly young *pakehas* from Wellington and Hawke's Bay. The MM eventually established its own subculture, based in part on the street-gang scene, before transforming further, at a time when 'immigration from the Pacific Islands and internal Maori migration created a social environment ripe for the formation of Polynesian gangs'. By the mid-1970s all street gangs had adopted the same organizational structure as the OMGs. The gangs spread quickly and led to the creation of another powerful gang, Black Power (BP), which would prove a 'counterbalance' to the MM.[42]

In the 1980s 'gangs became a permanent feature of New Zealand prisons.' According to one groundbreaking study based on the 1989 census, prison-gang members of that era tended to be 'younger, classified as requiring medium or maximum security custody, convicted of violent offences and serving longer sentences'.[43] Prisons were home to a medley of bikie gangs, street gangs and supergangs such as BP and the MM, and the most numerous were ethnic-based gangs.

Prison gangs in NZ follow the importation model, and there is scant evidence of any originating in prisons.[44] According to several reports and informal surveys, between 1982 and 1985 the total number of prison-gang members was 'remarkably stable'.[45] However, there was little light thrown on how gang members were being identified. As the decade ended, more systematic data collection suggested that the gangs had actually been increasing more than previously noticed. Institutional reports indicated that gang-connected inmates could be found in every institution except the special first-offender facility of Ohura in Central North Island, Ruapeho District.[46] The largest concentrations were found at medium- and maximum-security prisons on North Island, with the largest proportion of gang members located in Auckland Maximum, Auckland Medium, Waikeria and Wanganui, with numbers as high as 30 per cent of inmates.

By some accounts, gang members were regarded as a particular threat at minimum-security prison camps on the central part of North Island, due to low levels of staff supervision and lack of segregation facilities. Authorities were hesitant to bar gang members from these units, for fear that gang members might be reluctant to reveal their affiliations and create further problems once they were embedded, so it was decided not to make that distinction.

## Outlaw Motorcycle Gangs

In the mid-1970s ongoing conflict between the Hells Angels (HA) and other bikies led to an increasing number of bikers being incarcerated. Many of them ended up serving long sentences in the maximum-security prison at Paremoremo jail, Auckland, better known as just 'Parry'. By some accounts, their time in prison restructured the Hells Angels.[47] One of the unintended consequences of this incarceration was that it put bikers in touch with some of New Zealand's most hardened criminals and drug dealers. Taken as a whole, Parry had less than two hundred prisoners, but most were classified among NZ's criminal elite. It was there that the HA became 'involved in the black economy of the prison, dealing drugs and bookmaking, and gaining contact with various underground crime networks'.[48] During the 1970s the old convict code still took precedence among gang members, and was 'both learned and adopted by HA members' by the time they were back out on the streets. According to one HA who had been in charge of bookmaking while in stir, 'With the exception of one, who I met later on ... he really changed – they all learnt how to be criminals, proper criminals'.[49]

## The Mongrel Mob

The Mongrel Mob, comprising mixed or predominantly Maori and Polynesian members, was created in Hawke's Bay in the early 1960s. According to unsubstantiated gang lore, the name was adopted after a judge referred to a group of indigenous men before him in court as 'mongrels'. Members are easily recognized by their red-and-black colours and insignia, often featuring a swastika and a British bulldog wearing a *stahlhelm*, or German steel helmet. These identifiers were worn only by patched members. In other cases the insignia might be tattooed on the body or face and imprinted on their red bandannas, making them 'stick out like dogs' balls', in the words of one member.[50] The ex-MM leader Tuhoe 'Bruno' Isaac recounted in his autobiography, *True Red*, long after his active days, that 'Wearing the colour red, living by the law of lawlessness and having the patch with the emblem of the mighty bulldog' was what he regarded as being True Red, hence the book's title. For seventeen years his life revolved around the gang. He was so enamoured with it that he had the German helmet bearing the swastika, or 'Krautlid', tattooed on his back and elsewhere. When anyone asked him 'Why the British bulldog?' his stock answer was that it was a 'symbol of British colonial oppression that consumed the Maori people'. Remembering his turbulent gang years, Isaac noted:

> Being Maori meant nothing to us even though the majority of us were Maori; the only culture worth anything to us was Mob culture. The patch [insignia] replaced all ethnic or cultural dimensions. You never spoke the *reo* [Maori language] or performed a *hongi* [greeting by pressing noses] within the confines of the gang or gang pad. All that Maori stuff was to be left on the marae [tribal gathering

place] or wherever it was normally lived out . . . Dog [another term for MM] culture was the ruling power of my life.[51]

In 1975 Greg Newbold, the future New Zealand criminologist and penal authority, was sentenced to seven-and-a-half years in prison. He would serve two-thirds of his sentence, half of the time in maximum security. He recounted his experiences in his book *The Big Huey* (1982), the title referring to doing a long sentence, or 'doing the Big Huey Long'. Initially, Newbold was confined at Hautu, where there was much less tension between gangs, before being confined in Parry. Here the MM was the dominant gang. The only sporadic conflict was usually touched off by a gang member wearing the wrong colours in the wrong place. For example, the BP wore black sashes and the MM wore red armbands. Other prison gangs included the Head Hunters, Sinn Fein, Filthy Few and Highway 61, but their numbers were rather thin and there were not always enough members behind bars at any one time for them to call themselves a gang. The MM's membership easily topped the other gangs, because they recruited within prison walls. Newbold remembered hearing that in some jails, such as Rangipo, on the Central North Island, 'the Mob virtually ran the whole joint'.[52]

Similar to other prison gangs, the MM had developed a salute as far back as the 1960s. It is described as a 'three-finger salute', in which the thumb and pinky are extended with the other three fingers remaining clenched behind them. NZ gang expert Jarrod Gilbert suggested that the salute resembles the so-called '"shaka" sign common in surfer culture'. Others have argued that the extended thumb and small finger are meant to look like dog's ears, 'mimicking the bulldog the gang adopted as a symbol in the 1960s or early 1970s, when they also adopted the "guttural bark"'. A more interesting origin story claims that a Mongrel had lost three fingers in the 1960s in some type of industrial accident, so that when he 'waved or gave the Nazi salute, only his little finger and thumb were visible on his misshapen hand'.[53]

The route from prospect to officially recognized member of the MM was often a long journey of humiliation. Treated like slaves, prospects were expected to clean, cook and commit crimes that could lead to stints in prison. Until a prospect was formally accepted into the gang he was fair game for the rest of the gang; whether it meant being forced to drink excrement and urine from a boot or fighting three members at one time, the constant degradation was supposed to desensitize the

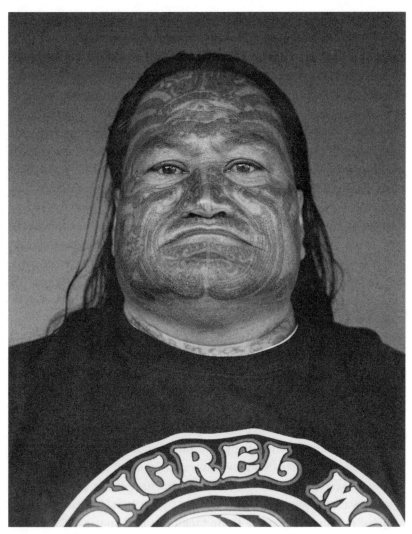

Jono Rotman, *King Willy New Zealand, President RIP, Manurewa*, 2014, C-type print, ed. 3.

prospective member to any type of intimidation or brutality he might be faced with by other gangs – in other words, to judge whether he 'had the stomach to be a Mongrel'.[54] Once inducted, any attempt to leave the gang was treated as a grave transgression.

The MM hierarchy comprised, in descending order, the president, vice-president, sergeant of arms, treasurer, patched and prospects. One former high-ranking member claimed: 'Prison was our second home; it meant free kai [food], a pillow and a bed.'[55]

In maximum-security Parry, members learned how to get along with other gang members and on some occasions even became friends. According to Tuhoe Isaac, 'there was a comradeship that developed amongst the inmates that sometimes went beyond my Mob thinking about comradeship. The brothers inside needed to unite if they were to survive within – comrades [were] aptly named Parry Comrades' to reflect an entity created inside to unite all those doing time.[56]

This brotherhood was symbolized by an insignia of two fists linked by a broken chain. The fists represented comradeship between gang members, criminals and lifers, while the broken chain stood for the idea that when you were in prison no authority ruled you and each man was free within the brotherhood.[57] Not all Mobsters were on the same page with this idea. Isaac did not like it, and made a point of hanging out with his own crew. Some time in the 1970s, while behind bars, he created a Paremoremo chapter of the MM with its own bulldog design that included 'a front view of a bulldog with no helmet . . . with the name MM on the top rocker rim and Paremoremo lined on the bottom rocker.'[58] Isaac claimed his crew was the first to create a new gang chapter within the country's prison system. This move solidified and distinguished the Mobsters inside from chapters around the country, and soon the idea of prison chapters was adopted in other institutions.

Prior to the formation of the Paremoremo MM chapter there was usually a kingpin who held sway over the prison; in most cases only the smartest and toughest ran the show. But as more and more MM came through the prisons, the kingpin was initially pushed aside and isolated, and then overwhelmed and mastered by MM. As Isaac put it, the old system 'was neutered and unrecognized by our boys'. Soon the strongest gang members ruled the roost, facilitated by a special relationship between the gang presidents and the corrections officers, who, some claim, allowed them to run the prison with little friction. The transition in prison culture meant 'being a Mongrel and doing a lag in prison gave you a certain status, a bit higher than the normal criminals.'[59]

Isaac could look back on a number of accomplishments when he left prison in 1985. While at Mt Eden Prison, for example, he was elected chapter president and, as mentioned previously, oversaw the adoption of a new symbol, a bulldog on its side without a helmet. All members of the chapter had it tattooed on their bodies, usually on the right shoulder to commemorate the very first Mobsters, who wore swastikas in the same place.[60]

By 2010 the Mongrel Mob 'was a collection of loosely affiliated, independent chapters with no national organization or president'. With more than 1,000 patched members in more than thirty chapters, it was NZ's largest gang. Prisons remained a fertile recruiting ground for new members. Members can be identified, in some cases, by their preference for facial tattoos, red bandannas and patches, typically featuring a German Second World War helmet and swastikas. Mongrel Mob members shout '*Sieg Heil*', bark like dogs and offer their distinctive hand salute.[61] More recently, one gang expert suggested that the use of the swastika was not meant to indicate racism but rather a 'symbolic defiance of social norms'. Thus, in terms of the MM moniker, the Nazi symbol stood for something despicable and terrible – 'it represented mongrelism'.[62]

### Black Power Gang

Black Power remains the MM's chief rival. It developed in much the same way as the MM did but it diverged from the MM in that it was inspired by the civil rights and black power movement in the United States during the 1970s. In its early years it made some notable progress in curbing antisocial behaviour, fighting and drinking, but these gains were short-lived. By most accounts it formed on Easter weekend 1970, when seven men formed a Maori gang they dubbed the Black Bulls. Two years later it changed its name to Black Power and a chapter was established in Auckland. In 1975 the gang came to national prominence.

Motivated by the African American black power movement in the United States, it adopted the clenched-fist symbol and the colours blue and black. Members greet each other with a clenched fist, and their main expression is 'Yo! Yo!' or the more prosaic 'Yo fuck yo!' They maintain that they have closer ties to Maori culture than the Mongrel Mob, but this is debatable. The gang has a loose structure and even has a women's section. BP espouses a 'quasi-political mantle', attempting to portray itself as a family-focused group. It was in that guise that, in the early 1980s, the gang reportedly formed a relationship with Prime Minister Robert Muldoon.[63]

In 1977 BP leader Rei Harris banned the wearing of Nazi regalia and geared the gang towards better connecting with its Maori roots as well as distinguishing itself from the MM. According to Gilbert, 'The rich irony of a largely Polynesian gang wearing symbols denoting white superiority was too great for a group named Black Power.'[64]

If some members are to be believed, there is a growing trend among certain prison-gang members to reform their ways from within the gang structure. One member of the vaunted Black Power, for example, is among a number of older members who are attempting to steer young men away from the gang life. BP member Eugene Ryder suggested that some blame for gang growth should be directed at the social policy of the 1960s and '70s that heavily discriminated against Maori children. As in other indigenous groups, young Maori men were much more likely to be institutionalized than their European counterparts for the same crimes. Ryder noted, 'We don't want that for our children.'[65]

Dennis O'Reilly, a lifetime member of the BP, joined in 1972 'because of my personal justice agenda'. While he admits that he has broken laws, he has never been imprisoned. He cites a fellow Maori gang member, who opined: 'Prisons are a breeding ground for gang activity enforced by the justice system and regulated by the prison population.' O'Reilly brought a well-respected outsider to meet his Maori colleague, who was behind bars. The outsider asked him, 'What do you do here?' He replied, 'I run the place.'[66]

By most accounts there is continuing parity between the number of MM and BP members, the leading prison gangs. Not surprisingly, the administration employs a strategy that prevents members of different gangs from sharing a cell. Back in the 1980s and '90s inmates were prohibited from displaying or owning gang-related materials, and gang members were expected to line up separately for work and the dining hall. The gangs had access to separate televisions in the recreation yard, which lessened the potential for conflict over entertainment control.

Early on, gangs provided inmates with a support system to work out problems behind bars. The MM and BP shared a number of characteristics with the constellation of other prison gangs around the world, ranging from hierarchy and class distinction to methods of achieving full member status. Once permitted to wear gang colours, the former prospect now had the power to direct the activities of prospects and affiliated supporters.

### Paremoremo and the End of the Convict Code

The Paremoremo maximum-security prison in Auckland opened in 1969. It soon followed that 'a distinctive inmate culture developed different from [that at] other maximum units.'[67] Between 1975 and 1978 the prison population was never allowed to exceed two hundred inmates, and the gang problem was negligible. During this era it was rare for inmates to violate the traditional social code of the prison. In fact, prior to 1978 there was 'no system of convict bosses ... nor observable hierarchy'. But as most of the old-time hard guys were released, or died, they took their code with them.[68]

In the late 1970s, an individual's prior or current gang connection was regarded as secondary to being part of the inmate population as a whole. According to Newbold:

> In Parry it was meant to be all for one and one for all. There were no gangs in the prisons. If you started that sort of thing you just got a hiding. I can remember a group of 12 Hells Angels in one of the blocks. But they never pushed their identity. However, there came a time when the traditionalists who insisted on the code were released. During the same period, more gang members started to come into the jail. They were very heavy guys ... quite different from the old guard that held the place together. For the first time gang members

Paremoremo Prison, Auckland, 7 February 1969.

began to wear gang insignia within the prison. It might, say, just be a red ribbon on the forearm to signal you belonged to the Mongrel Mob. But it was there. Prison culture began to be organized on gang lines. In the old days we were bonded against the system.[69]

By 1975 ethnic division was already an issue, but it would take several more years for racism and racially motivated violence between the Maori and *Pakeha* population to become more common. It wasn't until late 1978 that prison gangs were first mentioned in management reports, and in 1979 the first indications of a Mongrel Mob chapter of sixteen members forming at Paremoremo were revealed following the interception of a secret communique. One early study of NZ gangs credited a gang member who went by the name 'Kinch', and was serving seven years for several gang-related rapes, with 'bringing the latter day gangs to Paremoremo'.[70] Concentrated in B block, it didn't take long for the MM to become the dominant clique.

By the 1980s Parry was home to the prison system's most dangerous and troublesome inmates. An interesting phenomenon developed in which younger inmates who wanted to follow in their footsteps would exhibit the right amount of disruptive behaviour in other units in order to be incarcerated with their role models.[71]

The importance of following the inmate code was trumped by gang affiliation by the late 1970s. With conflict in the air, inmate interests were subordinated to gang loyalty. This transition meant that 'inmate solidarity had been broken and the power of the solitary man had been destroyed'.[72] One former inmate who had been stabbed in prison in late 1975 recounted after his release:

> In prison ten years ago you knew that if you had a fight with someone, the worst that was going to happen was maybe a kicking. But today you've got to size up each situation. 'Do I go on with this, or what?' Because it might be worth a killing. My own.[73]

A 1984 Christmas Eve riot at Parry between the MM and the Head Hunters left a number of inmates injured, and is considered the stimulus for a new policy that transformed the maximum-security prison. Previously there was regular interaction between inmates in the three standard cellblocks (A, B, C) at Parry. This ended and the units became 'discrete sub-units, each independent of the others'.[74] Henceforth, inmates would be subject to lockdowns and organized searches for weapons and contraband, and there would be restricted contact between prisoners in different cellblocks during visits, work and recreation. Prisoners were still permitted to use the gym, library and visiting room, but only at designated times for each block during the week.

While the Mongrel Mob was most prominent and virtually ran B block, members of the Head Hunters and Black Power were becoming more problematic and were confined to their own cellblocks (A and C respectively). Of the 43 inmates in B, 30 were MM members and the rest unaffiliated. Gradually problems developed as the MM exercised more and more control of its block and non-MM inmates began refusing to be housed there. Those who were already there sought transfers to other blocks, reporting MM extortion rackets that charged non-members rent and forced them to hand over canteen items and possessions, run errands, clean cells and collect meals for the MM.[75] Prison management responded by limiting the number of MM members in B to a dozen, filling the rest of the block with other inmates, including members of Black Power.

It took until 1988 to resolve the gang situation at Parry. Following a five-day hunger strike and a series of attacks on officers in 1986 and 1987, the restrictions directed at the MM were lifted and they had their former privileges restored with the caveat from administration that this was 'absolutely the final opportunity to show that they could live under normal conditions at the prison'. However, the respite lasted only six weeks. Once officials got wind of rumours of a possible hostage-taking in order to force a grievance resolution, the prison responded by removing all the MM from the block. As a result inmate assaults on officers at Parry dropped from 39 in 1986 and 43 in 1987 to just 14 in 1988.[76]

Former heavyweight boxing champ Mike Tyson wears probably the world's best-known Maori facial tattoo. Mongrel Mob members began wearing them in the early 1980s, which had 'obvious implications for members who might consider leaving'.[77] The introduction of facial tattoos wasn't accidental. It was in response to the banning of gang-related insignias and emblems in the 1970s and '80s. Of course prison officers could confiscate colours and drawings and cover up graffiti, but tattoos 'were impossible to regulate'. According to one leading chronicler of New Zealand gangs, 'Facial tattoos were not initially derived from jailhouse subculture or gang related.' In the 1980s they became 'larger and more obvious and gang specific'. During the '80s facial tattoos, which included

'MM', 'Mobster' or 'Mob' or incorporated the bulldog motif, often covered the entire face, and were referred to as 'masks' by gang members.
Black Power soon followed suit. One member of the MM who was sent to
Parry in the early 1980s was asked what indicated a prospect being ready
to be a full member, and responded, 'Give me his face.' Being marked
in such a perpetual and noticeable way 'place[s] limits on a member's
thoughts of leaving the gang, and his ties to it become that much harder
to break'. This phenomenon has been used to explain how the numbers
of the MM and BP were maintained in the 2000s.[78]

### Prison Gangs LA-style: The Twenty-first Century

As New Zealand's prisons become more crowded with 'patched' violent
young gang members, administrators are challenged to seek solutions to
bloody riots and conflict between gangs. The Mongrel Mob and Black
Power remain the most powerful gangs behind bars, with one observer
noting, '"Los Angeles-style" street gangs are gaining numbers fast.'[79]
The tradition of large, national, organized gangs dates back more than
fifty years. What has changed is the increasing development of 'smaller,
younger groups, closely tied to their neighborhoods and ethnicity'.[80]
Within these gangs, rivalry dominates day-to-day life. This phenomenon
has been transplanted into the prison system.

The Auckland-based Killer Beez gang, for example, increased its
membership behind bars by close to a third between 2011 and 2013.
Gilbert has suggested that they fit the LA-style model: 'younger men,
who without supervision of older members, tend to be more violent
inside ... The older ones learned the ropes, they know it's better just to
do the lag.' Gilbert, like other gang experts, notes that inmates need to
be occupied constructively: 'You can't leave them locked up in cages.
It creates disharmony that can lead to violence.' Gilbert foresees the
possibility that these new gangs, unlike their traditional counterparts,
could become a bigger problem than their progenitors, as new LA-style
street gangs spring up, inspired by the LA rap scene, flashy bling and
luxurious cars.

According to 2013 NZ corrections numbers, there were 934 Mongrel
Mob members behind bars, followed in descending order by Black
Power (697); Crips (street gang) (261); Killer Beez (138); Bloods (110);
Head Hunters MC (110); Tribesmen MC (108); Nomads (103); followed
in order by ten smaller gangs with less than a hundred members each

A Black Power gang member shows his patch tattoo during a protest against the banning of gang insignia in the city, 1 September 2009, Wanganui, New Zealand.

(from 74 down to 14). As the two leading gangs, the Mongrel Mob and Black Power are consistently at loggerheads. It is estimated that over 30 per cent of NZ's more than 8,000 inmates are affiliated with one of more than forty gangs. As is true around the world, prison gangs there are responsible for 'a disproportionate number of problems, covering a wide range of criminal behaviors including violence, intimidation, extortion and fraud.'[81]

The NZ prison-gang situation is quite different from Australia's. This can probably be best explained by differences in territorial size, and the number and diversity of inmates. New Zealand has a prison population approaching 9,000, including remand prisoners, while Australia has 43,000 inmates, of whom 30,000 are already sentenced. Not surprisingly, both countries have developed different strategies for dealing with the prison-gang problems. For example, with fewer than eight hundred gang members in total, it has been less necessary to separate them in NZ's institutions. It should also not be forgotten that British settlers came to NZ much later than to Australia. They were also much more impressed by the society they found there. Compared to the 'distinct indigenous "nations" of Australia', the Maori is a much more tightly knit group, with most sharing the same language. By most accounts, attitudes towards their native cultures are widely divergent between Australia and New Zealand. Segregation is still common in Australia, while New Zealanders 'tend to take more pride in their mixed heritage'. With growth in the popularity of tattoos, not surprisingly 'Maori tattoos are ubiquitous in mainly white suburbs.'[82]

Penal experts and officials continue to grapple with the prison-gang problem in Australia and NZ, particularly the number of indigenous people behind bars. Several strategies have been put into practice to alleviate the current situation. New Zealand, for example, offers the *Te Tirohanga* (Focus) programme, which constitutes a 'rehabilitation focused approach that attempts to interrupt the tendency of jails to act as recruitment centres and incubators for further criminality'. The programme also attempts to restore cultural links to a generation of young men and women who have been swept away by urbanization, which has gone a long way towards distancing them from their language and culture. The plan is education-orientated. By most accounts, too many Maori youths entered prison 'with a distorted view of what it is to be Maori, which is often used to justify offending behavior'. As one observer puts it, 'Nowhere are these identity distortions more apparent than in gangs and the scale of affiliation to the Maori dominated MM and BP gangs is inked in tattoos across bodies.' One official offered a 'classic' example of the distortion, which he said goes something like this: 'we come from a warrior race, we don't take shit from anyone, if I wants something I take it.'

Numerous factors have contributed to the rising prison populations and the over-representation of Maoris in the criminal justice system, including unemployment, poverty, poor health and family breakdown, which have hit them 'disproportionately'. Moreover, said one tribal elder, 'you can't look at a young Maori man in Paremoremo prison and divorce him from the history of what has happened to our people.' A Maori lawyer went even further, asserting that it is 'impossible to separate the place of Maori in the prison system from the impact of colonisation.'[83]

# 6

# ASIAN PRISON GANGS

When it comes to criminal justice systems, Asia tends to defy any overgeneralization. Until the eighteenth century, most penal sanctions in Asia veered towards physical punishments and fines. During the era of Western colonialization the prison was introduced to the region. In time, the penitentiary's form and structure evolved under various colonial regimes. Likewise, prison-gang subcultures appeared in Asian prisons in a variety of incarnations.

In the Philippines, prison gangs, or *pangkats*, emerged in the 1950s, characterized by their ethno-linguistic identities – distinguished according to whether members were Tagalog-speaking or non-Tagalog Visayans. Singapore's prison gangs, on the other hand, took the form of 'ethnic minority gangs'. The main exemplars include the Chinese Secret Societies and the Omega and Sarah Jumbo gangs, which are both racially restricted to Indian and Malay minority members.

The legacy of colonialism looms large, having impacted the development of most Asian countries. Among the countries of Asia, Thailand, which did not have a colonial heritage to speak of, is unique in its response to incarceration and was left free to develop its own criminal justice system. However, this was not without offering another version of prison gangs or groups, known as 'Homes', where inmates are intentionally *homed* with other convicts from the same places of origin. While there are prison gangs in many Asian prisons, data of any sort are hard to come by for many of them. The more prominent gangs are chronicled below.

## Bali, Indonesia

The Indonesian island of Bali summons up images of pristine beaches and hedonistic nightlife. But there is also a darker side, including a flourishing illicit drug trade and religious radicalization and terrorist attacks aimed at Westerners and Hindus. In recent years the country's street- and prison-gang problem has increased, as well. The largest street gangs have an unmissable presence behind bars. Of these, Laskar Bali (Bali Army) is the oldest and best known. Primed by the first Bali bombing in 2002 by Islamist extremists, which took dozens of Hindu lives, Laskar Bali went into operation as a 'Hindu defence league'. Today it dominates the nightclub business sector as well as many prisons. Some of its leaders come from a prominent provincial family, traditionally tied to the power brokers of southern Bali.[1] Members can be identified by horse-whip tattoos emblazoned on their chests. Lower-ranking 'foot soldiers' are marked between the thumb and forefinger on the right hand with a tattoo of the *trishula*, a logo that represents the weapon wielded in mythology by the Hindu god Shiva and used to sever the head of Ganesha.

If there are any doubts about the reach of Laskar Bali into the tourist sector, witness the saga of one restaurant diner who blogged about his experience at a Laskar-owned restaurant. His allegations included accusations of being overcharged for fish that was served with its entrails and all bones intact, 'so much fun to pull out in the dull candle light'. It did

Laskar Bali tattoo.

not improve from there. His party was next served squid that they had not ordered, which they decided to eat since it was too late to reject what the blogger described as being like 'eating this weird white car tire'. The alleged dinner rip-off continued. However, any ideas of making a scene or calling the authorities faded away when they noticed the trademark Laskar Bali gang *trishula* tattoos on the hands of everyone who worked at the restaurant. Apparently, the gang pays local taxi drivers to deliver tourists to the joint. This alleged incident took place in October 2018. Oh yes, not surprisingly they paid the meal tab.[2]

Other street gangs have splintered off from Laskar, including the second-largest gang, the Baladika Bali, with close to 25,000 members on the island. It is reportedly inspired by traditional Hindu notions of 'the sacred but divine warrior'. Less Hindu-orientated, Bali Youth United (PBB) is led by a member of the National Parliament. If these gangs were not trouble enough, gangs from Java and Sumatra have also entered the Bali gang scene. Nonetheless, according to one observer, Laskar is 'without doubt the most violent' gang in Bali.

### Hotel K: 'Bali's Drug Hub'

Of Indonesia's more than 460 prisons, none illustrates the emergence of prison gangs in Asia better than Bali's Kerobokan prison. Here, as in other correctional facilities, gangs offer beatings, plenty of addictive drugs and protection, but not much else. Almost all the inmates at Kerobokan are members of one of the gangs actively involved in extortion, protection and drug-supply control. One inmate says, 'Everyone joins or is forced to join . . . gangs recruit and indoctrinate especially young guys . . . they focus on building numbers . . . even guards are unofficial – and some are official [gang] members.'

In Kerobokan prison, otherwise known as 'Hotel K', each gang has its own turf, usually controlling one or more cellblocks. When new inmates arrive, gangsters either sell drugs to them or physically intimidate them. Heroin, crystal meth, ecstasy, cannabis and occasionally cocaine are available inside. It is said that Laskar members have a fondness for shabu (methamphetamine), 'Indonesia's most popular drug'. The market for shabu is very heavily controlled by gangs and competition by newcomers is rabidly discouraged.

If a convict feels threatened it is not uncommon for him to identify as a Laskar member for protection. One member who joined the gang

Kerobokan prison, Bali.

inside Hotel K, a former soldier doing nine years for murder, noted that 'We are part of security in prison . . . it can help control the situation because we work with the officers. It's about peace. Whenever there is Laskar there is peace.'[3] This is debatable when one takes into account deadly inter-gang clashes between Baladika and Laskar behind bars. In 2015, for example, rioting at Kerobokan prison left four dead, including two gang members. In an attempt to cool things down, administrators transported about a hundred Laskar members to other jails. Demonstrating the ties between prison and street gangs in Bali, the riot was precipitated by actions occurring outside the prison. It was reportedly touched off after members of both gangs appeared on the streets outside Hotel K fully armed with machetes and samurai swords, after hearing a violent clash was taking place inside the prison walls between gang members. These encounters are especially brutal, even by prison standards, with spears, machetes, knives and other homemade weapons the preferred method of doing battle. Following the skirmish, prison officials confiscated six rubbish bins full of weapons, several packages of methamphetamine, a bulletproof vest and a laptop computer.[4]

Laskar's power inside the joint evokes fear among prisoners and guards alike. Its control inside, by some reports, is so strong that there have been cases when it forced the lockdown of an entire cellblock, while gang members engaged in illegal activities such as indulging in drugs. There have even been reports of unsuspecting guards accidentally locked in the cellblock when this occurs and being forced to wait out the cell lockdown to get out.[5] Journalist Kathryn Bonella had access inside the prison and interviewed a number of foreign inmates doing time for various drug charges. One Italian inmate told her: 'Kerbo is the only jail where the prisoners totally run the jail. Prisoners have the key to the block.'[6]

Most of the inmates of Hotel K are doing time for drug offences, including many foreigners who had come to Bali seeking a decadent good time but instead became entangled in the illegal drug scene. However, if an inmate was worried about being able to feed a previous drug addiction inside the prison, he need not be. One observer suggested that locking a drug offender in the prison was comparable to sentencing a gambler to Las Vegas. By most accounts, drug transactions took place in every corner of the jail. Indeed, 'Hotel K was Bali's drug hub, its biggest and busiest drug market.'[7]

Prisoners look from a tower during a riot at Kerobokan Prison in 2012.

Testament to the gang's clout, after eight high-ranking Laskars were sentenced to Kerobokan, joining the twelve members already incarcerated, the prison 'dynamics changed overnight', and before long they controlled the prison. 'The guards no longer had any power. Laskar was the law.' According to the Italian inmate, 'What happened was that the guards just retired. They let them do whatever they wanted . . . as they pleased.'[8]

Laskar bosses flaunted their influence at every chance, ambling around speaking on mobile phones, while guards could only stand back and watch. Even the head of Laskar, Agung Aseng, was permitted to spend evenings out, knowing that 'nobody dares close his door.' However, the guards did not go unrewarded for their timidity. One foreign inmate recounted that 'Every night he had a party, barbecue, smoke marijuana, supply whiskey for guards. Every night.' Each morning, like clockwork, the Laskar boss returned to his cellblock.[9]

Like prison-guard counterparts around the world, Bali's officers are paid barely sustainable salaries. Therefore, the idea of earning extra lucre by collaborating with prison-gang bosses is attractive. The Laskars enforce their own rules and often join guards in battering other inmates. In some cases, if an inmate is caught escaping, fails to pay drug debts or has committed unacceptable offences, the gang will 'take Hotel K into their own hands'. The Laskars have numerous revenue streams behind bars, including selling drugs and protection. For example, they act as a de facto security force, helping inmates get back stolen items for a fee. According to Bonella, the largest source of income is protecting a major drug dealer, who is accorded the role of sole drug provider in the prison. Laskar members not only protected the drug kingpin from inmates and guards but also functioned as drug couriers, bringing drugs into bars and clubs throughout Bali. At the time she was researching Hotel K, Bonella estimated that the drug dealer earned between $13,000 and $39,000 each day, selling a range of products including shabu, heroin, ecstasy, ganja, hashish and cocaine. Ultimately, the entire cellblock worked for the drug boss and everyone in his orbit prospered financially. This autonomy could only be achieved with the help of the Laskar Bali.[10]

## The Philippines

There are over 1,300 types of correctional institution in the Philippines, not including temporary detention centres and lockups, which incarcerate those awaiting transfer to jails under court orders, or those under investigation. Located in police stations, it is not uncommon for these to function as known gang territories and recruiting grounds.[11] For example, the Laloma police station, in Quezon City, is a known territory of the Bahala Na Gang (BNG). Anyone detained there is 'instructed' to become a member. To seal the deal, gang members will promise new recruits that their gang affiliation would be respected and they could expect protection in case they were transferred to the so-called big house, or local jail. Once a prison gang becomes entrenched it is hard to get rid of. Gangs in the more prominent prisons, such as New Bilibid Prison, have been around since the 1940s and '50s, with an estimated 95 per cent belonging to one gang or another.

The prison a person is incarcerated in determines their choice of gang membership. Most prisoners in the Philippines are in jail on remand, awaiting trial – a process that can last years. Someone in Metro Manila, for example, will usually join one of the four largest Metro gangs: Sigue Sigue Sputnik (SSS),[12] Sigue Sigue Commando (SSC), Batang City Jail (BCJ) or the Bahala Na Gang.

In 2019, *World Prison Brief* ranked the Philippines prison system the most overcrowded in the world out of 205 nations. Much of the overcrowding has been associated with the lack of space to hold the thousands of prisoners awaiting trial since President Rodrigo Duterte began his punitive anti-drug campaign in 2016. Between June 2016 and December 2017, the nation's cumulative prison population increased from 96,000 to 165,000, meaning that the average facility endures 605 per cent overcrowding.[13] In the City Jail it is not uncommon for cells designed for 170 to hold up to 518 inmates.[14]

A new inmate is given a quick orientation. Once he understands what is expected of him, he takes an oath promising to follow rules and accept penal sanctions. Respect is considered 'the golden rule' and all prisoner debtors are required to pay all debts at a particular time, usually on Sundays. If the debt is not paid an inmate can expect to be beaten on his backside with a paddle every Sunday until he is paid up. In order to gather the funds to pay debts an inmate should exhaust all options at his disposal, whether it means cajoling family members to give him money or selling his own clothes and shoes.

*Ethno-linguistic Rivalries*

Gang rivalries based on ethno-linguistic identity are common in the Philippines prison system.[15] The two most prominent gang factions are the Tagalog-speaking Sigue Sigue gangs and the Visayan-speaking members of the Original Ex-convict Organization (OXO). These gangs rose to prominence in the 1960s, when they were mostly composed of Manilan members. The dominant language in the capital city, Manila, is Tagalog. One member of the Visayan-speaking Batang Cebu gang (BC) noted that Tagalogs 'get irritated when they do not understand what they hear from Visayans'. The predominance of Tagalog has made non-speakers '[feel] marginalized'.[16] Many of the Visayans have been transferred to Manila from the archipelago's southern islands. Tagalogs distinguish these inmates with monikers that testify to their outsider status.

Visayan gangs are perceived as lower caste and regarded as culturally below the Sigue Sigue groups, due to the fact that Manilan families tend to hire housekeepers and helpers from the Visayan-speaking population. The OXO originated in Batang City Jail, after earlier groups of Visayans banded together to protect themselves from the more predatory inmates, who reportedly robbed and raped them with impunity.[17]

Ultimately, Filipino prison gangs are distinguished according to variations in language and culture. These variations tend to generate 'animosity, interpersonal conflict and eventually, violence' between the two ethno-linguistic gangs. But the language divide is not the only distinction. Lifestyles vary as well, according to one Visayan: 'We like being quiet; they are loud. For food, we like vegetables and fish. Those from Bicol want spicy food. We think the Manila Boys [Tagalogs] always like barbecue, fried chicken.'[18]

The conflict between these gangs has been transported from institution to institution, and according to one source the Sigue Sigue (ss) and oxo organizations were 'pioneering' gangs that became the standard in terms of organization for other gangs that later challenged their respective hegemonies. The original ss would eventually give rise to the Sigue Sigue Sputnik, Sigue Sigue Commando and ss Puso subgroups.[19] In 1968, a Filipino Senate Committee Report listed these three gangs among the twelve major groups. The others ranged from the Bahala Na Gang to oxo-affiliated gangs that included Gestapo; Bicol Region/Ranger Masbate (BRM), representing Bicolandia; Genuine Ilocano Gang (GIG), from northern Luzon; Happy Go Lucky gang; Batang City Jail; Batang Samar and Leyte (BSL); and Batang Mananalo/Batman (BM). In the words of one gang observer, these gangs were identifiable by the 'provincial partisanship of [their] members'.[20]

Over the ensuing decades, gangs have become more distinct beyond the parameters of ethno-linguistic variance. Some gangs, for example, are less inclined towards violence than others, such as the BM, which focuses on escaping and rarely takes up arms against other prison gangs. This stance is also reflected in their real-world presence, where they mostly commit non-violent offences and tend towards confidence games and picking pockets.[21]

During the 1970s, a new dimension was added with the incarceration of more intellectually inclined political prisoners, better educated and better prepared to ameliorate conflict through mediation. With their additional bargaining proclivities they successfully won several concessions from the authorities, including the dropping of the prohibition against visitors in dormitories. This not only reduced stress, but also led to a drop in riots and sexual assaults.[22]

### Pangkats

The prison-gang subculture in the Philippines revolves around the *pangkat* system.[23] *Pangkats*, or gangs, emerged in the 1950s from the ethno-linguistic divisions between Tagalog and non-Tagalog speakers.[24] Even then, the prisons were dealing with inadequate provisions, tension between the keepers and the kept, and restrictive visiting policies, all of which would later contribute to 'escapes and violent riots between rival gangs'. *Pangkats* continue to accept most inmates – gay or straight, children and even women.

Estimates vary as to the number of inmates who join *pangkats*, but nationally the number is somewhere between 60 and 95 per cent. There is no 'specific ban on inmate groups', and the shared governance between gang members and staff is 'both officially and unofficially accepted'.[25]

The Filipino incarnation of the gang subculture favours the term *pangkat* over 'gang', because it implies the impression of brotherhood and self-help rather than mindless violent conflict. In contrast to American prison gangs, *pangkats* are not inherently violent or necessarily criminally orientated entities; nor are they selective regarding who joins. While some do adopt corrupt practices, use violence and traffic in drugs, these are usually regarded as individual actions rather than an entire *pangkat* action.[26] Similar to the American concept of prison gangs, *pangkats* have a leadership structure and an inmate code and are utilized to mediate conflicts when required.[27]

Members consider themselves *kakosa*, 'a term of endearment that cannot be used by inmates unless they come from the same pangkat'. As a brother, or *kakosa*, members become a 'surrogate family'. According to a three-year veteran of the BNG:

> We treat each other as brothers. But because I am a member, they automatically helped me. If kakosas are in need, we really help each other. I was like a vegetable when I came here. I could not walk. I was really traumatized, but it is my kakosas who patiently took care of me.[28]

By joining a *pangkat*, a *kakosa* can at least expect some access to scarce resources, including food, clothing, medicine and protection.

*Pangkats* are distinct 'from the Western notion of gangs' due to their problem-solving nature. Although they exhibit a number of similar features, their unique characteristics and the role they play in prisons are a counterpoint to the Western concept of the gang. It is common for *pangkats* to raise funds to support sick prisoners. Rather than being constantly at odds with other *pangkats*, they provide cell maintenance, offer rehabilitation programmes and mediate conflicts between *kakosas*. In contrast to their American counterparts, *pangkats* should be considered 'more developmental in nature', best exemplified by the comments of a two-year inmate:

> the jail will not run without the help of pangkats ... When inmates get sick, we are the ones buying medicines, not the guards, not the warden ... [and] we are the ones providing for the transportation of the inmates when they go home ... also, when the light bulb malfunctions, we are the ones buying the replacement. There are also inmates who are mentally ill; we are the ones who give an eye to them, making sure they won't be harming other inmates ... Our pangkat management [does] that.[29]

### Filipino Subculture: Tattoos

The Filipino version of the prison gang has developed a distinct subculture, featuring shared customs, dress codes, secret communication and physical identifiers such as tattoos and other markings. In fact, once a member is accepted into the gang, he is expected to be 'tattooed or tagged with the group's symbol to indicate dedication and commitment'. Tattoos might be formally prohibited, but prison administrators continue to rely on them informally for housing and classification purposes. Gang members can be identified by symbols tattooed on the right side of the body (it means nothing on the left side). The number of *tudoks*, or balls, indicates which gang inmates belongs to. Batang City Jail (BCJ) members are marked by four *tudoks* and a Bugs Bunny tattoo; SSC, three balls and a mustang; SSS by five balls and a spaceship; and the BNG, one ball and a Viking.[30]

It is imperative that at least some members of the correctional staff at each prison are knowledgeable about the prison subculture and identifiers. A small dot, or *malit na tudok*, can mean the difference between one gang and another. It takes a veteran inmate to interpret the signs. For example, a member of SSC might interpret a rose with three petals to mean any figure with three balls. But, in the Batang City Jail, a member might argue with this interpretation, claiming the rose's thorn is an additional dot, making it four balls.[31] Thus, when a new inmate is scrutinized during classification and cell assignment, it is imperative to assign him to the correct brigade. Problems have arisen over tattoos that combine symbols such as a spaceship and Bugs Bunny (BCJ). As a result, rival gangs might claim him as one of theirs. At Quezon City

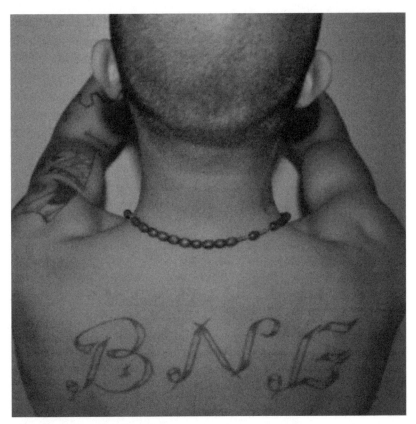

Bahala Na Gang (BNG) tattoo.

jail, if there is any confusion over membership, the prisoners will be transferred to Bicutan.[32]

*Pangkats* place great stock in numerical supremacy, always racing other gangs to garner more members. In some cases a new inmate might be automatically accepted into the gang simply by bearing the corresponding tattoo on the right side of his body. In other cases, correctional officers might be cajoled into supporting a particular gang by either becoming a member or helping a gang against rivals. This might include preventing gang rivals from getting out of cells during visitation times, adopting the ruse that the visiting area was too crowded.

### Pangkat *Criminal Activities*

When it comes to prison rules and regulations, gang members are experts at appearing to follow the dictates of the penal regime. A facade of order is created by avoiding outright physical conflicts and escape attempts. On the other hand, staying away from senseless antisocial activities is actually a cleverly thought-out strategy that allows them to avoid scrutiny, enabling them to pursue various criminal activities. Order and a stable environment are imperative if prison gangs intend to profit from various illegal revenue streams. Thus there are both 'financial and familial incentives' to keep prison disruption to a minimum.[33] As gangs generate income from illegitimate and legitimate enterprises in prisons, families often benefit from the lucre in the long run. Thus, it is vital that the very privileges that support sources of income are not withdrawn through potential punitive actions.

Family visitations are especially important on several levels. Although they exist to help inmates establish and maintain family support, on another level they are repurposed 'to acquire money and basic necessities' such as food and soap. Moreover, a *kakosa*'s wife or partner might play an active role in managing gang affairs, and if these privileges were revoked it could detrimentally impact sources of income. Family members are especially useful for carrying information and contraband back and forth through the prison gates.[34]

### Gang Conflicts

While rival *pangkats* are not averse to cooperating in certain business arrangements, problems occur when a member of one of them does not pay his debts. When riots break out between warring factions it is often bloody. Inmates rarely leave their cells without being armed. Weapons are always available and members are expected to be prepared to kill and maim when it is warranted, such as in the case of a riot. It is easy to bring raw materials into a jail. One can even purchase kerosene for cooking (or making Molotov cocktails) at jail cooperatives without raising any suspicion. At Quezon City jail weapons have included shotguns, big nails used as arrows, metal bolos, ice picks, metal saws, sharpened metal, bottles and wooden clubs.[35]

Conflicts between *pangkats* are not uncommon. Some are over more serious issues, such as territorial disputes over which group has the bigger cells, recruiting for the most members, and economic issues such as gaining a larger share of the underground economy. Other motives for conflict are related to retaliation. Riots are often provoked by corrupt jail guards and inmate leaders, known as *mayores*, or *mayors*, fighting over the drug trade. In other cases, corrupt guards have been known to provoke conflicts between gangs as a mechanism for expressing their displeasure with reform-minded prison wardens. In yet other instances, conflict can rear its ugly head internally as members vie for power and control of resources. Conversely, conflicts appear to be much less frequent in *pangkats* with little in the way of resources, drugs or money.[36]

### Querna: *Unaffiliated Inmates*

As in other prison systems with gang subcultures, not all inmates take part, preferring to retain a modicum of autonomy despite the implicit risks involved. The unaffiliated, or *querna*, regard gang members as pawns of the gang subculture and take a certain pride in their individualistic accountability and eschewing their participation in collective violence. However, most inmates would agree that there are more benefits in belonging to a gang. *Pangkats* protect members from other inmates as well as from jail and corrections officers. A senior *pangkat* enjoys respect due in no small part to his links to the prison staff. A member can also count on the availability of basic resources, which are often hard to come by. On the other hand, they must never leave their cells unarmed since rival gangs are always a threat.[37]

By contrast, since *querna* choose to be unaffiliated, there is no need to worry about rival gang members and they do not require inmate bodyguards as the *pangkats* do (especially for the inmate leader, or *nanunungkulan*).[38] The majority of *querna* (60 per cent) view the consequences of joining a *pangkat* as potentially lethal. One *querna* noted: 'In the querna, inmates are not armed . . . so when they fight, it is usually verbal and minor punches. Unlike in the pangkat, [whose members carry weapons that include] icepicks, knives, and other sharp pointed objects. So when they fight in the pangkat, it is really serious,' sometimes even using Molotov cocktails and improvised bows and arrows.[39]

### Magna Cartas

Similar to their American counterparts, which often feature a written constitution, Filipino gangs typically have an inmate code, a list of regulations that members are expected to follow and enforce. These 'magna cartas' detail rules about respect, not snitching, paying debts, prohibitions against stealing, and the amount of expected weekly dues and contributions to the gang. *Pangkat* members are expected to avoid criticizing other members, always consult leaders prior to taking action, respect visitors of gang members, and avoid voyeurism and affairs with spouses of inmates, which demands the maximum penalty.[40]

*Pangkats* have their own version of a disciplinary process, similar to a free-world judicial trial on some levels. Penalties for violating magna cartas range from providing personal services to gang officers for a period of time to swift physical punishments. In more serious violations a perpetrator may be expected to allow the gang leader or general shot-caller, or *bosyo*, to use his wife for sexual favours; refusal means death. But not all gangs enforce rules in the same way. In larger gangs, punishments and violations warrant dire consequences, while sanctions in the smaller oxo gangs are less punitive.[41] Among the more serious infractions is a member challenging the current leadership.

### Grievance Procedures and Punishments

To ensure law and order reigns in the prison, *pangkats* abide by a well-advertised set of rules and regulations, spelled out in the *patakaran*, or inmate code. Without a formal conflict-mediation and grievance mechanism, the '*pangkat* judicial system' fills the void. The *patakaran* elaborates the convict code, about giving respect to officers, fellow inmates and visitors; avoiding conflicts by prohibiting 'intrigues, excessive jokes, *baryo baryo* or cliques, and by settling obligations on time; participating in jail activities; observing cleanliness; and maintaining security'.[42]

Respect for visitors is of paramount importance. Visitors are the link to the outside world, and a more dependable source of money, food and supplies. Respect includes being on one's best behaviour, keeping one's area neat, looking one's best (hiding tattoos) and avoiding interacting with another inmate's visitors. To demonstrate the seriousness of violating the above: approaching a visitor at the Manila City Jail without invitation, or even winking at a visitor, can invite between fifteen and twenty-five lashes.[43]

*Querna* and *pangkat* members have devised a system of sanctions for infractions of the *patakaran*. The system, however, operates according to the status of the offender. At the Manila City Jail, where Sigue

Sigue Sputnik is powerful, members who fight are awarded five lashes, and if they draw blood while fighting, up to twenty lashes. Beatings are doled out with a 'lacquered wooden bat painted with Sputnik No. 1 on one side and on the other the commander's name'.[44] Some cells adopt different nomenclature to refer to their rules. For example, the BNG calls them the Ten Commandments of Tartaro (after those in the Bible).

Each cell has a *bastonero*, who functions as a sergeant-of-arms-cum-brigade chief. He is also the chief armourer and disciplinarian. The *bastonero* is named after the stick paddle, or *baston*, that he wields to hit the backsides of malefactors in a punishment known as *takal*. The *mayor*, or inmate leader, and the *bastonero* play an important role in the prison judicial system. When an inmate wants to file a grievance he must go through a chain of command until it reaches the *bastonero*, who is expected to hear testimony from both sides, as well as from witnesses.

The seriousness of the violation is taken into account. If it is egregious it will warrant a public-jury trial. Any vote must be unanimous, and if the inmate is found guilty the *mayor*, who is responsible for social, recreational and religious programmes, decides on the punishment. Before any penalty is administered, the *mayor* explains to the prisoners why the inmate is being punished. It is next up to the *bastonero* to implement the punishment. Each cell and *brigada*, or brigade, has its own set of penalties. For example, among the *querna*, the most common punishment is called the padlock. Protocol requires the inmate to be locked in a cell for between a week and a month. He is prohibited from conversing with other inmates. Another variation is called the *bartolina*, where the convict is isolated in an 'old barren room' for anywhere from one day to months. This is typically reserved for inmates who 'jeopardize' a planned escape attempt.[45] In the case of the *burahan*, a prisoner can be expelled from his *pangkat* and have his gang tattoo erased from his flesh with an iron.[46]

The more serious infractions are punished with the *takal*, and the inmate can be paddled fifty times, incapacitating him for the following few days. According to protocol, the offender is forced to lie down on a bench, with another inmate holding down his head and his feet. Once the punishment is completed the malefactor is expected to seek 'absolution' from the *mayor* and his cellmates.[47]

One of the most extreme punishments is the *basag*. This is reserved for an inmate who continues to break the rules after repeated warnings.

The offender is treated to a 'skull-breaking flogging', for such violations as looking at visitors, stealing from the cell fund, participating in a coup to overthrow cell leaders, and starting a riot without speaking to cell officers first.[48]

### New Bilibid Prison

In 1940 the New Bilibid Prison (NBP) was opened in Muntinlupa, to the southeast of Manila. The prison contains all the requisite conditions for the development of prison-gang subculture, featuring overcrowding, a paucity of correctional officers and a brutal regime. Here, by most accounts, corruption is the rule, rather than the exception. Any form of contraband is for sale, including sophisticated weapons and hard drugs. Prison raids have revealed a stock of lethal weapons, including automatic machine pistols and, in one case, during a riot, several M-16 grenades.[49] The ubiquity of mobile phones allows jailed kingpins to operate criminal networks on the outside.

The harsh glare of the media spotlight was focused on the facility in June 2011 after reports that prison gangs were 'lording it over at the National [sic] Bilibid Prison as they control amenities and resources within'.[50] As a result, an investigation was launched by the Department of Justice. At the centre of the inquiry was whether affluent inmates were receiving preferential treatment, such as the 'privatization of quarters, contraband proliferation and other corruptions'.[51] A subsequent investigation would explore prison overcrowding and the 'alleged underground criminal syndicates, illegal activities, and the gang culture at the NBP'.[52]

Almost 95 per cent of the inmates of NBP belong to twelve *pangkats*, each with its own specific turf.[53] Prison buildings are partitioned into dormitories (*brigadas*), where small cells (*butas*) are often shared by two or more inmates. There are dorms that also house non-gang members (*querna*), former soldiers or police officers, former Communist Party rebels (CPP-NPA) and the followers of two religious groups, the Christian Brigade and *Iglesio Ni Cristo* (Church of Christ).[54]

Originally designed for 5,500 inmates, by 2015 NBP was bursting at the seams with more than 14,000 convicts. Put another way, guards were outnumbered 80 to 1, making it 'one of the world's largest maximum-security facilities'.[55] The maximum-security compound can probably be best described as 'a 10-hectare diamond-shaped compound at the center of the sprawling 300-hectare New Bilibid Prison area'.[56]

The prison compound is organized according to *pangkat* society. Each building in the complex is divided up into living spaces for one of the twelve gangs and several 'marginal non-gang groups'. The compound has all the amenities of a human community, including a hospital, a kitchen, educational and training centres, churches, civic foundation offices, sports facilities and recreational facilities. Together with *talipapas*, so-called wet markets, selling fresh fish, meat and vegetables, and other types of food stall, these facilities 'give a sense of shared spaces'.[57]

The compound is further divided into two areas, the *carcel*, or jail, and the *presidio*, or prison. According to one leading authority, it is possible that these two labels 'were appropriated from the design' of the old Bilibid, constructed in 1865.[58] The old version contained a *carcel*, where jailed suspects awaited sentencing, and a separate *presidio*, housing those already sentenced. The two sections are separated by a thick wall designed to prevent riots between the main gangs. The Sigue Sigue-allied gangs mostly occupy the *presidio* side and the oxo-allied gangs the *carcel* side.

Filipino *pangkats* represent the yin-yang of prison organization. On the one hand they are rejected for their violent features and for undermining state authority to enforce prison order. On the other, the gangs are accommodated for their pragmatic function, often expressed as 'they police their own ranks'. According to one report to the Asian and Pacific Conference of Correctional Administrators, prison officials acquiesced to their 'good use', explaining: 'Though unorthodox in some jurisdictions that prohibit inmates from enlisting in gangs, the set-up actually helps prison officials maintain order in prison and put relatively unofficial organizations to good use.'[59] By most accounts the nation's correctional bureau 'makes no qualms in recognizing the co-management role of the pangkat in the Bilibid Max compound before the media'.[60]

### Pangkat *Hierarchy*

Each *pangkat* has a formal hierarchical structure, which some observers have likened to a 'military style of command'.[61] At the top of the hierarchy is the leader, or *bosyo*, who directs activities. He can earn this status through election by fellow gang members, who base their votes on several criteria, ranging from charisma and wealth to length of sentences (the longer the sentence, the more street credibility he has) and criminal accomplishments. It is common for the leader to have regular meetings with prison management to discuss a wide range of issues including prison conditions and general prison operations.

By most accounts, currently the major determinant for leadership is the individual's affluence and political connections. It also helps if he has a close affiliation with the former *bosyo*.[62] There are cases where a *bosyo* was previously proven weak and intellectually average, or had committed an 'immoral' act, but if he was wealthy enough that was no barrier to attaining higher rank. Affluence typically trumps one's rap sheet when it comes to respect.

The *tiradors* occupy an 'unofficial and highly secret position' that few, if any, prison guards are aware of. But recent research describes them as militaristic and responsible for maintaining an armoury of bladed instruments. They protect leaders and gang interests, and in case of a violent confrontation between gangs, the *tiradors*, as warriors, figure prominently.[63] When not engaged in these tasks, it is not uncommon for *tiradors* to run protection and extortion rackets or carry out reprisals for the *bosyo*. The number of *tiradors* in each gang varies according to gang size. For example, there are up to three hundred in the Tagalog-affiliated Sigue Sigue Sputnik, but less than ten in the Visayan-aligned oxo.[64]

Other members fit into the gang hierarchy according to their criminal history and the immorality of the crime, which of course is determined by cultural values and the convict code. Crimes against women and children, for example, bar a member from moving up in the hierarchy.[65]

### Mayors

Charged with maintaining cell cleanliness and in control of social, recreational and religious programmes, *mayors* enjoy several perks. Probably none is cherished more than their *kubols* (their own personal space; each *mayor* is entitled to least one of these). If an inmate has enough money he can buy the rights to his own *kubol*, making his stay behind bars much more comfortable. *Kubols* 'were initially started to maximize space by adding layers of beds' in subdivided cubicles, which were sold to inmates for various prices and were often made available as an enticement to newly recruited *pangkat* members.[66] Over the years the *kubol* concept evolved and they were regarded as a new revenue stream; they could be sold, rented or loaned.[67] *Mayors* are permitted to build a *kubol* or move into an existing one outside the building. There they sleep more comfortably, enjoy privacy and 'much needed personal space', and in some cases have air conditioning and televisions. The *mayors* have refined this as a revenue stream, operating them as hotels, whereby inmates can rent them for a short time when their partners and girlfriends visit. In other cases they have even been run like brothels, where prisoners pay for sex with transgender inmates or prostitutes brought in by guards.[68] Not surprisingly, *bosyos* and complicit guards earn a share from their construction and from the rental of *kubols*.

*Pangkats* manage revenue streams by approving which illegal and licit businesses take place in the jail. However, the *mayor* holds the power as to which ones are approved. According to one veteran inmate, a drug market was proposed in a prison. The *mayors* consulted with him. He told them that the NBP commander is vehemently anti-drugs and very strict; 'So I advised him not to trade drugs here in jail. So the mayors said no to the proposition of that inmate.'[69]

### Quezon City Jail

As the second largest and most overcrowded prison in the country, Quezon City jail is plagued by an officer–inmate ratio of 1:128. Jail can sometimes represent a homecoming of sorts for recidivist gang members. Recidivists, indeed, are among the more respected gang members. In some cases, repeated stints in jail can facilitate the rise of a multiple recidivist to the position of *tayman*, akin to a prison sage. Recidivists facilitate the expansion of criminal networks into the free world. In this warped universe, drug addicts will get to interact with large-scale dealers, petty thieves with bank robbers and kidnappers, and so forth.[70]

However, many who were in jail on drug charges might tell you they feel safer inside, where 'cops can't kill you' with impunity. Many gang members come in already affiliated on the outside. Quezon is home to four major *pangkats*, ranging in size, in descending order: Sigue Sigue Sputnik, Sigue Sigue Commando, Batang City Jail and Bahala Na Gang. Colourful murals mark each gang's territory. The vast majority of inmates belong to *pangkats*, with approximately 25 per cent remaining unaffiliated.[71] The BCJ is the most diverse *pangkat* in Quezon, with members representing more countries than any other. It was founded by 32 inmates, who challenged the older OXO in NBP.

Inmates sleep on the ground of an open basketball court inside Quezon City jail at night in July 2016. There are 3,800 inmates at the jail, which was built six decades ago to house 800, and they engage in a relentless contest for space. Men take turns to sleep on the cracked cement floor of the basketball court, on staircases, underneath beds and in hammocks made out of old blankets.

Many *pangkat* members came from free-world 'squatter camps', where membership was regarded as a status symbol and offered some type of street credibility in the criminal underworld. For example, if a gang boss wanted to put together a bank robbery crew, he would typically prefer *pangkat* members over others. Many inmates of Quezon City hail from the poorer neighbourhoods, and once released they return to their homes, marked by the identifying tattoo of the *pangkat*. One leading researcher noted that when they did return home to their families it was not uncommon for them to give their sons the same tattoo they had received in jail – ensuring that if any of them were locked up in the future, by virtue of the tattoo, they would automatically be accepted as a member.[72]

Not surprisingly, when a former police officer is sent to prison, he instantly becomes a target for retaliation, especially for criminals he might have put behind bars. The danger can be alleviated by joining a *pangkat*. If they are cleared of their crime, they will often remain a committed member when set free, and might help recruit new members.

The Quezon City prison compound houses prisoners sentenced to at least twenty years, inmates who were formerly housed on death row, and those serving several sentences or with cases in the appeal process. With the majority serving long sentences, most can expect to live with a relatively stable cohort of inmates for some time, 'a factor that explains the stronger influence of the pangkat in the compound, relative to its weaker presence in the Medium and Minimum security compound of the New Bilibid Prison'.[73]

### Political Structure at Quezon

As noted elsewhere, prison governance often ends up in the hands of its gang subculture. The Philippines fits this paradigm well, especially at Quezon City jail. With a paucity of staff, who are poorly trained, the *pangkat* and *querna* have created a political hierarchy to fill the void. Of all the positions, the most sought-after is that of the *panunungkulan*, who is expected to keep the peace and order in cells: 'Once a newly committed inmate enters his cell he is placed under his protective custody. He will then be responsible for anything that happens to the inmate.'[74]

Each *brigada* is composed of four *pangkats* and the *querna*, which has its own method of electing inmates to the position of *panunungkulan*. The jail warden chooses *mayors* and *mayor de mayors*, the leader of the cell *mayors*, for the *querna*; *pangkats* choose their own leaders. The BCJ gives the outgoing *mayor de mayor* 'blanket authority to select his successor, who appoints his own officials'. By comparison, the SSC does this by election and the BNG either by selection or election, depending on the wishes of the former leader.[75] Leaders do not have to be physically imposing or brutal; many have been former police officers, government employees and businessmen, and have experience that gives them qualities of leadership; such a one must be 'shrewd enough as to be able to discern the "criminal mind" of his constituents'.[76]

*Pangkat* members have devised a host of schemes to raise money behind bars. They of course vary from prison to prison, but typically run from the imaginative to the more traditional. At Quezon City jail, once gang members determine which inmates tend to have visitors, they assume this means they can get money from those visitors. Once this is established an inmate is expected to contribute P10 to cell funds each time one visits. However, this 'extortion' only applies to inmates who have been incarcerated for less than six months (cell leaders are exempt).[77]

Inmates, especially *nanunungkulan*, are permitted to run businesses in jail, including billiard tables, food stalls or even beauty salons. In return they contribute a percentage of their profits to cell funds. For example, cigarette purveyors pay P80 per week. Income is derived from stores maintained in all cells and brigades, which inmates are expected to patronize: 'Like cooperative stores [they] allow credits but on the appointed payday, usually settle accounts by Sunday.'[78]

By the 1990s the prison system in the Philippines was much more likely to be home to richer leaders with plenty of influence and political connections. It was at this time that attempts were made to reinvent the *pangkats* 'as formal brotherhoods and organizations'. While some did indeed reorganize, splinter groups from several gangs reunited and formed gangs with less ominous titles, more neutral in tone than sinister, with appellations such as 'Temple of Man', 'Love Foundation' and 'Sheep of the Lord'. Along with this new facade were some legitimate aspirations that conformed to the 'new' brotherhoods' goals, while still maintaining criminal activities.

By some accounts, membership 'follows pragmatic logic', leaving inmates to decide which gangs might be most advantageous to their individual needs.[79] At the start of the twenty-first century, most reports on Philippine prison gangs focused on the 'structural and cultural' ways of *pangkat* society. The prison system reflects 'the social inequalities of society'; *kubols* are reserved for inmates of high standing and with access to cash – only the most powerful members. This is often reflected by the practice of 'pairing impoverished inmates with VIP inmates who have access to resources'. This is one way to make sure everyone has food to eat and soap to wash with. As a result, it 'eventually recreates the patron-client relationship relevant in Philippine society inside the jail cells'.

With the increasing imprisonment of street-gang members, newcomers need to become familiar with an alien environment. In prison, *pangkats* tutor new inmates in the mechanics of crime and conflict-avoidance skills. Novice prisoners are carefully vetted for their physical traits. For example, if a new entrant looks thuggish, he might be directed into a bullying or harassment capacity, or ordered to attack a rival. He might even be recruited to fight in the boxing ring, where fights could be fixed by members of the gang.

'Inmate gangs have gained enough access to prison control "where inmates play a prominent role in the Jail's administration".'[80] The *pangkat* subculture continues to dominate the larger Filipino prisons, and according to one official, without a comprehensive ban on them their existence is 'unavoidable'. In recent years 'ethno-linguistic identity ceased to be the defining factor in membership'. According to Filomin Candaliza-Guttierez, membership 'follows pragmatic logic', leaving inmates to decide which gangs might best fulfil their needs.[81]

## India

Almost from the beginnings of its prison system in the years of British colonial rule, India's biggest obstacle to penal organization was establishing a prison system that could handle the diversity of castes, races and religions, in matters of diet, dress and labour. Prior to the advent of the modern prison, imprisonment was traditionally considered insufficient punishment and hardly a deterrent to most Indians, unless it was supplemented with sanctions such as branding with a mark or being transferred to overseas colonies. It was apparent from the beginning that the British did not understand the complexities of Indian culture, with its caste-related anomalies. By some accounts, Indian prisons did not follow European models and actually provided very limited prisoner surveillance.[82]

By the 1980s, the prisons were in shambles, with all classifications of inmate confined together within the same penal institutions, irrespective of age, status, background and the nature of the offence.[83] If there was any real segregation, it was separating under-trial or on-remand prisoners from those already convicted. With little differentiation between old and young inmates or recidivists and first-time offenders, 'everyone leaves it worse than he went in'. In some cases, prisoners were differentiated from one another by the severity of their offences. Bigtime robbers and murderers received top billing among the inmates when their crimes were 'considered prestigious enough to elevate one in the hierarchy'. The converse was true when it came to crimes against children. Like overcrowded and understaffed prisons around the world, many Indian prisons 'are run in [the] real sense, more by the inmates, than by the staff'. Conditions are made immensely worse by an absence of official orientation that can better explain to newcomers the unfamiliarity of prison life and the demands 'imposed by regimentation'. With little assistance from officials, first-time inmates are almost 'helplessly dependent' on veteran inmates, habitual offenders, recidivists and inmate leaders.[84]

*Tihar Jail*

Tihar Jail is located on 162 hectares (400 acres) in a working-class neighbourhood on the western periphery of New Delhi. When it opened in 1958, 'its design followed the idealism of newly independent India.' Initially, people could be forgiven if they mistook its carefully tended lawns, gardens and buildings for a 'high security college campus'. However, its facade deteriorated quickly over the next twenty years, reflecting the country's rising poverty and corruption.

Prison gangs were flourishing in India by the time Kiran Bedi took charge of the prison system as Inspector General in 1993. She recounted that the prison gangs 'were ritualistically named after their exalted leaders', such as the Tyagi Gang, Gujjar Gang, Saptal Gang and Dawood Gang.[85] For example, the Bawana Gang is named in honour of Neeraj Bawana, who ran a gang under his name inside prison. While some prison administrators like to downplay the proliferation of prison gangs, others have been more candid, with one source admitting, 'Gangs have existed in Tihar for decades. But of late, they have started functioning in a more organized manner. Most top gangsters in Delhi, NCR [National Capital Region] and Haryana [state] are behind bars and run their operations from the prison complex.'[86]

Since around 2010 it has become no secret that criminal gangs control cellblocks and that anything can be had for a price, sex and drugs included. In 2015, the Director General of the prison system admitted that 'there has been an increase in gang formations and activities . . . prisoners eventually make friends and groups within the jail, they are something we cannot control.' He blamed much of the gang behaviour on the ubiquity of mobile phones, but would not go as far as admitting that the Tihar gangs dictate criminal activity on the outside.[87]

As in other countries, in India it is almost mandatory to join a prison gang. Those who choose not to will always have to watch their backs. There is much to gain by joining beyond simply protection. One imaginative ruse allows inmates to get into desired cellblocks, with help from members strategically placed in the records office. Since lodging is decided alphabetically, an individual named Sanjay, whose alias is Pappu, can have this reversed so that he becomes Pappu, alias Sanjay, bringing him down lower in the alphabet and thus potentially gaining him much better lodgings. Besides access to food and lodging, gang members have ready access to pornography and mobile phones, the lifeblood of any prison gang.[88]

If there was any doubt as to the rivalry between prison gangs at Tihar, it was dispelled by a savage gang clash in May 2015 between the Chawanni and Beedi gangs. During a ten-minute brawl, six inmates were attacked by rivals with sharp blades and deadly 'improvised forks and spoons', leaving three seriously wounded and the main target dead. This was the seventeenth death in four months as the two gangs battled for supremacy over Asia's largest prison complex.

In 2015, journalist Raj Shekhar wrote one of the best accounts to date of the formation of Indian gangs.[89] His conclusions match up with their development elsewhere. He notes how the evolution of the gang began when inmates with similar criminal inclinations linked up and created what he called a 'seed' gang. In Uttar Pradesh's Dasna jail, thirteen inmates banded together and formed the Gore Khan Gang, which received media attention after it pulled off a sensational heist in January 2011.

Many inmates are drawn to each other due to similar criminal proclivities, so there are gangs of kidnappers (snatchers), murderers, burglars and so forth. Once the seed group is together they search for a VIP gangster whom they will seek support from and adopt his name as a gang moniker, such as the gangs Neeraj Bawana, Ravi Dabolia, Navan Bidi and Chawanna-Atthani, all named after respected and feared crime bosses. The gang next seeks to increase its striking power by adding new recruits. In order to lure new prisoners, leaders will promise them a panoply of perks including safety from rape and rival gangs, the choice of a cell on arrival, and access to luxuries such as cigarettes, drugs, mobiles, fans, coolers, blankets and medicines. And still better yet, access to homemade food.[90]

Tihar is home to at least twenty prison gangs and over thirty sub-gangs, all operating unimpeded in what was conceived as a high-security facility, making it 'a ticking time bomb', according to one observer. Gang members came from all quarters of India – particularly Hindus and Muslims, with some gangs containing both. One former inspector general noted that their 'ambit of crime specialization also covered vendetta, caste wars, gang wars, extortion, drugs and murder'. What's more, many have developed highly efficient communication networks.[91]

Until 1997, Tihar had 'its own sanctioned caste system', with politicians and white-collar criminals at the top and common criminals at the bottom of the hierarchy. Until this system was dismantled, the higher-status inmates ate better food in isolation from other inmates,

Inside Tihar jail, 2014.

and could expect requests fulfilled for extra sugar for their tea and more ghee (clarified butter) for their food. But the system has been replaced by a more rehabilitation-orientated regime. In a nation where caste and social standing are everything, criminal luminaries and prominent prisoners might have expected VIP treatment, but in recent years, despite the desire for luxury items and special treatment, most requests for air conditioning and food from home have officially been denied. One business executive went as far as going to court to demand access to his iPad.[92]

### Other Prison Gangs

Gang fights and riots are common in India's prisons. In 2018, a battle took place between more than a dozen members of the Bindar Gujjar Gang and the Rajesh Bawanna and Ashok Gujjar gangs in Bhondsi jail, Haryana's largest prison. It is well established that in prison, any minor disagreement can quickly morph into a bloody riot. In this case the beef was over which members were first in line to purchase food from the jail canteen. In lieu of customary prison-made knives, or shivs, and other cutting weapons, inmates tore off branches from trees inside the jail and began pummelling each other. The fight expanded after inmates contacted supporters in jail and continued the clash. After it was over, officers picked up 22 discarded mobile phones.[93] The major gangs inside Bhondsi jail are the Bindar Gujjar Gang, Sandeep Gadoli Gang, Kaushal Gang, Manjeet Mahal Gang and Ashok Rathi Gang. These gangs are far from monolithic, but are well connected on the outside.

In 2017 rumours of an impending gang war in Bhondsi led to the transfer of various rivals. According to one source, as members of free-world street gangs entered prison, it was not uncommon for them to link up with other groups. For example, when Manjeet Mahal arrived at Bhondsi he connected with Bindar Gujjap to eliminate rival gangs. Likewise, Sandeep Gadoli and Kaushal members joined forces.[94] As of late 2017 the consolidated gangs had refrained from war inside.[95]

Bihar's jails are considered among the worst in the country. In this state it is common for 'underworld dons to continue to operate from behind bars, thanks to mobile phones and lax security'. In the capital, Patna, almost every major crime is linked to crime bosses lodged in Beur Central Jail. Money inside jails 'attracts extortion gangs'. The biggest of these is the Bladebaaz Gang in Tihar jail, run by Romesh Sharma and believed to be affiliated with Dawood Ibrahim, East Asia's version of Al Capone. Anyone who refuses to pay extortion demands can expect to be attacked with surgical blades. This sometimes occurs in high-security vans on the way to court. Ultimately, prison staff are so outnumbered that most prisons 'let inmates do what they want, to buy peace with them. Bribes make things smoother.'[96]

Taloja jail, Mumbai, is home to members of the Bharat Nepali, Ashwin Naik and Salem gangs. Abu Salem, aka 'Captain', and Arun Gawli, aka 'Daddy', are the most notorious crime bosses held there. Surrounded by 6-metre (20 ft) walls, it opened in 2009. According to a Maharashtra Home Department official, the state government always sends Dawood gang rivals to Taloja to avoid showdowns at the congested Arthur Road jail, also in Mumbai. Taloja is close to the stronghold of Dawood's rival Chota Rajan, known as 'Navi Mumbai'. Both men run small empires from behind bars. Salem, who favours Marlboro cigarettes, walks the prison yard as though he owns it. He once told a jailer who asked him to hurry up a meeting with his lawyer in the common meeting area: 'Do you want to be shot inside or outside the prison?'[97]

Dawood Ibrahim in Sharjah, United Arab Emirates, 1991.

The Tihar jail is home to such gangs as the Jatav, Jat and Gujjar. One inmate recalled being protected by a gang member in return for becoming a 'waterboy' or *paniya*. His job included going for water for other inmates, 'the least dirty work . . . young, beautiful boys become wives in jail. And if a big dada takes a fancy to you that means you won't be touched by anyone else.'[98]

### Bladebaaz Gangs

Bladebaaz gangs exist in every Indian prison. Their extortion demands range from Rs 5,000 to Rs 10,000 to settle accounts. Bladebaaz members appear to be most threatening when they strike on overloaded buses taking prisoners to court. Police will generally not enter due to the security threat. On one bus 25 people were wounded during just one Bladebaaz cutting spree.[99] These gangs have earned a fearsome reputation inside the high-security Tihar prison. Their trademark knife attack usually leaves deep cuts on the faces of those who cross them. Even the most prominent inmates have had run-ins with them. In 2008, some 26 Tihar inmates wrote to the chief justice of the Delhi court, complaining about the gang's violent proclivities. These attacks are usually reported when they enforce extortion rackets and/or need to convince reluctant inmates to conduct menial jobs for them. Not surprisingly, as extortionists they target the wealthiest inmates with their protection schemes. Well-known prisoners targeted by the gang have included a former Congress member and a former policeman, as well as members of the Dawood gang. Adding to their lethality is the apparent complicity of various jail officials with Bladebaaz members. Non-gang members are hamstrung in their abilities to fight back since sharp weapons are banned.[100]

Two of the biggest Bladebaaz gangs in Tihar jail have been identified as being led by Jogo, alias Joginder Sansi,[101] and Krishan Solanki,[102] aka Billo Pehalwan. During the first decade of the twenty-first century there were approximately seventy members of Bladebaaz gangs in total. One study of the gangs identifies typical members as common criminals, often drug-addicted and bereft of family members. Extortion is one of the few methods available to earn money to pay for drugs. By some accounts, Bladebaaz gangs began around 2000, after prison officials ended physical punishments behind bars. Around 2006, between sixty and eighty Bladebaaz inmates were reclassified from 'general wards' to

'High Risk Wards (HRW)'. This transition to new status seems to have stimulated their vicious behaviour, contributing to an atmosphere of increased tension.[103]

In recent years Tihar's main prison gangs have added tobacco trafficking to their litany of criminal enterprises. As one observer put it, since tobacco was 'banned inside the capital's Tihar Jail', it remains a 'powerful commodity'. Rival tobacco dealers, who are usually Bladebaaz or gang associates, have clearly established their territories behind bars. Tobacco is smuggled with a variety of ingenious methods, sometimes packed into condoms and swallowed, to be regurgitated later, or in packets in the rectum. Tobacco is a powerful currency behind bars, often exchanged for other inmates doing menial work for the provider, washing clothes, giving a body massage, or even sex. In 2015, a packet of tobacco averaged at least Rs 500 (U.S.$7).[104]

Just as valuable, perhaps more, than tobacco, surgical blades have been smuggled in by attaching one to a long thread and then swallowing it (the other end is tied to a tooth). Others conceal blades in shoes. Few have mastered these techniques. Bladebaaz members are aligned with various affiliates who offer them a dependable supply of surgical blades. Prior to Tihar's use of X-ray equipment, the blades were usually transferred in cardboard files during court dates, smuggled inside shoes or in the mouth, concealed in the rectum or swallowed in condoms and vomited out once in a cell.[105]

Sometimes blades, as well as drugs and mobile phone parts, are smuggled inside tennis balls and socks. For a long time it was possible to throw tennis balls filled with contraband over the walls of prisons, but now nets have been installed to prevent this. Likewise, it is very difficult to smuggle items through the multi-layer security system at the gates. Not surprisingly, several wardens in 2014 were suspended for giving inmates SIM cards.

In 2011 one inmate noted:

Life becomes an even bigger hell when 'bladebaaz' are dumped in our ward. Lately the most notorious ones have come here – we have four to five of them out of 30 odd in the ward. These people who make life hell for others, slash people's face for any petty reason (not given enough respect, food or money or just for publicity).[106]

According to one observer,

A cut on both sides of the face is like trade marking that you've been inside. They come and ask, show me your face. If you give up meekly, then the cut is smaller. Else they will hold you down and give a bigger cut.

Standard operating procedure for the individual who ordered the attack is to take care of the assailant for at least several months if he is placed in a punishment ward. The slasher may get paid in cash outside prison, with the money sent to any person of his choice, but he must also be paid in kind. His employer is also expected to send the slasher boy three meals each day from the canteen for at least thirty days in the punishment ward. It is not uncommon for the victim of the cutting to send 'counter Bladebaaz' after the perpetrator, sparking a vicious cycle of bloodletting.[107]

## Thailand

The Thai prison system has more than 130 facilities and is always over capacity. An inmate–staff ratio of 25:1 leads to an abusive regime that often targets minority groups from Myanmar and Africa. Thailand has long been home to some of the world's worst prisons. None exemplifies this more than Bang-Kwang Central Prison near Bangkok, better known as the 'Big Tiger'.[108] The prison, completed in 1931, is almost 2,400 metres (8,000 ft) long, with walls that tower 6 metres (20 ft) (and 1 metre/3 ft below ground). The prison's most characteristic feature is its overcrowding and low staffing ratio. Having one guard for 25 prisoners has left it up to prisoners to create their own notions of governance. The prison administration has taken steps to maintain a semblance of order by using baton-wielding trusties, known as 'blue boys' or 'blue shirts', conspicuous in their blue uniforms. Trusties are best described as unpaid inmate guards given special privileges to ensure a patina of order.

Much of the overcrowding can be attributed to the drug war. Strategically located in close proximity to the opium-producing region of the Golden Triangle that includes Laos and Burma, Thailand has long been the epicentre for heroin trafficking and, more recently, rapidly expanding methamphetamine production. Over two thirds of the country's prisoners are incarcerated for drug-related offences. The Big Tiger houses those serving at least 25 years. Several dozen prisoners might be held in 6-by-4.5-metre (20 x 15 ft) cells at any given time. Besides the torment of a single unshaded light bulb that perpetually lights up the cell, new inmates must typically sleep on the floor due to a dearth of beds. And if they need a blanket or other basic necessity it has to be purchased from the poorly paid prison guards.

According to one study of five state-level prisons run by the Department of Corrections, inmates use the term 'Home' to refer to their inmate groups within the prison. Prisons with large numbers of 'demographically dissimilar inmates' usually find that groups will self-segregate and form a Home composed of inmates from homogeneous backgrounds. The name of each Home is determined by either former street-gang membership or shared home-town neighbourhoods. For example, an inmate group whose members are from the Bangkok area will have the name of their Home preceded by a specific neighbourhood moniker, such as 'Fung Thon Home' or 'Pathum Home'. In other cases a Home might be composed of inmates transferred from the same prison. So ex-prison names might include 'Bangkwang Home' or 'Klongprem Home'. One penal authority suggests that 'each inmate should have their "Home" like a gang membership'. The largest Home in a prison exercises the most power over its counterparts in the facility.[109]

Homes can range in size from fewer than five members to over a hundred. But, as recent research has noted, the variations in size depend on the type of prison and number of inmates as well as its zoning size, or area set aside for activities such as recreation, dining and general leisure. The larger Homes have adapted to their limited space inside prison by '[dividing] into 3–4 subgroups for convenience and accessibility of regular activities'.[110] When it comes to Thailand's prisons, there are basically two types. Prison gangs are more apt to be 'stable, organized, structured and with longer lasting association' in maximum-security closed prisons. In contrast, 'open prisons' house short-term prisoners or those waiting to go on trial, meaning the population is less stable as inmates are usually in flux, either being released on bail or being transferred to high-security prisons. Not surprisingly, older prisons are smaller and have fewer Homes. This is mirrored by the fact that there is typically only one powerful Home capable of preventing competing groups from developing. In the modern era, in Thailand's larger institutions, Homes 'are varied in both number and size'.[111]

*Group Structure and Hierarchy*

Prison groups are dominated by a leader with the charisma and clout to direct group members, and who in turn is respected as boss by his acolytes. If any conflict breaks out between groups, he is trusted with negotiating with other leaders. He is also responsible for the activities of his members, whether fighting with each other or other group members, or trampling on the rights of group members.[112]

Besides the leader, there is a consultant or secretary of the group, typically older and generally respected for his institutional memory and reputation. He is expected to assist the leader in managing members within the Home. He is imbued with the power to make decisions when the leader is not present. In the event a leader is transferred from the Home, the consultant fills his shoes, ensuring the perpetuation of the group.

Members of the Home abide by the group's regulations. The group leader decides the specialities of certain members, mostly related to day-to-day activities. A member might be selected to be the chef, laundryman, dishwasher, coffee-maker or delivery man, for example. Members are cognizant that they are under the scrutiny of the leader and consultant. According to one recent survey, each Home has a set of regulations that 'reflect the values of each group'. Among its tenets are numerous notions that are recognized in many other inmate codes, such as minding one's own business, paying your debts and not siding with prison staff.[113]

*Prison Gang Subculture*

Thai prison subculture typically includes a plethora of illegal activities, including smuggling drugs and mobile phones, gambling and the threat of violence commensurate with various extortion schemes. The additional income from these activities only goes to strengthen the gangs' control in prison. By most accounts these 'negative subcultures' are found among 'three major inmate groups': Oros, Samurais and the Vong Vian Yai gang. Some, for example, form gangs while in juvenile detention. In most cases they are associating with friends from the street, making it easier to bond together. Such is the case with other prison gangs that import their street subculture into the prison system.

Named after a famous Thai street gangster, the OROS Gang is considered the biggest prison gang. At one time, the Ban Ubekkha juvenile detention centre held at least a hundred OROS members. They exhibited all the hallmarks of the modern prison gang, tattooing their gang moniker on the hands and wrists. In like fashion, the Vong Vian Yai Gang boasts a tattoo of a 'V' on the same body parts to identify its members.[114]

One member of the OROS Gang chronicled his transition to gang member:

I am a member of the second cohort of the 'oros' gang. All affiliates should have tattoos of the word 'oros 02' on their hands. We all met each other in Ban Ubekkha and I have offered to be a leader since 2002. We committed a crime since we were at teenage [*sic*] because of low self-control. We could flight [*sic*] with other people only if we disliked them from first meet. We held that if we did not harm them, they would harm us. Everyone wants easy life and if we are rogues we will have easy life but if we fear them, we will have hard time.[115]

It is not uncommon for some members, mostly recidivists, to be tattooed on the whole body, face and head, but this is typically done only after incarceration. Similar to the Maori members of the Mongrel Mob, whose face tattoos were made famous by boxer Mike Tyson, once marked in such a way it is virtually impossible to find legitimate jobs and careers once they get out, cementing them to their criminal compatriots for ever. Not surprisingly, almost as soon as they get out they are rearrested and begin the cycle of imprisonment that marks the life of a career criminal. Not only does society abhor the tattoos and what they represent, but it is likely the family detests them as well.

In 2012 one drug gang in Nakhon Si Thammarat prison demonstrated its links to gang members in Bangkok's Bang Khwang Central Prison, in what was at the time 'the country's biggest drug network'. A major raid on Thammarat prison was spoiled when gang members were given a heads up just hours before. However, it did not keep police from seizing 284 mobile phones, 1,700 methamphetamine pills (*ya ba*) and a quantity of crystal meth from prison cells. As one high-ranking officer put it, 'They are not afraid of arrest, they work from prison.'[116]

The OROS Gang has demonstrated its ability to take its drug-trafficking networks from behind bars to the streets. In 2014, one member was arrested in a house in the environs of Chong Thong with 28,000 baht in cash and a variety of drugs, ranging from crystal meth (ice) to liquid ketamine and methamphetamine pills. The suspect was linked to the Thon Buri OROS gang, a drug-trafficking gang in Thon Buri prison.[117]

*Samurais*

When British citizen Billy Moore ended up in Chiang Mai Central Prison at the end of 2007 he lamented, 'If there is a hell, this must be what it looks like.' He was sentenced to three years for gun possession and handling stolen goods. Moore was not new to prison, having spent a stint behind bars in the UK, which, when compared to his new abode, was like 'the Ritz'. Diseases such as HIV, tuberculosis, dengue fever and hepatitis were rampant, and if they 'didn't find you, the gangs would'. As a *farang*, or foreigner, Moore was a 'constant target. He claimed the worst gang was the Samurais, a group of HIV-infected inmates who would make syringes from pens, taking them apart and using the sharp end to take out their

blood. That is what they would use to intimidate people.' A former drug addict and dealer, Moore fell back into his habit behind bars and was soon in debt to the gang for crystal meth. He later wrote, 'One day they pinned me to the ground and held a blood-filled syringe to my throat.' He was told he had one day to pay his debt or he would be infected with HIV. Somehow he convinced a Christian missionary to pay his debt in return for committing to the religion.

Transferred after eight months to Klong Prem prison, Moore discovered 'an ecosystem of organised crime'. Each gang had its own area. He found the prison-gang subculture significantly worse than Chiang Mai (his original stint). The HIV-infected Samurais sold drugs, mostly crystal meth, while Nigerian gangsters 'bought medication cheap and

Joe Cole as Billy Moore in *A Prayer before Dawn* (2017, dir. Jean-Stéphane Sauvaire), a film based on Billy Moore's memoir.

Klong Prem Central Prison, 2011.

sold it in bulk. And finally there were the Muslims, the money lenders of the prison. They were not to be messed with.' Pragmatic as always, Moore turned himself into a Muslim on the surface by adopting an Arabic name and wearing a skull cap. He had already given up drugs and now became a practising Muslim. He was eventually transferred to a prison in the UK.[118]

### *Drug-trafficking Groups*

Those who have been part of drug-trafficking networks in the free world typically enter prison with a higher status and are financially set. They will often band together in prison in order to 'gain influence'. Their funds allow them to buy anything they want behind bars, giving higher-status inmates superlative negotiating power with both inmates and prison staff. What's more, their illegal activities tend to be more lucrative and geared towards cushioning their stints in prison, allowing them to easily obtain mobile phones behind bars, open prison casinos and even expand drug networks beyond prison walls.[119]

In order to retain a degree of anonymity in prison, drug kingpins manipulate others into playing their roles. It is no secret that once a prisoner was marked as a gang boss it could lead to a prison transfer. One prisoner serving thirty years for drug trafficking recounted having

ten dependencies in my home. I needed money approximately three to four thousand Baht a month to support my team members . . . Culture inside prison included benefits, power, money and so forth. However, most real leaders usually hide themselves because of fear to [sic] being transferred and loss of interest.[120]

## Singapore

Like Australia, Singapore was initially a destination for prisoners transported from England to its colonies. During the colonial era the British subscribed to the Social Darwinism-influenced theory of racial division, wherein the people at the top are inherently superior and arrived there by merit. This theory was probably best exemplified by the racial division of labour, in which the 'docile' Indian Tamil labourer proved ideal for working on plantations and the 'indolent Malay peasant was best left alone in the fields'. By the colonists, the Chinese were regarded as 'self-reliant' and up to the task of pursuing 'commercial activities'.[121] These stereotypes and prejudices would be mirrored in the creation of the prison-gang subculture in Singapore, where the Chinese secret societies were regarded as the highest form of criminal organization. In the prisons the Malays are regarded not just as a 'minority group', but as a 'weak race, poor in money and education and intellectual equipment'. Historically exploited by the Chinese, the Malay Muslims of the Omega gang aimed to end this domination behind bars as well as to put a stop to constant bullying.[122]

As the colony grew in the twentieth century, so too did its crime rate, leading to the construction of Changi prison. Today it is considered the country's most secure maximum-security prison as well as the penal institution least likely to rehabilitate inmates. Inside the prison complex is the Moon Crescent Center, dedicated to holding political prisoners. Much of Singapore's prison-gang subculture is centred on Changi, one of fifteen correctional facilities in Singapore.

During most of the nineteenth century, Chinese secret societies (css) organized around Triad structures and strategy played an important role in controlling Chinese immigration to Malaya, where the css 'existed as an intermediate layer of extra-legal jurisdiction in regulating the social, economic, and political life of immigrants'.[123] This relationship is mirrored behind prison walls, where secret-society members dominate. Compared to the ethnic gangs composed of Indian and Malay inmates, the ideology of the secret societies 'deemphasizes ethnicity among members'. In contrast to the long history and strong institutional and organizational structure of Chinese Triads in Asia, the creation of the Omega and Sara Jumbo gangs, representing Malay Muslims and Indians respectively, was the result of personal experiences by individual members 'through accidental circumstances'.[124] Unlike the css, since the minority gangs developed without a pre-existing structure, it was incumbent on their leaders to be able to 'articulate personal charisma to ensure the gangs' expansion and sustenance'. Not surprisingly, the 'discourse on gangs was often couched in recognition of the mystic, masculine and invincible powers of their founders'.[125]

For almost a century there has existed in Singapore a symbiotic relationship between Chinese Triads and the police, a relationship that by most accounts continues. It was common for Triads to offer social, cultural, political and organizational assistance to poor, marginalized immigrants of Chinese origin. As one scholar put it, ethnicity, 'or more

The main gate of Changi Prison, 2019.

specifically Chinese-ness, used to be the main currency for recruitment and is still one of the chief variables determining social mobility in establishing secret societies.'[126] However, over time the ethnic exclusivity of the css was breached with numerous Indians and Malays joining, marking 'a dissolution of the character of triads and the evolution of multi-racial street gangs.'[127] Street gangs are usually referred to as secret societies in Singapore. More Malays and Indians are joining these gangs, including 'lower class ethnic Tamil minorities'. But no matter how the demographics changed, the Chinese remained in firm control. It was relatively easy to bring Indian and Malay minority street youth into the css fold, especially when they realized how much smaller and less structured their own minority gangs were than the css.

Singapore's two most important ethnic-minority gangs (Omega and Sara Jumbo)

> emerged primarily as a response to ethnic consciousness and racialization processes engendered within the prison institution, where racial self-identification becomes the only criterion in gang affiliation . . . The ideology of ethnic minority gangs stands in contrast to the criminality exhibited by the 'imported' (into prisons) csss [Chinese Secret Societies].[128]

## Chinese Secret Societies

One of Singapore's largest Chinese Secret Societies is Chap Puik Sio Kun Tong, or the 18 group. It also contains the most Malay members and has reportedly increased in numbers so that it has been necessary to create a new branch, Salakao, also known as 369 (add the numbers together and you get eighteen). In the early 1990s a small group of entrenched Malays in the 18 group decided to create their own Malay wing, Kun Tong Melayu. It was to be financed differently, and only Malays would be allowed in. However, this did not go as planned. A riot broke out after Chinese leaders took umbrage with what they considered a heretical move. As a result the Malays backed down and rejoined the Sio Kun Tong.[129]

A profile of a Sio Kun Tong member goes something like this. This case study involves a 28-year-old who had quit school and joined the group at the age of fourteen. He was arrested for stealing a motor vehicle and sentenced to eighteen months behind bars. It was at this point that he left the secret society to join Omega. Over the next five years he was arrested several more times and earned more time behind bars. In 2000 he was convicted of rioting in prison and came under the sentencing rubric of the country's Zero Tolerance Policy for Gangs. This earned him isolation for his active membership in a gang.[130]

Members of each prison secret society take part in some form of 'financial' activity. Some merely collect money from 'brothers' who work for wages in a workshop. Financial activities such as this are used to gather a gang fund. Several members are in charge of buying 'canteen', which refers here to commodities like chocolate, biscuits and other edibles. These can only be purchased by inmates who work. The canteens, or *akong*, will be dispensed to members locked in isolation or used as a recruiting tool. Messages between gang members are carried by teaboys or 'cookies', who 'function as taxis'. A cookie is an inmate who is recognized for good behaviour and placed in general maintenance around prison – performing jobs such as sweeping floors, picking up rubbish and taking inmate records from an office to interview rooms, 'since all interviews with inmates conducted by visitors are conducted outside the housing unit. Generally they work in the prison offices, under the direction and instruction of officers.' By contrast, tea-boys can be recognized for their T-shirts, with the inscription 'tea boy' emblazoned on the back. They are usually found in the kitchen area, cooking for the entire facility or serving drinks and food to officers and visitors when they aren't delivering meals to inmate housing units.[131]

*Initiation into CSS*

In order to be considered for membership, you need to be brought in by a 'headman' who will be responsible for your behaviour and 'will have to answer for you, vouch for you, back you up, or beat you up'. Upon joining, you are tested as to 'whether you are squeamish and whether you got guts'. This process, as related to one researcher, might involve killing a dog and removing its heart. The next test is even more onerous, forcing the new member to display his fighting abilities and bravery. The headman has to select another inmate, perhaps a rival gang member, and the new member is expected to beat him. Once both of these tasks were accomplished, the member was taken to a Chinese temple to complete his initiation:

> There were six people in the temple and they had handkerchiefs over their mouths like a mask. They just sat there through my initiation. I had to recite some oath in Hokkien, took three joss sticks, bow three times to Guan Ti, God of War with a black face. After that, I was offered alcohol and pork and I ate and drank.[132]

On the surface, by the time an inmate enters prison there is a good chance he has renounced his outside gang affiliations or links to secret societies. However, according to one inmate of Changi prison, ties to the underworld are 'a fact of life' in prison. This is best exemplified by the fact that as soon as a prisoner walks into the prison, officers check his tattoos for gang ties. Attempts are made to separate gang members whenever possible, but this does little to prevent them from communicating with each other through the prison grapevine. Not surprisingly, it is the younger gangsters and wannabes who cause the most trouble inside, so special attention is directed at them by housing them separately under heavy scrutiny. One veteran prison officer who spent more than a decade with the Singapore Prison Service agreed that prison gangs were 'part and parcel of prison life', but their numbers are low. A decline in prison-gang membership around 2011 was chalked up to the 2009 Gang Renunciation Programme, which facilitated the renunciation of gang affiliations in front of prison staff and inmates, with the pledge that they would be given protection on both sides of the prison walls. During its first couple of years, nearly four hundred inmates took advantage of this initiative. Singapore's zero tolerance towards gangs on the streets and in prison has reportedly had a hand in keeping prison gang activity 'low and under control'.[133]

Despite the government's efforts, prison gangs continue to flourish. However, in order to understand their continuance one must first comprehend the dynamics of the prison subculture in Singapore. At its core are the 'racial dynamics', where ethnic minorities operating in the wider society are marginalized and a constant focus of police scrutiny. Once ethnic Malays and Indians enter prison, their marginalization allows easy exploitation by the more numerous members of the css. This is exemplified by the over-representation of Indian and Malay members of csss on the street and in prison, where they are relegated to low-level and more danger-fraught positions such as 'Gi Na Kia (fighter)', or 'Gina (recruit)'. These positions are more likely to put ethnic-minority members in harm's way and under police observation than the more clandestine positions held by majority Chinese members. Thus, Indian and Malay gang members remain 'more vulnerable to detection, arrest and subsequent incarceration'. According to one ethnic-minority css member:

> It is a pity that we Malays have been taken to be fools working for the Chinese; we call them masters and devote everything I have to them . . . But I must say that they did take care of us, pay all of our expenses and recognized us . . . But only thing is that they ask me and my members to do all dirty things like whacking people and controlling businesses . . . the Chinese never want to dirty their hands.[134]

*Sara Jumbo*

The founder of Sara Jumbo characterized his power behind bars and the importance of ethnic background in prison-gang membership as follows:

> To me, first and most, I am an Indian. We are one family and because of this, every Indian is my brother, every Indian who enters prisons is Sara Jumbo. The membership is automatic. Whenever

we have problems with other inmates, I will go in and if I do, at least 10 people will be on the floor. This is the target I set for myself. The prison officers know this and that is why they do not try funny things with me. They will call me 'yogi kudu' for my fighting abilities. Only I can see the sop (Superintendent of Prisons) anytime and for a long time I never allowed them to shave my moustache and beard. If I remove my moustache, I am no longer a Man, no longer an Indian.[135]

The Sara Jumbo gang reportedly originated at the beginning of 1996, after its self-declared founder had an altercation with a dozen Chinese inmates inside one of the housing units in an unnamed prison. This was just one more example of Chinese power and abuse of Indian inmates, who until then were targets for rape and brutality by Chinese inmates supported by css. One ethnic Indian declared that 'They are everywhere in the prisons and they bring their "shirt" [slang for secret societies] when they come to prison. For Indians and Malays lack the protection of prison officials.'[136] By contrast with the Omega gang, Sara Jumbo has not exhibited any 'professed economic motive'. As recently as 2016, prison-gang authorities classified it as non-operational. However, as long as its members are marginalized and targeted in prison, it is only steps away from eventual revitalization.[137]

### Omega

Omega was formed by Yan Bai on 23 September 1989 in Singapore's Chia Keng prison, when seven Malay Muslims (mm) swore an oath of allegiance and pledged martyrdom upon the Koran. This took place in the aftermath of the so-called Seven Wonders defeat of Chinese gangsters controlling the prison. The group's primary goal is to protect the interests of mm inmates and prevent them from being victimized by css. By most accounts the acronym OMEGA stands for either Organization-Martyrdom-Encroachment-Gallantry-Admittance, or Only Malays Enter Gangster Area.[138]

Omega retains ethnically exclusive, restrictive membership, recruiting only mm. Prison has played a deciding role in both its formation and its expansion. The Omega gang is regarded as the more aggressive of the two major ethnic-minority gangs. Its structural and ideological motivations become clear as members proselytize and recruit others.

This can best be seen in the religious elements of the organizational principles of Omega, 'which take the form of swearing on the Quran as part of initiation rites, the adorning of a secret number of "535" signifying the Islamic practice of praying 5 times a day', and 'using a semantic structure where common enemies of the gang and street gang warfare described as "infidels" and "Jihad" respectively'.[139]

According to one leading authority, Omega's 'overtly aggressive recruitment policy . . . compounded by its antagonism toward Malay members of CSS (who are seen as betrayers of Islam) leads to an almost institutionalized conflict' between the CSS and Omegas.[140] Omegas target prospective recruits from among unaffiliated MM inmates as well as disaffected MM members of CSS. One of their proselytizing strategies is to explain how MM are relegated to the lowest positions in CSS, exemplified by the dangerous work they are tasked with. Within the CSS, Malays are mainly employed as fighters. The downside of this is that their presence in the forefront of violent skirmishes puts them squarely in the sights of the law-enforcement apparatus. Besides fighting, they are often called on to protect illicit activities and CSS investments.[141] MM are much more likely to be arrested than their Chinese counterparts. As one member put it, 'the Chinese don't want to go to jail. The Chinese only want to run their business, so they hire us to do the dirty job.' Another Malay was more pragmatic, stating prosaically that prisons were filled with Malays 'who are scapegoats of the Chinese. We always work for Chinese bosses and for every bone Malays get, the Chinese get a pound of meat.'[142]

Some Malay members of the CSS take umbrage when Omega members dress them down for consorting with the enemy. According to one member, 'Omega bastards run a campaign in the fucking prisons. Omega will *kutuk* [chastise] Malays in Chinese SS as betraying the Malay race, because we carry Chinese flags.'[143]

MM are over-represented both behind bars and as police officers in Singapore. Not surprisingly, CSS made every effort to recruit MM police officers when they landed in prison. It was hoped by the CSS that they might be able to use their former connections to bribe police, or at least look the other way when it came to active CSS on the outside. It did not take long for MM to recognize their 'economic marginalization' within the secret societies (SS). Few if any ethnic Malays would be given access to illegitimate economic activities.[144] One disaffected MM recounted:

I joined ss because they promised me money, ranking, businesses, I did everything the Chinese asked, rob, steal, smuggle, fight, kill, you name it I did it. I risk life and limb, trying to be a tiang (headman) in the underworld ... When I was in Mooncrescent Prison, I met Omega, I realize Chinese were fooling me, they never planned to [allow] any Malay [to] rise the ranks ... Chinese are not loyal to me ... So I joined Omega. I decide to protect and help out my Malay brothers instead, who are not out to make use of me. I am a martyr that protects the rights of my MM brother and prevent their further exploitation.[145]

The main shot-callers for Omega are called *traju*. Their role is to ensure orders from the upper echelons are carried out. They also function as recruiters and will typically pass on information to their superiors concerning new recruits.

Since the emergence of Omega more than two decades ago, it has transformed itself from 'an informal self-protection group' to a well-organized gang on a par with the css, featuring an intricate system of networks, relationships and offices akin to a criminal enterprise. It has been suggested that it has been able to extend its reach to the streets and its power behind bars 'by adopting a strategy of extreme violence'.[146]

### Asian Prison Gangs in the Twenty-first Century

Large swathes of Asia house tens of thousands of prisoners, both gang members and unaffiliated, in various types of correctional facility. However, except for the handful of Asian countries chronicled in this chapter, little is known about what goes on behind the prison walls. In China, North Korea, Myanmar and a number of other developing Asian countries, the prisons remain more an enigma than a source of statistics or a laboratory for research into prison populations. Some of these societies are heavily regulated and are not faced with the high prisoner-to-guard ratios so familiar in other parts of the world. So, the prisons might be crowded, but in many cases governance is in the hands of the authorities rather than the inmates.

# 7

# PRISON GANGS OF EUROPE

Europe contains more sovereign nations than any other continent, but is smaller than all the others except for Australia. Its more than forty countries are home to perhaps one-seventh of the world's population, and it is surpassed only by Asia in population density. Most European countries are comparatively prosperous, with lower rates of crime and incarceration than other countries chronicled in this book. Not surprisingly, the prison-gang phenomenon is not heavily rooted in Western European countries. Some might have high crime rates, but they are more likely to rely on alternatives to incarceration, hence fewer examples of overcrowding or for the need for prisoner self-governance.

Sweden is home to the Brödraskapet, one of Europe's more identifiable prison gangs. Prisons in Denmark and Sweden house outlaw motorcycle gang members from the Hells Angels and Bandidos. Inmates have been quick to emulate the motorcycle-gang culture by starting similar gangs inside prisons, albeit without bikes. Conversely, in France, there is a tendency to eschew the word 'gang' in favour of the more overarching and inclusive term 'organized crime'. In the Czech Republic, prison officers have uncovered plans for mass escapes organized by Russian gangsters, including a case where Russian inmates used smuggled mobile phones to organize cars and helicopters, and had more than U.S.$20,000 stockpiled for the break.

But researchers hoping to find a vast repository of information on European prison-gang subcultures will find this phenomenon rather elusive. In order to examine this subject, it is necessary to look beyond the parochial frame of just 'prison gangs'. There are several reasons for this. Continental Europe has not suffered from the after-effects of historical events such as colonialism or conflict with indigenous tribal cultures. Moreover, none of its countries has undergone the colonialization process that influenced the historical development of prison gangs in Africa, Asia, Oceania and the Americas. Prison-gang and group subcultures in Western Europe tend to be more connected to political and religious radicalization, whether it be the paramilitary groups imprisoned in Northern Ireland or the recent evolution of Muslim gangs in several European prisons. The prison-gang phenomenon and prisoner self-governance are rare in Europe, where the typical precursors of overcrowding, poor management, sparse oversight and racial and ethnic stratification are usually missing.

The persistence of much smaller prison populations in Europe helps explain 'why gangs have relatively little influence in many English and European prisons'.[1] Unlike in the United States and elsewhere, there are few massive big-house prison fortresses in Western Europe. Most European prisons are much smaller, making them easier to supervise and control, thereby keeping inmates safe and secure for the most part, alleviating the necessity of joining gangs for protection. Moreover, there are fewer opportunities for organizing contraband networks.

## Sweden: Brödraskapet

Despite the Scandinavian reputation for convivial prison environments, Sweden's first prison gang, Brödraskapet (BSK), 'The Brotherhood', formed in response to a stricter correctional regime implemented in the Swedish prison system beginning in 1993, as crime rates began to rise. The Brotherhood originated at Kumla maximum-security prison in 1995. Opened in 1965, Kumla was designed to hold 435 inmates behind its imposing 6.4-metre-high (21 ft) walls. The new punitive prison regime instituted several unpopular changes, including the abolition of early parole. Following in the footsteps of other nations that have seen crime rates soar, in Sweden this meant more people being imprisoned, and longer sentences.

Since its formation the BSK, like its counterparts in other countries, has spread beyond prison walls and boasts at least seven hundred members nationwide. Its criminal activities include drug and weapons trafficking, robbery, murder and extortion. Even before it was officially established, inmates were at war with a system that, by 1994, was considered too punitive. Tension between correctional officers and inmates burst into riot in the summer of 1994, resulting in the torching of parts of

Brödraskapet gang member.

the high-security Tidaholm prison. By most accounts, the leaders of the riot would become 'some of the founding members of the Brotherhood'. In response to the unrest, prison administrators resorted to the now familiar tactics of relocating inmates to other prisons, delaying parole and the widespread use of solitary confinement. Like other prison gangs, the BSK has been branded an organized crime group by regional author- ities, in this case the European Union.

### *Daniel Mark Michael Fitzpatrick, aka 'Danny the Hood'*

Daniel Mark Michael Fitzpatrick is considered the founder of the BSK. He was born in Kenya to British parents on 26 February 1953. It is unclear when he came to Sweden. During his criminal career, 'Danny the Hood' was tied to several high-profile crimes, including the killing of a police officer during an armed robbery. He served eight years for armed robbery and was linked to drug trafficking, blackmail and other crimes. While in prison he recruited from a growing clan of hardened thugs, as he assembled the fledgling BSK. Gang rules behind bars followed the usual litany of regulations and membership requirements, including having served time in a secure prison and refusing to take part in rehabilitation programmes or give urine for drug tests. For security purposes, prospective members had to show court documents that demonstrated they had not been informants. In an effort to break up the gang, prison officials tossed several members into solitary confinement or transferred them to other prisons. However, this proved counterproductive, enabling the BSK to spread into other institutions during the mid-to-late 1990s. At its zenith, the BSK had perhaps eighty to ninety members. However, their influence over officers and other prisoners belied their relatively small numbers. Inside prison, the BSK used violence and murder to extend its influence and control the drug trade.

Although outlaw motorcycle gangs (OMGs) are somewhat outside the purview of this book, it is worth noting that Fitzpatrick was involved in the so-called Nordic Biker Wars of the 1990s. In 1995 the ASA, a Scandinavian motorcycle gang, teamed up with Brotherhood OMG members who had recently been released from prison to form the first BSK chapter outside prison walls. With the Brotherhood chapter on the outside embracing the *nom de guerre* Wolfpack, members still behind bars adopted it as well. Testifying to the gang's violent nature, during a 1998 celebration of the release of Fitzpatrick from Hall prison, one club defector was shot in the leg and another gangster was struck in the head with an axe.[2] Embroiled in turf wars with both the Hells Angels and the Bandidos OMGs, Fitzpatrick was assassinated on 18 June 1998 as he drove on a roundabout in downtown Stockholm. His funeral and burial in Stockholm were a rather subdued affair, attended by thirty members of the BSK, with 'not a single Harley Davidson in sight'.[3]

Once the Brotherhood started recruiting outside prison, it made the decision to induct new members who had not served previous stints in security lockups. In the first decade of the 2000s, the BSK retained a strong presence in Swedish prisons as it expanded its outside operations and affiliations. Despite a relatively small number of members, its predilection for violence and criminal sophistication has served as a force multiplier.

In the early 2000s the BSK continued to expand its membership beyond prison walls, founding new chapters in a number of cities and recruiting members inside the walls. In 2002, only about one-third of its membership was incarcerated. Two years later a police crackdown in the

Gothenburg area led to twenty members being convicted and imprisoned for a litany of serious crimes. With so many members in prison at the same time, recruitment increased as well. Soon there were more members on the inside than outside. Over the next few years, the BSK feuded with other gangs in prison while it tried to increase its hegemony. Although it is considered mostly a prison gang, its membership inside and out fluctuated, but by most accounts, by 2010 it had strengthened its power in prison.

## Poland: Grypserka Subculture

In 1969 Poland adopted a penal code considered one of the most punitive in Europe. Under the Communist regime, prison conditions ranked low in administrative priorities. Moreover, prisoners had little hope of having grievances and appeals addressed. With the end of martial law in 1993, Poland had to create a new system to handle its large prison population. Poland has one of the largest prison populations. That said, prison occupancy stands at around 92.1 per cent, making it 137th out of 205 countries. This is a good indicator that the prisons do not face overcrowding to the same extent as in most of the countries examined in these chapters.

The Polish prison system and its subculture were influenced by some of the features of the Soviet Gulag system. There is evidence that the 'grypsman' culture, Poland's version of the prison-gang subculture, was imported into prisons following 'the political thaw' of 1956, which halted the flow of political prisoners. There are few detailed accounts of Polish prison life after the end of Communism. Previous accounts were the products of educated political prisoners who had been thrown in with the criminal population. According to one of the best accounts, there are 'similarities between the codes of Polish thieves and grypsmen'[4] and the Soviet thieves-in-law, including the adoption of a code of honour, initiation rituals, similar slang, behaviour norms and conflict-resolution practices.[5]

The Polish prison community, except for inmates 'with transitory status', is divided into three classes: in descending order, grypsmen, suckers and fags. A prisoner is consigned to one of these categories following his arrest. The majority in Polish jails, holding short-term prisoners waiting to go to trial, are grypsmen; this is less the case in prisons, which hold those already convicted. But any inmate has the opportunity to become a grypsman. This prison subculture shares with others a set of rules, prohibitions and expected behaviours. According to grypsman expert Marek Kaminski, a grypsing group operates according to five codified principles, which include demonstrating solidarity with other inmates, non-cooperation with authorities, assisting weaker inmates, perpetuation of the honour code and observing strict personal hygiene. These expectations might vary in different prisons and only apply to grypsmen.[6]

Grypsmen are the largest and most dominant caste in prison, followed by 'an intermediate caste', called suckers; at the bottom of the heap are the fags, prisoners who have provided or presently provide sexual favours to other convicts. In other cases, they have been previously raped or sexually humiliated. Suckers are less numerous than grypsmen and perform certain functions such as cleaning cells and performing services for the higher-caste inmates. The rules of contact are especially strict; a grypsman is not permitted to shake a sucker's hand or eat at his table. However, he has the freedom to take anything he wants from him. It is not uncommon for a grypsman to be demoted to sucker for violating one of the group's rules.[7] The fags, or male prostitutes, are the smallest faction, representing only 1–2 per cent of a jail's population.

Like other prison gangs and groups, grypsmen are tightly bound by a shared argot. The secret language is called *Grypserka*, which one researcher describes as 'the anti-language of Polish prison inmates'.[8] Besides the slang, every prospective recruit is expected to learn all the prison group's rules and principles. Polish prison subculture is sometimes referred to as 'second life' in the 'Polish professional literature', but inmates prefer the term 'grypsing': a 'prison code transmitted and enforced by the largest group in prison. The code of grypsing appears to be stronger and more informal than the inmate code that has been observed in American prisons'.[9]

One leading authority on Polish prisoners argues that a 'relative peace' is maintained by the 'self-sorting of inmates into "tougher" grypsmen and "softer" suckers'.[10] This goes a long way towards alleviating the unpredictable violence that is part and parcel of most prison environments. Indeed, this system is much like the systems of self-governance found in other prisons.

Whenever a new prisoner enters a Polish cell he is asked, 'Are you a grypsman?' Before answering he must make some 'strategic' decisions.[11] Once he says yes, an investigation is triggered: if he lied he is lucky to get away with a light beating; if he lies again he could become a sucker or fag. His best choice is to abstain from yes or no and reply, 'Ask other grypsmen.'[12] From now on the vocabulary he uses and the way he conducts himself are closely scrutinized. He cannot imitate a grypsman by frequent cursing or playing the tough guy. Mimicking a grypsman 'is the most dangerous action one can undertake'. The longer the time it takes to uncover the imposter's ruse, the harsher the retaliation. Always subject to secret background checks, the new prisoner can be accepted into the upper echelons only once confirmation as to his bona fides has come from any previous prison that he might have been incarcerated in. This is accomplished through 'grypses', secret messages that are passed around a prison or between prisons in order to receive verification of one's credentials. In a worst-case scenario, when an imposter is discovered he can expect severe punishment and then assignment to his proper caste. Punishment might come in the form of a gang rape by his cellmates. If no punishment is allotted, an entire cellblock may be downgraded into suckers.[13]

Once the prospective member has been 'authenticated', a process that takes weeks or even months, he must pass a series of initiation tests. Until he passes these, he is in a sort of limbo, closer to the sucker caste. Inmates who are child molesters, drug addicts, Communist Party members or law-enforcement officers are rejected outright.[14]

When a rookie is accepted as a prospect, he must pass a series of other tests that reveal his toughness and ingenuity. During this 'interim period', while he is evaluated and tested, he is described as living in 'America'. According to Kaminski, the term America 'reflects both the traumatic experience of Polish immigrants in a new society and the wry sense of prison humor, juxtaposing the promised land with a rookie's miserable status'.[15]

Once a rookie passes the requisite tests and is accepted as a grypsman, he enters the final phase of matriculation, 'a secret training' called *bajera*, shorthand for 'prison university'. During this phase, a series of instructors teach him clandestine knowledge and all the details of the secret code, ensuring that its traditions continue. Marek Kaminski suggests that 'grypsing studies could constitute a minor field at an eccentric college.'[16] Among the most important rules are those governing interactions with convict counterparts, such as prohibitions against getting into someone else's business and the requirement to stay neutral during conflicts and fights. Moreover, since it is a universal prison tradition that everyone is 'innocent' behind bars, a prisoner should not question or make fun of an individual who claims to be innocent.[17]

A grypsman expresses his solidarity in several ways. He might come to the aid of a fellow inmate who is being assaulted by suckers, fags or other prison groups. In other situations he might join a raucous response to a fellow grypsman being beaten by officers by hitting his cell gates with stools and other furniture until the guards stop. Likewise, if a riot or protest breaks out, he is expected to take part (that is, if there is a good reason for it).[18]

Besides a special argot, grypsmen are usually tattooed. Kaminski recalled one individual referred to as the 'illustrated man', describing 'his face, cheeks, neck, even his tongue [covered] with little pictures, partially hidden under his beard. On his eyelids are two "sleeping" dots. On his neck are two red lips', and so forth. Grypsmen are always ready for a good joke. Tattooing a special phrase in a special place can contribute to the levity, such as in the case of guards checking an inmate's feet at bedtime only to find 'Fuck Off You Dirty Dick, It's Clean' neatly tattooed on the soles of his feet.[19]

Scene from *Symetria* (*Symmetry*, 2003), directed by Konrad Niewolski.

### Paramilitaries, Religious Radicalization and Prison-group Subculture

Paramilitary groups held in European prisons over the past few decades bear little resemblance to the 'classic' gangs that we have encountered elsewhere. However, as one authority has pointed out, 'many of the underlying dynamics present in cases of criminal prison gangs operate in the case of jailed members of militant groups.'[20] One important difference is that, while most prison gangs use jail as an opportunity for recruiting new members, ideologically based paramilitary groups are less likely to recruit behind bars. Moreover, convinced of their political prisoner status, they are more inclined to remain separate from the common criminals. This was perhaps best illustrated by the British government's strategy of purposely trying to integrate paramilitaries with common criminals in order to deny and dilute their militant status, as in the case of the Irish Republican Army (IRA).[21] A similar strategy was used by the South African government at Robben Island during apartheid, where Number gang members were mixed in with political prisoners. However, as noted earlier, this backfired, and the political prisoners began inculcating gang members with ANC ideology (see pp. 102–3).

Among the most prominent examples of paramilitary groups behind bars in Europe are the cases of the IRA and Spain's Euskadi Ta Askatasuna (ETA/'Basque Fatherland and Liberty'). For both groups, prison and imprisonment played a significant role in the radicalization of individuals and organizations.[22] According to one Rand group study, the perceived treatment of ETA members in prison played a 'central role in the group's ideological and doctrinal outlook.'[23] Their purported abuse at the hands of the prison administration behind bars became 'an important source of propaganda' as the organization sought support in the Basque Country.

When prisons are tasked with imprisoning groups of individuals, it becomes a challenge as to where and how to contain them. Do you concentrate them in a few institutions or disperse them throughout the prison system? As will be seen later in this chapter, the difficulties of housing opposing paramilitary factions in one prison make this conundrum even more problematic. With membership concentrated in particular sections of the Maze prison in Northern Ireland, for example, groups were able to take control of prison wings, segregating themselves from rivals and common criminals. However, this situation only lasted as long as they were treated as political prisoners, separate from the general population.

Radicalized Muslim prison groups have a very different attitude to recruiting in prison. They actively recruit there, which contrasts sharply with the nationalist IRA and ETA policy of deliberately avoiding recruitment behind bars. Indeed, jihadist-orientated groups 'appear to regard recruitment in their prisons as [their] prime objective'.[24]

As ETA and Irish paramilitary factions were incarcerated in ever-increasing numbers, the prisons, by default, became central to the political-military struggles waged on the outside. By the 1980s the Spanish government was expressing concern at the amount of control the ETA was exercising over other prisoners. To counter this, the government introduced a policy of 'social reinsertion', in which ETA prisoners were offered reduced sentences and early release if they disavowed violence. More than half of the five hundred ETA prisoners took advantage of this offer. The policy not only reduced violence but also undermined ETA cohesion, as the organization began targeting for assassination members who took early release. To further disrupt their hegemony behind bars, in 1989 the Spanish government began dispersing ETA members throughout the prison system. Not surprisingly, this strategy was met with vociferous and violent protest.[25]

## Prisoner Radicalization

Since the 9/11 (2001) World Trade Center attacks, prisoner radicalization has become an issue throughout the world's penal systems. In Europe this phenomenon has increasingly tested the law-enforcement community beyond the walls, as some criminal-turned-jihadist prisoners were released and went on to commit terrorist attacks in Western Europe.[26] There is a long tradition of prisoners being radicalized behind bars. Moreover, as in the cases of future despots Adolf Hitler and Joseph Stalin, who both served time in jails, prisons have long served as recruitment centres and headquarters for ideological extremists. Behind prison walls in their respective countries, both future dictators had plenty of time and solitude to foment extremist philosophies and recruit others to their mode of thinking.

There is ample evidence that most prisoners who become radicalized behind bars enter prisons with little to no religious calling. In time, charismatic leaders convert inmates to their theological positions and a very small number of them become radicalized extremists or go on to join terrorist groups on the outside. As prisoners search for an identity beyond 'convict' they become more receptive, in some cases, to jihadist propaganda. This has been especially true among non-European inmates, who might not be conversant in the local languages and culture. Extremists are quick to pounce on these potential recruits, whom they often find easier to mould into religious followers. In some cases, prison radicals '[operate] like street gangs where prison gangs are generally drawn along racial and ethnic lines. Prisoners prior to incarceration who are affiliated with certain gangs may naturally gravitate towards similar gang organizations in prison where members have each other's backs.'[27]

## The United Kingdom: England and Wales

One journalist opined, 'Prison gangs do not exist in the UK, at least with anything like the sophistication or reach of those in California and Texas.'[28] That may well be true when it comes to the 'classic' American exemplars, but prison-gang-like subcultures increasingly operate inside British prisons. However, the dimensions of these gangs are still not well understood, perhaps because of the lack of an adequate definition for a prison gang. Definitions of American prison gangs run the gamut from three or more people making up a Security Threat Group (STG) to a criminal organization operating behind bars.[29] Presently, Welsh and English prisons regard a prison gang as a 'group of three or more prisoners whose negative behaviour has an adverse impact on the prison that holds them'.[30] By most accounts, gang culture is imported into the prison system. Or, another way of looking at it is that prison-gang members get out and spread their activities into new neighbourhoods while street-gang leaders introduce their gang culture into prisons when they are incarcerated. Prisons in the UK have much smaller populations than in the United States, leading one to conclude that 'inmates may have less demand for extralegal governance'.[31] However, there are signs that this is beginning to change.

Since 2016, Her Majesty's Prison (HMP) Birmingham has been under pressure to suppress its overall violence and growing gang scene. Videos have been produced inside on mobile phones and sent to journalists and others, testifying to the increasing presence of gangs and lack of administrative control. Some of the problems at the prison are attributed to it being run by the multinational security firm G4S, which in

2011 was awarded a contract to run the prison for fifteen years by British Home Secretary Theresa May; it was the country's first privatized prison. However, a series of scandals and serious violent incidents has led the government to take back control. Some of the problems are related to the lack of trained guards, the ubiquity of mobile phones and a thriving drug market. Some inmates had even isolated themselves in their cells for protection. According to one report, 'inmates have more power than staff'.[32]

Around the same time that inmates were hiding inside their cells, reporters revealed that eight gangs were battling to control the drug trade inside the 1,200-inmate all-male prison. One source lamented, 'It's a toxic mix. The staff are being forced to smuggle in drugs or just turn a blind eye . . . The prisoners are almost running the place themselves at times.' Gang members have resorted to using petty criminals to smuggle in drugs. One account has gang members paying common criminals to get arrested for minor crimes such as shoplifting, crimes that have short sentences, meaning they will probably end up in Birmingham. Before being incarcerated they are instructed to swallow packages of narcotics to be sold inside.

With jailed gang members getting younger, they are also setting up 'their "branded" franchises', including the 'Badder Bar Boys', or B21, after its local postal code, and the 'Baby Johnsons'. One recently released convict noted that the gangs are getting more violent as the prison becomes overwhelmed with synthetic drugs. Spice and Black Mamba, synthetic cannabinoids, are the most popular drugs, and have such serious side effects they have been referred to as 'zombie drugs'. Compounding the drug problem is the inexperienced and untrained prison staff.[33]

After the scandals at Birmingham became prominent, officials placed netting over the prison to end the delivery of drugs by drones. However, prisoners are innovative, and before long they found other ways to bring in drugs, including the soaking of letters and other correspondence in Black Mamba. Increased bullying and intimidation have been linked to the rampant use of this drug and a catalogue of other paranoia-inducing drugs.[34] But the drug explosion is not the only problem plaguing prison chiefs as they seek to regain control of HMP Birmingham. Among the identified gangs causing havoc is a Sikh gang known as Shere-Punjab and its rival, a Pakistani group known as the Muslim Panthers. Their rivalry reportedly goes back decades. Another gang, the Lynx, has been linked to Islamic extremists, and has been attracting converts from minority groups. If there is any doubt as to the existence of gangs in British prisons, in July 2019, an inmate's relative told a reporter, 'The prison has a big problem with gangs.'[35]

Recent research into UK prison groups has found few parallels with America's highly structured, hierarchical gangs that exercise substantial control over prison regimes. The groups found in UK prisons were more inclined to be loose collectives of prisoners, bonded through their shared conditions. Most evidence points to the importation of gang subcultures into prison, rather than their formation behind bars. Since there are rarely enough prisoners from a specific street gang in a cellblock at any one time, it is almost impossible to recreate the gang inside. Ultimately, an individual's neighbourhood and outside attachments trump former gang connections. It also comes down to achieving numerical supremacy inside prison. Unlike in other countries, there is no substantive evidence that gang-involved prisoners control aspects of the prison regime and economy, such as contraband markets.

Observers inside and out of British prisons argue that 'organized prison gangs' are rare behind bars. If one is using the 'classic' monolithic gang as a reference point this might have some validity. However, this does not mean that gang activity does not take place. Most prison groups in England are neighbourhood-based, an arrangement that affords a group protection on the inside. Put simply, if you have a problem with one member, you have a problem with the whole group. This neighbourhood orientation allows prisoners to find 'meaningful relationships and conversations covering mutual friends' and so forth. One inmate described the 'tribal' practice of prisoners calling out their postcodes after evening lockup. Another convict suggested 'it don't matter what you are in for it's just who you know and what area you're from.'[36]

According to one recent study of London's Thameside Prison, there was 'no evidence that gang-involved prisoners are simply recreating gangs within the prison'. Rather, groups formed according to territories, or neighbourhoods they came from on the outside. They would often bring their enmities against rivals into the prison. As a result, 'Gang related conflict' escalated as the number of prisoners claiming loyalty to one area or another demonstrated loyalty for each other. These disputes between rival gangs have been described as 'almost post coded'.[37] Ultimately, this study did not find pre-existing gang structures migrating into penal institutions. Where someone is from is used as a shortcut to decide who can be trusted, making inmates feel they have something in common and will be able to trust each other in the long run. One Maidstone Prison inmate reported:

> I lived a life of crime and I've lived with criminals for thirty years ... prison is a mini city ... out there on the landings there, that's your streets, and the wings ... are housing estates ... you've got the people that brews hooch, you've got your drug traffickers, you've got your pimps, you've got your prostitutes, you've got your violent gang, you've got your gangs that traffics drugs, gangs that goes and collects debts.[38]

## Muslim Prison-gang Activity

It is common for non-Muslim inmates to exhibit a large degree of hostility towards Muslim inmates, particularly as their numbers surge behind bars. Some research suggests that part of the animosity is a certain resentment of the fact that the Muslims exhibit a 'universal and supreme unity of Muslim solidarity'. This reinforces a narrative that assumed solidarity among them, which is 'loosely characterized in gang terms'.[39] Whether this is true or not, outsiders presume a built-in collective propensity for mutual aid, group loyalty and protection among them. With little understanding of the complex nature of the Muslim prison population, non-Muslims 'tended to ignore [the religion's] internal heterogeneity' and simply view all Muslims as a gang, while in actuality there are many variations among the Muslim collectives. Some inmates converted for protection, while others were more attached to national, regional or local origins.[40]

As one prisoner put it, a non-Muslim inmate might envy the fact that if you pick on one of them, the rest will help, while lamenting the fact that 'If someone hits a white person, the rest of the white people ain't gonna do nothing, they'll say you sort it out yourself'. The common conceit is that Muslims 'walk around in tens' and 'always stick up for each other'.[41]

A 2019 study of eight high-security prisons found that prisoners will join gangs for a variety of reasons, including solidarity and a sense of belonging, excitement, and to further criminal activity. The pragmatic convicts in this survey were masters at recruiting and converting prisoners to Islam. One strategy was to befriend a new prisoner and, if they could not convince him to convert, begin spreading rumours about him so that he would be ostracized and physically punished.[42]

In another study of high-security prisons in England, researchers found group mechanics in the Muslim communities to be rather complicated. On the one hand, there was a large 'heterogeneous' group, whose main objective was to practise their religion in peace. Conversely, there was a smaller group operating as a gang and using religion as a facade. This group had much more in common with the prison groups that have been the focus elsewhere. These groupings offered members opportunities to engage in anti-establishment and criminal behaviour, to exert power and influence and provide protection. This research supports other studies that have found that Muslim gangs operate in British prisons with similar motivations and behaviours to those found in other prison gangs. Moreover, the study 'identified a clear hierarchy in the gang with defined leaders and followers along with roles of recruiters and enforcers who served to perpetuate the gang's dominance and control'.[43]

The aforementioned Muslim gang earned a reputation for its disruptive influence and was associated with much of the bullying, intimidation and violence on the inside. While the gang did not enforce anything resembling the 'blood in, blood out' practices featured in American prison gangs, there were consequences for those attempting to leave the gang, ranging from being ostracized and bullied to serious violence. The most severe penalties were reserved for those who committed apostasy, denouncing Islam. In this study, each of the three high-security prisons had gang leaders who communicated with each other. It seems that Muslims living in this type of prison rarely left the group while incarcerated, instead making the break upon release. Behind bars, it was more likely that one would leave the gang after being transferred to a lower-security facility, where there was much less of a Muslim presence. One Muslim inmate put it like this:

> Once I go to a category B prison, I'll say goodbye to Islam. If I said I didn't want to be a Muslim, I'd need to watch out in case someone stabbed me. It's very dangerous to denounce Islam. It'll be nice to be true to myself.[44]

The study also revealed the existence of Muslim gangs that 'formed for criminal purposes'. This should not be confused with the fact that most Muslims join groups for support and companionship, rather than traditional gang activity.[45] It is not uncommon for Muslim inmates to 'operate as a gang under the guise of religion'. When they do, the gang demonstrates a hierarchy that includes 'leaders, recruiters, enforcers, followers and foot soldiers'. Moreover, these gangs are regarded as chiefly responsible for 'the circulation of the majority of contraband goods' in prison.[46] Muslim gang recruits share with their secular counterparts similar reasons for joining, including protection, power and criminal opportunities.

The hierarchy of a typical Muslim gang in a high-security prison in the UK is led by an individual who is often conversant in Arabic and born into the religion. Others respect his knowledge of the religion. But Muslims outside the group take issue with this perception, with one noting, 'People who're leading them aren't intelligent. They read the Koran and make it fit with their life and their own beliefs. They don't fit their life around the religion.'[47]

By most accounts the leaders, or at least senior members of the gang, have committed terrorist crimes, earning them street credibility among younger inmates. One non-Muslim inmate offered a profile of a typical gang leader:

This will be someone whose offence has validity. It could be for high profile terrorism . . . They will either be born to the religion or converted a long time ago, before they came into prison. Prison converts would not have the legitimacy to become leaders. Nothing will happen without the say so of the leader. If you speak Arabic or learn passages of the Koran, this will allow you to get up the ranks.[48]

Recruitment is handled by members tasked with increasing the size of membership. Compared to traditional American prison gangs, recruitment is 'relatively indiscriminate', with street-gang members particularly sought out for their violent proclivities. In other cases, prisoners who are deemed most vulnerable are sought out as well. However, there are cases of coercion and violence being brought to bear in order to convince an inmate to join.

The most numerous factions of the Muslim gangs consist of 'followers' and 'foot soldiers'. Most join for the criminal enterprises that gangs represent, or simply for protection. When violence is required on behalf of the gang, it is the foot soldiers to whom the gang turns. These members are more likely to have converted to Islam while behind bars. One study cites black inmates sharing that, once they joined the gang, they 'felt exploited and discriminated against by senior members, always perceived as having lower status'. As one Muslim inmate put it, black members are enticed to join by the Muslim hierarchy, who know that 'they can push their buttons to do things. Blacks don't get the same invitations Asians do. If you're Asian they'd be cooking for you.'[49]

Foot soldiers called on to act in the role of 'enforcers' are tasked with making sure members adhere to the teachings of Islam. Moreover, it does not matter which faith prisoners subscribe to; inmates are prohibited from cooking bacon or taking showers without wearing underpants. Violence and terrorization are doled out to those who transgress.[50]

Gangs are especially alluring to vulnerable prisoners and those being threatened and extorted. The younger and less experienced inmates and those who have committed sexual offences on the outside are especially susceptible. By most accounts they only come to the faith for protection and typically leave it when they get out. Others, particularly street-gang members, join because it gives them a cover for continuing their street thuggery behind prison walls. No matter the motivation, prison staff, some of whom have racially biased views, report Muslim gang members to be especially troublesome and more difficult to supervise than non-gang-affiliated inmates. One veteran staff member saw through the group dynamics, noting that members were 'criminal offenders who want power and influence to be disruptive and they happen to be Muslim . . . this is about power, status, criminality, not faith.'[51] Ultimately, from the perspective of the prison-gang subculture, Muslim gang members often control contraband revenue streams, ranging from mobile phones to drugs, and profit from extorting taxes from other prisoners.

### France: Terrorist Cell or Prison Gang?

As shown throughout this chapter, there are a variety of prison groups in Western European jails. Some are the product of a long and contentious cultural, social and religious history in which the British Isles are distinguished from other regions. Over at least the past decade, Muslim-centric gangs have infiltrated French prisons, including its largest, Fleury-Mérogis. Located south of Paris, it holds more than 4,000 prisoners in a facility built for 2,855. This prison was home to several groups of jihadists who went on to commit terrorist attacks once freed. This begs the question: 'Can a terrorist cell be included in the conversation about prison gangs?'

On 9 January 2014 former inmate Amedy Coulibaly murdered four Jewish hostages at a kosher supermarket in Paris. By most accounts he was radicalized in prison by the jihadist Djamel Beghal, who also reportedly mentored the *Charlie Hebdo* attacker Chérif Kouachi during his time in prison.[52] There are an estimated 35,000 Muslims in French prisons, and a growing fear that inmates are being radicalized and forming cells before they leave prison. By most accounts, in recent years French prisons have proved to be effective incubators for Islamic extremism.

Following the 2015 *Charlie Hebdo* attack in Paris, new measures were proposed in France to counter prison radicalization, especially after it became known that two of the suspects were 'products of the French penal system'. More than half of the country's inmates are Muslim, offering a ready supply of new recruits. One observer suggested that 'The u.s. problem that you have with high rates of Afro-American [*sic*] and Hispanics populating the prisons seems to be like how we have a high rate of Muslims living in the prisons.'[53]

Individuals convert to Islam for various reasons: some to rediscover their religious and cultural roots, others for protection and still others for the camaraderie, and the chance to fit in with a peer group. One political scientist explains that most individuals confined to cellblocks often have nothing to do but speak with each other. Like American men who join gangs in prison for the same reasons, these might be individuals who are not part of a violent criminal enterprise or a jihadist network on the outside; 'There is a simple gang logic [at work] that we find in many other types of settings in prisons in the u.s. or Europe.'[54]

As French prisons grow increasingly overcrowded, it becomes almost impossible to prevent communication between Muslim adherents, whether verbally, through messages or via mobile phones. Officials have considered taking a similar tack as that used against the paramilitaries, placing them in separate institutions conceived for Islamists trying to radicalize others. As a large, overcrowded prison, Fleury-Mérogis is a perfect example of how conditions such as these can lead to the creation of prison subcultures and groups. The role of this prison in the Paris attacks redoubled European concern that its jails are recruitment centres for violent jihadists.

Terrorism and religious experts remain divided over the extent of prison radicalization, as well as what can be done to prevent or at least monitor it. Unfortunately, much of the evidence is anecdotal. But some observers have suggested that isolation in a separate prison basically 'forms a cell in prison'. Alternatively, the UK and other countries have tried to avoid segregation, hoping that mixing with other inmates might lead potential terrorists to disavow violence and pointing out that many more are radicalized online than in prison. Some observers blame French prison conditions for the increasing climate of indoctrination. What's more, the nation's well-entrenched secular traditions prohibit the government from gathering information on the religious persuasion of prisoners, in effect stifling intelligence gathering at the prison level.[55]

The recent ISIS-inspired attacks in Europe were carried out by what one Belgian counter-terrorism expert described as the 'fourth wave' of jihadists, 'bitter, alienated young Muslims who turned to crime and were largely recruited while in prison'. Indeed, there is a growing body of evidence that prisons have become key incubators for a new generation, leading the expert to assert that 'street gang dynamics and . . . foreign fighters' networks have much in common'. According to one report there is a 'complete connect between jihadist groups and criminal organizations across the continent that comes together in Europe's prisons'.[56]

## The United Kingdom: Northern Ireland

Prison violence has been a feature of Northern Ireland's prisons since the 1970s. Like that associated with prison-gang rivalries elsewhere, much of the violence in Ireland is attributable to feuds between gangs and groups, often divided along ethnic and religious lines. As one expert put it, 'The dangers of holding such large numbers of paramilitary enemies in close proximity had led to predictable outbreaks of violence between rival factions'.[57] This was particularly true in the 1970s and '80s, as authorities attempted to integrate loyalist and republican inmates. Whether described as a faction or a group, these groupings share a number of attributes with more traditional exemplars of prison-gang subcultures.

It is not possible to state the exact number of prison gangs operating in Irish prisons. In some cases, individuals have been associated with two different gangs. Besides various paramilitary groups, there is always a variety of feuding rival gangs, Traveller groups and small numbers of foreign nationals, including Chinese and Eastern European gang members.[58]

Between 1968 and 1998, an era known as 'the Troubles' in Northern Ireland, the nation's prisons were a maelstrom of turmoil as paramilitary prisoners fought for the status of political prisoners. Much has changed since then. Today, Ireland boasts a much smaller share of prisoners than England, Wales and Scotland. By most accounts, its incarceration rates (the number of people incarcerated as a proportion of a nation's total population) are more in line with those of Norway and Sweden, where penal reform is usually on the docket. Moreover, Northern Ireland's incarceration rate is just above Germany's but below that of France, Ireland, Scotland, England and Wales.

The Irish prison-group experience is best exemplified by the activities of Northern Ireland's paramilitary groups beginning in the late 1960s, as well as sporadic gang rivalries. Members of Protestant- and Catholic-affiliated groups, typically under thirty years of age, were often behind bars for politically motivated malfeasance, such as disorderly conduct and rioting, as well as more criminal activities such as larceny, breaking and entering and assault, the majority serving less than nine months. With the incarceration and internment of more and more paramilitary operatives and associates in the 1970s, in order to make up for the paucity of prison staffing and housing, it was necessary to innovate. In response, in 1971, an abandoned British Royal Air Force field was turned into a detention camp and the prison administration launched a robust recruitment drive for staff. Originally named Long Kesh, or 'long meadow', five years later it would be replaced by the notorious H-blocks[59] that became known as the Maze prison.

### Long Kesh/Maze Prison

Soon after the beginning of the Troubles, paramilitary groups controlled aspects of prison life, in no small part because of the British policy of detaining large numbers of individuals in an attempt to diminish the civil turmoil on the outside. Not surprisingly, the prison administration was unprepared to handle such a quick increase in population. Between 1969 and 1974, the average number of prisoners rose from 617 to 2,517.[60]

Long Kesh operated without a formal prison regime, allowing inmates to wear their own clothes and to work only if they wanted to. At their own request, republican and loyalist prisoners were separated into their own compounds. Expansion projects eventually saw 2,000 prisoners housed in 22 compounds. Exclusive compounds were maintained for splinter groups. Among the most prominent paramilitary factions were two IRA groups, the 'Originals' and the newly organized

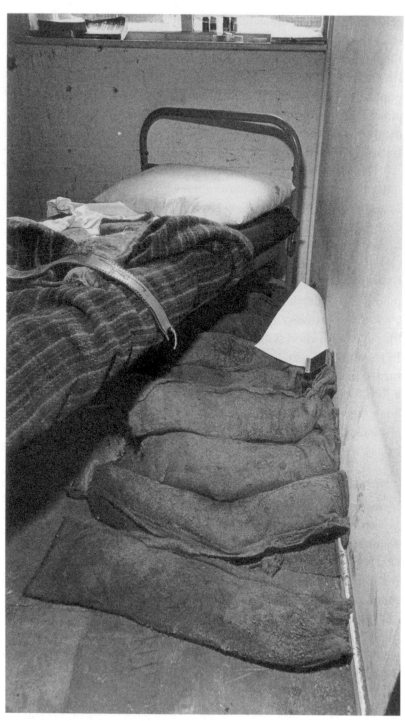

Inside HM Prison Maze, 1974.

'Provisionals'. Conversely, the loyalists were divided into the Ulster Defence Association, the Ulster Volunteer Force, the Ulster Freedom Fighters and the Red Hand Commandoes. Prison security was provided by the British military, with four guards assigned to each compound. In 1972 Long Kesh was rechristened HMP Maze.[61]

Within five years, the makeshift structures of Long Kesh were abandoned for the newly constructed H-blocks that would become known as Maze prison. It consisted of eight H-blocks, guarded by twelve 9-metre (30 ft) watchtowers.[62] Named after a nearby village, Maze means 'plain' in Irish. Opening in 1976, it achieved global attention in 1981 during an IRA hunger strike that led to the starvation deaths of ten prisoners. Built close to the Long Kesh internment camp, it was located on 109 hectares (270 acres) of boggy, low-lying land. During the thirty years of sectarian conflict, 10,000 prisoners would pass through the gates of these two institutions.

In the 1980s, the government introduced several reforms. These included detaining paras according to affiliation. The groups were organized along military lines and maintained such tight control over their respective cellblocks that prisoners could be murdered over political differences. Despite strict security, in 1983 some 38 prisoners, many serving life sentences, broke out in the largest jailbreak in British history. During the ensuing escape one guard was killed and five injured. Half the inmates evaded capture. During its first two decades the Maze earned a reputation for brutality. A number of Northern Irish prison guards, as well as IRA and loyalist leaders, were murdered at Maze and Long Kesh. Between 1974 and 1993, paramilitary group members also killed 29 Northern Ireland Prison Service employees.[63]

Prisoners were initially permitted to elect their own officers and to form a council to parley with prison officials. But from the outside, Maze's corrugated-iron huts made it a sinister presence. Surrounded by barbed wire and secured with floodlights and guard dogs, it could easily pass for a prisoner-of-war camp from a previous era. Like most prison gangs, this gang subculture was imported into the prison system, and 'their influence on the prison system waxed and waned depending on the wider political, social and economic climate.'[64]

In 1972 a political decision recognized the different paramilitary groups, allowing them self-government and holding them apart from common criminals. Observers hoped this might lead to an end of hostilities in the community, but it failed. In 1976 this policy was reversed, after prison authorities recognized that the strategy lessened staff control over IRA militants, while strengthening the influence and control of groups inside prison. After losing 'quasi-political status' in the prison system, they were no longer treated differently, housed separately or allowed to self-govern. Indeed, a new cellular prison (Maghaberry prison) was built to lessen the control of paramilitaries after twenty prison staff were murdered by paras in the community as retaliation. Now they were treated as common criminals and consigned to the general prison population, a strategy 'to demoralize and delegitimize their armed resistance in the public eye'. Like other prison-gang strategies, the results were disappointing. Henceforth, IRA prisoners refused to wear the prison uniforms of common criminals, instead electing to remain in their cells wrapped in blankets. Before long this devolved into the notorious 'dirty protest', in which they refused to wash and spread human waste in their cells and hallways.

In 1981 IRA members, as a form of resistance to prison governance policies, began a hunger strike to drum up public support. International and national responses to the strike after ten starved themselves to death would help the paramilitary groups win limited free association. IRA leaders point to this so-called prison war as the source for the revitalization of the republican movement and its later political achievements. Although the IRA bore little resemblance to a classic prison gang, it did transform prison into an arena of confrontation with the state.[65]

Part of the paramilitary prison strategy was to pressure authorities for more access to the public areas of the institutions. In the early 1980s they won free access to their own separate wings. Nevertheless, they wanted more. Between 1986 and 1989 they earned another victory, winning permission for inter-wing associating. However, prison officers saw through this strategy, with one commenting, 'They were always wanting more territory, they had the cell, then they had the landing, then they had the dining hall. They wanted to have control over the areas that we thought we controlled.'[66]

In 1991 an outbreak of prison violence featured bombing attacks inside the walls of the Crumlin Road Gaol in Belfast. In November the IRA detonated a small Semtex bomb in the dining wing of the prison's C-wing. The bomb was triggered by a timer, killing two loyalists. Republican inmates knew that the hall would be occupied by loyalists at the time, since both sides self-segregated at specific times of the day in the dining hall. Knowing which alternative day would be appropriate, the device was placed by the IRA the day before the explosion during their lunch period. The loyalists retaliated by launching a rocket-propelled grenade at the IRA members using the dining hall, but it missed, without any casualties. These attacks illustrated the 'interplay between the broader objectives of the paramilitaries regarding their desire to achieve segregation, the reality of their ongoing military campaign against each other . . . which led respective factions to devote resources to prison-based attacks.'[67]

As with neighbourhood gangs that bring their local conflicts into prison with them, conflict between imprisoned paras was often connected to activities on the outside. By some accounts, the IRA decision

H-block monument in the Free Derry area of the Bogside, Derry, in memory of the hunger strikers in H-Block of Long Kesh prison in 1981.

HM Prison Maze, 2007.

to plant the bomb in the dining hall corresponded to a loyalist attack on a Republican minibus carrying prisoners' families to Crumlin Road several months earlier. Prior to this there was an unwritten agreement between the two groups that families were off-limits. The IRA would later report that the attack was 'in direct response to [a series of] outside attacks upon republican prisoners and their families by loyalists'. But the attack on the bus was regarded by most observers as 'one step too far'.[68]

Between 1998 and 2000 an accelerated prisoner-release programme led to the release of many prisoners, and in September 2000 the last four inmates were transferred to other prisons and the Maze was closed.

### Maghaberry Prison: Racial Conflict

In recent years, Maghaberry prison, near Lisburn in Northern Ireland, has been the scene of racial conflict, pitting loyalist prisoners against Chinese drug traffickers, or 'drug mules'. Most of these were Chinese nationals incarcerated for running cannabis factories for Triad gangsters.

In a rapidly globalizing world, it should not be surprising that the Irish prison system is now more diverse. The loyalist faction was led by Rab Colgan, a Nazi supporter and noted 'church bomb hoaxer'. In 2015 violence between the gangs led to solitary confinement and special supervision units for some of the actors. According to one prison source, 'The last fight between the gangs was mental – they used brushes, snooker cues, anything they could get their hands on . . . They beat the living daylights out of each other and wardens in riot gear had to pull them apart.'[69]

Tension had been brewing for weeks between the inmate groups, beginning with 'complaints from the loyalists about the personal hygiene of the Chinese prisoners', if one source is to be believed. The Chinese inmates were accused of 'not washing and of not clearing up after themselves'. Moreover, there was resentment over perceived favouritism of the Chinese, who had their own cook and access to satellite television that permitted them to watch shows in Chinese.

These conditions brought out the worst in the 'Hitler-loving' Colgan, who bore a tattoo of a swastika on his chest. He used these cultural differences to 'whip up a race hate storm', convincing his gang to attack the Chinese. He was apparently surprised when they did not take the attack lying down, as they reportedly 'gave as good as they got'.[70]

### Republic of Ireland: Mountjoy Prison

In 2018 the Irish Prison Officers' Association let it be known that 'violent gangs operate international criminal empires from inside Irish prisons'.[71] Most of the prominent gang activity in Eire takes place in the country's prison system. At Mountjoy prison, Dublin, for example, there have been recent accounts of clashes involving thirty different factions. Between 1924 and 1962, 'it was rare for Mountjoy to be without a political prisoner', with republicans 'an almost constant political population'.[72] This pattern persisted into the twenty-first century. Prison administrators were well aware of the growing problem, with the general secretary of the Prison Officers' Association reporting:

> gangs in prison over the past number of years have become a huge challenge for people working in our prison system, currently we have up to thirty gangs in Mountjoy, and the logistics of keeping them separated apart is very difficult for people working on the floors of our prison.[73]

Criminal activities flourish inside and out, with many operations directed from behind bars, including murders. Like their counterparts elsewhere, gang members 'control the prison population in the way they control their outside territories'. Strategies have been implemented to disrupt the gang hierarchies by splitting up the membership across different prisons, but with little success.[74]

As reporter Conor Gallagher noted, it is not uncommon for a prisoner 'to hear a scream and suddenly a fella's pumping blood'. He suggests that violent prison gangs have 'existed for as long as there have been prisons', citing ongoing feuds between the Ballyfermot and Coolock gangs, the feud pitting the Crumlin gang against the Drimagh, and the Keane-Collopy versus McCarthy-Dundon feud. In other cases, various paramilitary groups have been at each other's throats for at least half a century. While these prison gangs have little resonance outside Ireland, recent years have seen a surge in powerful organized crime groups behind bars, along with concomitant violence and drug use.

One of the more prominent feuds of recent years has been between the Hutch and Kinahan gangs. One observer noted that the Kinahans have a level of organization in and out of prison 'that hasn't been seen

Cumann na mBan protest outside Mountjoy prison during the Irish War of Independence, 1921. Placards read: 'Mother of God, open the prison gates; Release our Fathers and Brothers; and Mother of Mercy, pray for prisoners.'

before'. Prison staff seem to agree, asserting that the gang and its associates control entire landings at Mountjoy prison, as well as most of the prison's drug trade.[75] In some cases Kinahans have taken advantage of the official confusion over gang membership by having one of their members claim to be a Hutch, in order to be placed in with them to commit an assassination, before being dragged out.

One official stated: 'In the past, gangs came and went. Now there seems to be a more permanent structure to it, there seems to be a significant hierarchy within the prison.' The Irish Prison Service estimated in 2018 that there were 'significant gangs operating across the prison system with approximately 100 close associates, many of whom have to be kept separate at all times'. So far, the prison service has not tried diluting gang strength by splitting gangs up across its fourteen prisons, fearing further recruitment. Their only alternative at the time was to segregate gangs on individual landings.

Irish prison gangs have become increasingly sophisticated and are able to reach beyond prison walls, arranging various gang hits and creating drug-trafficking networks. For example, in 2013, a shot-caller named Brian Rattigan was convicted of organizing a €1 million heroin deal from inside Portlaoise prison in County Laois, Ireland. However, the gangs of Eire have a long way to go to match American prison gangs in terms of sophistication and power. So far, the little that is known about the Irish prison gangs is that they do not have 'rules, initiation and hierarchies and are much less likely to be organized along ethnic lines'.[76]

### Northern Ireland: The Assassination of Billy Wright

In 1997 Protestant Loyalist Volunteer Force (LVF) member Billy Wright was sentenced to eight years in prison after committing a series of criminal offences. On the outside he had operated under the moniker 'King Rat', and had been linked to several Catholic murders in Ulster. He was initially housed in HMP Maghaberry. Several months later he was informed that the republicans had put a hit out on him, and he was transferred to the Maze. There, he 'demanded an LVF section be created in the C and D wings of H-block 6 (H6) for himself and 26 other inmates'. At the time members of the Irish National Liberation Army (INLA) were lodged in the A and B wings. Its political arm, the Irish Republican Socialist Party (IRSP), warned there would be violence if the LVF members were not segregated. While behind bars,

Wright directed the LVF activities of a membership approaching two hundred. But conditions became increasingly tense at the Maze, and INLA inmates told staff they intended to destroy LVF's imprisoned membership if given the chance.

While measures were put in place to prevent the two groups from interacting, there were serious concerns over security measures in their cellblock. Although a ceasefire prevailed between the IRA and the Ulster Volunteer Force (UVF) on the outside, neither the LVF nor INLA had agreed to it. Both factions opposed the peace process and had been cleaved with deadly internal schisms, linked to criminal activities that included selling hard drugs, which in effect damaged the factions' credibility in the Catholic community.[77]

In December 1997, Wright was killed by three INLA members who had had several guns smuggled in to them. Wright was assassinated on Saturday 27 December at 10 a.m., as he sat in the back of a prison van heading to a meeting with his girlfriend at the visitors' complex. After shooting him seven times, the assailants surrendered to prison guards and handed them a statement that Wright had been executed for directing and waging his campaign of terror against nationalists from his prison cell in the Maze. His death would have 'considerable political significance to his killers and the broader community'.[78] Sentenced to life, the three assailants would serve only two years, getting an early release thanks to the Good Friday Agreement.

It was not long before speculation was rampant that the authorities had colluded with the INLA inside the high-security prison. An inquiry in 2010 failed to substantiate any state collusion. The £30 million inquiry found fault with the security inside, specifically how the guns were smuggled in and the decision to house both groups in the same H-block. There were other glaring security faux pas as well, including a non-functioning CCTV camera just days before the killing, the circulation of a visitors list showing Wright's schedule, and so forth. One of the killers boasted to *The Guardian* that security inside the prison was 'a joke', claiming the guns were smuggled inside nappies.

Western Europe's evolving prison-gang and group subcultures do not yet approach the classic American model. One researcher prefers to view prison-gang-related subcultures as 'racketeers' who operate collectively behind bars. Rather than a highly structured gang or group, these collectives should more properly be viewed as part of 'a more diffuse arrangement . . . with many entrepreneurial individuals operating to maximize profits as well as some small groupings using "runners" to distribute goods and seek repayment'.[79]

Maghaberry prison was dubbed the 'most dangerous in the UK' in 2015. Critics compared Northern Ireland's only high-security prison to a Victorian-era institution, and it was branded 'unsafe and unstable' by a joint assessment of HM Inspectorate of Prisons and Criminal Justice Inspection Northern Ireland (CJINI). Her Majesty's Chief Inspector of Prisons in England, who was commissioned to assist the CJINI inspection team, said it was the most dangerous prison he had ever seen, adding that the prison would struggle to meet United Nations minimum standards for prisons worldwide. At the time of the report, Maghaberry was home to almost 1,000 prisoners, including around fifty with loyalist and republican paramilitary affiliations, who were held in separated housing. The report claimed that 'efforts to manage separated houses containing paramilitary-linked prisoners were having a disproportionately negative impact on the rest of the prison, with staff and management resources drawn away from the main prison population.'[80]

Since 2015 there has been a noticeable surge in violent conflict between inmates and assaults on staff in the Republic of Ireland. Officials blame it on the 'prevalence of crack cocaine' and low staffing numbers. Between 2016 and 2018, serious attacks doubled at Dublin's Mountjoy prison (from 12 to 24), and at Limerick jail (4 to 8) and Midlands prison (7 to 13). Some observers have blamed it on the unforeseen consequences of the successful Garda (police) campaign against the Kinahan and Hutch gangs that has put so many of them behind bars, allowing them to affirm their authority inside.[81]

Muslim gangs continue to dominate the conversation about prison gangs in parts of Europe, as well as several other countries, including France. A 2019 report brought to light the activities of Muslim criminal gangs in Britain's high-security prisons. As in the past, they purportedly still use violence to force inmates to convert. To confuse investigators, inmates operate under the banner of the ideological Muslim Brotherhood movement (but are separate). The so-called Brotherhood has a hierarchy of leaders, including recruiters, enforcers, followers and foot soldiers. Most troubling is that those who are jailed for terrorist charges typically play a more senior role in the gangs. Like Maoris and other indigenous peoples in Oceania, and African Americans and Hispanics in the United States, Muslims are over-represented in prisons. In 2015 there were almost 180 convicted terrorists among the 13,008 Muslim prisoners in England and Wales. Most evidence suggests that Muslim inmates involved with gangs tend to be less interested in theology than those who practise their faith peacefully. In some cases inmates have used their purported conversion to Islam as a device to exert control over non-Muslim prisoners. One journalist observed that the behaviour of ganged-up Muslims contrasted sharply with their actual lack of allegiance to Islam, illustrated by their willingness to uphold the tenets of Islam, in some cases stopping prisoner behaviour if it is at odds with Islam.[82]

As a postscript, several serial killers have sought protection behind bars by converting to Islam. In 2016, aged around seventy, the infamous Yorkshire Ripper, Peter Sutcliffe, became affiliated with a Muslim gang for protection. The ageing multiple murderer had been transferred from a psychiatric hospital to HMP Frankland, which houses some of England's most dangerous criminals. As one newspaper reported, 'HMP Frankland is ruled by gangs and you are either in a white gang, black gang or Asian gang.' By most accounts, the only gang that would accept a child murderer or rapist was the Muslims, 'but you have to convert'.[83] Sutcliffe was warned that he was marked for death and his only way to survive was to join a gang. In furtherance of this, an Asian gang member set up a meeting with a Muslim imam, who explained the quid pro quo expectations. In October 2016 Sutcliffe had second thoughts about converting when he was told he would have to be circumcised first, and never went through the ordeal.[84]

If Sutcliffe had actually gone through with the conversion, he would have joined child killer Levi Bellfield, who had already converted and joined the gang. In March 2018 it was reported that the notorious murderer of Milly Dowler in 2002 had 'joined [the] biggest Muslim jail gang to impress terrorists'. Bellfield, in his newest incarnation, now calls himself Yusuf Rahim and, if the *Daily Star* can be believed, strictly follows Islam in HMP Frankland, referred to by insiders as 'Monster mansion' for its notorious population of thugs and religious extremists.[85] Bellfield rose to ignominious prominence for murdering three people, earning him the moniker 'the Bus Stop Killer'. According to authorities, the budding serial killer might have converted to Islam to receive 'the approval of the Muslim terrorists and extremists locked up at the Category A maximum security jail, in County Durham'. One prison source told a reporter for the *Daily Star*, 'He's under the umbrella of the biggest gang

Frankland prison walls, 2013.

in jail at the minute . . . That's the Muslims and it's a big umbrella. In prison everyone belongs to something.' Although he is held in a special wing for 'vulnerable prisoners', Bellfield is offered the opportunity to meet 'with Muslim inmates at weekly Koran readings and Friday prayer meetings'. Nevertheless, it has been reported that he has fooled no one and 'doesn't get any respect at all' from those he has tried to impress.[86]

# 8

# PRISON GANGS OF NORTH AMERICA

Although prison gangs are best known as an American phenomenon, American prison gangs are relative neophytes compared to the Italian Camorra, the South African Numbers and the Russian thieves-in-law, which pre-date them by decades. Unfortunately, there has been little debate by researchers over which American prison gang was the first. The vast majority of researchers have cited the elusive 'Gypsy Jokers' in Washington State Penitentiary (WSP) in Walla Walla, some time in the early 1950s, as the first, with little in the way of substantiation.[1] More recently, the veracity of this claim has been brought into question by several researchers.[2] It is curious that this assertion has been accepted as fact for so long by so many, since very little is known about the gang except that it was a motorcycle gang established in San Francisco in 1956, only arriving in Washington State in 1967. The motorcycle gang still exists, and has expanded internationally.[3]

The majority of research conducted in search of the first American prison gang has been limited in scope, relying on mostly secondary evidence or just parroting the Gypsy Jokers claim. For some reason, researchers have neglected to undertake even a cursory search of newspapers prior to the 1950s. If gang researchers had combed through the *New York Times* microfilm from the 1930s, they would have found information about the existence of prison gangs in the New York State prison system decades before the accepted Gypsy Jokers saga.

American Prison Gangs: 1930s

There is plenty of evidence that prison gangs operated in American prisons during the first era of massive prison overcrowding in the late

1920s and early 1930s. Lewis E. Lawes (1883–1947) knew a thing or two about prison subcultures. The son of a correctional officer, he entered the penal profession as a guard at New York's Clinton Prison in 1905. His prison career took him from chief guard at Auburn Prison to superintendent at the New York City Reformatory and then to warden of Sing Sing prison. Speaking to an audience of prison wardens at the 1931 meeting of the American Prison Association in Baltimore, Lawes lamented that he had to run Sing Sing while contending with '132 different gangs represented in his prison'. Moreover, he had to watch over the inmates 'within the walls of the institution as carefully as the police watch the activity of their associates outside'.[4] These comments indicate that there were indeed gang members in prisons with associates on the outside. There is not much more specific information on gang monikers and other characteristics that marked them as early counterparts to more modern prison gangs. But most of these accounts suggest that these gangs were extensions of their gang affiliations on the outside. Essentially, they imported their subculture into prisons. What is most notable is that they were ethnically restricted, like more modern prison gangs. Reflecting the immigrant demographics of another era, the gangs were essentially Neapolitans versus Sicilians and Italians against Irish gangsters.

New York State's prisons were a hotbed of inmate conflict throughout the first decades of the twentieth century. Auburn, Dannemora, the Tombs, Sing Sing and so forth are some of the most storied American prisons. By the 1930s there were reports coming out of the lesser-known Welfare Island Penitentiary that prison gangs were 'ruling Welfare Island' and were heavily involved in prison drug trafficking. During the last week of January 1934, a series of articles on the front pages of the *New York Times* testified to the existence of prison gangs behind bars. Much of the research for these articles had been conducted in 1932 by a former research director for the New York State Crime Commission.[5] Journalists relished the corruption scandal brewing inside the prison, with headlines such as 'Prison Gang Chiefs Served by Valets'. Most of the focus of authorities and investigators was on Joe Rao, considered an 'ally' of prominent mobsters and bootleggers Ciro Terranova and Dutch Schultz. In one case, the research director observed the warden spending half an hour 'getting a lot of lemons for Rao, in order that Rao might have lemonade ... The Rao group, in return for the many favors conferred by the warden, always did the noble thing'. This referred to the

Rao gang's predilection for decorating the warden's office with flowers before he came back from vacation or sickness.[6]

Rao was considered the 'head of the Italian inmates' and Edward 'Wolf' Clearly the 'head of the Irish prisoners'. Both bosses were served by valets, who pressed their clothing, shined their shoes and cooked them meals. The gang leaders might not have been patched or wearing gang symbols, but

> The average prisoner on the island could recognize the gang leader and prison boss by the sharp crease in his trousers, his polished shoes, the good cigars he smoked and his general bandbox sleekness that bespoke the best personal attention.[7]

At mealtimes only about 1,200 out of the 1,700 inmates showed up at the mess halls. The rest, 'the leaders and their satellites, or the ones who paid for the privilege – enjoyed the cream of the commissary'. While they feasted on steaks, chops, cakes and pies, the rest made do with 'a greasy stew with next to no meat in it'. 'Men who were not in with the gang, but could pay for the food', once they became connected with the Rao and Clearly factions, could live 'just as well as [they] would at home'. The most privileged prisoners ate in their cells, much like their elite counterparts in prisons in Latin America and Asia today.

The gang bosses apparently had the run of the prison, with the Rao and Clearly factions converting the entire prison hospital (except for one ward) into their private quarters. The most important 'rackets' in the prison were 'controlled by the Rao-Clearly mobs'. These included narcotics trafficking and the sale of stolen food, inmate clothing and privileges.[8] The gangs had a prisoner responsible for picking out the best clothing left behind by newcomers, who upon beginning their incarceration had to trade in their free-world clothes for prison uniforms. The gang member was permitted to sell these clothes and take anything of value that he discovered in the pockets. Inmates were expected to pay bosses for soft jobs as well.

Most prisons offered the rudiments of free-world vice, particularly gambling and drugs. Gambling was controlled by 'the captains', gangsters who occupied the 'strategic positions in the dormitories, the wings of the prison blocks, and other parts of the institutions'. Bosses received a '"cut" of every play and averaged about $15 a day, in cash and in commodities such as cigarettes . . . So complete was the gangsters' control that they had their own wiring systems for radios and private telephones.'

On the morning of 24 January 1934, a secret raid led by the nation's commissioner of corrections, Austin McCormick, revealed the scale of corruption and scandal at Welfare Island prison. Narcotics were found in cells and on inmates, while weapons ranging from axes and hatchets to pipes were discovered. Two gangs, led by 'notorious racketeers', were revealed as 'having virtually run the prison'. Rao and Clearly were taken out of their dormitory and tossed into cells. Joining them were 66 'of their henchmen, who also had been living lives of ease and luxury'.[9]

Further investigation revealed that Rao and Clearly ran a prison dope ring thanks to narcotics smuggled into prison. One of their more ingenious methods of transporting small amounts of drugs and messages was using pigeons. Both bosses could keep 'flocks of homing pigeons'. Clearly's bird house was built in the prison dormitory. Not surprisingly, when the rest of the inmate population was alerted to the raids, they rejoiced and applauded. Once the cells were cleared, tier by tier, a search turned up a large amount of paper soaked in what some believed was some type of heroin solution. Also found were eye droppers and a hypodermic needle. Prisoners would often steal food from the prison kitchens and trade it for drugs.[10]

Throughout the news coverage of January 1934, the Rao and Clearly factions were referred to as 'gangs'. One headline read, 'Prison Gangs Face a Federal Inquiry; Clean-up Pressed.'[11] In this same article, mention is made of questioning prisoners in an effort to determine the extent of the power of the two gangs headed by Rao and Clearly. A district attorney promised to make a 'sweeping investigation of the system of gang control'. The prison gangs had gained so much sway over the prison food supply that many inmates were 'slowly starving because of the exactions of the 200 members of the prison gangs'.

## The Purple Gang

Michigan State Prison in Jackson, or 'Jacktown', was a sanctuary for the notorious Purple Gang in the 1930s.[12] Several of the gang's foremost members, including Harry and Phil Keywell, were imprisoned there, continued running their street activities from inside the prison and controlled most of the prison rackets. They were reported to have brought bootleg liquor, drugs and even women into prison. Purples exerted influence not just on other inmates, but on the guards and wardens as well. Like prison-gang bosses in many developing countries, gang members were often permitted to leave the facility at weekends, thanks to prison guards who loaned them civilian clothes to visit brothels and illegal speakeasies.[13]

## Reform-school Gangs

Historian Joseph F. Spillane used detailed prison records to study youth gangs in the 1930s and '40s. Through detailed examination of reform-school records in New York City, he discovered that youth gangs during the first half of the 1940s began to adopt gang monikers, clothing and language, as conflict between ethnic cliques emerged at places such as the Coxsackie Reformatory in New York State, which opened in the 1930s. In the case files he found the story of Jack E., who showed up behind bars in 1943, and 'is "case one" of the new youth gang culture at the prison, the first case of the sample who fit the new profile'. Jack E. was a West Indian immigrant from Harlem and a member of the street gang called the Socialist Dukes. The Dukes 'were the first of many named gangs to be represented there'.[14] By the 1950s, self-segregation was the unspoken rule on the yard. As inmate Sonny Carson recalled, 'All of the blacks were concentrated on one side and all the whites, with Puerto Ricans intermingled, gathered on the other side.' Early on, new arrivals 'found themselves forced to assume their assigned place in the racial geography' if they wanted to survive. Carson would always remember that 'the dominance of gang associations was something that prisoners soon knew if you wandered' into the wrong corner.[15]

Carson describes a reformatory yard in the post-war years that would be instantly recognizable to any prison gang today. As he learned his place on the yard, he described the turf boundaries:

> On the right side of the yard, where the first group of blacks were located, you were told it was the Turk's turf . . . from 118th Street in Harlem. A few feet on, the area belonged to the Brothers from Buffalo, Rochester, Syracuse and all other upstate areas . . . Then the wildest sector in the center of the black-populated area was set aside for all the Brooklyn groups. Even though we were not united in Brooklyn, we were united in this place: The Robins, Beavers,

Bishops, Socialistics, both Dukes and Gents . . . We intermingled and stood together against our foes.[16]

## 'Classic' Prison Gangs

One researcher has dubbed the prototypical race-based prison gangs 'classic' prison gangs.[17] A number of these long-established gangs, including the Mexican Mafia, Aryan Brotherhood and Black Guerrilla Family, are covered in this chapter. Desegregation and the political awakening among inmates in the 1960s and '70s made these watershed years for the expansion of prison gangs. With politicization came polarization between racial and ethnic groups, diminishing the more traditional and stable prison culture that had prevailed in the days of the 'convict code'. Adding to the demographic changes in prisons was the American 'War on Crime' that contributed to the growing racial disparity among prison populations beginning in the 1960s.

Gangs quickly spread into the new liberal prison environments that prevailed after Cooper v. Pate, the U.S. Supreme Court decision in 1964 which established the precedent that inmates could sue state officials in federal court, ending the era of omnipotent wardens who ran their institutions as their own feudal realms. The liberalization of the prison environment gave inmates the enhanced ability to meet in groups, as long as they demonstrated some type of religious affiliation. This facade was an important contribution to the development of American prison gangs. Prior to the ruling, only Washington and California reported the presence of gangs; by 1984, more than 60 per cent of state and federal prisons reported gang activity. The growth was spurred in part by the free-world crack trade. Tougher sentencing laws in the 1970s and '80s ensured that an unprecedented number of street-gang members ended up behind bars and in the process transferred street gangs from the outside to the inside.

This transformation, however, was not entirely new, as James B. Jacobs noted in 1977 in his seminal study of Stateville Penitentiary, Illinois, which was dominated by ethnic gangs, particularly Italians affiliated with Chicago's Taylor Street mob. However, under the administration of Warden Joseph Ragen, there were no laws mandating the coddling of prisoners, and authorities had a free hand in breaking up and controlling gangs. There were few restraints if the authorities wanted to separate inmates, censor mail, monitor visits or lock up prisoners in solitary confinement.[18]

Meanwhile, as early as 5 November 1973, the FBI reported that:

> California penal institutions are violently experiencing the powers of criminally oriented groups now operating both within and outside the correctional system. Individuals have grouped themselves into organizations that reflect their ethnic background and language and are directed at prisoner self-protection and control of illegal activities within prison walls and on the streets. These formal tight-knit organizations are composed of convicts and ex-convicts and are known to involve narcotics, extortion, contract killing, robbery, forgery and receiving.[19]

This account is virtually a description of prison activity in the twenty-first century, more than thirty years later.

### Prison Gangs as Security Threat Groups

Today, American prison officials and police organizations increasingly refer to prison gangs as Security Threat Groups (STGs). The American Correctional Association defines an STG as '2 or more inmates acting together, who pose a threat to the security or safety of staff/inmates and/or are disruptive to programs and/or to the orderly management of the facility system'.

More recently, the Gangs and Security Threat Group Awareness organization has asserted that there are six prison gangs nationally recognized 'for their participation in organized crime and violence'. These are Neta, Aryan Brotherhood, Black Guerrilla Family, Mexican Mafia, La Nuestra Familia and Texas Syndicate. Besides these groups there is an ever-expanding population of apolitical street gangs, including the vaunted Bloods and Crips. Although white, black and Hispanic gang members adorn their language with racist rhetoric to ensure racial solidarity, a close examination of the larger prison gangs suggests that 'it is often the desire for power, profit and control that really drives the gangs to action'.[20] Meanwhile, there is little historical coverage of Native American prison gangs, many of which have been around in certain prison systems for decades. It is hoped that this chapter will rectify this oversight.

Prison gangs, for the most part, operated below the radar of law enforcement for years by using racially charged language to obscure the true nature of their enterprises, including extortion, drug trafficking and assaults. The best evidence of the profit motive trumping the racist one is the fact that several white supremacist gangs have formed alliances with black or Hispanic prison gangs to increase profits. The following gang portraits demonstrate instances of these unexpected alignments.

Prison gangs have been around in the u.s. for close to a century. What has changed is that in recent years some have evolved into organized, highly structured gangs, capable of reaching out to victims beyond the prison walls. Originally the gangs developed or were restricted along racial lines, but as they matured, they went to war over lucrative prison rackets, including extortion, mayhem, murder-for-hire, prostitution, gambling, drug trafficking and weapons manufacturing. Until very recently, almost without exception, American prison gangs formed according to racial and ethnic backgrounds.

## Prison-gang Communication in the United States

One of the biggest challenges for members of prison gangs in the United States and around the world has been communicating with each other in the prison system and with affiliates on the outside. Despite intense scrutiny and security, leaders collaborate with subordinates and allies with all manner of coded messages. Some simply pass these messages to other cells, others tap out Morse code on prison bars, and still others coerce orderlies and sometimes staff to pass communications. Another technique uses rhyming coded language called 'carnie', which they whisper through wall vents to each other.[21] Others have women pass on messages during visits, or after visits to outside compatriots. Some codes are very sophisticated, with one based on a bilateral cipher invented by the sixteenth- and seventeenth-century philosopher Sir Francis Bacon.

Except for Hispanic gang members, who are likely to be conversant in Spanish and English, most inmates are not fluent in more than one language. That said, most have some familiarity with a form of encryption. For a time, the Black Guerrilla Family was known as Jama, or 'family' in Swahili. Many members learned to communicate to some degree in this East African language. Other African American prison gangs have adopted Nubian and Arabic languages. White supremacist groups such as the Aryan Brotherhood have experimented with Ogham or Runic languages, and Hispanic gangs are known to use some of the rudiments of Nahuatl or a Mayan numeric system of tattoos and dots.

These are often incorporated into *Sureño* (southern California gang members) and Mexican Mafia tattoos.

## Race-based Prison Gangs

In the racially and ethnically stratified prisons of the modern era, after a new inmate hears the gate of freedom slam behind him, he enters a subculture that few first-timers are prepared for, no matter how much they think they are. Typically, he will have to navigate the various inmate cliques. Prison yards are usually broken down into distinct racial categories, where segregation is strictly enforced. In a large state prison complex the new 'fish' is likely to become familiar with the 'woods', short for peckerwoods, or the whites; the 'kinfolk', or blacks; the 'Raza', or Americans of Mexican descent; the 'paisas', or native Mexicans; and in some prisons the 'chiefs', a Native American contingent. It is essential that newcomers become familiar with the unwritten rules of the prison yard pertaining to inter-racial relations. For example, it is acceptable for individuals from different races to play on the same teams, but there is a prohibition against playing individual games, such as chess, outside your race.

Inmates can be in a cubicle with another race 'if the situation warrants it', but never sit on each other's beds or watch each other's televisions. They can attend the same churches but not pray together. However, if these rules are accidentally broken the consequences are usually not too grim. Worst-case scenarios include getting a talking to from one of the leaders (who can claim an exception to the rule), or a punch in the face. When it comes to the dining halls rules are sacrosanct. Races are never supposed to dine together, and violations are harshly sanctioned. An inmate could expect a severe beating, and if he eats off the same tray as an inmate of a different race, he'll 'end up in the hospital'. Eating from the same piece of food can lead to death.[22]

## Mixed-race Inmates: 'Which One Do I Join?'

Naturally, not everyone fits neatly into a racial or ethnic category. It is not uncommon for a new inmate of mixed race to face the conundrum of 'which gang do I join?' In some cases it depends on geographical location, in most others on the prison's established inmate culture. In California, New Mexico and Arizona inmates self-segregate by race.

Gangs run the whole gamut – Caucasian, Mexican American, Mexican nationals, African American and Native American. So, typically, someone of mixed race would pick one of the above.

There have been occasions when inmates of Washington State were required to declare their racial preference, and if they did not, a guard would choose for them. In Arizona, Asian convicts usually side with the Mexican American population, but are not actually obligated to join. However, they would be expected to follow gang rules and to align with Mexican Americans if there were a riot.

In the Midwestern states and on the East Coast it is common to find 'hybrid gangs' composed of members of several street gangs from a geographical area. In New York, if an inmate were mixed race (white/black), he would usually join a black gang. As one observer put it, 'to whites you are not white, to blacks at least partially black.' Opinions vary by prison. Some former inmates assert, 'If you are black, look black, or have any African American features that could be construed as such, you are with the blacks'. One prison has its own section where inmates from the Pacific Rim, Hawaii, the Philippines and others of Far Eastern heritage are housed. In some cases, a Hispanic who hangs out with whites and has English as his first language gets to choose between the two racial groups, usually going with whites.[23]

An ex-con from California's San Quentin prison recounted an interesting example of the above challenge:

> Funny thing I saw when I was at San Quentin. A white man, and I mean really fair-skinned, with red hair[,] ran with the Blacks. He grew up in Palo Alto and hung around blacks his whole life so that's who he chose to run with while serving time. Very rare to see that especially in California state prisons where races are segregated ... Hell he was even playing basketball with the blacks. And to see that at sq where the basketball courts are for blacks only was a sight to see.[24]

When a Jewish inmate enters prison, he has little choice if he is white but to make peace with the 'woods'. According to one Jewish inmate,

> I am always the last person to eat. It's part of the compromise I worked out with the skinheads who run the western state prison complex where I am incarcerated. I am allowed to sit at the whites'

San Quentin prison, 2010.

tables, but only after the 'heads,' and then the 'woods,' and then the 'lames,' have eaten. I am lower on the totem pole than any of them, the untouchable. I should feel lucky I am allowed to eat at the whites' tables at all.[25]

Perhaps one California gang member explained the conundrum of races mixing behind bars best: 'The races don't officially mix. That's true but you can buy drugs from whoever and the leaders control that stuff. I've had a cigarette with some white guys and the Mexicans . . . It's not as cut and dry as you think.'[26]

## Hispanic Prison Gangs

What distinguishes California's Hispanic prison gangs from each other is whether or not members are affiliated with northern or southern Californian street gangs. Originally the name *Sureño*, or 'southerner', was brandished exclusively by youth gangs in East Los Angeles, before being adopted by thousands of Hispanic gang members in the United States and into Central America. However, in the mid-1980s Californian Hispanics locked up in the state's correctional system diverged into two opposing factions – southerners, or *Sureños*, and northerners, *Norteños* – and entered a bloody internecine conflict that continues to this day.

The dividing line between the two alliances at one time was considered to be the city of Bakersfield, California. However, over time, the movement of *Sureños* into the north has forced the demarcation line further north, to Fresno. Non-aligned prisoners were pressured to join either faction. Gang experts suggest that the *Sureños* are better acclimated to the 'prison-gang environment' because most of them had been actively involved in the gangster lifestyle in the barrios of East Los Angeles.[27]

*Norteños*, however, were considered 'less sophisticated in gang ways and had values more closely related to agriculture and family'.[28] Many had in fact worked as farm labourers and in related occupations at one time or another in California's Central Valley. *Sureños* mocked them as *farmeros*, or farmers. It became common for Hispanics inside and out of prison to adhere to an allegiance with one faction or the other. For this reason, the *Sureños* became the dominant clique, with most newcomers to the state adopting *Sureño* tattoos. Some of Los Angeles' most powerful Hispanic gangs – the 18th Street Gang, Sur-13 and White Fence – claim they are allies of the *Sureños*. However, this relationship never precludes gangs within each alliance from warring with each other.

*Sureños* number in the tens of thousands, but this attests more to the ease of gaining membership than to any great criminal acumen. Like other large gangs, its 'made members', those who have killed or completed a 'mission', number only in the hundreds. What was once just a California phenomenon has spread to other cities.


The Mexican Mafia

The Mexican Mafia (MM) has long been the most prominent Hispanic prison gang in the United States. It is generally agreed that its origins can be traced back to California's Deuel Vocational Institution (DVI)[29] in 1957, where 'already tormented teens honed criminal skills and acted out against enemies from the barrios', earning the institution a reputation as 'Gladiator school'.[30] DVI opened in 1953 on the periphery of Tracy, California. Ironically, it was named after a progressive politician, California State Senator Charles Deuel, who crusaded for better re-entry programmes for adult convicts and a juvenile diversion curriculum aimed at rehabilitation. Just two years later the unit was designated a long-term housing location for all violent disruptive juveniles in an effort to put 'the worst of the worst of teenage criminality' in one place.[31]

By most accounts there were no active prison gangs in California in 1955. Much of the credit for the inception of the idea of a 'Mexican Mafia' and 'the gang of gangs' has been given to several teenage inmates. Foremost among them was a seventeen-year-old named Luis 'Huero Buff' Flores, a street-gang member from the 'Hawaiian Gardens' section of Los Angeles. Some insiders claim, although there is little evidence to support this, that the moniker 'Mexican Mafia' was selected with the calculated purpose of emulating the Sicilian Mafia, as the gang sought to control prison black-market activities. On the other hand, a Los Angeles Police Department gang expert has suggested that DVI guards began calling the young DVI gangsters the 'Little Mafia' and that 'Little' was later dropped and replaced by 'Mexican Mafia'.[32]

Credit has been given to Flores for coming up with the notion of uniting all southern California's Mexican American gangs into 'one supergang'. One of the motivations was to operate as 'brothers', damping down street-gang rivalries in prison, allowing the gang to control the heroin trade and protecting members from black and white gangs. Some sources have gone as far as suggesting that the MM was 'the first prison gang to have nationwide ties'.[33]

Initially street-gang members, who already had local street credibility, proved unwilling or at least unaccustomed to being ordered around in jail, except perhaps by the so-called shot-callers in their free-world neighbourhoods.[34] According to one researcher, 'Forming a prison gang from street gangsters was an odd concept,' in no small part because

Members of the Mexican Mafia.

longtime gang rivals hated each other as much as they did police and informants. Some rivalries, in fact, went back decades and even beyond living memory.[35]

Early LA street-gang members were much less inclined towards violence than their modern counterparts, largely preferring sticks, fists and rocks to guns and knives. One observer suggests that these street thugs 'were only marginally criminal, dabbling in petty theft, joyriding, drinking and marijuana.'[36] It was a time before drive-bys, when neighbourhood warfare rarely escalated to murder. When Flores brainstormed the MM concept, gang warfare between Hispanic neighbourhoods was a fact of life for young men, with many street rivalries already well established. It was from the increasingly violent East LA street gangs that the MM would recruit.

Flores, who spearheaded the development of the prison gang, recognized that it was probably counterproductive for him to assume the leadership mantle or to devise some type of rigid controlling body. Very pragmatic for a young man, he settled on the idea that members would have to earn their ranks over time. Unlike the Sicilian or, for that matter, the Italian American Mafia, from the beginning an egalitarian ethos was perpetuated, where all men were equal, each casting one vote, effectively adopting a majority rules system. Merging various Los Angeles street-gang members into a 'supergang' was intended to overcome turf rivalries on the outside by 'bestowing the immediate honor and recognition to the LA street neighborhoods they represented'. Moreover, 'becoming a "made" man became a more ambitious gang aspiration'. The core group of charter members in time would be regarded as 'original gangsters', or 'OGS'.[37]

As the young gangsters increasingly became custody problems, DVI administrators took steps to accommodate them elsewhere. Several of the more prominent ones were transferred to San Quentin, where the youths were given adult (A) and young adult (YA) numbers. They were among the first to be given dual commitments. Contrary to the goal of ameliorating their behaviour, by placing them with more hardened adult convicts to control their criminal activities, the reverse occurred, as they 'became the oppressors rather than the victims the CDC [California Department of Corrections] hoped for.'[38]

*Carnales*: Cadena and Flores

Among the dual commitments in the state prison were MM stalwarts Flores and Rudolph 'Cheyenne' Cadena. In the prison laboratory of San Quentin, the two DVI 'veterans [reorganized] the gang's infrastructure to include a formal and binding induction process and a structured set of rules for its members. The implementation of a 'death oath' elevated each member to a higher level of commitment. Any member who had joined MM prior to its reorganization was given the option of rejoining *hasta la muerte* [until death] or leaving with no punitive consequences'. In the past, when gang members were released, they were allowed to rejoin their street gangs. Now, anyone who joined the MM inside was expected to help expand the group outside upon release.[39]

By most accounts, the MM was created in part as protection against larger white gangs. A major concern in its formative years was that the term Mexican Mafia 'lacked a distinctive Hispanic flavour'. According to one leading chronicler of the gang, it was Cadena who coined the term '"EME", the Spanish pronunciation of the letter "M"'. Moreover, it was Cadena's 'knack for conflict resolution and keeping of the peace through charismatic leadership' that made him the right guy at the right time for creating a prison gang'.[40]

Flores and Cadena also officially adopted the terms '*Carnal*' and '*Carnales*' (Spanish slang for brother). A *carnal* was synonymous with being a 'made member'. In this way they sought to emulate the street gangs of the era, which had no clearly defined leaders. The Mexican Mafia was among the first prison gangs to adopt the 'blood in, blood out' doctrine; you spilled blood to get in, and died to get out. A *carnal* joined for life. Over time, other rules were imposed. While members could not be homosexual, it was considered acceptable to rent out and control non-gang male prostitutes as a business venture. *Carnales* were expected to stay physically fit, practise good hygiene and keep orderly cells. Recreational drug use was tolerated, addiction not so much. Convicts recognized the potential liability of having a drug addict privy to the gang's inner sanctum. Hence, heroin addicts were subject to a range of sanctions from banishment to death.

By most accounts, between 1957 and the mid-1960s 'the Mexican Mafia ruled the California prison system'. Part of the explanation for their domination was that from the very beginning the Mexican Mafia was distinguished for the quality of its members; put another way, the excellence of its members trumped achieving numerical superiority.[41]

In order 'to prevent internal conflicts' the MM instituted a 'no politicking' policy, basically prohibiting a *carnal* from disrespecting another member. It was also considered bad form for a member to lobby the sanctioning of another member unless it was for good reason, such as snitching or failing to carry out an assignment. According to one leading expert on the MM, 'The hope was to abolish personality conflicts that could lead to infighting and weaken the group. That theory rarely worked in practice.' What did seem to work for almost twenty years was a secrecy pledge, which prohibited any member from speaking about or even acknowledging the existence of MM, except to another member. Violation of this pledge meant death.[42] Its goal to become the most feared group in prison would succeed beyond its founders' wildest dreams.

Long stretches in prison gave inmates plenty of time for contemplation, with many trying to learn about their ancestry. Some gang members adopted monikers in honour of ancient Aztec or Toltec roots, while others preferred more recent Apache and Yaqui exemplars, such as the legendary names Geronimo, Chato and Indio. Still others found inspiration in the nicknames of iconic American gangsters such as Al 'Scarface' Capone and 'Machine Gun' Kelly.[43]

## Joe Morgan: 'Caucasian by Birth, Mexican by Choice'

In the 1970s, the MM expanded beyond the prison walls and moved closer towards becoming an organized criminal outfit, specializing in extortion, drug trafficking and so forth. In 1971, Joe Morgan became the godfather of the MM. It was the same year that the MM first reached out into the streets, committing its first street execution, that of Alfonso 'Apache' Alvarez in the suburb of Monterey Park. Morgan was a forbidding presence, even with only one leg. He was tall (1.9 metres/6 ft 2 in.), bald, muscular and, peculiarly, of Croatian or Hungarian descent. He was supposedly blessed with a 'near genius IQ', although his rap sheet consisted of numerous convictions for murder, bank robbery and other crimes. Besides the distinction of being of either Hungarian or Croatian descent in a Mexican gang, he also entered prison at the advanced age of forty. One writer described Morgan as 'Caucasian by birth but Mexican by choice'.[44]

Convicted of second-degree murder while still in his teens, Morgan was sent to Folsom prison. He had already lost his right leg from a gunshot wound and wore a prosthesis, earning the infrequently used nickname 'Pegleg'. According to a 1977 article in *New West*, he lost the leg to a bone infection and it was amputated below the knee, but somehow, he still became the prison handball champ.[45] By the late 1960s he had been christened with the Aztec moniker 'Cocoliso'. He almost immediately began hanging out with the Hispanics in the yard. But the 1950s was a time when the convict code and subculture had not yet been riven by racial gangs and politics. Although inmates were segregated by race in their living accommodation, there was not yet the racial animosity that would dominate prison yards in the 1960s. Most of the convicts in Folsom were white in this era.

Morgan was paroled out in 1955. In 1961, when he was sent to San Quentin, he had attained almost legendary status, having escaped prison four times, brandished a machine gun during a bank robbery and served fourteen years mostly at Folsom prison.[46] At the zenith of Morgan's power he was referred to as the MM 'godfather' by law enforcement and the media.

### Sureños and the MM

In the late 1960s, the emergence of La Nuestra Familia, the Black Guerrilla Family and the Aryan Brotherhood cut into MM control and established competition for various prison rackets. But the increasing incarceration of young Hispanic street-gang members from southern California, the *Sureños*, revived the strength of the gang at a time when it needed increased support. MM members have been identified in prisons across the United States. There has been some confusion among authorities and researchers as to the actual relationship between the *Sureños* and the Mexican Mafia. Prison experts today consider these two separate phenomena.

In order to become a true member of the MM, a prospect must kill or seriously injure a target identified by group leaders. More prominent MM members display the symbol of a Black Hand, or *La Eme*, in some form on their bodies. Conversely, there are few requirements for becoming a *Sureño*, apart from being of Hispanic heritage. Many are born in gang neighbourhoods and effectively 'born into the gang', stepping into a tradition established by relatives. Others simply relocate from south of the border and join the gang. Its street-gang members are often identified with the symbols XIII, X3, 13 and three dots – all inferring the 13th letter

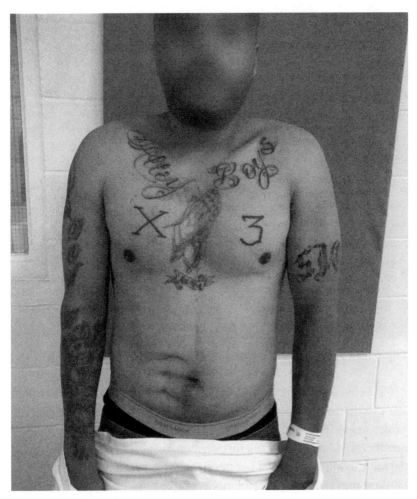

A *Sureño* gang member arrested near Rio Bravo in 2018.

of the alphabet – M, for Mexican Mafia. Other identifiers include the colour blue and the words *Sureño*, *Sur* and 'Southerner'.

One gang authority asserted that 'La Eme [M, short for Mexican Mafia] was the foundation of the Sureños,' whose name would become shorthand for southern California gang members.[47] La Eme issued an edict to southern California street gangs in 1992, ordering them to pay a percentage of money gained from illegal activities to the gang. This tax was ostensibly to help each gang's members when they went to prison. Many of the gangs were cowed by the MM control of the drug trade and its brutal reputation, but some Latino gangs, such as Mara Salvatrucha (MS-13), were not intimidated and did not share their lucre.

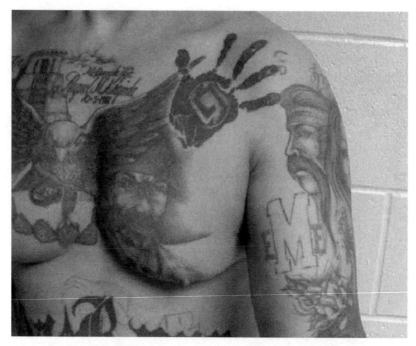

Tattoos of a Mexican Mafia member, including the Black Hand symbol.

This led to conflict between MS-13, the MM and the gangs that paid MM tribute. To maintain its status, MM put a 'green light' on non-paying gangs, essentially declaring open season to kill or injure any of their members. According to gang investigator Al Valdez, 'The opposition to paying the Mexican Mafia tax nevertheless grew to a point that some Latino gangs started calling themselves "green lighters".'[48] They revelled in their 'tax-free' status, going as far as advertising their stance with tattoos that included words such as 'tax-free' and 'green light'. It was not uncommon to see graffiti in some areas boasting that they were a 'tax-free neighborhood'.[49]

It was during this era that Joe Morgan gave out an order to *Sureño* street gangs 'to stop drive-by shootings and other gang violence, a development the media helpfully publicized.'[50] From the outside this was translated as some type of 'gang truce'. However, gang defectors would later admit that the edict was a ruse to allow the MM 'to infiltrate every street gang and put a representative in place to enforce the collection of taxes'. One defector admitted: 'we really had it planned out that California would be carved up . . . into slices, with each member receiving an organizational turf'. Thus, 'by monopolizing the use of violence', the MM sought to extend control over street gangs and control drug traffic in southern California.[51]

However, if there was any hope that the violence would calm down, in 1992 some 803 gang-related murders were recorded, compared to 771 the year before. Nonetheless, the MM remained influential. Indeed, between April and September 1992, in the aftermath of the edict, there were no drive-by shootings in East Los Angeles, a phenomenon rare for the era. In 1993 MS-13 had settled the tribute issue with the MM and aligned itself with other *Sureño* gangs. The MM and MS-13 cliques soon shared the number '13' as an identifier along with their gang name to signify gang alliance.

MM members have at one time or another partnered up with Italian syndicates and the Aryan Brotherhood. The MM's foremost prison rivals are the Black Guerrilla Family, black street gangs and its main enemy, La Nuestra Familia. As previously mentioned, it often throws in its lot with the Aryan Brotherhood for business and security purposes. Interestingly, it reputedly provides protection to imprisoned La Cosa Nostra members, such as the late John Gotti, former boss of the New York City Gambino crime family. Women and relatives play an important role as couriers for drug and financial activities. The gang's main criminal activities include drug trafficking, extortion and maintaining internal discipline. The MM has won a hard-earned reputation for violence and horrific contract killings.

### Rene Enriquez: From *Carnal* to Informant

One of the best-known and most controversial members of the MM was Rene 'Boxer' Enriquez. He spent a decade (1993–2003) in the Security Housing Unit (SHU) at Pelican Bay. Sentenced to three consecutive life terms for carrying out hits at San Quentin and Folsom, he next attempted another hit in the Men's Central Jail in Los Angeles. Returned to state prison in 1993, he was sent directly to the SHU at Pelican Bay, a place he described as having the 'smell of despair, depression . . . a place where people come to die'. Even in solitary he was able to pass messages to visitors, using letters labelled 'legal mail', which indicated correspondence with his lawyer and were thus exempt from censorship. From the solitary confinement of the Pelican Bay SHU, Enriquez had the clout and wherewithal to orchestrate a gang ceasefire and an end to drive-by shootings. By initiating some stability and peace, it allowed

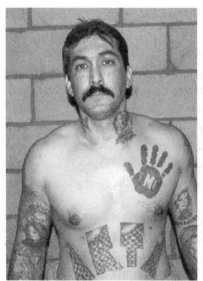

Left: Rene Enriquez at Wasco State Prison in 1997, with the Black Hand tattoo on his chest and the word ARTA on his stomach (short for his original street gang, Artesia 13). Right: Photo of Rene Enriquez in 2015 from the California Department of Corrections and Rehabilitation.

the MM to better control more profitable drug dealing. He was even able to maintain his own heroin habit, finding creative ways to have it smuggled in to him. More importantly, solitary confinement meant he was safe from rivals who wanted him dead.[52]

By his ninth year in total isolation, having had no physical contact with friends and family, no sight of the sun or moon, and having survived a heroin overdose, Enriquez became increasingly frustrated with the gang's 'arbitrary targeting of families' by *carnales*, and was in the throes of what he described as 'mob fatigue'. In 2002 he contacted gang investigators and instantly put his life in jeopardy as he was debriefed on the secrets of the MM. News of his defection spread rapidly through the prison grapevine and he was moved into protective custody. According to a special agent with the California Department of Corrections and Rehabilitation, 'For the first time we had a Mexican Mafia member defect that was really able to lay out for us how the organization works, the organizational structure.'[53] Over the following year, Enriquez collaborated with law enforcement, listening to and decoding MM wiretaps, testifying as a witness and expert, and even leading conference and training sessions for law enforcement across the U.S. His story is well

Aerial shot of Pelican Bay State prison, 2009.

documented in Chris Blatchford's 2008 book *The Black Hand*, and in several reference books Enriquez co-authored.[54]

### The FBI and the Mexican Mafia

During the late 1960s and early 1970s, the FBI was enmeshed in a campaign against numerous left-wing organizations. By the 1970s, according to the FBI, the MM had become increasingly sophisticated, '[putting] together an efficient intelligence organization, pools of sympathetic lawyers ... [using] revolutionary groups for its own ends, and [taking] over respectable Mexican-American social action groups'.[55] Early on, the federal agency recognized a number of its signature rules, including 'blood in, blood out' status and membership restrictions. Notwithstanding the fact that the FBI understood that the gang represented 'truly organized crime in its embryonic stages', in one teletype to the San Francisco office of the FBI, the MM was also referred to as 'a Mexican revolutionary group in CDC allied with Aryan Brotherhood'.[56]

As it quickly expanded in the 1970s, the MM made the transition to a criminal enterprise. By the early part of the decade the FBI was investigating it for organized crime activity, including loan sharking, drug trafficking and the use of violence to enforce their activities.[57] In the mid-1970s, MM brothers and affiliates began targeting drug rehab centres that were funded by local and federal agencies. In the early 1970s, MM took in millions in federal grant monies destined for drug rehab programmes, thanks to its perspicacious co-founder Cadena. They hired parolees as drug counsellors and 'ghost workers', who were paid but never showed up for work. It also gave them access to hundreds, perhaps thousands, of heroin addicts to whom they could sell dope.[58]

In the 1970s the FBI began investigating the MM as an extremist group, as is made clear in a memorandum relating to Cadena. The special agent in charge of the San Francisco office sent FBI director Clarence Kelley an enclosure referring to the Mexican Mafia and its 'Participation in civil disturbances, anti-U.S. demonstrations or hostile incidents against foreign diplomatic establishments'.[59] This report related to an investigation into the Mexican Mafia's possible 'violation of Title 18, U.S. Code, Section 2383 (rebellion or insurrection), and Section 2384 (seditious Conspiracy)'. However, the investigation was based on a confidential source 'who has furnished reliable information in the past'. The informant reported that the MM 'uses force and violence in connection with racial problems, advocates violent attacks and disruptive activities against California's Department of Corrections authority, and engages in rebellion, insurrection and destruction at San Quentin prison'.[60] What stands out about this FBI memorandum is the early mention of MM's reach 'outside the correctional system'. The 'reliable' source reported a month prior to the FBI report that the members had 'grouped themselves into organizations that reflect their ethnic background and language'. Moreover, the group was established to both protect Hispanic prisoners and maintain control of illegal activities within prison walls and on the streets, including narcotics, extortion, contract killing, robbery, forgery and receiving. Also, it was able to control the narcotics traffic and so forth through 'crimes committed by members on the outside'.[61]

In 1974 Kelley reported to the U.S. Secret Service that the MM was 'potentially dangerous' and engaged in 'activities inimical to the U.S.' Until his death Cadena was probably the most respected member of the gang, and if FBI informants in the gang could be believed, he had a 'long range plan for the organization to first gain the confidence and support of the Mexican American community of East Los Angeles, by assisting in the "Chicano" movements'. If his scheme went as planned, the gang 'would move into the criminal activity, using the total community as a "front"'. Put another way, the 'Chicano movement was a good mask to conceal the operations of the Mexican Mafia'.[62]

In 1971 the first known MM-authorized hit on the streets targeted an inactive member named Alton Alvarez, also known as 'Apache', a founder and director of Los Pintos La Raza (Convicts of the Mexican People). By most accounts this group was a front for MM. According to the FBI informant, Alvarez was executed for muscling in on drug traffickers under the name of the MM and was collecting extortion money without sharing with members inside.

FBI reports in the 1970s reflect the turbulent times and paranoia on the part of the government whenever an organization was linked to revolutionary activity, whether it was the Black Panthers or the MM. One of the most exaggerated memoranda asserted that 'Maoists have captured the interest of the gangs, who see themselves as oppressed members of the third world ready to join the revolution'. The Marxist-Leninist-Maoist group the Venceremos,[63] formed in 1970, purportedly wrote to MM members telling them 'to stop their warring and kill "pigs"'.[64]

Although the MM has a fearsome reputation on the streets, 'For most of its history it was primarily a prison gang'.[65] Unlike modern-day outlaw motorcycle gangs, which try to recruit members without a rap sheet, the MM rarely inducted a new member who had never been incarcerated in the LA County Jail. By most accounts, older MM members still refer to the facility as 'headquarters'. Among its most lucrative prison rackets are drug smuggling and collecting cell taxes from other inmates. The influence of the MM behind bars is significant in California, leading one correctional officer to admit, 'We don't run the prison. They do. We're not the enemy, we're just referees' providing housing and services.[66]

### American Me

The making of the film *American Me* demonstrated that when it came to the Mexican Mafia there was no such thing as literary licence. It opened in 1992 to little acclaim and crashed at the box office. However, it garnered much more attention after it 'triggered a wave of unexpected aftershocks, drawing [actor Edward James] Olmos into a real-life drama that echoes the treachery he portrayed on the screen'.[67] Soon after its release three of the film's consultants were murdered

*American Me* (1992), directed by and starring Edward James Olmos (centre).

execution-style. Since the killings took place in the violence-ravaged barrios of East Los Angeles, it was not immediately clear if they were related to the movie.

This fictional portrait of the Mexican Mafia was considered blasphemous by its members.[68] Eagerly anticipated by the *Sureño* community, the opening of the film introduced the Mexican Mafia's power outside the prison walls to a much larger audience. A thinly veiled film about the creation of the MM, it was given the typical Hollywood makeover, rife with embellishment and exaggeration. Following its release Olmos, its star and director, was alerted by the U.S. Marshals Service that the MM had placed a contract on him and several of his consultants. Several months later he had a meeting with MM contract killer Ramon 'Mundo' Mendoza to get an 'insider's assessment' of the danger he was in. At the time, Mendoza was living under the government's witness security programme after testifying against the MM in court.

Mendoza informed Olmos that he had 'insulted his former comrades' sense of honour, depicting one of their most revered leaders being sodomized in jail, impotent with a woman and knifed by his own brothers – sacrilege to a secret society that equates disrespect with death'.[69] He warned Olmos not to underestimate 'these people . . . If they are obsessed with getting to you there's nothing you can do to stop it.'

The three murders linked to the film began on 25 March 1992, when Charles 'Charlie Brown' Manriquez was shot dead in a Los Angeles housing project by an MM member. He was shot six times with a 9mm weapon, but it had probably been only a matter of time till he met his maker, since he was already on the gang's hit list for having failed to complete a hit at Chino State Prison. Manriquez had survived a prison stabbing, but once paroled out he was shunned by his former brothers. At the time of his death, he was a homeless drug addict, and might have remained a low priority on the hit list if he had not been hired by the film-maker for 'technical advice'.

The next victim was ambushed and killed outside her home on 13 May 1992. Ana Lizzaraga was a prominent gang counsellor, and was preparing to drive to her mother's funeral in Utah when she was shot. She had been working as liaison between gang members, community representatives and the police, and had been suspected for years of relaying gang intelligence to the Los Angeles Police Department. Lizzaraga was known as the 'gang lady' to the 'Big Hazard' gang members who had the contract on her. She had made the mistake of falsely claiming she had visited Morgan in prison and had received permission to consult on the film if Morgan was not portrayed with a limp. Apparently, the film-makers made light of the prosthetic limb.

The final victim, Manuel 'Rocky' Luna, long known as the 'godfather' of the 'Big Hazard' gang, was executed on 7 August 1993. Until he became a crack addict and assisted on the film, he had been a respected gang member. It is worth noting here that all three victims had existing political issues with the MM or the Hispanic community at the time of their deaths.

The irony over the bloody fallout from the film was that the film-makers had hoped the fictionalized portrait of the gang would act as a deterrent to gang recruitment, but the converse occurred, as more prospects came into the orbit of the gang thanks to the unintended consequences of the film. It should probably be no surprise that the film was banned inside prisons. On 19 April 1993, Morgan sued Olmos and Universal Studios for $500,000 over his depiction. It is unknown whether this was ever satisfactorily settled.

## Norteños: La Nuestra Familia

The MM thirst for power and control did not go unchallenged. Not as well known as La Eme, but just as deadly, La Nuestra Familia (NF), 'Our Family', emerged in the California state prison system some time in 1967 or 1968. Tired of being extorted and manhandled, a group of northern California Mexican inmates responded by forming a new prison gang at Soledad Prison. While some of its earliest members might have come from Los Angeles, most were from the more rural communities of northern and central California. At its peak it was among the most organized prison gangs in America. Its structure was inspired by the military. As it became more structured, its rules grew more rigid, enforcing strict standards of dress, hygiene and conduct. In the 1970s it grew and expanded on to the streets of northern Californian cities, particularly in its home base in Fresno.

While the Mexican Mafia and other *Sureños* held the upper hand initially, the *Norteños*-linked NF responded by adopting a paramilitary set-up made up of a general at the top of the command structure, followed in descending order by captains, lieutenants, squad leaders, squad members or soldiers and recruits. A constitution was also created. *Norteños* can be identified by the number 14, representing N, the 14th letter in the alphabet. Other symbols include vIv, x$ and four dots.

## La Nuestra Familia in the 1970s

The NF had roughly six hundred members and associates by the mid-1970s, and, like its main rival, the MM, it adopted a policy of quality over quantity when it came to increasing its ranks. By this time the prison gang was well situated in rackets that included protection, extortion, prostitution and drugs and weapons trafficking. Following a particularly bloody showdown between the two gangs, they were separated into different Californian prisons, which, as demonstrated in other chapters, only resulted in a boom in recruitment for both gangs.

In 1976, the NF branched out to the hard streets of Fresno, where it organized a 'regiment' led by recently released *carnales*. Once outside, veteran gang members entered into an alliance with local Chicano street-gang members. Unrestricted by the prison regime, NF members trained the earnest gang members in how to extort business owners, using the NF reputation to sell street protection. The NF also began taxing street dealers. By controlling drug trafficking in the area, the gang's wealth rose as well. Co-opting prison staff to traffic drugs inside the prisons, NF members received a return of four to five times that on the streets. However, by bringing their organized crime activities to the streets, it was only a matter of time before they attracted the attention of the authorities, and in 1982 some 25 NF members were indicted for a litany of acts including extortion, robbery, drug trafficking, murder and witness intimidation. The NF became the first prison gang federally indicted for violating the Racketeer Influenced and Corrupt Organizations (RICO) act.[70]

What facilitated the government's case was the testimony of defectors, and in the end, only a handful of gang leaders escaped indictment. The RICO indictments and the testimony of informers were a hard lesson, but one the NF would learn. A strategy was conceived to better insulate leading NF members. By most accounts, a 'diversionary' NF was created in the hope that the Feds would take to their scent, allowing the real power structure to operate in peace. The decoy NF, however, was trusted with vetting the ever-ready recruitment pool. This 'Northern Structure', as it was originally dubbed in the 1980s, was expected to evaluate any potential recruit closely before allowing him to join. Later some members sought out another name that would put it more in line with the gang's Hispanic roots, calling it Nuestra Raza, 'Our Race'. At the time it was hoped the 'name would throw off law enforcement while its members forged the NF's first ties to the streets'. Once able to run street activities from behind the walls of Folsom, they would be able to share the illicit income generated on the streets.[71]

### Restructuring of NF

In the meantime, NF was restructured under the direction of Robert 'Black Bob' Vasquez. The new scheme featured a Regimental Security Department (RSD) as its new security arm. The RSD provides intelligence and security for the gang by maintaining contact on the outside with associates who gather information for the inmate members. It is not uncommon for wives or relatives of members to find employment in government offices, such as the Department of Motor Vehicles, law-enforcement agencies, correctional institutions and utility companies, where they can gain access to confidential information that might shed more light on prospective and current members. In so doing, they can tap into any number of databases and establish a 'foolproof' system for vetting new members or gaining information that could be used to blackmail adversaries.[72]

The RICO case against NF made the gang's shot-callers more aware that law enforcement was almost able to destroy the organization simply because gang members at all levels were privy to gang leaders and their enterprises. This was a major flaw that needed correcting. The first step was to establish three levels of rank, in an effort to obscure the identity of ranking members. Category I comprises new members or returning members, who are given the opportunity to advance, but are barred from knowing the identities of higher members. At this point, prospects receive their basic training and education, which includes reading Sun Tzu's *The Art of War*. Promotion to Category II leads a member to advanced training in the criminal arts and the appointment of squad leaders, but recruits at this level are still cognizant of the membership of the bottom two categories.

The leading NF cohort belongs to Category III, which includes RSD staff, lieutenants and commanders. At Category III, *familianos* make decisions to be passed down the food chain. The next highest level is La Mesa, dominated by no more than ten captains. According to gang expert Bill Valentine, at the turn of the twenty-first century, all the captains were housed at the Pelican Bay maximum-security prison.

On the highest rung of the hierarchy is the General or Nuestro General, who is typically selected by the outgoing General. He has the power to sign treaties, start wars and promote or demote officers. Those in Category III are the only members with knowledge of the entire organization. The rank of lieutenant is attainable for a soldier who makes a name for himself by completing several hits.

The gang maintains a detailed enemies list, or directory, known as the 'Bad News List'. It typically contains the names of defectors, snitches, witnesses and enemy gang leaders who are to be systematically eliminated. Protocol is for the gang shot-caller to check the names of new prison arrivals against the record book. When a soldier is transferred to another prison a copy of the directory is sent with him.[73]

Ultimately, the NF's targeted recruitment pool includes proven street-gang members, preferably ex-convicts from northern California, whose 'papers' can be easily checked, establishing their bona fides such as prior street-gang membership, crimes committed and murder victims. These have to be checked and approved by the gang recruiters.

The NF's constitution and its list of fourteen rules state that only northern Hispanic recruits are welcome. Members refer to each other as *carnales*, Cs or *familianos*. They follow a 'blood in, blood out' policy, and members are expected to go to war at any time. But before one is fully accepted, he is expected to finish a prisoner education programme in which he is taught how to manufacture and conceal weapons, carry out defensive strategies and lethal striking techniques, escape from handcuffs, use non-verbal communication, and employ coded writing for business and security purposes.[74]

The NF's paramilitary leanings require a member to present a well-groomed appearance, make his bed each morning, wear shoes when awake and not fall asleep before lockdown (for personal protection). *Carnales* can be identified by the colour red and have a standing policy to attack MM on sight. For anyone who shirks their responsibilities, shows cowardice or attempts to leave the gang, death is waiting. NF soldiers have been known to hit friends and even brothers. There are few places to hide when you are targeted for a hit. Rival gang members have been killed on the prison yard while being escorted by officers. One ploy adopted to complete an unfinished hit is for a prospect who did not kill the assigned target on his first attempt to ask to be placed in protective custody, where he can finish the blooding that will lead to his full membership.

### The Texas Syndicate and the Mexican Mafia of Texas

The Texas Syndicate is a Texas-based prison gang that includes mostly Hispanic members and on rare occasions allows Caucasian members to join. More so than the MM and NF, the Texas Syndicate has been associated or allied with Mexican immigrant prisoners; the others tend to associate with U.S.-born or -raised Hispanics.

Texas street gangs have a long history and have influenced the development of prison gangs in the state. By the 1960s, the old-school norms of prison life were rapidly fading. Some recent researchers have suggested that Fred Carrasco, aka 'the Heroin King', 'bridged the era',

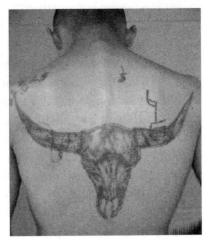

Texas Syndicate tattoos.

ushering in the age of 'extreme and merciless tactics of prison gangs'.[75] Carrasco's influence was especially evident in the 1980s, when Texas prison gangs were operating on both sides of prison walls. During these years, the prison system was dealing with the incarceration binge brought about by the continuing drug war's increasingly punitive policies. This was timely for the development of gangs, because the surge in inmates ensured a ready supply of potential members, leading to the 'fiercest and most capable barrio criminals' taking charge of these gangs. Chicano prison gangs emerged much later in Texas than in California, but when they did they were on the top rungs of the hierarchy.[76]

The Carrasco syndicate introduced some of the strategies used to terrorize the competition and discipline those within the ranks of the organization in the 1970s, a 'brand of violence that would become widespread among Chicano prison gangs in Texas throughout the 80s and 90s'. Moreover, 'one of the most compelling arguments to support this theory was the strong geographical connection between the Carrasco group and the most prominent of the Central Texas prison gangs, Mexikanemi.'[77]

San Antonio is the home base of the Texas MM. The researcher Mike Tapia found that children of the 1950s and '60s barrio gang members became prison-gang members in one of three major groups operating in the area in the 1980s – MM, Texas Syndicate and Los Pistoleros. But there is still much debate over whether the MM in Texas grew out of the Carrasco group. Some argue that it was more a case of Mexican gang members emulating the California Eme model, which had originated more than twenty years earlier.[78]

Mexikanemi (Free Mexicans), better known as the Mexican Mafia of Texas, formed in early 1984 in the Texas prison system. Highly structured at first, at its peak it had an estimated 2,000 members, mostly Mexican nationals or Mexican Americans living in Texas at the time of their incarceration. When it was created, the Mexican Mafia was considered the largest gang in the Texas Department of Corrections (TDC). According to the TDC, it originated as a group of inmates interested in becoming more aware of their cultural heritage. However, it quickly morphed into a criminal organization more concerned with extortion, drug trafficking and murder than cultural heritage. It wasn't long before it was committing these acts inside and out of prison. Its Constitution states upfront:

In being a criminal organization we will function in any aspect of criminal interest for the benefit or advancement of Mexikanemi [La Eme]. We will traffic in drugs, contracts of assassination, prostitution, robbery of high magnitude, and in anything we can imagine.[79]

Similar to the original MM, it is structured along paramilitary lines with a president, vice-president, and generals mostly responsible for the rules and guidelines they are bound to. According to an early informant, there were initially three generals, each of whom was responsible for a specific geographical region of Texas. At this time lieutenants were selected by the president or vice-president to oversee certain cities as well as specific TDC units.

## White Supremacist Prison Gangs

In the 1960s white supremacist prison gangs were created in the U.S. to protect Caucasian inmates from non-white inmates. Over the years they have engaged in murder, assault and identity theft, and have been prominent in meth trafficking. Although the Aryan Brotherhood is the main example, there are numerous smaller Caucasian gangs scattered in prisons across the country. Among them are Dead Man Incorporated, founded in the Maryland Correctional System; European Kindred, founded in Oregon; and Public Enemy Number One, considered by some observers as the fastest growing of them all. Its four to five hundred members are allied with the Aryan Brotherhood and the Nazi Low Riders on the streets of California and elsewhere.

### The Aryan Brotherhood

A journalist once described the Aryan Brotherhood (AB) as 'the most murderous prison gang in America'.[80] In its halcyon years this was certainly true, but times have changed, and many of its leaders are now cloistered in maximum-security prisons. However, few would argue that the AB was, at one time or another, the most prominent white supremacist prison gang. Its influences range from Irish/Celtic folklore and neo-Nazi ideology to Satanism, exemplified (perhaps) by the popularity of the 666 tattoos. Sinn Fein, Gaelic for 'we stand alone', and the political wing of the Irish Republican Army at one time, also carries weight. With shaved heads, physical conditioning, tattoos and so forth, ABS are

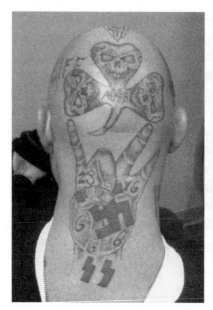

Tattoos of members of the Aryan Brotherhood.

instantly recognizable behind bars, where nothing is more important than being recognized by friends and foes in prison corridors and on the yard – emphasis on appearance is a must.

The AB originated in San Quentin prison in the mid-1960s, at a time of acute racial tension. Its membership is restricted to whites and it was initially formed to protect them from minority inmates. Best known for their racist inclinations, the ABS 'are motivated less by furthering their die-hard racist ideology than satisfying their crude greed'.[81] In the early 2000s the group was considered one of the nation's most violent prison gangs. It has had a long alliance with the Mexican Mafia against their mutual enemies in La Nuestra Familia and the Black Guerrilla Family. In recent years diverse authorities, from law enforcement to the Anti-Defamation League, have likened the AB to a criminal syndicate responsible for violent attacks, drug trafficking and other illegal enterprises.

*Precursors of the Aryan Brotherhood*

The AB originated as the Diamond Tooth Gang, so called for the practice of embedding diamond-shaped pieces of glass into their teeth. Its next incarnation was as the Bluebird Gang; all members were required to have a bluebird tattoo on their necks. In 1968 the AB was formed out of the hardcore Bluebird members, together with assorted bikers and neo-Nazis. It was then that they gravitated to white supremacist ideology and adopted a paramilitary structure. AB members are recognizable for a tattoo of a three-leaf clover, with the number 666 across the leaves and underscored by the letters AB.[82]

Unlike most other prison gangs, which continually recruit to increase their numbers, the ABs limit their membership to the most powerful and violent inmates, who are expected to kill on command. Being more cloistered than other gangs allowed the AB to slip under the radar, effectively operating with impunity for years.[83] Like many other prison gangs, the ABs have a 'blood in, blood out' rule.

Numbering only about one hundred, the original AB group managed to stake its claim as the deadliest prison gang by declaring 'open season' on all black inmates regardless of their affiliations. By the early 1970s, California's prison system was beset by an unparalleled spate of murders and violent gang assaults instigated by ABs. Along with establishing its dominance, the AB also took over most of the prison rackets, including protection, extortion, drugs and weapons trafficking, and contract killings.

Until 1977 the ABs were active only in the California prison system. However, as several of its leaders were convicted of federal racketeering this led to its expansion inside the federal prison system as well. It was at this point that the Aryan Brotherhood was divided into the California AB and the federal AB.[84] This expansion allowed it to take control of existing gambling and drug activities in the federal prison system by taxing these existing rings under the threat of death.

The AB has also allowed the creation of unaffiliated splinter groups, which use the name of their state with the AB moniker, as in 'Aryan Brotherhood of Texas'. The Texas version of the Aryan Brotherhood has perhaps 3,500 members, mostly outside prison walls.[85] However, ABs in federal and California prisons do not regard them as true members and have even gone so far as to threaten violence if 'copycat members' do not cut or burn off AB tattoos. In October 2014 one member was sentenced to fifteen years in federal prison for using a blowtorch to burn tattoos off the ribcage of a former member.[86] In another case, he was part of a crew that made a non-member burn an AB tattoo off his own body.[87] It should be remembered that while members wear tattoos such as neo-Nazi symbols (swastikas, lightning bolts), the most coveted is the patch.

The blowtorch victims boasted tattoos with a shield and a sword, and a swastika with the letters A and B above it and 'Texas' below.

Prison authorities once dismissed the AB as a 'fringe white supremacist gang', but eventually awakened to the fact that the gang 'had gradually taken control of large parts of the nation's maximum-security prisons, ruling over thousands of inmates and transforming themselves into a powerful criminal organization'.[88] By the 1980s, the AB, or 'Brand', had established drug-trafficking, prostitution and extortion rackets in prisons throughout the nation. Perhaps one member put it best, explaining that the gang was 'no longer about destroying the minorities of the world, white supremacy and all that shit. It's a criminal organization, first and foremost.'[89]

By the 1980s, the gang had a well-established reputation for violence. Even when housed in isolation units, members were able to lure enemies into close quarters for fatal stabbings. In other cases members have been tied to the murder of federal prison guards and coordinated executions of civilians by recently released members.[90] Between 1970 and 1987 over three hundred inmates were murdered in the California prison system, a disproportionate number of them at Folsom prison. These numbers did not drop until the late 1980s and the 1990s. Beginning in the 1980s newly released members began forming street-gang operations. Originally a 20 per cent flat-tax policy was created, requiring one-fifth of the lucre derived from AB-affiliated operations on the street to be deposited into accounts supervised by a 'de facto banking system', and laundered through a variety of legitimate businesses.[91]

In 1992 the AB's street activities were given increased credibility after Gambino Mafia boss John Gotti was sentenced to life in prison at the maximum-security federal penitentiary in Marion, Illinois, 'a longtime AB stronghold'. It was there that Gotti hired ABs to protect him, allowing them to coordinate street activities with Mafia crews. One former AB leader characterized this rapprochement as follows:

> We could tap into his resources up in New York, so when we needed glassware or whatever to set up [methamphetamine] labs, hey, his crews have righteous [legitimate] businesses through their unions that can get all the glasswork, all the chemicals, and you know, the beat just went on from there.[92]

Since the mid-1990s, prison authorities have been able to disrupt many of the AB's criminal activities. In response, the gang began recruiting young white males imprisoned in juvenile institutions to act as middlemen. In so doing they created a new gang that became known as the Nazi Low Riders. Their association with the AB allowed them to extend their power in prison and on the outside, basically conducting the criminal activities that the AB could not accomplish in isolation at maximum-security prisons.

By the late 1990s law enforcement noticed that the AB had expanded its racketeering activities outside the prison walls. The AB recruited paroled members and affiliates to operate drug- and weapon-trafficking schemes, and to commit contract killings. Although the ABs are racist this has not prevented them from using black associates to buy and sell drugs to black prisoners, once again proving that the gang's ideology often comes second to promoting criminal activity.

In 2006 four alleged leaders of the AB went on trial on racketeering charges. The federal prosecutor told jurors that the gang ordered members to start a war against a black gang that left two dead within twelve hours. Prosecutors described how two federal inmates received a letter in 1997 with a message written in invisible ink, ordering them to begin a war against a black gang. When the note was heated the inmates read the message: 'War with D.C. from T.D.' The initials referred to the DC Blacks, an African American prison gang that started in the Washington, DC, area, and the first two initials of AB leader Tyler Davis 'The Hulk' Bingham, currently in prison for robbery and drug trafficking.[93] According to the indictment, it was alleged that gang members had been involved in 32 murders and attempted murders since the mid-1970s, most of them directed by the men on trial. More than a dozen other defendants faced the death penalty at trials coming up, and nineteen others had already accepted plea bargains. The attorney for one of the suspected ringleaders noted, 'The reality is, federal penitentiaries are violent and dangerous places and all of these guys – white guys – are a small minority and they're just trying to survive.'[94]

According to AB recruitment policy, emphasis is on physical appearance, including a shaved head, tattoos and a well-conditioned body. Contrary to popular belief, members apparently do not get on with the Hells Angels, although they share similar white supremacist views. The AB is paranoid about informants, so prospective members must show 'government-issued proof of their criminal credentials', which means their FBI-issued arrest records that include convictions and sentences.[95] The AB has used a classic self-defence strategy when accused of murder, which involves allowing members to act as their own lawyers. When this strategy works, it permits them to oversee subpoenas and witness lists and coordinate efforts to get other members into courthouse holding cells, where they can plan and carry out violence against potential witnesses.[96]

### Aryan Brotherhood of Texas

Founded in Texas in the 1980s, mainly as a criminal enterprise, the Aryan Brotherhood of Texas does not have ties to the original AB. Despite claims of solidarity, members have been arrested for hurting fellow brothers, going as far as torching tattoos off bodies, hacking fingers off corpses to keep as trophies, and ordering the deaths of informants to be as 'messy as possible'. Members are rewarded for these acts with sought-after tattoos that include the AB motto, 'God Forgives, Brothers Don't.'[97]

Like its national incarnation, the Texas version is very militaristic in structure, with generals, majors and officers who command soldiers. As with most prominent prison gangs, any member who ignores instructions can expect punishments ranging from fines to death. The Texas ABs are careful to weed out potential informants before they even join the gang. Like the national AB, ABT prospects have to offer their so-called 'resumes of bad deeds' to ensure they are who they say they are.[98] In the 1980s prospects were required to be Texas natives. While the gang tolerated killers, kidnappers and drug dealers, by most accounts child molesters and rapists were regarded with the highest disdain and would do well to avoid AB members in prison.

The bureaucratic process of joining the ABT includes an application form that mimics its free-world counterparts. Called a Form 12 (the 1 is for the A in Aryan and 2 for the B in Brotherhood), it is expected to accompany an FBI criminal-history background check, as the gang leaders probe deeper into the backgrounds of prospective members. Years behind bars have given veteran gang members the acumen to spot red flags or signs that a prospect has snitched during previous jail stints. This is done by checking the amount of time someone served for the crime he committed. If he was released early (or easily), he would probably be perceived as a government informant who made a deal for early release.[99]

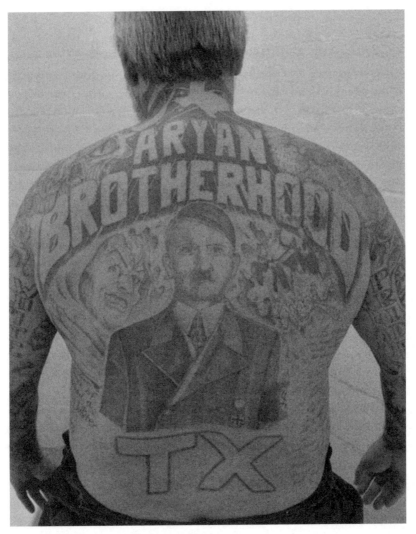

A member of the Aryan Brotherhood of Texas.

The Texas AB divides the state into five territories. Heavy emphasis is placed on physical sanctions, with the worst punishments doled out to members who cross the gang. One member and his girlfriend, for example, were shot in the head. Joining the gang is never taken lightly, since it is a lifelong proposition, as is made clear by the signing of a 'Blind Faith Agreement', in which the member promises to follow all rules and be a member for life.[100]

*Nazi Low Riders*

According to the Anti-Defamation League (ADL), the Nazi Low Riders (NLR) originated as a skinhead gang in the California Youth Authority in the late 1970s and early 1980s. Its rise in prominence has been helped along by its alliance with the Aryan Brotherhood. It is considered one of the newer incarnations of white prison gangs, and while it does promote white superiority, it is probably just as driven by lucrative criminal activities that include extortion, armed robbery and drug trafficking. By some accounts the gang adopted its moniker as 'an act of one-upmanship', by taking the term 'low riders', associated with Hispanic gangs.[101]

Once the California Department of Corrections had 'successfully suppressed AB's activities', the NLR went from middlemen for the older gang to filling the void left by the AB in California's prison-gang hierarchy. By 2000 there were, according to the FBI, at least 1,500 NLR members behind bars and hundreds on the streets. Their tattoo identifiers include swastikas, ss lightning bolts and 'NLR'. Some members prefer other Nazi-related adornments, while still others stick with tattoos of eagles, skulls, demons and references to Hitler, such as 88 and HH. Less noticeable are various white-power abbreviations such as WSU (White Student Union) and AYM (Aryan Youth Movement).[102]

The gang is known for its ferocious attacks on individuals of colour in California, and continues its 'status-seeking violence' behind bars as well. In 1999, two NLR members being held in a holding cell with a black inmate were able to slip their shackles and slash his face and neck. In the indictment that followed, the two gang members, while they did not actually succeed in killing the black inmate, were charged with assaulting him 'for the purpose of maintaining and increasing their positions in the NLR'.[103] When the California prison system changed the NLR classification to 'disruptive gang', authorities were free to implement a more restrictive regime to impede their activities. Members were taken out of the general prison population and housed separately, allowing the authorities to cut off their drug-trafficking and extortion revenue streams. In response the NLR allied with Public Enemy Number One Skins (PEN1skins), who acted as middlemen for the NLR operations (as with the way the alliance between the AB and the NLR began). And, like the NLR, the PEN1skins increased their prominence on the streets and behind bars.

The NLR operates according to a 'three-tier hierarchy'. The most common structure is for an NLR unit to be led by seniors, many tracing their membership back to the California Youth Authority. In order to reach this level, one must be an active member for five years and be selected by three other members. Next in descending order are the juniors, who do not have the clout to bring in new members. Finally, it is the seniors who bring in and mentor new recruits called 'kids', usually associated with white supremacist gangs such as the PEN1skins.[104]

Although the gang has a predilection for Nazi iconography, the ADL suggests that anti-Semitism 'has not figured in its actions'. The term Aryan Brotherhood instead is used 'to flaunt its whiteness'. Since the ABs have been segregated from the general prison population, there are members of the NLR who view all white prison gangs as subordinate to them. Nonetheless, the links between the two groups remain strong, despite a growing number in the NLR (but still a minority) who advocate breaking ties with the AB and seeking independence, claiming that the older ABs are 'out of touch with the current scene'.[105]

*Aryan Warriors*

The Aryan Warriors (AW) can trace its origins back to 1973, when a Nevadan convict became familiar with Aryan-influenced prison gangs while doing a stint behind bars in California. The story goes that he later ended up in the Nevada State Prison, where he began spreading the white-power doctrine and tried to begin a prison gang. However, he was disappointed to be rejected in his attempts to receive a charter membership from the California AB. In response, the Nevada group adopted the moniker 'Aryan Warriors'.

With little direction, the gang seemed to be treading water and about to fall apart when a lifer who went by the name of 'the Pope', and had spent several years in California's prisons, began teaching his fellow convicts the cornerstones of white supremacist prison gangs. He promoted physical conditioning, meaning all were expected to 'drive iron' or lift weights and be ready to police other white inmates. This forced the prison administration to put child molesters, snitches and whites who palled up with blacks into protective custody. The Pope emphasized the idea that the gang's enemies were the black inmates, not the guards.[106]

The next step was adopting some form of structure. All the original AWs became soldiers and were awarded a pair of lightning-bolt tattoos inside the left bicep. Any white who wanted to join had to be sponsored by a 'bolt-holder'. His main test for being accepted into the gang was committing a bloody attack on another inmate, or a drug rip-off of a non-member. Once the mission was satisfactorily completed, he earned his bolts. The AWs had a reputation as skilled weapons-makers. Helping to solidify the membership was a member's knowledge that by paying dues he was confident that if he was moved to a different lockup he would be supplied with tobacco and other small luxuries.

The aspiration of any new member was to be a 'horn-holder', just below the leader in rank. They were identifiable by a Viking helmet with horns and the letters AW tattooed on the left upper chest. To earn this distinction the member had 'to commit an attack of great violence', typically targeting a black inmate or someone on the AW hit list.

As the leader of the AW, the Pope created a council of six horn-holders to sit below him. Under the council were the soldiers and prospects. The top shot-callers began angling to take control of the prison rackets, as the gang continued to elaborate on its rules and punishments. Following a poorly conceived hit in 1980, on a suspected informer, fissures began to breach the former solidarity of the membership as several turned informant. It soon spread throughout the prison grapevine that the AWs were falling apart. Other white gangs mocked the turncoats, branding them the 'Aryan Witnesses'.[107] In response to this unexpected turn, members began disassociating themselves from the gang, and even had their bolt and horn tattoos covered with less specific images. Those who turned state witness gained early release; others remained behind bars, wary of their reputation as prison informants (snitches) should they find themselves with former members. Meanwhile, there were members who continued to wear the horns and bolts. By the end of the 1990s there were still some hardcore supporters who hoped there would be a recrudescence, which has yet to come to pass. During its heyday, unlike the Aryan Brotherhood, the AW did use a blood-in mission to join, but members could apparently drop out without fearing reprisals.[108]

To make matters worse, some correctional officers had helped the rival gangs, the AW and the *Sureños*, 'distribute sheets of construction paper saturated with methamphetamine'. Each sheet sold for between $75 and $100. According to one AW who turned state witness, guards would carry compact-disc cases loaded with white powder into prison and slide them under the cell doors of certain prisoners. In other cases, they were accused of opening cell doors so that AWs could attack other inmates, and of passing messages between members.[109]

*Simon City Royals*

Mississippi's Simon City Royals is one of the newer prison gangs on the scene. However, it is distinct from other white prison gangs. It was a white supremacist organization until 1980, when it united with the African American street gang the Gangster Disciples. For most of its existence, since its emergence in Chicago, the Simon City Royals has been mostly prominent as a street gang. Between 2010 and 2015 the gang's membership in Mississippi had risen from 1,200 to 2,000, and it is especially powerful in the southern part of the state. By some accounts the gang is active in thirteen states.

According to an interview with an active member, the Aryan Brotherhood '[tends] to shy away from us. They never understand what Royals are. They think we're white boys that want to be black . . . We usually show out [*sic*] to let them know just cause we're country don't mean we're stupid or that we won't go.' Since it is not uncommon for the Royals to get along with black gangs, some others, such as the Texas Aryan Brotherhood, 'didn't like the fact that I had black homies. We don't carry it like that in Mississippi or in the Simon City Royals.'[110]

Asked to explain how the gang smuggles contraband into prisons, the aforementioned Royal pointed to guards 'trying to be one of us. We've got him convinced we're gonna put him down with us. He's

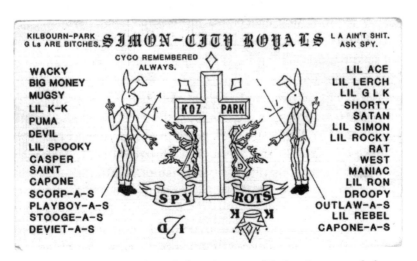

An early Simon City Royals card, featuring one of their primary symbols, a cross with three slashes above. Behind this is a broken flaming cross representing the Almighty Gaylords (a longtime rival gang).

bringing in all kinds of shit: cell phones, weed, meth, whatever we told him ... then he would bring it in.' This particular guard apparently saw how the gang was using him and stopped bringing contraband to the pick-up point at his girlfriend's house. After driving to his girlfriend's house he got out of his car. The guard noticed the house was being watched and ran for his car, but not fast enough, and was hit by a van driven by a Royal. 'After that shit got sweet. The guards were spooked.'[111]

## African American Prison Gangs

The growing politicization of prison inmates in the 1960s, particularly African Americans, was fostered by Black Power and Black Pride, as well as the influence of the Black Muslim movement. At a time when most prisons were segregated, the emergence of the Black Muslim conscious-ness in the 1960s within the nation's prison systems coincided with a newfound appreciation for organization, discipline and politics among black inmates. Prison administrators were so alarmed at the growing solidarity that they began separating Muslim inmates from the rest of the prison population. Threatened by the growing stature of the Black Muslims, in 1962 the American Correctional Association termed the group 'a race hatred group' that was therefore 'unworthy of the recog-nition granted to bona fide religious groups.'[112]

In 1962 a 22-year-old African American inmate named Thomas Cooper, serving a life sentence in Stateville prison (Illinois) for murder, and a recent convert to Islam, changed his name to Thomas X. Cooper and sued the prison's warden, Frank Pate. Cooper had been held in solitary confinement for years and had been denied the use of a Koran. He filed a religious freedom complaint and, against all odds, appeared before the u.s. Supreme Court. In 1964, the court issued the historic ruling *Cooper v. Pate*, a landmark decision with an impact on all the nation's prisoners. The case was followed by an avalanche of prisoner lawsuits protesting at the often barbaric conditions of the prison system, and led to an unprecedented liberalization of the country's correctional institutions.

Prison desegregation and the political awakening among inmates in the 1960s and '70s made these watershed years for the development of prison gangs. With politicization came polarization between racial and ethnic groups, diminishing the more traditional stable prison culture. As a result, prison gangs based on race flourished. However, according to one prison scholar, 'The line between being a political organization or a race based prison gang [was] often blurry, in administrations' perception even if not in practice.'[113]

### Black Guerrilla Family

The Black Guerrilla Family (BGF) originated in San Quentin prison in 1966, founded by the former Black Panther George L. Jackson as the Black Family. Many of its early members had belonged to other revolutionary groups in the 1960s. Jackson was the best-selling author of *Soledad Brother: The Prison Letters of George Jackson* (1969) and was 'a behind-bars affiliate of the Black Panthers'.[114] During his two stints in San Quentin in 1962–8 and 1970–71, he earned a reputation as one of the most dangerous inmates to walk a California prison yard. After having several parole requests denied, and during his continuing indeterminate sentence behind bars, he made the transition to revolutionary. His frustration found intellectual release in the writings of radical theorists such as Karl Marx and Frantz Fanon. Between 1966 and 1971, members of his reading group joined the BGF. Jackson saw the BGF as a revolutionary group, with many of its affiliates maintaining ties to the Black Panther Party. The BGF targeted the rampant racial discrimination of the era while paying close attention to revolutionary theorists.

Following Jackson's death during a failed prison escape attempt in 1971, a power struggle erupted within his gang, with one faction wanting to pursue a more political agenda and the other gearing itself towards organized crime by controlling various lucrative prison rackets. Eager for financial gain, the BGF began shaking down prisoners selling protection. The group soon moved into selling drugs and weapons, extortion, gambling, prostitution and contract killings.[115]

The initial structure of the BGF was designed along paramilitary lines, with one leader, who functioned as the supreme commander, a central committee and a rigid chain of command. Membership was restricted to blacks, and members were expected to make a lifetime commitment with a death oath.

One BGF member described the advantages of joining the gang, claiming the group controlled the prison population where it was located 'by offering protection of numbers, protection of comradeship'.[116] Moreover, any member could expect a range of benefits that included such perks as cigarettes, sweets, pies, canned food and canned

**ONE YEAR AFTER ASSASSINATION: THEY HAVEN'T KILLED GEORGE JACKSON**

SEE ARTICLE PAGE 2

Cover of *The Black Panther* newspaper on 19 August 1972, featuring George Jackson a year after his death.

meat – all from their 'private stores'. One selling point was that you would receive commodities even if 'you were short', and 'wouldn't have to double up [pay interest on borrowed goods]'. And if an inmate was lonely, the BGF would get him a pen pal on the outside. This largesse would continue to the streets, promising community liaisons for those who had contact with individuals on the street.[117]

The BGF is usually found in adult prisons, although authorities have cited instances of it operating in juvenile facilities. It is centred in California, but also operates in Arizona, Georgia, Indiana, Minnesota, Nevada, New Jersey, Texas, Washington and Wisconsin.[118] Its written constitution runs to sixteen pages of single-spaced type, and clearly indicates the gang's intent to engage in armed conflict. The constitution reveals that the Aryan Brotherhood and the Mexican Mafia are its arch-enemies, describing them as 'tools' of the prison administration.

The BGF is considered the most politically astute of the major prison gangs, but lacking in originality.

In recent years the BGF has also been known as Jama, or 'family' in the East African language Swahili, a language in which many of its members have learned to communicate. Although it is still centred in the Bay area, the gang is active in several other states and in the Federal Bureau of Prisons. The BGF has become increasingly radicalized and members consider themselves political prisoners or prisoners of war. The group has earned a reputation for its propensity for attacking officers. The BGF reportedly shares intelligence with other politically orientated groups such as the New Black Panther Party and the Nation of Islam, and is still allied with La Nuestra Familia.[119]

The BGF has continued to exhibit its reach in recent years, demonstrating a hierarchy complete with a 'minister of education' responsible for testing members on the requisite gang literature, as well as a 'minister of finance', who 'manages the profits that are sent by cellphones from behind bars'.[120] The prison gang's criminal enterprises include smuggling strategies to raise bail to free members who do not have the financial resources to do so themselves.

Prison authorities got a rare insight into the gang in 2014 when one leader, who reportedly 'impregnated' four guards, testified to the controlling influence of the BGF inside the Baltimore City Detention Center, recounting how he directed correctional officers to smuggle in mobile phones and drugs in return for sex and money on the outside. He even used guards to help him discipline inmates who resisted his authority. The prison gang also maintained its monopoly of prison rackets by taxing any contraband goods smuggled in by non-members. It originated in California half a century ago, but today its prison presence is national in scope, and especially strong in Maryland.[121] At the time this scandal was made public, most of the prison guards were women, many of whom came from the same communities as the inmates. One search revealed graffiti painted on the wall, listing the names of fourteen guards willing to have sex with inmates for $150 per tryst, including two of the women impregnated by the aforementioned gang member. One had a child with him and his name tattooed on her wrist; another had two with him and had his name tattooed on her neck.[122]

*Gangster Disciples*

One new inmate and inactive member of the Gangster Disciples (GD) recalled his first day in Cook County Jail (Chicago), when he was approached by two men while in the bathroom. 'They asked me if I was hooked up', and he responded that he was GD. Later that day the first c (coordinator) and the gang's top leader in the unit of the jail came to check his references and deliver a 'poor box' of toiletries. If the inmate had not been in the gang's good graces he could have expected a severe beating, but he checked out and was soon immersed behind jail walls in GD literature that he was expected to study. He also learned the creed, considered a homage to its leader, Larry Hoover, referring to him as 'our honorable chairman' and speaking of 'the vision of our great leader'. Hoover directed a multimillion-dollar organized-crime empire from behind prison bars for almost thirty years as he was shuffled from prison to prison in Illinois, where he was serving life for killing a competing dope dealer in the 1970s.

Members are required to attend regular meetings to discuss security and to pay weekly dues, so incoming GDs receive 'poor boxes' (as noted above). GDs will usually walk together to such places as the recreation room in tight formation to prevent non-members from cutting into the line. It is common for violations of GD laws to be physically punished, sometimes leaving the malefactor hospitalized with significant injuries. But in the world of the GD, this type of sanctioning 'instilled discipline in the thousands of their members behind prison and jail walls and formed a more powerful gang when paroled out'.[123]

At the turn of the millennium, GD had risen to the top of Chicago's African American underworld, and by 2013 it was probably the biggest gang. Gang members on the streets are responsible for hundreds of murders each year. According to the authorities, this is due to the factionalization within the gang, leading to more internecine conflict, and the fact that 'a new generation of gangbangers [are] more willing to strike out on their own without respect for traditional hierarchies'.[124] In recent years the GD has relaxed its black-only restriction and has initiated white and Hispanic youths into the fold. Although membership is probably in the tens of thousands, the conviction of most of the gang's leadership has cast its hierarchical structure into disarray. It is worth noting the legitimate entrepreneurial side of the gang, which also enjoys revenue from its own clothing line and music-promotion company.[125]

## Native American Prison Gangs

More than 70 per cent of America's Native American (NA) population lives in urban areas. However, the rest live on wretched Indian reservations that are perhaps the poorest communities in the United States, plagued as they are by poverty, alcoholism, unemployment and a host of other social problems. Over the past twenty years NA street and prison gangs have appeared in several states, most notably Arizona, Minnesota and Washington. By 2011 there were close to 15,000 NAs behind bars, some bringing their street-gang credentials with them and others joining in prison. Recent research suggests that there are several types of these gangs, with more than four hundred exemplars and 28,000 members, some living on tribal lands, others in urban areas. Of these, reservation gangs are the smallest, with 25 or fewer members. For the purposes of this book, we will look at the so-called hybridization of these gangs in prisons. Indeed, gangs such as the Warrior Society, Native Nation and Native American Brotherhood 'began as prison gangs'.[126]

In contrast to their African American, Hispanic and white counterparts, NA gangs inside and out of prison are a relatively new phenomenon, tracing their roots to the 1980s and '90s, when city gangs introduced themselves to Indian Country and began recruiting. When it comes to these gang members, there is a diversity of backgrounds to consider; some are involved with native cultural and spiritual practices, others are refugees from broken homes, and still others have nowhere else to go.

By most accounts, the larger street gangs are most likely to have affiliate organizations behind bars, and as members return home from prison, they bring their knowledge of the various gangs they have been exposed to, thus 'cross-pollinating' the nature of NA gangs from one location to another. As pieces of gang culture are transplanted from one race or ethnicity to another, the 'process of hybridization expands'. The convergence of various gangs brings together those representing reservation gangs, urban gangs and other criminal groups; some mimic major urban gangs and are named after them, as in the case of the so-called Tre Tre Crips gang on the Pine Ridge Reservation in South Dakota. Hybridization can be discerned in the gang's name and structure. The name Tre Tre Crips indicates they were probably exposed to members of a Denver street gang of the same name when they were incarcerated. Once released they adopted some of the more urban Denver gang's characteristics and introduced them to others when they returned to the reservation.

Similar to the way African American gangs were influenced by polit-icized groups such as the Black Panthers, NA gangs were inspired to some degree by the American Indian Movement (AIM), which formed in 1968. (Interestingly, the 250 original members of AIM initially flirted with naming the new group 'Concerned Indians of America', but must have had a good laugh when they realized the folly of its acronym, CIA, several weeks later.) AIM's first meeting took place in Minnesota, home to urban Indian populations 'large enough to register on the radar of city government, the press, and the public'.[127] AIM adopted some of the tac-tics used by the Black Panthers in Oakland, California, in order to raise funds to 'equip cars with two way radios, cameras, and tape recorders so they could monitor arrests by the police department'.[128]

AIM has long restricted membership to Native Americans, eschew-ing involvement with other races and ethnicities.[129] But when it came to gangs, members were much more pragmatic than the AIM. For example, in the mid-1990s several Indians became associated with the Vice Lords, one of the country's more prominent street gangs. Due to inner conflict the groups diverged, leading to the formation of NA criminal street and prison gangs, variously known as the Native Mob and the Native Mob Family. This became notable as one of the few Native American-based street gangs with an organizational hierarchy.

Most NA prison gangs 'are closed and secretive, and their members', like the Mexican Mafia, typically deny that they are a gang. Rather they assert that they are a brotherhood, a cultural group, a warrior society merely seeking to protect their brethren and honour cultural traditions. Despite all the links to criminal activities, 'to some degree the motiva-tion for membership may actually be about this.'[130] In prisons where they are low in number, they usually align with an existing gang, typ-ically Hispanic. However, the Oklahoma Department of Corrections is the exception, where members of the Indian Brotherhood gang have been known to align with the Aryan Brotherhood. As one observer put it, it is 'about strength in numbers' and protection from black and Hispanic gangs.[131]

Conversely, in prisons containing significant numbers of native peo-ples, it is common for them to establish a stand-alone gang. Often these are merely extensions of street gangs they were involved with prior to prison. In Minnesota, for example, the Native Mob is active both inside prison and on the streets. NA prison gangs tend to be more organized and disciplined than their street counterparts. As with other race-based gangs, it is also not unusual to have regulations and rules, rank structure and leadership hierarchy. The Indian Brotherhood exemplifies this, with members expected to strictly follow a set of by-laws and an organized hierarchy. Likewise, the Warrior Society and Dine Pride in the Arizona prison system have rules, qualifications for admission, specific signs and symbols that are culturally based.[132]

There is a general notion among certain gangs that the prison gang will probably not stay active on the streets. But this is not always true, and some ex-prisoners take their gang affiliations with them when they leave, transplanting behaviours to reservations or urban communities. Oklahoma's Indian Brotherhood, Oregon's Indian Pride, South Dakota's East River Skins and the Native Nation in North Dakota all originated in prison and have become active in tribal locations.[133]

### The Native American Brotherhood: Warrior Society

Most NA inmates entering the Arizona prison system join the Native American Brotherhood (NAB), a group that unites Indian people inside the prison system to 'ensure the religious practices and ceremonial beliefs can be met'. Within the NAB are 'younger, stronger, more aggressive inmates' who are considered the elite NAB and are referred to as the Warrior Society. Like so many other race-based gangs, the main purpose of the group was to protect its members from other inmates and security threat groups (STGs) in their units. Prior to the emergence of the Warrior Society, NAS were often victimized by other prison gangs. The Society has written by-laws expressly stipulating that all members be NA, stay loyal unto death, put in at least two to four years of full-contact martial-arts training and abstain from drinking and partying (except on members' own time), and prohibiting marriage to non-Native Americans.[134]

In the summer of 2001 the Warrior Society was certified as an STG in the Arizona prison system,[135] joining a black, an Aryan and five Mexican and Mexican American gangs that had reached this status. Certification as an STG is a thirty-day process 'that allows other inmates and staff to be aware that the gang is going to meet severe punishment for its activities. It warns other inmates who have not affiliated with the group to stay clear of the group.' Inmates suspected of gang membership are classified either as members of a 'disruptive group' or as a 'security threat'. The Warrior Society had formerly been tagged as a disruptive group. The guiding state prison philosophy is to 'identify, validate and isolate' them.[136]

First noticed by prison officials in 1982, after a gang fight on an athletics field, the Warrior Society originated as a gang of about 120 Arizona prisoners who were charged with committing acts of violence against employees and other inmates, as well as extorting family members of inmates, work crews and the mail system in order to smuggle in drugs. One administrator went as far as branding them 'an elite group' of convicts.[137] Warrior Society members can be identified by 'the tattoo of a war shield on the right side of the neck with two feathers hanging down over the upper chest'.[138]

### The Native Mob: Minnesota

Minnesota is home to the Native Mob gang, which is active in prison and has ties to reservations in four states. The Mob is considered 'a well-structured, highly organized gang', with influence reaching from the Twin Cities to reservations throughout Minnesota, North Dakota, South Dakota and Wisconsin. It was established in Minneapolis some time in the 1990s, and by 2012 its membership was around two hundred. According to federal court papers, in 2012 an incarcerated leader, Wakinyan Wakan McArthur, aka 'Kon' and 'Killa', was found to be directing gang activity on the outside as well as holding Native Mob meetings for inmates. He had begun a sentence for second-degree murder in 1999. One informant revealed that McArthur was working on a succession plan while behind bars, including training a replacement leader to work on his behalf if he (McArthur) returned to prison. 'Killa' had a long rap sheet beginning at the age of eleven, for crimes that became increasingly serious, including a second-degree murder (prosecutors failed to prove intent) charge at sixteen, for which he received probation and time in a juvenile facility. Those sanctions did not work; at the age of nineteen he was charged with murder.

By the time McArthur was 33, the feds accused him of directing 'a widespread criminal enterprise'. Among the court records testifying to his prison activities was a letter from 2004 describing his plan for the Native Mob, which included the 'need to hold people accountable, foes or our own. Discipline and fear is the quickest way to progress our case.' Another letter, two years later, explained to a member how he was recruiting new members and holding gang meetings in prison.[139]

According to an interview with 'Boots', who claimed to be a Native Mob member, 'A commitment to the gang is a life commitment.' Boots claimed that by the seventh grade he was a fully fledged member and quickly fell into line, following a strict code of conduct, respecting the hierarchical structure and willing to enforce rules and regulations with violence if required. One of the most common punishments was 'getting violated', whereby an offender's hands were tied above his head and he was given a choice: get beaten from head to toe for two minutes or get beaten neck to toe for five minutes. If he fell over or passed out during the pummelling, the clock started again. Boots claimed, 'I always chose neck to toe,' because he didn't want his face marred. Frequently, members are violated for breaking rules against the use of pills and other hard drugs (marijuana and alcohol are acceptable). Out on the streets, members even need authorization to shoot someone. The Native Mob's main gang rivals include the Native Vice Lords, Native Disciples, Bloods and *Sureños*.[140]

### The Indian Brotherhood: Oklahoma

The Indian Brotherhood (IBH) is composed of members of NA descent and operates inside and out of the Oklahoma Department of Corrections (ODC). It has a defined structure as set out in its written by-laws, which outline expectations and commands that must be followed by each member. The IBH consists of numerous individual Tribes, each controlled by a War Chief, who, with certain limitations, makes command decisions concerning actions to be taken by his Tribe. The IBH uses this structure to coordinate the distribution of controlled substances, the collection of drug debts, and the protection by force of other members and drug-trafficking interests in and out of the ODC.[141]

In one case in 2017, several members of the McClendon Drug Trafficking Organization were found guilty by the U.S. Department of Justice for conspiracy to distribute methamphetamine and assault. Cody Lee McClendon III, aka 'Cody-Mac', and Michael David Lincoln, aka 'Linc', were charged with distribution in eastern Oklahoma and elsewhere while behind bars, serving twenty years and thirty years respectively for robbery and manslaughter. These crimes were facilitated by a smuggled mobile phone. Both members are War Chiefs of the IBH and used their positions to enlist other members and associates on the streets (as well as one corrections officer) into the drug-trafficking conspiracy. What's more, they used violence and the threat of it as a method of coercion and to further the success of the IBH. The operation that led to the arrests, dubbed 'Home of the Brave', was exposed during a joint investigation by the Organized Crime Drug Enforcement Task Force and the Eastern District of Oklahoma.[142]

### Dine Pride: Arizona

*Dine* is Navajo for 'the People'.[143] By most accounts the prison gang Dine Pride was created around 2001. Initially, membership was only open to NA inmates from the Navajo Nation, but in recent years it has changed its rules to include other tribes. It maintains a strong relationship with the AIM, with some observers suggesting that its display of AIM's 'Shadow Warrior' tattoo indicates the association. It is among the more powerful gangs, and one of its purported goals has been to get recognized as the representative of the NA inmate population. This has only deepened its conflict with the rival Warrior Society population. In Arizona, both gangs are considered STGs. The Warrior Society maintains several by-laws, including (in common with some of the Hispanic prison gangs and the South African Number gangs) mandatory education. Those who are 'painted' or 'patched' are expected to be knowledgeable about the history of the group. Other regulations

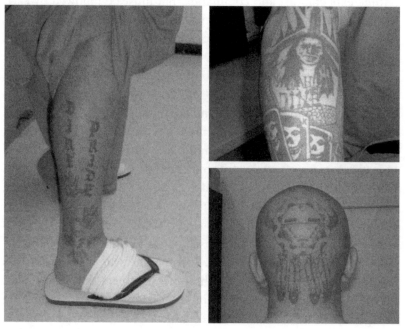

Tattoos of the Dine Pride gang, Arizona.

prohibit alcohol and drug use, gambling and disrespecting brothers. Self-control and discipline are expected at all times, and involvement with a religion is a must.

### The Silent Area Warriors: Utah

One way to discover the structure of a prison gang (when all other ways fail) is to peruse its constitution, if it has one. In Utah, the Silent Area Warriors (SAW) have a constitution known as 'Philosophies and SAW Laws and Codes of Conduct'. It offers insight into the gang's structure and the duties of the leaders. The SAW are led by commanders, responsible for managing the gang, determining who is accepted and decreeing new laws. Under the commanders are the generals, who act as spokesmen for the gang when it comes to interacting with prison administrators. The generals report to the commanders and are expected to conduct meetings each week dealing with current issues and troubles. Under the generals are majors and captains. The majors inform generals which inmates have violated conduct expectations; the captains are more involved in recruiting new members and dealing with security issues and report to the commanders.[144]

Under the captains are lieutenants, who have many of the same responsibilities as captains. When physical force is required the SAW turn to sergeants and enforcers, who control 'arms and preparation of all personnel for combative situations'. Moreover, they take the lead when 'suppressive or preemptive actions' against SAW's rivals are necessary. Those without rank are called warriors, and are expected to be lifetime members. According to one study, these 'structures are unlikely to be followed too closely'. What's more, 'Internal power struggles, lack of members and apathy, more often than not, preclude a gang from actually achieving the hierarchical, military-like ranking to which they might aspire.'[145]

### Prison Gangs in Canada

Canada's prisons are ranked 47th out of 223 in the world in terms of number of prisoners. However, the United States – at number one globally, with more than 2 million inmates – has about the same occupancy level (103.9 per cent of the capacity it was designed for) as its counterpart (102.2). Over the past few years, Canada's gang population has become increasingly diverse and difficult to manage. About 10 per cent of its inmates are tied to STGs, including indigenous gangs, Asian gangs, motorcycle and street gangs. The Correctional Service Canada also recognizes members of cults, terrorist groups, white-supremacy organizations and other hate groups.[146]

Unlike in the United States, in Canada it is not uncommon for inmates to belong to more than one gang. According to one recent chronicler, 'The security threat group population has become increasingly fluid, which has made the ideas of groups, members, associates and the compatibilities of each, increasingly difficult to identify definitively.' Moreover, 'the rivalries and alliances that are present in the community and on the street do not necessarily translate to the institutional setting or mirror those within federal institutions.'[147]

Most indigenous gang members can be found in the Canadian prairie region, including the Native Syndicate, the Manitoba Warriors and the Indian Posse. Many are affiliated with street and biker gangs. It has become increasingly difficult to identify prison-gang members in Canada, since many eschew tattoos and patches and other signifiers that were so important to gang investigators in times past. By one count, there are an estimated 65 different STGs, as gangs splinter into new gangs, allegiances change and old gangs are subsumed by newer ones.

The Decline of Traditional American Prison Gangs

Between the 1970s and the end of the century, prison gangs adhered to traditional standards of behaviour, criminality and structure. However, as American prisons have become more overcrowded with younger inmates unfamiliar with these traditions, leading prison gangs such as the Mexican Mafia, the Texas Syndicate and the Aryan Brotherhood have found themselves on the decline, due in no small part to the fact that recent gang members refuse to follow the traditional principles, disrespecting other convicts and guards alike. A new generation of gangster has come of age on the streets, where loosely structured gangs are united more by one's home town than by racial or ethnic pride.[148]

Until recently, a prison-gang member needed to seek authorization from a higher-ranking member before initiating an attack on another prisoner. In stark contrast, younger members tend to act on impulse and eschew the approval process. One of the newer gangs is the Texas

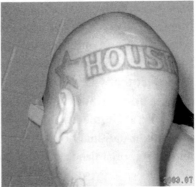

Tango Blast Houstone
gang-identifying tattoos.

prison gang Tango Blast. One observer compared it to 'the headless horseman', adding: 'Tango will take anybody.'[149] Without a true leadership structure or even shot-callers, Tango Blast and other new gangs are far less organized and aggressive than older STGs, but create many more problems, robbing, assaulting and extorting protection money from inmates.

## Tango Blast

In 2015 the Texas Department of Public Safety (TDPS) branded Tango Blast (TB) the 'top gang threat to Texas'. In its most recent gang-threat examination, the TDPS attributed TB's growth to its lack of delineated hierarchy, its lack of constitution/by-laws, and especially its lack of 'blood in, blood out' mandate. TB membership now outnumbers that of older prison gangs. Further distinguishing TB from its precursors is the fact that when members of Mara Salvatrucha or *Sureños* enter a Texas prison where none of their fellow members are residing, they can join TB. Ultimately this has facilitated the possibility of expanding across international borders. In any case, 'Due to its liberal guidelines and loosely organized structure', its membership will continue to exceed that of its rival prison gangs.[150]

The evolution of the TB prison gang and of the Tango Blast Houstone (TBH) street gang in Houston, Texas, America's fourth largest city, offers insights into the relationship between modern prison gangs and their street counterparts. By most accounts the two groups have joined forces to increase criminal profits, obviously taking advantage of the more numerous opportunities on the streets. According to one recent study of TBH's 100,000 members statewide, almost a quarter of them reside in Houston. Of these, close to a third are considered a 'loose affiliation' of ex-TB prison inmates. The Houstones are considered a 'subgroup of TB' and are distinguished from groups such as the Mexican Mafia by a lack of structure. As we have seen, TB is also distinct for operating without a 'true leadership structure – no shot caller'.[151] Although there are Tango Blast affiliates in most large cities in Texas, most rejoin their original gangs when they leave prison. TB's leadership vacuum by no means diminishes its ability to adapt. Many TBH members have been altering their 'public appearance', which screams out 'gangster', leaving their traditional coloured bandannas at home and making better use of social media instead.[152]

# 9

# PRISON GANGS OF LATIN AMERICA

As European prison populations continue to decline, and American incarceration rates level off, Latin America is experiencing an unprecedented rise in its prison populations. Several penal scholars suggest that this region has become 'the new mass carceral zone'.[1] Military dictatorships, bloody civil conflicts and overcrowded prisons have all contributed to the expansion of Latin American prison gangs over the past half-century. However, the recent surge in prison populations in the region is also being driven by punitive drug-prohibition policies that have overwhelmed prisons with detainees waiting to go on trial for drug-related offences.

Most Latin American prisons, overcrowded and poorly staffed, would have a hard time operating without the 'self-governing systems of aid and protection' provided by a variety of prisoner collectives and 'cellblock mafias'. Prison gangs and subcultures play an important role in not just regulating informal economies behind bars but assisting both prison administrators and prison inmates in their day-to-day activities.

The region's prisons are among the most dangerous and fetid in the world. If one has any doubts as to the dangers of prison life in the region, one has to look no further than the 30 July 2019 Brazilian prison brawl that left 62 prisoners dead, as members of the Red Commando and the Comando Classe A clashed in the northern prison of Altamira, in the state of Pará. Sixteen of the victims were decapitated. And if the gangs don't kill you, in many cases fire will. For example, a fire in Honduras in 2012 killed more than 360 inmates and, two years later, 81 died in a Chilean prison fire. One observer suggested that 'bad prisons are a feature of most Latin American countries. Too much violent crime translates to too many violent prisoners,' made worse by lack of funding for penal institutions. No country illustrates this better than Brazil.[2]

As noted above, much of the increase in prison populations is the result of the implementation of various hardline security policies, better known as *mano dura*, or 'iron fist', targeting drug-trafficking networks and the growing street-gang problem. It is a common response by Latin American countries, but has had little impact, except to transfer the street-gang problem into the prisons. In the process it has increased the hegemony of the larger prison gangs, as the prison systems of the region have 'become a prime incubator for organized crime'.[3] Meanwhile, prison facilities cannot be built fast enough to meet the inward flow of prisoners, a large proportion of whom have not even been convicted yet. Nonetheless, the penitentiary has been central to the social-control strategies employed in many Latin American countries.[4]

The Cold War played a major role in the way gangs developed in prisons. Many were born during the ideological conflicts that ravaged much of the continent. What's more, many of these wars were played out under various military dictatorships that feared political insurgency more than common criminals. However, once the dictatorships transitioned back to democracies, that gang problem became uncontrollable, leading to what one observer has described as a transition from the Cold War to crime wars.[5]

## Bolivia

While Brazil and Venezuela are home to the most structured and sophisticated prison gangs in Latin America, other prison systems have seen an expansion of the prison-gang subculture in recent years. Bolivia, for example, has proven to be a 'fertile breeding ground for criminal gangs'. Most prisoners are in preventive detention (84 per cent in 2011), thanks in no small part to an inefficient court system that operates at a glacial pace. In 2012 Bolivian authorities surmised that more than ten criminal organizations were being run from behind bars in cities such as La Paz, Cochabamba and Santa Cruz. These networks are able to operate thanks to family members and affiliates who visit gang leaders in prison regularly or communicate using mobile phones. Meanwhile, gang leaders are dependent on 'lieutenants' who keep them up to date with operations on the streets.[6]

Fears are increasing of growing Bolivian gang sophistication as inmates form organizations known as 'councils'. Their members do what organized crime does best: extort money and tax other inmates. Although the authorities have tried to whitewash this phenomenon as money for 'collective welfare', knowledgeable observers suggest that it is no more than an extortion racket. Meanwhile, in Bolivia as in its neighbouring countries, new prison construction is always outpaced by demand for larger capacity.

Funding for corrections officers remains tight, resulting in increased 'inmate governance', achieved through prison leaders known as 'delegates'. Delegates extort fees from inmates for privileges such as having one's own cell, family visits and access to televisions. In November 2011, prison officials broke up an extortion network in several Cochabamba prisons, where prisoners were forced to pay 'life insurance fees', ranging from $100 to $500. Reluctance to pay in some instances was met with torture and death. Similar internal-control mechanisms exist in prisons in Mexico, Venezuela and El Salvador. Ultimately, prison stints allow organizations to strengthen hierarchies, as they use time in jail to develop their networks on the outside.[7]

## Ecuador

As in Bolivia, the Ecuadorian prison system remains understaffed and underfunded, leading to widespread corruption. In Ecuador, 1,500 guards are expected to handle 40,000 inmates; meanwhile, salaries have not increased since 2005. It is not uncommon for guards to be fired for smuggling in contraband to earn some type of subsistence wage. In recent years the rapid increase in the prison population has been linked to the 'overuse of preventive detention' and the country's growing importance as a drug-transit nation, demonstrated by increased cocaine seizures in the early 2010s.[8]

By the end of the 2010s armed forces were being deployed to various Ecuadorian prisons to improve security and to deal with the unintended results of having left organized crime groups to thrive unchecked within the penitentiary system. On 14 May 2019 the armed forces were sent in to reinforce security outside prisons, while police reinforcements tackled gangsters inside jails. These operations were unleashed as two of Ecuador's gangs, Los Coneros and Los Cubanos, waged a war to control drug trafficking on the streets and in prisons. In one case, the mother of a suspected Cubanos member received an audio recording indicating that her son was to be murdered. Soon after came word that two rival gang members had mortally stabbed him 31 times in a regional prison in Latacunga, south of Quito.[9] Nonetheless, the country's prison-gang subculture problem pales in comparison with the happenings outlined below in Brazil, Venezuela, Central America and Mexico.

## Brazil

In 2019 Brazil had the third-largest prison population in the world. Since 2000, the nation's prison population has quadrupled to almost 800,000 prisoners, trailing only the United States and China.[10] With one of the highest urban crime rates in Latin America, Brazil has adopted an increasingly punitive approach to justice, leading to prisons teeming with violent young men. According to one leading expert, 'all major gangs in Brazil started out [as] and continue to be foremost prison organizations.'[11] Compared to Brazil's major prison gangs, their American prison-gang counterparts seem rather quaint. The country's prison gangs, or groups, are so prevalent that many of the country's penologists who contend that criminals run Brazil's prison system are not far off the mark. As far back as the 1950s, prison administrators never employed enough staff to run a prison adequately without the full cooperation of prisoners.[12]

To understand the evolution of Brazil's prison subculture it is necessary to go back to the Cold War era. The United States was busy in Latin America during this period, as leftist candidates took office in a number of countries. In 1961, João Goulart, also known as Jango, took the reins of Brazilian leadership. His critics warned that he 'was Castro in sheep's clothing.'[13] In 1964, still paranoid after the 1962 Cuban Missile Crisis and what followed in Cuba, the United States backed a military coup leading to a military dictatorship in Brazil. In the wake of the coup the prisons were flooded with the 'first wave' of political prisoners (a mix of trade unionists, soldiers and sailors), many supporters of the overthrown president. Almost from the very start, the political prisoners did what they could to disassociate themselves from the legions of criminals who filled the jails. Not surprisingly, the general population branded them 'elitist'. But as the prison regime became more brutal, it eventually led the two factions to seek common ground.

Both factions seemed to have agreed that some type of internal structure was needed to control so many inmates. Surprisingly, the

Cell with capacity for 36 prisoners housing 281 detainees, almost all of whom are temporary, in the Department of Judicial Police of Vila Velha, Espírito Santo, Brazil, 2009.

politicals convinced other prisoners to accept rules that would at least organize their lives and give them a chance to mount a defence against the powers that be. As one leading expert put it, 'this is a driving force behind prison gangs in Latin America. Inmates organize to survive.'[14] Not all the prisoners were convinced that a new order was required. But after a prison official wrote a report about the murder behind bars of six bank robbers, he grasped at some nomenclature that might distinguish the alleged killers from the rest of the inmates, and as the story goes the 'prison director baptized them' as 'Red Commando'.[15]

Brazil's prison system had been in freefall since the early 1960s, when the federal government withdrew much of its funding. Before the decade was out, the National Security Law was passed (1969) in response to a rash of bank robberies and the increase in anti-government groups. During the 1970s political prisoners became inextricably linked behind bars with the general prison population, creating an apprenticeship that apparently worked both ways. Indeed, leftist insurgents and political ideologues offered intellectual tools and action strategies to the prison population as the most dangerous criminal organizations emerged in the states of Rio de Janeiro (the smallest of the 27 states) and São Paulo.

### Red Command/Comando Vermelho: Rio de Janeiro

A number of non-political bank robbers sentenced and imprisoned under the National Security Law established a gang known as Falange Vermelho, later rebranded Comando Vermelho (CV), or Red Command. With the passage of the 1979 Amnesty Law, the political prisoners were released, but the rest had to return to their cells and the criminal community. Having broken bread with the politicals for almost a decade, the criminal element had absorbed enough ideology and organizational prowess to become one of Brazil's most powerful prison gangs. As one scholar put it, the 'integration of the reds with the rest of the prisons changed the system dramatically' and should be considered a 'definitive moment in the history of the consolidation of the prison gangs'.[16] From this point on, the CV vowed to 'live according to a collectivist ethos, promulgating a prison code barring rape and theft, prisoner on prisoner violence, except when ordered by decree by collective'.[17]

In 1979 the moniker Red Command appeared in newspapers and a government report for the first time. As with most other sagas of prison-gang creation, there are several versions of the Red Command chronicle. However, most 'concur on a central detail': that it was born in the era of the Cold War and Brazil's military dictatorship, which ruled from 1964 to 1985.[18]

By some accounts, the gang began after numerous small-time street criminals were incarcerated with leftist insurgent fighters allied against the military regime. This led to a melding of middle-class intellectuals with different degrees of criminality, both common and hardcore offenders. Although the guerrillas wanted to be treated as political prisoners and held separate from common criminals, the regime thought it might teach the intellectuals a lesson by throwing them into the Ilha Grande maximum-security island prison (closed in 1994 and now a popular tourist destination), where it was hoped they would be raped and beaten into submission by the criminal subculture. However, as with what occurred in apartheid-era South Africa, when political prisoners were tossed in with the Number gangs at Robben Island, the opposite occurred. (The regime was worried that if they were given political prisoner status they would be legitimized.)

The unintended consequences of this strategy had the intellectuals inculcating the criminal castes with 'revolutionary ideas'. Together, the two factions integrated the guerrilla cell structure and politics with the violent predilections and street connections of gangsters. According to one journalist, 'The Red Command's unique political influence from the guerrillas gave it its name and quasi-Socialist discourse.' It would soon morph from just several dozen inmates in one wing of a prison to a prison-system-wide phenomenon.[19]

By the end of the 1970s the political environment was such that the military regime decided to install a new president, who let it be known that he wanted the country to move back towards democracy. In 1985, with the dictatorship ended, former guerrilla leaders rose to prominence in national politics, breaking off any relationships they might have had with Red Command. Nonetheless, the group spread into every prison in the state of Rio, as well as the impoverished favelas. The group reduced violence, restored order and 'provided an alternate authority that guards could deal with'.[20] As Ioan Grillo sagely noted, a 'paradox of the Latin American crime wars' was that 'prisons are meant to stop gangsters from committing crime. But they became their headquarters.'[21] Brazil resorted to the strategy of moving the Red leaders to distant jails, only facilitating the construction of new chapters wherever they went. Soon they had expanded not just through Rio's state prisons but through the national prison system as well.[22]

Not all prisoners approved of the new rules. One group of inmates known for their violent proclivities hailed from the slums of Jacaré, adopting the name 'Falange Jacaré' in due course. Jacaré remained at odds with the CV over several issues, particularly how a slush fund from inmate taxes was being dispersed. Other dissidents joined Jacaré, leading to a bloody showdown in April 1983, when the CV killed all the main representatives of Jacaré. Transferring leaders to maximum security in the hopes of lessening its power only made CV stronger, giving it even more control over Rio de Janeiro's inmate communities, until it became, at the time, the biggest gang in the Brazilian prison system.

But Falange Jacaré was not a spent force yet, renaming itself Terceiro Comando (TC), Third Command. Both CV and TC were prison-born, before migrating to the streets. Fear was a good ally for gang members, since they by now understood that once they were released, they were expected to follow gang dictates on the streets. They knew it would only be a matter of time before they reoffended and were back behind bars, where they would be answerable for any gang violations they might have committed in the free world.

Much of cv's expansion in the 1980s can be attributed to its increased involvement in the region's cocaine trade. As part of its organization the gang created a prison book that listed the names of all offenders and their profiles. Some referred to it as the 'Ten Commandments'. Its rules to live by would be familiar to most prison subcultures: don't snitch, do not accuse without evidence, do not covet your neighbour's wife, be humble, strengthen the poorest, be part of the collective and do not kill in vain. Anyone who violated these commandments risked the death penalty. This heavily armed group joined a coalition with São Paulo's First Capital Command (Primeiro Comando da Capital, PCC) in 2006 that lasted for close to a decade.

At the beginning of 2017 a spate of prison massacres left more than a hundred inmates dead in Brazil's northern and northeastern prisons. The decapitations and disembowelments of many victims were widely publicized, the result of a gang war between the PCC and a local affiliate of Rio de Janeiro's cv. The gangs had been allied for more than ten years, until the PCC declared war on its former ally in September 2016, 'citing cv betrayals'. Just weeks later, PCC-led prison

Inmates are seen during confrontation between the cv and PCC gangs at Alcaçuz Penitentiary Center near Natal in Rio Grande do Norte, Brazil, on 19 January 2017. Stick-wielding inmates hurled stones and lit fires in a jail where dozens were previously massacred, as authorities struggled to contain a spreading wave of gang violence.

riots in three states killed about twenty people, 'foreshadowing [the] January bloodletting'.[23]

More recently a cleavage between the older CV and its newer members has emerged. Younger members are more likely to indulge in crack cocaine and commit over-the-top violence, eschewing rules and ideology.[24] However, one feature that has not changed is the malice reserved for rapists. In similar fashion, bus thieves and those who neglect to pay child support are considered the lowest of the low. One inmate explained, 'Because our families ride the bus, and my mother could have been on that bus.'[25]

### The Collective

Inmate communities, or collectives, a term given to them by political prisoners in the 1960s, are today dominated by drug gangs, who control all routines and transactions within the prison. Every day the collective takes part in a ritual prayer at 6 p.m. Each cellblock has a 'Circular', a type of newsletter that accounts for day-to-day activities in the cell. These are later discussed by the 'summit' leaders. In the prisons of Rio de Janeiro it is common to have a summit consisting of 21 leaders who supervise a collective. At the head of the summit is a president, a vice-president and a spokesman (*frente da cadeia*). They maintain contact with each other and report directly to the leaders of organized crime groups ensconced in 'federal custody' at Catanduvas prison, in southern Brazil.[26]

By most accounts, the directors of maximum-security prisons appreciate the role of the collective, with one relating:

> Hierarchy is useful on a daily basis, I use it for my advantage, and you call two or three of them and say what you want to say and they are responsible [for] passing it on to the collective. Otherwise, I would have to go gallery to gallery and say the same thing over and over to [more than seven hundred inmates].[27]

The collective controls every facet of prison life, including work assignments. For recidivist criminals, 'there is a sense of familiarity' when they are reincarcerated, as they catch up with familiar faces, old partners and friends, and have a chance to get closer to the gang's shot-callers. With prison a regular component of criminal lives, rejoining the collective can be an institutional reunion of sorts. As one member put it, 'While jail is high school, prison is the university of crime.'[28]

Among the main strategies of the collective is to obtain loyalty by promising protection and dominating the prison through the 'physical elimination' of troublesome prisoners during 'opportunistic' riots. Once a prison gang has consolidated its power behind bars there is typically a decrease in violence between inmates. Beginning in 2006, the PCC and the CV issued a prohibition against 'spilling blood' with knives and similar instruments. One way of executing an inmate, one that was designed to make the death simulate suicide, was the 'Gatorade strategy', which consists of forcing the victim to drink water laced with cocaine and Viagra, which in high enough doses will lead to cardiac arrest.[29]

According to one inmate, anyone not involved in the collective typically endures 'extreme hardship and [has] to, sooner, or later, affiliate with the organized criminals to live'. As one inmate put it, 'I have actually starved in prison. If you do not succumb to the narco criminals, and if you do not have family visits, you can become a mendicant in prison, what the collective call the *caidinhos*,' shorthand for inmates who are never visited and have no access to cash, thus making them more vulnerable to gang extortion. 'Either you get involved or you leave. I decided to leave.'[30] Of course there are always prisoners who will never be able to adapt to the collective. They have alternatives, such as undergoing a religious conversion and entering the Evangelical category. Conversion is perhaps the most respected way to get out of joining a collective. Although there is still some well-founded mistrust by the criminal community, the decision is often respected. Others, however, remain unconvinced, especially if the convert has broken community rules and is just seeking the easiest way out of his predicament. But compared to American gangs, at least it is possible to leave the Red Command and other Brazilian groups without the ultimate retribution.

The main formality for getting out of the gang is called the *tocque de cadeia*, or 'prison call'. The departing inmate must first write a retraction to leaders of the group, all of whom are in federal prisons outside the state of Rio, and wait for a response. The *tocque* is always done in writing and must include a solid reason for leaving and proof of the leaver's next step (beginning a formal job, entering the clergy, leaving the state and so on). Moreover, he must demonstrate proof that he has organized his duties and accountability concerning drugs, weapons and personal matters; that all are in order and that he has not forgotten the statute of commandments, regarding never talking about the group to anyone, under threat of the death penalty: 'Secrecy is the most important part of detachment.' What's more, he is prohibited from leaving prison with any business profits accrued while he was inside. The next step in the protocol is for the leader to respond to the *tocque*, digging for more specific information. It is after this that he will agree to a decision, and both parties must stick to the decision once it is made.[31]

### Jumping

Among the chief concerns about someone leaving a collective or other prison group is whether the prisoner might 'jump' to another group. Various explanations have been offered for why this occurs, anything from internal disagreements, fights and discussions to betrayal and errors. However, when the inmate makes the decision to jump, it is understood that this does not mean there were prior negotiations before the *tocque* (though that is usually the case). As one observer put it, 'One can negotiate and check out possibilities and create oneself an offer.' New groups typically welcome jumpers, considering it a small victory, simply because it is 'one less [gang] member to kill'. However, there are limits to jumping and a prisoner can only do it once. As one inmate put it, 'This is a business, not a game.'[32] In recent years jumping has become more common both on the streets and behind bars, leading to an environment of almost constant tension and distrust among gangsters, who are constantly watching each other's actions.[33]

### Primeiro Comando da Capital

With one of the highest urban crime rates in the world, in the 1990s Brazil embarked on a punitive approach to crime control and the burgeoning drug trade, leading to prisons bursting at the seams with violent young men. São Paulo's Primeiro Comando da Capital (PCC), or First Command of the Capital – also referred to as 'the Command', 'the Party', 'Fifteen' and 'the family' – originated in the early 1990s and spread rapidly throughout the country's notoriously brutal and corrupt prison system. There is still no consensus as to its actual origins.

Several creation sagas have been offered for the birth of the PCC. One popular backstory has it forming after 111 inmates were massacred by police and correctional officers during a riot at the now demolished

Carandiru prison in 1992.[34] More recently, in his book *Snakes and Lizards* (*Cobras e Legartos*; 2004), the São Paulo reporter Josmar Jozino claims to put to rest any other creation stories with his account. He cites a soccer match on 31 August 1993, in an annexe of the Casa de Custódia e Tratamento de Taubaté jail. The game pitted a loose association of prisoners, Comando Caipira (Redneck Command), against the PCC. Two members of the Comando Caipira were killed in a melee. Fearing payback from either the aggrieved gang or the prison administration, after the bloodletting, members of the PCC signed an agreement that if any of their group were punished for this transgression it would be met by a 'serious response by the entire team'.[35]

One of the co-founders of PCC put together a constitution that stressed the importance of organizing the jailhouse to end the legacy of prisoner maltreatment by authorities. Ultimately, it was successful in ameliorating an environment of almost constant warfare, where 'everyone was for himself' and the 'survival of the fittest' formed the basis for prison life. Put another way, any disagreements or insults could lead to 'decision by the knife'. It must be understood that prior to the emergence of the PCC, sex and violence were everyday occurrences in Brazilian prisons. The PCC, as it became more formidable, successfully eliminated rival gangs and terminated the extortion rackets, rapes and mindless killings.

The PCC campaign to introduce a new ethos gathered support on both sides of the prison walls. The Command controls its members and all other prisoners serving time in São Paulo's vast prison system. Much of the country's crime activity used to take place in São Paulo, which, with more than 20 million inhabitants, is among the world's largest cities. At one time, crime was so widespread that business executives were afraid to travel by car. Therefore, the city became home to more heliports than New York City and the world's largest purchaser of armoured cars for civilian use. However, observers suggest that the PCC's virtual monopoly on organized crime in the city has been a strong contributing factor in the tremendous decline in murders between 1997 and 2019.[36]

Since the start of the new millennium, murder rates for the region have dropped substantially. In 1999, the São Paulo region had a homicide rate of 44.1 per 100,000, with a population of just over 55,000 prisoners. During the PCC's growth over the next decade, the homicide rate plummeted, reaching 15.4 per 100,000 in 2009, with three times as many prisoners (153,056). Moreover, the decline was matched by the decline of murders in other cities where the PCC was active.[37] Although the authorities would claim that successful security strategies were responsible for the homicide drop, a substantial number of others have attributed the decline to the PCC.

However, for most of its existence, the PCC remained largely invisible to the free world, thanks in large part to official censorship that prohibited any mention of it. In 1979, the acronym PCC was revealed publicly by a reporter covering a prison rebellion. Not surprisingly, the authorities challenged the veracity of this report, claiming that police investigations revealed that rather than some monolithic organization, it was only a small group of convicts with little clout inside or out of prison. This was followed up by transferring PCC leaders to prisons in distant regions. Of course, this just facilitated further expansion into other states, allowing it to build alliances with other criminal groups, including Rio de Janeiro's Red Command.[38]

On 8 February 2001 the Brazilian government could no longer deny the PCC's existence and their power inside its prison system and on the streets after a 'megarebellion' was fomented at 29 prisons in São Paulo state. Nineteen inmates were killed, mostly by prison-gang rivals. Prison officials acknowledged that this could not have been planned and coordinated without mobile phones, and vowed that this issue would be addressed. However, this never came to pass. It turned out that until the deregulation and privatization of telecommunications in 1997, São Paulo had unreliable mobile-phone coverage. Over the next two years, more capacity was built around the prisons where 'the usage was high'. The government was not aware of this until after improvements had been made, at which point it ordered the telecommunications companies to 'shut down their services within range of the prison walls'. The companies 'resisted, as they resist today, in the name of the greater good provided by a truly free market'.[39]

In October 2002 Marcos Willians Herbas Camacho, better known by his monikers 'Marcola' and 'Playboy', became the undisputed leader of the PCC after a power struggle that left fifteen senior PCC leaders dead. Serving a 44-year sentence for bank robbery, the 39-year-old self-styled intellectual was purportedly versed in Sun Tzu's *The Art of War* and Machiavelli's *The Prince*, but neither of these kept him from spending more than half of his life in prison. Over the next four years, Marcola directed the rapid expansion of the PCC's membership so that by 2006, about 90 per cent of São Paulo's state prisons were PCC members. He now controlled an

estimated army of close to 140,000, including 125,000 behind bars and more than 10,000 on the streets. With its expansion, PCC set its sights on carving out some type of presence in the political system. Accounts have surfaced of members taking competitive exams for civil service positions that they hoped might lead to running as candidates in future elections.[40] Like other prison gangs around the world, the PCC was created for self-defence and better prison conditions, but soon gravitated to creating various revenue streams to fund its operations. In 2006, some accounts pegged it as 'probably the largest gang in the Western Hemisphere.'[41]

*Salve Geral* (Time of Fear, 2009, dir. Sérgio Rezende), a film based on the real violent attacks by the PCC gang against security forces and some civilian targets in São Paulo in May 2006.

The PCC once more demonstrated its strength on 11 May 2006, when it instigated an even larger megarebellion than the one in 2001. That night, heavily armed gang members launched more than fifty ambushes, bombings and drive-by shootings. São Paulo's 74 prisons were ordered to take part in the uprising simultaneously, and street soldiers attacked police forces and security services in the state capital. Once again, mobile phones facilitated the well-planned rebellion. The following day they bombed eleven banks and other targets. By 15 May, close to one hundred police and civilians had been killed. However, the riots and attacks were ended apparently after Marcola made a deal with officials. Ultimately, the megarebellions gave the PCC the prestige and respect it sought as it spread across the Brazilian prison system. Having demonstrated that it could paralyse the country's largest city, it was now free to impose more rules of conduct and use indiscriminate violence as it expanded its business into neighbouring countries.

By the second half of the 2000s, even Marcola admitted there was no hierarchy or single leader, so that 'today the PCC lacks leadership. Everyone is the boss ... where there once existed a command ... Marcola has now decreed that anyone who wants to rebel should rebel, that each and every Brother would be responsible for his own actions.' This new ethos of equality, although it did not occur all at once, or 'evenly in all prisons', distinguishes São Paulo's PCC from other prison-gang subcultures, notably the Red Command in Rio. However, this generalization does not necessarily apply to all prisons in São Paulo, as the prison ethnographer Karina Biondi has asserted:

> this shift is not felt in the same way across prison units. In fact there exist great differences in the politics and rhythms of different prisons, since whether large or small, the changes that occur in one jail do not necessarily migrate to other locations.[42]

By the 2010s, the PCC had evolved into a formidable criminal organization, displaying a high degree of coordination, integration and management of its members, leading a Brazilian official in 2012 to describe it as the country's largest criminal organization. It is fair to say that the PCC controls most of São Paulo's prisons, and it has a policy of non-communication with guards, whom members have dubbed 'Germans' (Nazis). According to one human-rights lawyer, even Brothers (members) cannot speak with other inmates without the boss listening in.

There is no consensus as to the number of PCC members, who are expected to pay dues – an equivalent of U.S.$23 per month for inmates and $230 a month for those on the outside. When members are unable to pay, they are required to take part in risky attacks on police officers.

In 2001 alone, the PCC was involved in 24 riots; in 2005 they killed five of their fellow inmates and tossed the decapitated heads from the roof-top. By most accounts, it is common for prisoners to pay the dues just to keep in good stead with the Command. Conversely, the PCC 'also buys loyalty by helping prisoners get lawyers, medicine, and by handing out the best jobs and cells inside the prison.'[43]

An interesting development has been the merging of criminal and political activities, a phenomenon common in other Latin American countries. For example, shortly after the turn of the twenty-first century, the PCC entered a relationship with Colombia's leftist paramilitary ter-rorist group, FARC, which offered its 'kidnapping expertise' to the PCC and went into a drugs-for-weapons exchange with it.[44]

In 2006, further demonstrating its internationalization, federal police documents suggested that the PCC was protecting inmates of Lebanese origin housed in Brazilian prisons, in exchange for weap-ons provided by Hezbollah, through transnational weapons-smuggling networks.[45] The PCC has also been linked to Italy's 'Ndrangheta cocaine-trafficking network.[46] More recently, police in Paraguay arrested four members of a PCC cell active along the border between the two countries.[47] In 2015 a gang of bank robbers, mostly members of the PCC, was linked to a series of crimes in eastern Paraguay, including bank, ATM and armoured-car robberies.[48] Perhaps most troubling are recent inklings of PCC cooperation with Chinese smugglers, just as Brazil increases its economic trade with China. Financial investigations have revealed that the PCC maintains bank accounts in the United States and China as a strategy for laundering drug-trafficking profits in order to buy guns and drugs.[49]

Like many American prison gangs, the PCC adheres to an ideology, in this case prisoner solidarity, and in 1993 it outlined a sixteen-point manifesto under the motto 'Liberty, Justice and Peace'. The manifesto listed discipline guidelines, specifically prohibiting mugging, rape, extortion and the use of PCC power to resolve personal problems. Some experts have indicated that its 'fundamental reason to exist is to improve the rights of prisoners.'[50] But this does not preclude its criminal activi-ties, and the PCC has long been involved in drug trafficking and other criminal activities in order to raise money to support family members and even put former prisoners through law school.

### Brothers

In the PCC, once a Brother always a Brother, at least theoretically. Inmates with a significant rap sheet are most likely to be accepted as Brothers. The higher security a prison, the more likely there will be many Brothers, since that is where the hardest criminals are housed. Once it is determined that the convict is set to serve a long sentence, he has the option to be baptized as a Brother. However, it is 'a decision without return', since once in you cannot stop being a Brother. Once accepted, if you break any rules or act 'inappropriately' you might 'take a hook': be suspended from your position for one or two months. Although an individual cannot just leave the group of his own volition, there is a way out, a calculated manoeuvre to say the least. If you 'take a hook' too many times you might forfeit your status as a Brother, so, not surprisingly, members have figured out that you can purposely misbehave so often that you will be forced out of the PCC, but still have your life to look forward to.[51]

Once an individual is selected for baptism to brotherhood, he must first have a sufficient criminal résumé, then exhibit a talent for persuasiveness and negotiation. The process for determining prospective members begins when two Brothers recognize the potential of a standout inmate and recommend him after having observed him for a while. When the invitation is accepted, the two Brothers who proposed entrance become his de facto godparents, or *padrinhos*. Once a Brother, he becomes equal with the other Brothers, all responsible for maintaining order in prison. This distinction, that everyone is considered equal and not part of a hierarchical scheme, is a rarity in the prison-gang subculture.

Not everyone can be a Brother, or must become one. Those barred from entering the PCC include snitches, hired killers affiliated with the police, members of other factions and those who have committed crimes such as rape, parricide and infanticide and have been forced to serve time in protective custody. Brothers refer to them as 'things'. Other prisoners who are permitted to live in cells controlled by the PCC are regarded as 'Cousins', or *Primos*.[52]

### The Faxina, Pilots and Towers

The key to understanding how Brazilian prisons operate is the *faxina*, or cellblock leader, better known as the 'housecleaner'. Dating back to at least the early 1950s, Brazilian prison supervisors have not had enough staff to run prison facilities without the assistance of prisoners. When a prisoner first enters a prison wing, he immediately meets with the cell-block leader, the *faxina*, who asks him what he is in for. The *faxina* can be understood as a coterie of prisoners responsible for maintaining their wing, or pavilion, of the prison. The term *faxina* itself refers to both the cellblock and the prisoners within. Another way to look at the *faxina* is as a group of 'housecleaners' or a 'clean-up squad' that directs the daily internal administration of a cellblock. Their responsibilities include delivering food, serving meals, opening and closing cells, overseeing sanitation and mediating disputes within a cellblock. Housekeepers are 'usually responsible for medicines and prescriptions', and fulfil medical needs for inmates when necessary, such as requesting medication from prison administrators.[53] Both Cousins and Brothers have operated in this important capacity. If a jailer or official needs to speak to the inmates of a prison wing, it can be done only through the *faxina*. In the modern era of mass incarceration, prison guards are rarely required to enter a cellblock, unless to unlock or lock the doors.

On occasion there are issues that impact a larger number of inmates. In these cases, a pilot, or *piloto*, will need to be brought into the conversation. The pilot takes responsibility for an entire prison wing. He is typically involved in presenting petitions or brokering understanding between the keepers and the kept. As a result of their importance, pilots are never housed in a housekeeping cellblock. This tactical manoeuvre is a safety mechanism, since when authorities decide to transfer inmates from one cellblock to another prison after a rebellion or strike, all the inmates are transferred en masse. Too many transfers of pilots can leave a void in the command structure. Like other positions, that of pilot is transitory. Once a pilot leaves a unit where he was elected, another is elected in his place. Only Brothers are permitted to vote for and nominate pilots.

The tower, or *torre*, is a high-ranking Brother who often has the final decision in matters concerning the violation of the modern PCC ethos. For example, if someone murders another gang member or non-PCC member without permission, he will have to answer to the *torre*. All major recommendations and directives come from the towers. However, like the Brothers, the pilots and the *faxina*, the towers should best be understood as 'a political position, or mode of positioning, rather than an identity'. Moreover, since the PCC ethos precludes 'individual identity' or differences between the various positions, communiqués released by the towers typically reflect 'the desires of the collectivity'.[54]

### The Família do Norte

Based in the Amazonian hub of Manaus, the Family of the North (FDN) is Brazil's third-largest prison gang. Despite its lack of prominence, FDN has emerged as a violent competitor over the past few years. The gang has earned prominence for recent internecine conflict that has left dozens of its own members dead. The bloodletting revolves around a turf war between the founders of what is now considered 'northern Brazil's most powerful crime group'.[55] The war stems from a coup against FDN boss José Roberto Fernandes Barbosa, aka Ze Roberto da Compesa, led by João Pinto Carioca, better known as João Branco, after Branco funded a splinter group dubbed FDN Pura (Pure FDN). Over two days in May 2019, more than fifty prisoners were murdered, many of them strangled in four FDN strongholds in prisons in the state of Amazonas.

According to texts intercepted by investigators, the attack by the FDN began in the Anísio Jobim prison in Manaus before spreading to other prisons across the state, in what has been described as a 'tit for tat fight'.[56] The other afflicted prisons included the Antonio Andrade penal institute, the Puraquequara and the Male Provisional Detention Centre in Manaus. Although the leaders of both factions are housed in the distant states of Mato Grosso and Paraná, their ability to create strife in prisons so far away speaks to their reach across the Brazilian prison system.

Much of the inter-gang conflict has been blamed on the decline of power and drug sales under Barbosa. Probably more important was the fact that the FDN's long alliance with the Red Command had ended in 2015 following a three-year truce with CV over control of drug-trafficking operations in the Amazon region.[57] The alliance with the Rio de Janeiro-based CV was crucial, with the FDN controlling drug-trafficking routes along the Amazon River and into neighbouring Colombia, Bolivia and Peru.[58]

The May 2019 infighting was particularly brutal, fought with sharpened toothbrushes and a panoply of choking devices. Much of the blame can also be placed at the feet of President Jair Bolsonaro's punitive strategy of mass incarceration. He memorably quipped, 'I'd rather a prison cell full of criminals than a cemetery full of innocent people.' Since he launched his incarceration campaign in May 2019, the country with the third-largest prison population in the world has acquired at least 800,000 prisoners in space designed for half that number. Some accounts describe cells so crowded that inmates must sleep standing up, a feat that can be accomplished only by lashing oneself to the cell bars to keep from falling. Any chance of beating the prison gangs had been thrown away by previous administrations, using the now debunked strategy of sending gang leaders far from home. As a result of this failure, local gangs could develop a national reach as prisons became recruiting grounds for prospective members as soon as they entered prison gates.[59]

The recent violence has echoes of the January 2017 massacre at Anísio Jobim prison, which left 56 inmates dead. The victims were mostly PCC members and were killed by an FDN and Red Command alliance. In its aftermath another 140 inmates were killed in retaliatory strikes in Amazonas's prisons.[60]

## Venezuela

Thanks to a lethargic justice system that leaves 70 per cent of inmates on remand for extended periods, overcrowding has long been the bane of the Venezuelan prison system. It is not uncommon for prisoners to wait years for court dates, and meanwhile they are expected to pay gang bosses for the privilege of going to court. One explanation for the 'astronomical rates of pre-trial detention' in Venezuela is that imprisonment remains 'the only means of official punishment'.[61] Exacerbating the problem is the fact that only one new prison was built during the thirteen-year rule of Hugo Chávez, and only three detention centres out of the 24 promised by the Minister of Popular Power for Penitentiary Matters in 2012 have been opened.[62] One of the few instances of prison expansion took place at Yare Prison, where Chávez had been incarcerated in 1992 after leading a failed military coup.

Between 1999 and 2014, there were 6,470 murders committed in 35 prisons holding 49,000 prisoners in space designed for less than half that. This does not include the 33,000 held in police cells intended for 5,000. In recent years it has not been uncommon for inmates to claim they feel safer in prison than on the outside, as the country's homicide rate has reached unparalleled highs. In 2017 alone, there were 26,000 violent deaths, giving the country a homicide rate of 89 per 100,000, a rate only exceeded by two conflict zones, Syria and Somalia.[63]

In 2011 Chávez established a special Ministry of Penitentiary Services. However, it provided few services, so few in fact that the 'only effective form of social control depends on the inmates themselves'.[64] More recently, scholars have documented 'the existence of a distinctive Venezuelan prison subculture'.[65] What makes it so is its 'unique hierarchical structure', the 'pervasive use of violence' and 'the existence of an indigenous system of norms that governs the interaction among inmates and others [similar trends have been spotted in Bolivia and Brazil]'.[66]

### Prison Subculture

One of the more anomalous characteristics of Venezuela's prison subculture is the existence of a 'meticulous regulation of vocabulary and speech'. The reasons for this regulation run counter to the general perception that prison life is rife with verbal bullying and abuse, compounded by sexual innuendos and uncouth double entendres. However, even prison community members have recognized how easily misunderstood words can lead to violent clashes. Thus, prison jargon is heavily proscribed. Moreover, anyone who violates these rules faces a severe reprimand. Behind this distinct set of regulations is the fact that in order to improve an already volatile environment, any attempts at eliminating or minimizing sources of tension are valuable for 'inmate governance'.

An idea of how well this has been thought out is given by the particular words that are most regulated. The Venezuelan prison subculture has gone to great lengths to come up with safe words that leave little doubt about their intended meaning. Forbidden words are typically common ones. For example, the words for egg, yucca and milk are prohibited because their alternative connotations refer to semen and male genitalia. As a result, instead of using *leche* for milk, in its place *vaquita* (little cow) is used, to avoid its more pejorative connotation as shorthand for semen. Likewise, the words for egg (*huevo*) and yucca have been used as Spanish vulgarities for the testicles and penis. Instead of *huevos*, the preferred word is *yenci*. Similarly, yucca is replaced with *raiz*, or root.[67]

Words and expressions that are part of the lexicon used by police and government officials are forbidden. Instead, inmates will conjure up new words, creating an 'original slang unintelligible to outsiders'. Any violation of the rules carries a penalty dubbed *chinazo*, or being 'hit from a stone thrown by a slingshot'.[68] Other prohibitions are more familiar. The Venezuelan code of the inmate maintains strict bans on any 'unnatural physical contact with others', since even the 'slightest accidental touch' may be misconstrued as either some type of sexual advance or an 'unacceptable act of humiliation by cellmates'.[69]

Prisoners are always watching each other for 'any conduct, act, or speech that may appear ambiguous, suspicious, or that is perceived to potentially disturb the fragile order of prison'. Such behaviour can include being caught shaving one's own legs. A sentinel on watch in the bathroom has permission to shoot the inmate if this occurs; the same goes for catching someone masturbating or engaging in a sexual act.[70]

### *The* Pran

The existence of a prison subculture in Venezuela is best exemplified by the *pran* system. While there is no consensus as to where the term originated, and it has no known Spanish meaning, some suggest that it is an acronym of the Spanish *Preso Rematado Asesino Nato*, which translates to something like 'natural born double killer prisoner'.[71] Others offer that it is shorthand for the term 'principal', denoting rulers in the community.[72] By most accounts, *prans* are not democratically elected or appointed by any internal organization; instead, they usually rise to power through violence against a predecessor or following the death, release or transfer to another prison of another *pran*.[73] During the interregnum between *prans*, there is usually a great deal of bloodshed and instability in the prison.

The *pran* or *pranato* operates as a separate entity in the prison, parallel to the director and his correctional officers. The *pran* rarely interacts with inmates and enjoys perks that other inmates can only dream of, including special foods and electronics. The *luceros*, or lieutenants, of a *pran* make up a *carro*, shorthand for a prison's 'criminal governance structure'. When any attempt is made to change the *carro*, it is treated as an attempted coup and often results in bloodshed. The *pran* structure has evolved over time, gaining collections services, a social committee and a security wing. Ultimately, a *pran* can be deposed only when he is killed by another *pran*.

The *pran* and his *carro* are tasked with enforcing social behaviour and making sure inmates follow regulations. There are no written documents cataloguing infractions and punishments, but most inmates are familiar with the rules. Under the *pran* is a chancellor (*canciller*), who mediates conflicts. Meanwhile the *pran* is protected by bodyguards, who are collectively known as *los perros*, or 'the dogs'. But it is the *luceros* of the *carro* who are responsible for doling out punishment to anyone caught in the act of violating prohibitions.

By most accounts there are two distinct sanctions for violating regulations, both designed according to the nature of the prison subculture. Being caught in the act is severely punished, particularly when a night watchman, or *garitero*, is caught asleep or distracted during his shift, putting the entire prison wing at risk. The sanction is dubbed *Sueño de la Muerte*, or 'Sleep of Death', referring to the fact that the offender will never see his demise coming. There are seldom witnesses to the act, since anyone in the vicinity follows a general order to hide until after the act has been completed.[74] But executions are rare. Those punishments that are publicly carried out occur when the *pran* wants to send a message to his constituency, always 'mindful of his precarious position at the top'.[75] Much consideration is given before any death penalty is ordered, since there is always the distinct possibility that it will lead to 'negative attention' and 'create internal tensions' that might result in a coup against the leadership.[76]

Most *prans* are also cognizant that the number of followers usually decides which *pran* is more powerful, so eliminating or executing a member of the community cuts into the number of soldiers available in a crisis. Moreover, there is an economic motive as well, since the elimination of one person means one less contributor to the group's tax base. More likely scenarios might be to banish an individual from the territory of the *pran*. As one recent examination of the *pran* system put it, those typically kicked out 'are the deadbeats or delinquent tax payers', who contribute little to the group.[77]

Besides the traditional codes of prison conduct, one's sartorial choices and accessories are heavily regulated, as exemplified by the ban on sunglasses when women are present. In the machismo prison culture, an inmate is expected to remove his sunglasses any time a female is visiting another prisoner, fearing that he might appear to disrespect the woman by staring at her with eyes hidden behind dark shades. Similarly, prisoners are prohibited from revealing their unclothed torso or from staring directly at another inmate's spouse, girlfriend, mother or other female relative.[78]

*Carros* vary in size and function, often according to the size of the prison. A smaller facility might have just one *carro*; larger institutions might have one per major section. *Carro* members are the only prisoners allowed to carry weapons inside. While state officials are often visible, their authority goes only so far, 'exercising minimal control over the population'.[79]

The prison population is only allowed to own homemade knives, which are to be used only in community-approved duels between inmates or when called upon to fight off attacks by rivals or wardens.[80] But, ultimately, the *pran* holds the power to decide to wage war against other groups, adjudicating disputes between inmates, imposing punishments to protect and support the legal order, and making collective decisions such as riots and protests.[81]

### Wilmer José Brizuela

Wilmer José Brizuela, better known as 'Wilmito', helped develop the prison-gang subculture of Venezuela around 2005. Over the ensuing year he went from running one section of his prison to taking over the rest of the institution, until he was considered the top shot-caller at Vista Hermosa prison. By 2009 Wilmito was bringing in an estimated $3 million in profit each year. The more he earned as a *pran*, the more he rose to prominence. By most accounts, the turning point for his success was in 2008, when prison visitation rules were vastly expanded, allowing families to spend nights at Vista Hermosa. This was followed by an explosive growth in smuggling contraband and offering services for sale, enhancing and expanding the prison economy.

To most observers, the decision by the Minister of the Interior and Justice to allow families to stay the night created the *pran* system. Many would arrive on Fridays and not leave for days or even weeks.[82] This smoothed the way for prostitutes and partiers who wanted access to the prison demi-monde. These interlopers were the keys for smuggling in the alcohol and drugs that spurred the *pran*-driven criminal economy. Moreover, all these visits were tied to the collection of more and more extortion profits, since every visit had to be paid for by inmates.[83]

The way the extortion system works is that each prisoner pays a fee, or *la causa*, to the *pran* each week. Ignore it and you risk death or a vicious beating. If a prisoner wants a nicer cell or a new television, he has to pay a 'tax'. Such taxes can make the cost of commodities behind bars ten times higher than in the free world. The numerous prison-owned businesses, including barbers, restaurateurs and merchants, pay the *pran* to stay in business. At Tocorón prison in the state of Aragua, the most populated prison in Venezuela, the 7,000 inmates are said to pay taxes close to $2 million each month.[84]

While the *prans* controlled the *carros* on the inside, they also oversaw a parallel criminal structure known as *trenes*, or trains, on the streets. It was common for *prans* and their *luceros* to replicate prison structures on the outside once they were released. One recent report claims they have been 'instrumental' in creating 'megabandas', criminal syndicates made up of hundreds of members, which remain active in various parts of Venezuela.[85]

The year 2011 was a turning point in the relationship between the Chávez regime and the *pran* prison subculture. That year 4,700 inmates of El Rodeo prison in Guatire, near Caracas, fended off close to 4,000 soldiers during a battle between rival *prans*. Rather than the prison-made knives that dominate violent conflict in American prisons, this battle was waged with semi-automatic weapons. It took the government 27 days to put down the conflict and regain control of the prison. After the violence ended, authorities found 20 semi-automatic weapons, 7 assault rifles, 5 shotguns, 8 grenades and 45 kilograms (99 lb) of cocaine in one building. These were only smuggled in after paying 'tolls' to officials. The system of taxes meant it cost $2,300 for an assault weapon, $70 for a pistol and $45 for a grenade.[86]

In the aftermath of the conflict at Rodeo prison, Chávez appointed a 'socialist firebrand', Iris Varela, minister of prisons. During her term she befriended a number of *prans*, allowing them to consolidate power inside the jails. As a result of government outreach, Varela set off a 'system of Pax Mafiosa', which 'gave birth to a new generation of organized crime structures and prans, trains and megabandas across the country'.[87] Indeed, the deal gave the *prans* control inside, but only with the understanding that gang violence would not 'spill over the walls and into the media'. Another theory regarding the emergence of the *prans* suggests that national officials, such as Varela, created them 'because it was easier to negotiate with just one or a few people rather than negotiating with all the inmates at once'.[88]

Following the death of Chávez in 2013, organized criminal enterprises rapidly expanded. However, despite their criminal proclivities, the *prans* and *carros* operated much more efficiently than the administration that followed. Supermarket shelves remained bare in the free world, while *prans* ate behind bars to their heart's content. There are numerous instances of residents going to the nearest prison when they were unable to find food on the outside.

Since 2016, the government of Nicolás Maduro has been filling the country's jails with political opponents and critics – criminalizing free speech. Many of the prisons remain under the de facto rule of criminal gangs. In recent years, Maduro's ill-advised economic policies have put much of the nation on the verge of starvation, with the world's highest inflation rate (2,700 per cent per year). However, the inmates still seem to be well fed. One inmate, asked in 2018 whether Maduro's policies had affected prisoners, replied: 'Yes, the price of hookers has shot up.'[89]

### *The Venezuelan Steve Jobs: Teófilo Rodríguez Cazorla*

Teófilo Rodríguez Cazorla, better known as 'El Conejo', or 'The Rabbit', has been described as 'a visionary prison boss who personi-fied Venezuela's social and political breakdown'.[90] He was released after twelve years from Margarita Island's San Antonio prison in 2015, and killed months later. In 2011, *New York Times* journalist Simon Romero explained how Cazorla was able to turn the island prison 'into a hedo-nistic moneymaker', comparable to a 'Hugh Hefner-inspired fleshpot', offering four swimming pools, a disco, a cockfighting arena and a never-ending supply of crack cocaine and cannabis.[91] The island even became a fashionable destination for vacationers looking for a beach resort. There they could feel safe, gambling away their money and just relaxing. Meanwhile, the profits filled the coffers of El Conejo. It is not hard to miss the Rabbit allusions on the mainland, where taxi drivers emblazoned their vehicles with 'his trademark Playboy bunny sticker ... visual evidence that drivers had paid their protection money'. If there was any doubt about who ran the prison, take the word of a British army veteran incarcerated there for drug charges. Having served a decade in the military he was impressed by the arsenal of weapons available to inmates: 'I've seen some guns in here that I've never seen before. AK-47S, AR-15S, M-16S, Magnums, Colts, Uzis . . . You name them, it's in here.'[92]

### Central American Prison Gangs: The Northern Triangle

During the second half of the twentieth century, Central America was ravaged by bloody civil wars, marked by scorched-earth policies, mass

Murals in San Antonio prison, Margarita Island, of 'El Conejo' and Hugo
Chávez (left), and the trademark Playboy bunny sticker (right).

graves and the aerial bombardment of civilians. By the 1980s the region
was considered 'a place where the Cold War turned red hot'. When
it came to bloodletting, it went 'well beyond the counterinsurgency
of Brazil'.[93] The deadliest conflict took place in Guatemala, following
a CIA-organized coup against leftist president Jacobo Árbenz in 1954.
In the 1980s paramilitary forces and government troops were on a
mission to wipe out support in indigenous communities. Honduras
was saved from internecine conflict by a strong dictatorship and weak
opposition.

'Prison is where the present gang leadership in three countries of
Central America was established.'[94] Moreover, thanks to the punitive
anti-gang policies of the region, the incarceration of so many gang members ensured that they would establish links with organized crime and
drug-trafficking operatives. Much of the rising incarceration is attributable to the tough stands taken by the governments of El Salvador,
Honduras and Guatemala, collectively known as the Northern Triangle.
These three small neighbouring countries see an almost constant flow
of gang members crossing their borders. The most prominent gangs
inside and out of prison in this region are Mara Salvatrucha (MS-13) and
the 18th Street Gang, also known as Barrio 18. Both were established in
Los Angeles by young Salvadorean immigrants whose parents fled that
nation's brutal civil war in the 1980s. Deportation and the migration of

gang members from the United States played a major role in the development of the gangs in El Salvador and Honduras, but this was less true in Guatemala, where most gang members had 'never been outside the country'.

While it is not uncommon for prison gangs to spread through a national penitentiary system, in Central America, this 'propagation' occurred on a transnational basis beginning in the 1990s, when the u.s. exercised a policy of mass deportations of undocumented immigrants to El Salvador and Honduras from southern California, in response to the growing gang violence in California's urban centres. This policy had the unintentional consequence of returning to Central America hardened gang members who introduced the LA gangster style of the 'Mexican Mafia's prison-based rule' from California. In 2016 it was estimated that Central America was home to at least 70,000 hardcore gang members.[95]

## El Salvador

Between 1980 and 1992 El Salvador endured one of Latin America's bloodiest armed conflicts, in a civil war that claimed at least 75,000 lives. In its aftermath came a major crime wave, as many demobilized war veterans returned home to few opportunities. It also created an exodus of almost half a million refugees, most heading towards the United States. Many ended up in the gang-infested streets of Los Angeles in the late 1970s and early 1980s, and formed their own gangs, or *maras*. According to one journalist, the term came from a 1954 Charlton Heston film, *The Naked Jungle*, which was a huge hit in El Salvador. The American film was oddly translated in Spanish as *Cuando Ruge la Marabunto*, or 'When the Ants Roar'. In the journalist's telling, young Salvadoreans adopted the name *Mara* as shorthand for 'a group of friends, who like ants, protect each other'.[96] Another source suggests the term is meant to summon up a 'fierce, tenacious type of Central American ant'.[97]

Initially, the *maras* were drawn to rock and heavy metal music and called themselves 'Mara Stoners'. This contrasted sharply with the Barrio 18 gang and other southern California Hispanic gangs that preferred 'cholo-style buzzed heads, wife beaters and loose fitting pants'.[98] Their well-known 'horn' hand signals came from their appreciation of Black Sabbath, whose early line-up used the trademark 'throwing the horns', in which horns are created by extending the index and little fingers and holding down the middle fingers and thumb. *Mara* members could often be seen leaving concerts flashing the 'devil signs', which they later flipped upside down to make an 'M' for *mara*. As investigative reporter Ioan Grillo put it, 'In the bizarre world of gangs, a symbol that started at Black Sabbath concerts would become connected to massacres, bus bombs, and a government truce,' as MS-13 came into being.[99]

Barrio street gangs had been a fixture of East Los Angeles for decades by the time the *maras* landed. They were initially regarded as easy marks, with their hippie wardrobe and ways. However, around 1984 the gang began developing into a more threatening presence, changing its gang moniker to Mara Salvatrucha, not just to reinforce its Salvadorean identity, but to make the name sound more dangerous. There is no consensus as to the origin of the second part of the moniker, but some have speculated that it might be a combination of the words *Salva*dorean and *trucha*, which translates to 'street smart'. Another translation of *trucha* posits that the gang name's origins reside in El Salvadorean slang meaning 'reliable and alert'. Still others argue that they adopted it because 'it just sounded good.'[100]

As the *maras* grew in numbers, they adopted their iconic weapon, the machete – symbolic of their pastoral lives back home – essentially turning a tool designed for cutting down crops into a sword for cutting down rivals. As more and more Central American immigrants found themselves in California's prisons, they had to change their rather myopic street territorial dynamics and join forces along ethnic and regional lines, as they were forced to fend off the Aryan Brotherhood and the Black Guerrilla Family. MS had one more adaptation to make, and that was to swear allegiance to the *Sureños*, dominated by the Mexican Mafia.[101] It was at this point that the *maras* added the number 13, referring to the thirteenth letter in the alphabet, M. This also meant that once back on the streets they were expected to pay tribute to those in prison, a gang insurance policy if you will; it was a good trade-off in order to earn respect.

Following a truce in 1992 between the El Salvadorean government and the Farabundo Marti National Liberation Front, the American government was more than happy to deport imprisoned gang members to what was then asserted was now a 'peaceful and prosperous nation.'[102] It was not long before aeroplanes from California, chock-full of *maras*, were dumping gang members into El Salvador, 'covered in tattoos and buff from lifting weights in penitentiary gyms'. This was paralleled by a decline in homicides in LA the following year. With a new immigration policy, it was now expedient to deport foreigners who committed

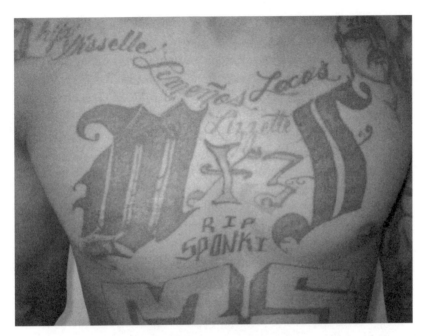

MS-13 tattoos.

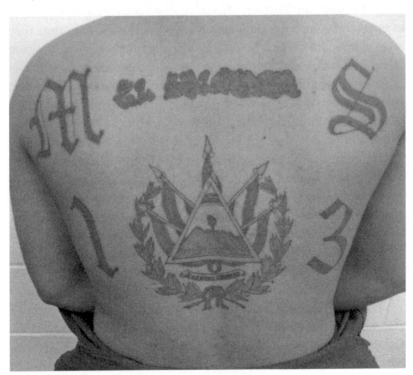

Tattoos of an MS-13 gang member, Atlanta, 2010.

minor crimes. The problem was that El Salvadorean authorities were unaware that many returnees were already hardcore gangsters. Once they hit the streets with their East LA mystique, they quickly developed a following among the legions of homeless and rudderless teenagers, as well as battle-toughened war veterans, who shared their expertise in murder and torture. The demobilized vets ended up taking the lead, offering an organizational scheme and sharing battle strategies with eager-to-learn *maras*.[103]

It didn't take long for members of MS-13 and Barrio 18 to end up in the country's overcrowded prisons after its civil war ended. Until their arrival, beginning in the 1980s, political prisoners affiliated with insurgent groups ran the prison, albeit not without problems. Like MS-13 and Barrio 18, they soon began to turn on each other.

In 1991, most political prisoners were released. At almost the same time 'a young MS13 member wrote in a diary from his jail in San Francisco Gotera, the first reference to the modern-day street gangs in the prisons.'[104] Once the political faction was gone, the more traditional prison gangs filled the vacuum. Among the most prominent actors was one Bruno Ventura, aka 'Brother'. Charismatic and discerning when it came to using force, he led a gang clique known as La Raza. In time they reigned over La Mariona, El Salvador's largest jail. From there, the gang reached into other institutions. At the time of Ventura's emergence, Barrio 18 and MS-13 were mere shadows of what they would become. Moreover, Brother preferred to eschew tribal warfare, recognizing that conflict is never good for business. He ran a tight ship, with every prisoner familiar with the rules and behaviour limits under his rule. If they forgot, he had a brutal system of punishment to remind them. Among the prohibitions under La Raza were injunctions against drug dealing, murder, robbery and attacking visitors and other inmates, rules that seem especially anachronistic considering what would follow in the coming decades. Ventura's special gang rules prohibited tattoos that could be seen on the body, as well as any other gang-related graffiti. His punishments came under the neutral-seeming nomenclature of 'appointments with the psychologist' – shorthand for beatings administered with a wooden rod.[105]

With the return of more than 80,000 deportees from the United States between 1998 and 2014, the prison-gang population exploded, eating into the power of Ventura and La Raza. Most of the gang members were absorbed by El Salvador, Honduras and Guatemala, and by the end of the 1990s gangs were fighting in almost every prison where they were incarcerated. Following strategies used in other parts of the world, officials were under the illusion that a policy of gang segregation would put a stop to the gang warfare behind bars.

As previously mentioned, Brother advocated peace between gangs, especially MS-13 and Barrio 18. At one time this could be assured by sending members to 'the psychologist' every time there was conflict or when more than four of them convened in one location. However, his presence would be missed by the peacemaking element after he was transferred from La Mariona to San Francisco Gotera jail in 2002. Once he was out of the picture, prison life became chaotic, as knife attacks became the rule rather than the exception. Salvadorean jails would never be the same again.

Seeking to bring back some sort of stability, the general prison population was able to convince the administration to remove either MS-13 or Barrio 18 to another facility. MS-13 became the odd man out and was transferred to Ciudad Barrios maximum-security prison, beginning a

A gang member incarcerated in Sonsonate prison, El Salvador, displays the tattoos that cover most of his body.

The town of Sonsonate in western El Salvador is home to a prison housing more than eight hundred inmates. Like many of the prisons in this Central American country, Centro Penal de Sonsonate incarcerates only gang members.

de facto policy of separating gangs inside the adult prison system. With MS out of the way, La Mariona was now divided between Barrio 18 and Brother's La Raza. A battle between the two saw Barrio 18 get the short end of the stick, with the losers awarded the worst cells and food. All this did was escalate the bad blood between them. Both gangs rearmed and prepared for a second battle.

With La Raza under the leadership of José 'Viejo' Posada Reyes, Barrio 18 received contraband weapons from visitors, including a grenade. On 18 August 2004 the concussion from a grenade signalled an attack on La Raza. Caught unprepared, despite having the numbers over Barrio, La Raza was hit the hardest, with 24 out of the 34 deaths being La Raza members (and dozens wounded). Fortunately, Posada saved himself, having the foresight to arm himself with a pistol before the blood began flowing.

### Mano Dura

The El Salvadorean government's adoption of the strong-hand policy, *mano dura*, beginning in 2003–4, accelerated the gang control of prisons even more. Not only did it strengthen gang ties and distinctiveness, but also their coordination and criminality. By indiscriminately locking up suspected gang members and concentrating them in a special prison, it amplified the power of the gangs.

The jails were overrun with thousands of new inmates, each one a potential gang recruit. Between 2000 and 2016 the number of prisoners swelled from 7,754 to 35,879 inmates. Police officers were free to stop and frisk anyone suspected of gang associations. Often a tattoo was reason enough to begin the process. Ultimately, the gang separation strategy might have quelled violence, but at the same time it 'granted de facto control of the penitentiary system' to individual prison gangs. Safe from attack, leadership could pour their efforts into restoring control and command, and revisit gang rules and regulations.[106] Put another way, prisons 'gave gangs a headquarters from which to recruit and expand influence', putting unaffiliated inmates, often first-timers, under the thumb of the gangs, bringing 'a broad range of street-level actors – anyone who might be sent to a given gang's wing if incarcerated – under the gang's "coercive jurisdiction"'.[107]

There were several Central American street gangs, or *pandillas*, prior to the emergence of MS-13. But *maras* were distinct for their ability to organize in a more traditionally hierarchical manner, allowing them to manage activities across parts of North and Central America. With the gangs increasingly ensconced in separate lockups, it allowed shot-callers to systemize their criminal activities out on the streets.

Among the most lucrative ventures was the methodical extortion of bus and taxi cooperatives, propane tank supply and other distribution services. This began around 2010, when Honduran gangs, particularly Barrio 18, began taxing 'anything with wheels, including buses, taxis and motorcycle taxis – a "war tax"'. Since this gang strategy started, more than 1,500 Hondurans working in the transport sector have been murdered. Victims have been strangled, shot and even 'cuffed to the steering wheel and burned alive while their buses are torched . . . If anyone on a bus route stops paying[,] gangs kill a driver – any driver – to send a message.' It is not uncommon for bus drivers to go to a prison to drop off extortion payments. When asked recently to help control this extortion, an anti-extortion official responded that 'they just can't touch MS-13 or 18th Street. They know people in the government are with them.'[108]

By 2015, one-third of El Salvador's prison population consisted of gang members. As with prison gangs in the United States and elsewhere, going to jail became a 'rite of passage' and offered the potential of moving up the ladder of the gang hierarchy. Conversely, incarcerated leaders had new contacts with whom they could expand their financial opportunities.

### *Ranfla*

In the early 2010s, most of El Salvador's MS-13 leaders had experienced American jails and were able to step into positions of leadership thanks to the cachet afforded them by their deportee status. The leaders, or *ranfleros*, have been able to use the horrible prison conditions to their advantage, 'to exert [incredible] control over other gang members'. MS-13 has a firm hierarchy, in which every prison has a *ranfla*, or 'council', of fifteen gang leaders (*ranfleros*) which allows it to control contraband and resources coming from outside. These resources might be legitimate, such as water, clothes, food and visitation rights, or illicit commodities, including drugs, liquor, weapons and mobile phones. Without the phones, the 'sometimes shaky hierarchy' is harder to control.[109]

In descending order, other *ranfla* stalwarts include lieutenants, or *corredores*. Each one of them is part of a programme which controls several cells or cliques. These factions have lieutenants responsible for

Inmates at Zacatecoluca Prison, El Salvador, January 2019.

their individual clique. Moving down a rung are homeboys (members) and then lookouts (*chequos*). To ensure gang solidarity and discipline, strict rules have been developed, along with an accompanying punishment for any infraction. Severe penalties are most commonly given for disrespecting the gang, a wife, girlfriend or visitor, or stealing from other members.[110]

In 2011 the highest level of *ranfleros* were inside the Zacatecoluca Prison, which some have dubbed 'Zacatraz'. This maximum-security prison is the most constantly supervised prison in the country. Today, El Salvador's prison system remains the 'headquarters of the country's largest gang'. It is also a battleground where MS-13 leaders fight each other for control.

### Gang Truce

The government brokered a gang truce in 2012, in which gang members agreed to disarm. This was followed by a substantial drop in the country's homicide rate. But the truce didn't last long. In 2014, the government, after pressure from public opinion, decided to back off from the truce and begin putting gang leaders into maximum-security prisons, triggering assaults by the gangs on three fronts: against the state, citizens and each other. However, this policy reversal was widely supported by citizens who felt that all the truce had done was make a mockery of the justice system, and that it had 'bolstered the bona fides of gangs who seemed powerful enough to offer a truce'.[111]

While the ephemeral truce might have halted murders, it had little impact on the gangs' main revenue stream, extortion. By most accounts, the truce offered a respite that allowed MS-13 and the 18th Street Gang to rearm (after they had turned in their weapons). By 2015 the murder rate was twenty times more than the U.S. rate, meaning El Salvador overtook Honduras as the 'most violent country on earth bar those that are at war'.[112]

### The Death of El Chory

In 2015, a plan was hatched in the Zacatecoluca jail to kill the main leader of MS-13, Walter Antonio Alfaro, better known as 'El Chory'.[113] The forty-year-old Chory had a prestigious résumé, having earned respect on the mean streets of Los Angeles before being deported. In 2014 he had convinced several gang factions to support him in his 'mini rebellion'. He would be a difficult target for his antagonists to kill, and soon assumed a bit of grandiosity by calling himself an 'MS-13 Revolutionary'.[114]

The plan to eliminate Chory offers some insight into the machinations of modern MS-13 prison politics. Chory was a middle-level leader, and along with several others of high status was vocally critical of the upper brass, who he believed were using the gang for their own gain. There was apparently a long-held belief that the leadership had sold out to the government during the ill-fated truce years earlier. Chory went against protocol by organizing a meeting to judge the high command of MS-13, the so-called historical leadership, or *ranfla*. According to Chory, the *ranfla* had disrespected the 'core ethos', or *barrio*, by taking millions of dollars from political parties to help them win elections. He hoped to expose what he regarded as hypocrisy. Chory's strategy would undermine the *ranfla*'s hold on the group.

Among the most prominent leaders at the time of the ill-fated coup was Borromeo Enrique Henríquez Solórzano, 'El Diablito de Hollywood'. When El Chory instigated his rebellion, he was initially backed by pledges of support from thirteen programmes, or factions. However, before the rebellion could be launched, El Diablito warned its targets, and on 6 January 2016 Chory was ambushed and killed.

## Honduras

Beginning in the early 2000s, Honduran prison directors started segregating prisoners according to their gang affiliations, a policy considered imperative in order to diminish violence between MS-13 and Barrio 18, the country's largest gangs. The policy was equally important for gang members, since it protected them from armed death squads known to clandestinely penetrate prisons, targeting gang members for elimination. Prison authorities, to their credit in some cases, were complicit in protecting gang communities by ceding entire barracks to the gangs, minimizing official access within and permitting the gangs to fortify themselves against the death squads. At Marco Aurelio Soto, the country's largest penitentiary, MS-13 moved into a 'traditional barracks' and Barrio 18 took over a former factory where many inmates had previously produced fabrics in bulk for sale in the capital city.[115]

The prisons of Honduras are just as unsavoury as those in neighbouring countries. As the *mano dura* in El Salvador put pressure on the *maras*, many crossed into Honduras. Behind bars, most prisoners would be described as *paisas*, a generic term meaning no affiliation to a larger group. Each inmate is responsible for his own protection, and by some accounts many pack either a handgun or a machete. Prisons such as San Pedro Sula are divided by type of inmate. In Honduras, gangs are not 'well organized and leaders do not have the same authority over rank and file members as in El Salvador'.[116]

Walking into San Pedro Sula Prison, after you move through the layers of police and soldiers, you find yourself winding through what has been described as a 'prison-run ghetto', where inmates have the run of the prison, unhindered by anyone resembling a guard, free to walk around, cook their own meals, run shops and have days-long visits from wives and girlfriends. San Pedro Sula is a microcosm of the prison-gang situation in Honduras. In this facility there are countless internal conflicts between different cliques. It is not uncommon for gang members to just leave the gang. Those who desert are branded *pesetas* and forced to live separately from their former colleagues in the cellblock, typically sharing space with the *paisas*. As one observer put it, 'If you are a peseta, [the authorities] can't put you where your [former] gang is [because] they would chop you up immediately, and [you] can't [be] put in the other gang's area because the same thing would happen.'[117] As a result, *pesetas* from different gangs have formed

Members of the Mara 18 (M-18) gang, pictured at a prison in San Pedro Sula, 240 km (150 mi.) north of Tegucigalpa, in May 2013.

their own group and are considered the power in the *paisas* section. Taking control of the unaffiliated sector means that they now exert the same powers that their former gangs had in their respective sectors. They are now free to tax visitors and prisoners who run various criminal enterprises.

In 2008, following the assassination of a powerful leader, a new group was established in San Pedro Sula prison led by Francisco Breve, or just Don Breve. Under the new leadership, and to tone down violence, weapons were prohibited, so it became much more difficult to hire a killer. Don Breve was able to forge a closer relationship with the prison administration and was soon dubbed 'inmate general coordinator', a title that legitimized his position. He became the go-between for the inmates and the administration, and he alone was responsible for passing on directives from officials.

In his role of coordinator, Don Breve operated as a combination of gang boss and emissary to legitimate channels. Indeed, the 'entire prison economy passe[d] through the hands of the coordinator and administrator', who hand out licences to those running businesses in the corridors, restaurateurs and workshops. They had the power to determine whether one could build a new room and install cable television or provide rooms for prostitutes and visitors.[118]

However, the peace brokered by Don Breve would not last. After he was released there was no one to fill his shoes. He promised to 'continue his good governance' from the streets, leaving a representative in his stead. But as 'general coordinator', his representative, Mario Henríquez's, regime was plagued by terror and violence, with extortion the least of the problems. Henríquez used his authority to steal food from the poorest inmates and resell it in the shops along a prison corridor dubbed 'Zone of Death'. But he crossed a line that was sacrosanct when he raped the young girlfriend of another prisoner, a cardinal sin in the eyes of the *pesetas*. Within a month a coup d'état was underway, punctuated by the killing of Henríquez. His eyes were shot out and his decapitated head tossed from a prison rooftop. And peace returned to San Pedro Sula Prison.[119]

In the aftermath of a national political coup in 2009, the growing independence of Honduran criminal gangs altered the daily lives of Hondurans, both inside and out of prisons, as organized crime groups attempted to create a new revenue stream from mass incarceration. The following year prison administrators reported that the crime networks were taking control of the prisoners' system of self-governance, with one official noting that embryonic criminal syndicates were now entangling gang leaders, non-gang members, organized crime groups and corrupt state actors 'into far reaching criminal networks', where they have taken over entire prison sections, generating huge profits through various extortion schemes.[120]

In June 2019 the government came down hard on incarcerated MS-13 and Barrio 18 members. In order to get a handle on the gangs, a mobile-phone crackdown was implemented, forcing inmates to 'adopt desperate measures to communicate' with the free world. Innovative writing tools such as toilet paper, toothpaste, scraps of plastic and medicine were adapted as writing utensils. This subterfuge was revealed after authorities discovered thirteen 'handwritten coded messages', or *willas*, inside the stomach of a soon to be released Barrio 18 gang member. In addition, telephone service providers were ordered to disable coverage and remove phone booths from all prisons.[121]

The crackdown amplified what inmates thought was a 'drastic increase in repression, citing the banning of visits, not being able to go outside and "see the sun"', prohibitions against books and electronic devices, football, walks and so forth. Following the interception of another 26 messages written on transparent plastic and swallowed, a plastic-free policy was instituted. Prisoners are, if anything, an inventive lot. One message that was intercepted ordered associates to 'send out drones equipped with radio reception to hover just outside prison walls'.[122]

## Guatemala: Committees of Order and Discipline

In recent decades, Guatemala's adult prisons have housed close to 9,000 prisoners, most from the lower classes, with close to 75 per cent waiting to go to trial.[123] In 2018, Guatemala had the fourth-highest occupancy level based on official capacity (357.6 per cent), surpassed in descending order only by the Philippines, Haiti and Bolivia. As would be expected in any overcrowded prison, the conditions were miserable at best. In the 1990s, 'groups of inmates took over the internal functioning of some prisons' as a 'response to the disastrous state of affairs inside them'. Their answer was to organize *Comités de Orden y Disciplina* (Committees of Order and Discipline, or CODs). They made the institutions safer for visitors and inmates, implemented stricter disciplinary codes and demanded fees from prisoners to pay for cleaning equipment, prison security against internal theft, and the salaries of COD staff. The most prominent COD was at the El Pavon prison. Its main goal, initially, was to stop the relentless robbery and sexual assault of visitors. Over the years it created what has been described as 'a country within a country' or 'small town run by inmates'.[124]

The Pavon COD restored a sense of security, as it efficiently ran illegal prison rackets and reduced internal strife. It not only supplied contraband such as alcohol, drugs and prostitutes, but managed the collection of fees from inmates who ran the prison's 'lively commercial center', which included a pizzeria, pool hall, call centre and butcher's shop, and arranged for the sale of 'homes' built by departing inmates. Observers claimed it 'brought a sort of peace'. But behind the scenes this '"prisoner power" consolidated the control of a small minority of inmates' who ran roughshod over the most impoverished prisoners.[125]

Due in large part to the policy of segregating gang members in the same prisons and cellblocks, by 2002 'the gang presence had become concentrated within the system', essentially beginning 'a new stage of Mara history'. Guatemala's overcrowded facilities hold anywhere from 1,500 to 2,000 inmates. As a result of the rise in incarcerated gang

Inmates of Centro Preventivo, Zone 18, during a visit by *La Hora* journalists, 2011.

members in such close proximity with each other, the prison system became 'the most important place for mareros in Guatemala society'. Put another way, prison has become the axis of 'sociability par excellence', where inmates can immerse themselves in their gang identities, while staying in contact with other gang members and leaders thanks to the ubiquity of mobile phones and regular visits from family and friends. 'In those closed shared spaces,' according to historian Deborah T. Levenson, 'they can recuperate their fantasies . . . use gang language and signals, get new tattoos and shave their hair off over and over . . . they are together day and night.'[126]

Tensions are ramped up whenever prison authorities are set to transfer gang members to other jails, sometimes resulting in riots. This is often a matter of survival, since there is safety in numbers, and sometimes gang members are reassigned to jails considered rival strongholds. Despite the numerous gang members throughout the Guatemalan prison system, it must be recognized that these are mostly young men from impoverished backgrounds, thus 'their power in prisons is limited.' In the early 2000s, except for several jails, the cohorts of young gang members were mostly bereft of political connections and well-heeled lawyers. As a result they never represented a real threat to competing groups of more powerful prison cliques, which included 'incarcerated state agents and members of the Colombian and Guatemalan mafias' and other outside competition.[127]

Around 2001 Captain Byron Lima Oliva, a former member of the presidential guard, imprisoned for killing a human-rights reformer, was able to link up with a number of ex-soldiers on remand and take control of Guatemala City's Centro Preventivo, Zone 18 jail. It did not take long for them to take over the COD and begin extorting payments from inmates in exchange for providing security, cable television, food, water, cigarettes, upkeep and so forth.[128]

### Byron Lima: King of the Prison System

After Guatemala's bloody civil war, numerous military veterans were tried and sent to prison. Some were members of the Kaibil, a powerful elite military unit.[129] None was more representative than Captain Byron Lima Oliva. Lima was sentenced to twenty years for the killing of Bishop Juan José Gerardi in 1998. Once behind bars he was a marked man, despite his network of friends in high places and his career fighting leftist guerrillas. As a former intelligence officer, he used his experience to develop his own human intelligence networks that reached into the prison community and administration. He had cobbled together an army of loyal acolytes who were ready to die for him if necessary, and was able to eliminate enemies by using his political connections to send them to other institutions. Lima was soon lionized, to a certain extent, by journalists who dubbed him 'king' of the prison system.[130]

In 2001 Lima and his co-defendants, who included his retired army father, were ensconced in the Centro Preventivo, Zone 18. Still wearing military uniforms initially, they were confronted by the prison boss, who demanded extortion payments from both Limas. In Guatemala this is known as the *talacha*. The practice reportedly goes on unchallenged and sometimes even overlooked by the authorities, if they have received their cut of the extortion money. Prison wardens have created their own revenue streams by collecting a 'tax' from the boss of each prison sector. The amount is computed according to the number of prisoners in each sector, and the types of special privilege that are granted. In order to come up with the taxes, the sector bosses tax the inmates in their sector. The *talacha* can be paid in cash or labour, depending on the financial situation of each prisoner. As one inmate put it:

> if you don't have any money, [it] means cleaning. But not the usual cleaning ... It means cleaning the floor with a mop in your hands, sometimes squatting, in your underwear or even naked. It also means cleaning the toilets, where everyone has taken a shit, with your hands. After a while you can't even stand up because your legs have gone numb, and if you try to get up, you'll fall on your ass. That's hard and you have to do it twice a day.[131]

Some inmates have been turned into *talacheros*, 'the equivalent of an indentured servant', after their families could not come up with the cash to pay extortion fees. Those prisoners who are without outside support and lack any resources of value are dubbed *rusos*, or Russians, or together as a collective as *La Rusua*, Russia.[132]

Coming from a military background, in the politically charged environment of the era, Lima and his father were constantly on the lookout for assassins. Even though they could come up with the *talacha*, prison shot-callers harassed them continuously. In one case, Lima had to fall back on his martial-arts skills to fend off attackers. Over time he gathered power and support to force the drug bosses out of his sector. (He expressed a particular disdain for crack cocaine.) He then set about creating his own extortion rackets and began 'treating the prisoners in his sector like he had treated the soldiers in the army'. Prisoners unaccustomed to discipline must have had a rude awakening when they were put on a regime of waking at dawn, exercising and demonstrating some type of constructive behaviour for the rest of the day, 'such as [building] something, work or exercise'.[133]

It was not long before the former Kaibil ordered all graffiti to be replaced with the Kaibil emblem, a skull gripping a knife between his teeth. Underneath was the group's motto: 'If I go forward, follow me. If I stop, push me. If I retreat, kill me.' But Lima's most revolutionary move was to prohibit further collection of extortion money, much to the gratitude of the *rusos*. Meanwhile, under the noses of the other prison bosses he was putting together his own army.

With his expertise in military intelligence and counterinsurgency, Lima began to move into other sectors of the prison, claiming he was doing so for humanitarian reasons. This was after several inmates came to him with horror stories from other sectors, of prisoners unable to pay *talacha* being forced to copulate with dogs or having their cells flooded as punishment. Lima intended to win the hearts and minds of the inmate population to further his power. However, that power only went so far. There was a special wing that he could not influence; this contained members of the MS-13 and Barrio 18 gangs, or *pandilleros*.

It was de rigueur for prison bosses to do all they could to marginalize gang members and confine them to the worst sectors because they were, in their estimation, too problematic to be mixed in with the general population. This occurred in several prisons. Resentment over their treatment led to an explosion of gang violence at Pavoncito prison just outside Guatemala City, the country's most dangerous prison. Much of the blame was directed at the warden, who earned a reputation for gleefully torturing gang members. But, as one member noted, 'The truth is that that dude had given the homies so much shit.' Both gangs agreed to put aside their rivalry and form an alliance in the prison.[134]

On 23 December 2002 they launched an offensive later dubbed 'a kill or be killed' attack. It took just hours for them to take over Pavoncito prison. Emboldened by their success, the gang members agreed that the next target should be Lima. But he was transferred to Boquerón prison in 2003, before they could put their plan into action, blamed for poisoning the food of the gang members at his former prison. While none died, at least one hundred became ill.

Next, Lima was moved to Pavoncito. All the gang members had by now been transferred to Escuintla, so he was free to create his own regime and establish his hegemony over the contraband markets. He had accrued enough clout that in 2008 he was able to have four high-profile MS-13 leaders transferred to his prison, where they were decapitated and had their heads put on display.[135]

After a former classmate, Otto Perez Molina, took over the Guatemalan government in 2011, Lima did what he could to ride his coat-tails, exercising extraordinary power from prison. He was able to arrange the transfers of prisoners and extort drug kingpins (some awaiting extradition to the U.S.), who were tortured or otherwise humiliated if they didn't pay. However, his transgressions proved too much and too public. By 2013, accompanied by guards, he was regularly leaving prison to see friends and family. More troubling was the fact that he soon had political ambitions of his own as he burnished his cult of personality.

In 2016, along with his brother Luis, Lima established the National Refoundation Party, whose slogan was 'Take Back the Constitution.' He saw the presidency in his future. Never lacking confidence, Lima let it be known that he had no fear of gangsters. However, there were those who did not like the fact that he had intervened in their lucrative crack business, which, Lima told anyone who would listen, was the 'worst thing there can be within a prison.'[136]

Lima strode through the prison corridors of Pavoncito usually flanked by a coterie of bodyguards. These men were considered powerful in their own right. He rotated his guards as a security precaution, since many were bosses of various wings of the prison, and so potential rivals. This proved to be a weakness in his security plan. One day in July 2016, he was walking to breakfast accompanied by a female friend and his bodyguards. He was evidently distracted long enough to be ambushed. He was killed along with his companion and several bodyguards. In the aftermath of his assassination, the killers and their associates began settling scores, killing a total of fourteen inmates; four were beheaded, probably in retaliation for the MS-13 decapitations. Lima had amassed a number of powerful enemies over the years. Surely, there were those behind bars (or on the outside) who remembered his brutality in the insurgency against leftist guerrillas. Others probably did not forget his use of connections to have rivals transferred to other prisons, or his elimination of the *talacha*. His brother denounced the state for the murder, claiming Lima was killed because he knew too many secrets. Whoever it was got away with it.

In April 2019 Howard Wilfredo Barillas Morales was dubbed 'king' of Pavoncito. Although confined to an 'isolate sector', he had ten inmate bodyguards and an alleged army of sixty prisoners who maintained his operations, extorted new arrivals and bribed guards. In 2019 he was charging a 10 per cent fee for all items smuggled into and sold in jail, from bread to cannabis. He took over after the killing of Lima in 2016. Lima had served as a mentor of sorts to Morales, who was sent away for 31 years for a kidnapping in 2012. There is no telling how long he will reign. He may have amassed an arsenal, but bragging that he is not afraid of cartels, especially the Mexican ex-military members turned drug traffickers known as the Zetas, does not necessarily ensure a long lifespan. Nonetheless, Morales apparently revels in his nickname, 'Matazetas', or 'Zetas Killer'.

## Mexico

Throughout its history, Mexico has been burdened by economic inequality that put most of the nation's wealth in the hands of perhaps several dozen families. During almost seventy years of one-party rule, the Institutional Republican Party often rigged elections, which became a 'significant factor in promoting criminal activity' at all levels of society. What's more, Mexican organized crime flourished thanks to a culture of corruption that characterized the country's military and politics for decades.[137] Despite recent attempts at reform, Mexico remains mired in corruption. No part of the country's justice system exemplifies this more than its prison system.

Mexican drug cartels and drug-trafficking organizations flourish on both sides of the border with the United States. The power of various cartels has waxed and waned since around 2000. But since 1992, when drug-trafficking routes were moved from the Caribbean to Mexico, the country's prison population has more than tripled. Estimates of how much of the prison system is run by gangs range around 60 per cent. In more recent years, Los Zetas, and the Sinaloa, Gulf and Juárez cartels, have been the most prominent gangs, fighting each other over drug routes and the monopolization of various illicit revenue streams. In terms of prison-gang subculture, this conflict often takes place behind prison walls, aided by smaller ephemeral prison gangs. There are several smaller gangs that have sided with one cartel or another, but other than the Barrio Azteca, Los Mexicles and Artistas Asesinos, there is not a lot of verifiable information to allow us to trace any historical continuum beyond the past few years. What is known is that factions have engaged in bloody warfare in a number of Mexican prisons, using weapons ranging from homemade shanks to automatic weapons.

### Barrio Azteca

What distinguishes the Barrio Azteca (BA) gang is the fact that it was created in Texas prisons around 1986, before expanding into Mexican jails. Much of this transmission took place between the bordering towns of El Paso and Ciudad Juárez. It has a reputation for organization that has allowed it to increase its membership on both sides of the border. What has helped it expand is the increasing deportation of Mexican criminals from the United States. Just after the turn of the millennium, the gang controlled most prisons in the state of Chihuahua. By 2013, there were an estimated 5,000 members of BA in the vicinity of Juárez alone (and more than 3,000 in the U.S.).[138]

BA burnished its reputation in the early 2000s by backing up the Juárez cartel in its war with the Sinaloa organization for control of Ciudad Juárez. By most accounts, this alliance was made possible thanks to 'La Linea', the armed wing of the Juárez cartel, which recruited members to fight. The gang finds many of its prospects in Juárez jails, apparently 'attracted by the strict order that the gang enforces on members'.[139]

BA has adopted a hierarchical structure that has been compared to that of the military, complete with a committee of 'generals' at the top, who rule on both sides of prison walls 'by consensus'. In descending order below them are captains, lieutenants, command sergeants and soldiers (*indios*). In 2012, it was reported that 60 per cent of Mexico's 430 jails and prisons were 'self-governed' by gangs.[140]

BA maintains communication through coded letters, contraband mobile phones and the distribution of membership rosters and hit lists. A number of its members have learned to communicate in a secret language based on Nahuatl. Most of the gang's power resides in the prison system, leading some to suggest that its operational capacity is hindered when all the leaders are incarcerated. On the streets, BA members will contact imprisoned gang leaders to verify the status of any

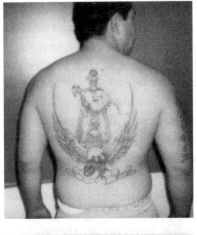
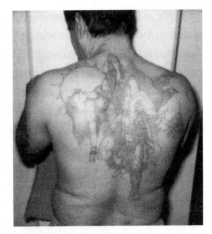

Known Barrio Azteca gang members who have been arrested in Texas.

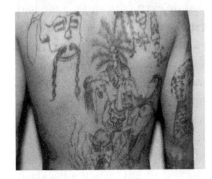

individual operating under the mantle of the BA. If it turns out that the individual is not in good standing, he will probably be killed. BA taxes independent drug dealers in El Paso, west Texas and parts of eastern New Mexico. Once the money is collected it is typically deposited in the bank accounts of imprisoned bosses, usually by wiring it under false names or to female associates.[141]

The operations of Mexican prison gangs typically come to light after major bloodletting between rival gangs behind bars. In March 2009, for example, a bloody clash between BA and a gang known as Los Mexicles broke out early in the morning (after all conjugal visits had ended). The Mexicles were allied with another prison gang, known as Artistas Asesinos (Murdering Artists), which had worked as enforcers for the Sinaloa cartel. Apparently, BA members were able to steal cell keys from a prison guard, allowing them to free their members before launching an attack on the cells holding rival gang members. After taking a number of guards hostage, BA soldiers went into the high-security blocks and forced guards to open cells, allowing them to murder at least twenty inmates with knives and homemade guns. While no one could point to why the brawl broke out, the longstanding feud between the BA and the Artistas was well known, since they are often at odds regarding control over weapons, drugs and contraband in whichever prisons they are in.[142]

### The Zetas

The Zetas have usually been the most powerful prison group wherever they have been locked up in sufficient numbers. At Saltillo's Centro de Reinserción Social Reform Institution, the warden was murdered in 2011 and the Zetas took over. Everything was taxed. If one wanted to work in a certain shop or factory, purchase timber for construction or for fuel, or have access to soap, food or even education, a fee had to be paid to the imprisoned Zetas. If one wanted to buy drugs from a gang member, one had to pay to leave the cell to make the purchase. Practically everywhere one turned in the prison there were paintings on the wall of a 'giant clown with blood-red shoes and a demented smile, the tag of the commandante'.[143] It did not take a genius to figure out that the symbolism meant that the Zetas were always watching.

In 2010 Gomez Palácio prison, located in the state of Durango, permitted Zeta inmates to carry out murders, including a massacre of seventeen. However, the tables were turned in 2017 when a backlash from inmates and members of their longtime rival, the Gulf Cartel, in northern Mexico's Cadereyta Prison, successfully fought back to ward off the gang's domination. What distinguished this episode was the reluctance of the prison population to allow the Zetas to take over. The prison grapevine was rife with stories of the prison director bringing the gang in to help him control the prison. Most doubts were dropped when a banner was spread across a wall proclaiming, 'We don't want a Z director'.[144]

### Piedras Negras State Prison

No prison exemplified the 'self-government that criminal gangs enjoy in Mexican prisons' more than Piedras Negras state prison in Coahuila between 2009 and 2012, when it was used as an 'extermination camp' by the Zeta drug-trafficking organization. Zeta leaders, adorned in prison-made uniforms complete with bulletproof vests, acted as the institution's 'de facto security force'. Until 2012, their activities went under the radar. But the prison hit the headlines that year when 131 inmates escaped through its front door, in Mexico's largest jailbreak. Later that year the authorities closed it down and transferred the inmates to other prisons.[145] The Zetas used Piedras Negras as a headquarters of sorts, where they were free to manufacture uniforms and lock up kidnap victims until they were killed and cremated in containers of diesel fuel. With the security of having a prison to themselves, Zetas had plenty of time to modify stolen or purchased vehicles for drug smuggling, installing secret compartments and, if necessary, fitting them with new VIN numbers. Meanwhile, military-type uniforms in green and sand colours, Navy uniforms, Rapid Intervention Force (GAFE) uniforms and uniforms of the Federal Investigation Agency (AFI), all used in Zetas operations, were being manufactured in the sewing workshop. The gang also manufactured covers for plate carriers, tactical webbing and police-type belts, slings for rifles, holsters for pistols and spare magazines. Every week a car would pick up everything that had been produced. In a welding shop, devices for puncturing tyres, *ponchallantas*, were made in preparation for future conflicts with state police forces.

The prison also proved a fertile recruiting ground for hitmen, better known as *sicarios*. There was little resistance from the state officials. Zetas were so comfortable in the prison that free-world leaders would hide out there and entertain guests at parties where cows were slaughtered and cooked. It was common for Zeta leaders to be escorted outside by guards for coffee, to 'shoot at people for fun' and to have sex with the wives of other convicts.[146]

Most kidnap victims arrived at the prison alive, and were killed there with either a hammer blow to the head or a gunshot. Their dismemberment took place under the noses of the guards in the tower above. The victims were usually drug traffickers unaffiliated with the Zetas; some owed them money, others were relatives of targets and still others had no ties to the underworld. No one challenged the Zetas.

Aerial shot of Piedras Negras prison near the border with Texas, 2010.

According to the testimony of one boss in 2014, 'When they cooked up the people [cremated them in containers of oil, as above] they would get smaller and they would hit them with a metal bar until there was nothing left – later they would tip over the barrel to dump what was left on the ground . . . and there was very little.' One of the most delicate tasks was destroying remains at night in diesel fuel, which would earn the worker $300 each time. During its short run as a Zeta operations centre, at least 150 victims were killed at Piedras Negras. Meanwhile, the gang was earning a reported $75,000 each year. Guards walked the grounds unarmed, while close to a hundred prisoners working for the Zetas carried guns.[147]

The head of the Zetas at Piedras Negras, David Loreto Mejorado, better known as 'El Commandante Enano', ran the prison from 2009 to 2012. He instituted an organization that revolved around 92 'collaborators', including lieutenants, bodyguards and messengers. He made it clear that his priorities for running the prison were drug smuggling and modifying vehicles, developing 'war equipment' and the 'destruction of bodies'. Discipline was maintained by an iron-clad system of punishment, typically the *tablazos*, which was a beating on the buttocks with either a wooden board or an aluminium bat. One inmate suggested that the boss even gave the prison director a dose of this penalty.

Inside the prison compound, the Zetas maintained their own jail, 'El Monte', in the maximum-security area. Inmates who committed transgressions and victims who had been abducted and were still negotiating ransoms were kept there. The Zetas were constantly on the lookout for new revenue streams. El Commandante made this clear in 2010, when he used the state of Tamaulipas' Nuevo Laredo prison as an example of a prison that brought in plenty of lucre, commenting that they made money 'fucking the inmates with extortion and fines'. This was supplemented by weekly fees and the renting of prison cells.[148]

### The Caribbean: Puerto Rico

The best-chronicled prison gang in the Caribbean is the Puerto Rican Neta or the Neta Association, founded in the 1970s by Carlos 'La Sombra' Torres-Irriarte in Río Piedras Prison. The gang reportedly adopted its name from the popular celebration of a baby's birth, when Puerto Ricans traditionally chant 'Neta! Neta!' Others suggest that it is actually an acronym for 'Never Tolerate Abuse'. Prison authorities chalk its development up to a strategy to reduce violence between inmates at that prison. In any case, it is now a major force in the island's drug trade.

Ideologically, Neta sees itself as part of the Puerto Rican independence movement, and members see themselves as oppressed by the u.s. government. It is affiliated with street gangs and with members of the Los Macheteros terrorist group seeking independence. However, most observers debunk this 'cultural' association as a facade.

Carlos 'La Sombra' Torres-Irriarte, photographed by Wilfredo Freddie
Toledo.

There are an estimated 40,000 Neta members in Puerto Rico and another 20,000 in the United States, with a further 30,000 across the globe. The gang earned prominence in the aftermath of a savage attack on the leader of the G27 gang, when Netas broke into his cell, stabbed him more than 150 times and chopped him into 84 pieces. By some accounts, body parts were sent to various individuals, including his mother and G27's second in command. Neta is notorious for its secrecy, and members will never admit to belonging.

Neta is active in a number of American prisons on the east coast, from Florida to New England. Each member is expected to find twenty potential members, and on the 30th of each month the group comes together to recognize the dead. Gang-member affiliation is reflected by the colours red, white and blue, although black sometimes fills in for blue. Members often display the Puerto Rican flag and carry membership cards. Colours can be recognized through clothing or beads. Probationary members wear only white beads until they become official members. The gang is very restrictive regarding who joins, and its ability to stay in the shadows has allowed it to operate under the radar for years. The Neta preoccupation, at least in the United States, with keeping a low profile is in stark contrast to other Hispanic groups, which are constantly the focus of officials.

From a historical perspective, 'inmate self-governance' has 'deep and strong roots in Latin America'.[149] Meanwhile, prison gangs continue to evolve and operate, providing self-governance to the region's overcrowded and understaffed prisons. Overcrowding continues to set the stage for all sorts of violence between prison gangs and other locked-up rivals. This was made clear in March 2018, when 68 prisoners died in a fire in an overloaded Venezuelan jail. The fire reportedly began after gangs running a party fought with guards and took a hostage. The party was masterminded by Venezuelan *prans*, who, as mentioned previously, have long operated extortion rackets inside with impunity. In this country, and the rest of the region, where 'tragedy has become the norm', tens of thousands of prisoners sit neglected in overcrowded cells, mostly waiting to go on trial.

# EPILOGUE

Over the past half-century mass incarceration has become increasingly common in both the developing and the developed world. As a result, overcrowding, paucity of prison staff and a lack of budgeting and oversight have combined to create a vacuum in authority within many prisons and prison systems. With the ratio between the keepers and the kept becoming increasingly disproportionate, it should not be much of a surprise that these power vacuums are being filled by various incarnations of the prison-gang subculture.

Whether one uses the identifiers prison gang, gang in prison, security-threat group, prison group, institutionalized gang, prison-based criminal organization or any others depends on one's perspective and favoured use of nomenclature, as well as the diversity of cultures.[1] In some cases this might include emphasizing certain criteria and disregarding others, as the Arizona prison system does. Gang cultures inside and out of prison are dynamic and shape shifting as they evolve over decades. What becomes clear is that, despite variations between prison gangs and terminology, there are enough points of similarity to recognize the phenomenon if one has adequate information on individual prison groups.

Although the image of the prison gang remains a sinister one, summoning up the worst that prisons have to offer, such groups can also be constructive. In the article 'Why Prisons Aren't All Bad', the authors explain that because of gangs, some prisons run more smoothly than others, while dispelling the notion that prison gangs are not 'exclusively about crime'.[2] The Philippine *pangkat* system, for example, is 'functionally important' to both administrators and inmates, by providing a system of governance and network of social support. Similarly, the *pran* system in Venezuela, Homes in Thailand and indigenous prison gangs in the United States, Australia and New Zealand perform similar functions. As early as 1850, William Gladstone, a British Member of Parliament, noted how Neapolitan prisons were being run by the prisoners, commenting, 'they are a self-governed community'.[3] Indeed, modern Latin American prisons would have a difficult time operating without cellblock mafias and prisoner collectives that provide 'self-governing systems of aid and protection'. One journalist recently noted the 'paradox of the Latin American crime wars', in which prisons that were 'meant to stop gangsters from committing crime ... became their headquarters'.[4] Likewise, thanks to the strong hand, or *mano dura*, of the region's justice systems, the prisons of the so-called Central American Triangle of El Salvador, Honduras and Guatemala have given rise to modern-day gang leadership of the *maras*, such as MS-13 and the 18th Street Gang.[5]

All prison gangs offer some type of creation saga. Some trace their origins to cultural and social change resulting from the European colonial experience and its impact on indigenous cultures, such as the Number gang in South Africa and the Mongrel Mob in New Zealand. But the older their origins, the more obfuscated and debatable the stories become. Even in the United States, home to the world's most-chronicled and best-known prison gangs, there has been little debate or research to verify the country's first prison gangs. In fact, there has been virtually *no* debate over the long-accepted notion that the elusive Gypsy Jokers gang was the first, in 1950. However, a perusal of archives and newspaper microfilm reveals a robust prison-gang culture in New York state prisons decades earlier.

As far back as the 1930s, members of free-world bootlegging syndicates, as well as Irish, Italian and Sicilian groups of prisoners, had banded together and self-segregated to do what their modern counterparts do behind bars – run gambling operations and drug networks, and create hierarchies. The Federal Bureau of Prisons was aware early on of the potential of gang culture being imported into prisons, and attempted to counteract it by sending members of the Chicago Capone syndicate and New York's Luciano gang to different prisons in order to prevent them from organizing and fraternizing. The study of prison gangs has long been the purview of criminologists, criminal justicians, political scientists, anthropologists, sociologists and economists. This book adds a new dimension to the examination of prison gangs by utilizing a mixed approach that is heavy on historical research.

Prison-gang research in the United States has been dominated by coverage of the legendary gangs of California – the Aryan Brotherhood, the Mexican Mafia, La Nuestra Familia and the Black Guerrilla family, which gang researcher Benjamin Lessing refers to as the 'classic gangs'.[6] These were established according to the racial and ethnic backgrounds of members, making racial solidarity their key ingredient. Almost without exception, the early California gangs of the 1960s were divided by race and ethnicity. This left a conundrum for anyone of mixed race as to which gang to join, especially in the case of Jewish, Asian and Native American people and those who were of mixed racial and ethnic heritage. Despite the self-segregation and general hostility between groups, according to one inmate, while the 'races don't mix,' it is 'not as cut and dry as you think'.[7]

The study of prison gangs as a global, national and state phenomenon has been challenged by the lack of consistent nomenclature and of generalizable definitions. However, a historical survey of prison groups reveals a number of commonalities, including a familiar slang, tattoos, initiation protocols, written and unwritten rules of behaviour, and the reliance on extortion as an important revenue stream and recruiting device.

While the Neapolitan Camorra was born in Italian prisons, today the prisons of Western Europe are outliers in comparison to other prison systems. Where prison gangs do exist there, they are more likely to be associated with political (Irish paramilitaries) and religious radicals (Muslim, Catholic and Protestant), and in some cases the free-world outlaw motorcycle gang culture imported into prisons. With lower crime rates and smaller prison populations, lacking the harbingers of overcrowding, racial and ethnic stratification, and sparse oversight, self-government is rare in European correctional facilities. Neighbourhood connections trump traditional gang organization behind bars, often importing conflicts from outside into prisons, exemplified by the ongoing Kinahan–Hutch feud. Nonetheless, there is evidence that more permanent structures and hierarchies are now being identified in the prisons of the United Kingdom.

Recent years have seen a decline in European prison populations and a levelling off of inmate numbers in the United States, but a substantial and unprecedented rise in prison populations in Latin America, mostly due to glacially slow justice systems that leave thousands of young inmates to wait months and even years to go to trial. Like the American incarceration binge, the region's punitive drug policies have overwhelmed the prisons with pre-trial detainees for drug offences.

Prison-gang subculture continues to evolve. The Russian thieves' world is a case in point. By the 1970s, without the Gulag system, the prison subculture virtually disintegrated, and with the collapse of the Soviet Union, prison subcultures and the 'world of thieves' did not fare well in the new capitalist Russia. In its Soviet heyday, the subculture stretched further geographically than any other prison subculture. Although the thieves' culture still influences prisons in Russia and the states of the former USSR in the twenty-first century, after the fall of the Soviet Union it lost most of its cultural relevance.

Likewise, the South African Number subculture discarded most of its traditions after apartheid ended. Beginning in the 1990s the impact of drug trafficking and kingpins inflicted chaos on the traditional prison-gang culture. While there is still debate over how much the Number and other gangs control prisons today, there is evidence of the breakdown of this tradition-based culture in post-apartheid South Africa as old loyalties fray and a new criminal economy challenges the Number system for hegemony.[8]

Asian prison gangs and groups defy any attempt to overgeneralize them. The legacy of colonialism has a strong presence in places like Singapore, which is home to ethnic-minority gangs comprising Indian and Malay members. In Bali, Indonesia, many prison gangs are linked to Hindu groups, such as Laskar Bali, who control Bali's largest drug hub, in Kerobokan prison. One inmate told a journalist that it's 'the only jail where the prisoners run the jail'.[9] In the Philippines, where prison-gang culture revolves around the *pangkat* system, 'shared governance' between gang and staff is officially and unofficially accepted.

Prison gang cultures and groups will continue to provide self-government in regions where prison systems are overburdened, under-staffed and underfunded. Other factors suggest that this will be the case for the foreseeable future as a much larger supply of potential gang recruits' looms on the horizon as the world's population gets younger. Most recently, it was announced that there are 'more young than ever before'. Put another way, 41 per cent of the global population is under the age of 24.[10] This does not bode well for the world's penal institutions, as a large portion of these young men and women reside in impoverished countries boasting increasingly punitive criminal justice regimes.

# REFERENCES

PROLOGUE

1 George M. Camp and C. G. Camp, *Prison Gangs: Their Extent, Nature, and Impact on Prisons* (South Salem, NY, 1985), p. 20. It was not until recently that the claim was challenged, after one study suggested that it originated as a motorcycle gang six years after it supposedly started in the Washington State Penitentiary. See Carter F. Smith, 'When Is a Prison Gang Not a Prison Gang: A Focused Review of Prison Gang Literature', *Journal of Gang Research*, XXIII/2 (March 2016), for an overview of the search for America's first prison gang.
2 'Penologists Back Wickersham Data', *New York Times*, 23 October 1931, p. 17.
3 'Prison Gang Chiefs Served by Valets', *New York Times*, 25 January 1934, p. 1. Samples of more supporting evidence for 1930s prison gangs can be found in the following *New York Times* articles: 'Welfare Island Raid Bares Gangster Rule over Prison: Weapons, Narcotics Found', 26 January 1934, pp. 1, 3; 'Prison Gangs Face a Federal Inquiry; Clean-up Pressed', 26 January 1934, pp. 1, 3; 'Jail Inquiry Turns to District Leader', 28 January 1934, p. 20; 'Head of Jail Gang Threatens Suicide', 30 January 1934, pp. 1, 4; 'Three Felons Stabbed at Great Meadow', 27 January 1933, p. 3.
4 Joseph F. Spillane, *Coxsackie: The Life and Death of Prison Reform* (Baltimore, MD, 2014).
5 Benjamin Lessing, 'The Danger of Dungeons: Prison Gangs and Incarcerated Militant Groups', in *Small Arms Survey*, January 2010, p. 161.
6 Kayleen Hazlehurst and Cameron Hazlehurst, *Gangs and Youth Subcultures: International Explorations* (New Brunswick, NJ, 1998), p. 7.


1 PRISON-GANG SUBCULTURES

1 David Skarbek, *The Social Order of the Underworld: How Prison Gangs Govern the American Penal System* (Oxford, 2014).
2 Michael D. Lyman, *Gangland* (Springfield, IL, 1989), p. 48.

3 The American Correctional Association defines a prison gang as 'two or more inmates, acting together, who pose a threat to the security or safety of staff/inmates, and/or to the orderly management of the facility/system'. American Correctional Association, 'Gangs in Correctional Facilities: A National Assessment' (Washington, DC, 1993), p. 1.

4 George W. Knox, 'The Problem of Gangs and Security Threat Groups (STG's) in American Prisons and Jails Today: Recent Findings of the 2012 NGCRC National Gang/STG Survey', National Gang Crime Research Center, www.ngcrc.com/corr2012.html (2010), defines a prison gang as 'any group of three or more persons with recurring threatening or disruptive behavior (i.e., violations of the disciplinary rules where said violations were openly known or conferred benefit upon the group would suffice for a prison environment), including, but not limited to gang crime or gang violence (i.e., crime of any sort would automatically make the group a gang, and as a gang in custody it would logically be an STG).'

5 Benjamin Lessing, 'The Danger of Dungeons: Prison Gangs and Incarcerated Militant Groups', in *Small Arms Survey 2010: Gangs, Groups, and Guns* (Cambridge, 2010), p. 159.

6 Ibid.

7 John M. Hagedorn, 'Global Impact of Gangs', *Journal of Contemporary Criminal Justice*, XXI/2 (2005), pp. 153–69. Hagedorn suggests that this form of prison subculture 'persists despite changes in leadership (e.g. killed, incarcerated, or "matured out"), has organization complex enough to sustain multiple roles of its members . . . can adapt to changing environments without dissolving (e.g., as a result of police repression), fulfills some needs of its community (economic, security, services), and organizes a distinct outlook of its members (rituals, symbols, and rules)'.

8 *National Gang Intelligence Center Report* (Washington, DC, 2013), p. 7. The National Gang Intelligence Center (NGIC) expanded the definition to include 'criminal organizations that originated within the penal system that have continued to operate within correctional facilities throughout the U.S., including self-perpetuating criminal entities that can continue their operations outside the confines of the penal system'.

9 The Arizona Department of Corrections (2004) applies the tag 'prison gang' to 'any organization, club, association or group of individuals, formal or informal (including traditional prison gangs), that may have a common name, identifying sign or symbol, and whose members engage in activities that would include, but are not limited to, planning, organizing, threatening, financing, soliciting, committing, or attempting to commit unlawful acts or acts that would violate the department's written instructions, which would detract from the safe orderly operations of prisons'.

10 Clarke R. Jones, Raymund E. Narag and Resurrecion S. Morales, 'Philippine Prison Gangs: Control or Chaos?', *RegNet Working Paper*, LXXI (2015).

11  Clarke R. Jones and Raymund E. Narag, 'Why Prison Gangs Aren't All Bad', CNN, https://edition.cnn.com, 11 December 2014.

12  Ibid., and quotations above.

13  Ibid.

14  Michelle Butler, Gavin Victor Slade and Camila Caldeira Nunes Dias, 'Self-governing Prisons: Prison Gangs in an International Perspective', *Trends in Organized Crime*, 30 March 2018.

15  Ibid.

16  David Skarbek, 'Covenants without the Sword? Comparing Prison Self-governance Globally', *American Political Science Review*, CX (2016), pp. 845–62.

17  Gresham Sykes, *The Society of Captives: A Study of a Maximum Security Prison* (Princeton, NJ, 1958), p. 79.

18  Donald Clemmer, *The Prison Community* (Boston, MA, 1940).

19  Sykes, *The Society of Captives*.

20  Quoted in Skarbek, *The Social Order of the Underworld*, p. 67.

21  John Irwin, *Prisons in Turmoil* (Boston, MA, 1980).

22  Ibid., p. 12. Cited in Carter F. Smith, 'When Is a Prison Gang Not a Prison Gang? A Focused Review of Prison Gang Literature', *Journal of Gang Research*, XXIII/2 (March 2016).

23  Gresham Sykes and S. L. Messenger, 'The Inmate Social System', in Richard Cloward, Donald Cressey and G. H. Grosser, eds, *Theoretical Studies in Social Organization of the Prison* (New York, 1960), pp. 6–8.

24  Irwin, *Prisons in Turmoil*. See also John Irwin, *The Felon* (Englewood, NJ, 1970).

25  Quoted in Eric Bronson, 'Medium Security Prisons and Inmate Subcultures: 'The Normal Prison', *The Southwest Journal of Criminal Justice*, II (2006), p. 62.

26  Benjamin Lessing, 'Study Shows Prison Gangs Rule Much More than Penitentiaries', www.insightcrime.org, 30 September 2016.

27  Kathleen Harris, 'Street, Indigenous, Biker Gangs Flourish behind Bars, but a Growing Number of Groups Evade Classification', www.cbc.ca/news/politics, 25 March 2018.

28  Quoted in Rebecca Trammell, 'Values, Rules, and Keeping the Peace: How Men Describe Order and the Inmate Code in California Prisons', *Deviant Behavior*, XXX (2009), p. 748.

29  Meyer Galler and Harlan E. Marquess, *Soviet Prison Speech: A Survivor's Glossary* (Madison, WI, 1972), p. 23; Mark Galeotti, *The Vory: Russia's Super Mafia* (New Haven, CT, 2018), p. 66.

30  Diego Gambetta, *Codes of the Underworld: How Criminals Communicate* (Princeton, NJ, 2009), p. 12.

31  Charles Van Onselen, *The Small Matter of a Horse: The Life of 'Nongoloza' Mathebula, 1867–1948* (Johannesburg, 1984).

32  Sou Lee and Raymund Narag, 'Fanning the Flames: Understanding Gang Involvement among Philippine Prisoners', *International Journal of Offender Therapy and Comparative Criminology*, LXIII/3 (2019), https://doi.org, 5 September 2018, p. 83.

33 Marie Rosenkrantz Lindegaard and Sasha Gear, 'Violence Makes Safe in South African Prisons: Prison Gangs, Violent Acts, and Victimization among Inmates', *Focaal – Journal of Global and Historical Anthropology*, LXVIII (2014), p. 42.

34 Steven Dudley and James Bargent, 'The Prison Dilemma: Latin America's Incubators of Organized Crime', www.insightcrime.org, 19 January 2017, p. 2.

35 G. David Curry, Scott H. Decker and David Pyrooz, *Confronting Gangs: Crime and Community* (New York, 2014), p. 161.

36 Raymund E. Narag and Sou Lee, 'Putting Out Fires: Understanding the Developmental Nature and Roles of Inmate Gangs in the Philippine Overcrowded Jails', *International Journal of Offender Therapy and Comparative Criminology*, LXII/11 (2018), https://doi.org, 3 December 2017.

37 Sacha Darke, 'Inmate Governance in Brazilian Prisons', *The Howard Journal of Crime and Justice*, LII (July 2013); Sacha Darke and Maria Lucia Karam, 'Latin American Prisons', in Y. Jewkes, B. Crewe and J. Bennett, eds, *Handbook on Prisons* (Abingdon, 2014); C. T. Garces, T. Martin and S. Darke, 'Informal Prison Dynamics in Africa and Latin America', *Criminal Justice Matters*, XCI (2013); Lee and Narag, 'Fanning the Flames', p. 24.

38 George Knox, 'The Problem of Gangs and Security Threat Groups (STG's) in American Prisons and Jails Today: Recent Findings from the 2012 NGCRC National Gang/STG Survey', *Journal of Gang Research*, XX/1 (Autumn 2012), p. 52.

39 David C. Pyrooz and Scott H. Decker, 'Motives and Methods for Leaving the Gang: Understanding the Process of Gang Desistance', *Journal of Criminal Justice*, XXXIX (2011); James B. Jacobs, 'Street Gangs Behind Bars', *Social Problems*, XXI (1974), pp. 395–409.

40 'Kiwi Model', *The Economist*, 1 December 2018.

41 The Attica riot was not actually a riot, but a hostage-taking rebellion following years of awful conditions. The most recent chronicler of the uprising suggests it was the result of a 'misunderstanding more than anything'. Of the 43 deaths, including ten guards, all but one was killed by friendly fire in the taking of the prison by the assault team that came in firing weapons. This bloody event had more in common with Brazilian prison uprisings, such as the Carandiru massacre, where most of the 111 deaths were at the hands of those retaking the building. Like the Brazilian prisoners, some of whom would be inspired to create the PCC, the inmates were in this together, rather than factions fighting over territory and drug trafficking. For the best account of this four-day siege see Heather Ann Thompson, *Blood in the Water: The Attica Prison Uprising in 1971 and Its Legacy* (New York, 2016).

42 Trammel, 'Values, Rules, and Keeping the Peace', pp. 746–71.

## 2 THE CAMORRA

1 'Alfano Holds Stage at Viterbo Assizes', *New York Times*, 1 April 1911, p. 5. See also in *New York Times*, 'Camorra Treasurer Heard at Viterbo', 6 April 1911, p. 4, and 'Don Ciro Vitozzi's Tears Move Court', 7 April 1911, p. 6.

2 'Court the Camorra Chief', *New York Times*, 10 November 1912.

3 It is now common for most prisons containing numerous prison-gang members to determine gang affiliation before classifying the individual and placing him in a cellblock.

4 Arthur C. Train, *Courts, Criminals and Camorra* (New York, 1912), pp. 168–9.

5 Ibid.

6 Ibid., p. 150.

7 Gaia Servadio, *Mafioso* (London, 1976), pp. 22–3.

8 Ibid.

9 John Dickie, *Blood Brotherhoods: The Rise of the Italian Mafias* (London, 2011), p. 42.

10 Tom Behan, *See Naples and Die: The Camorra and Organized Crime* (London, 2002), p. 19.

11 Henner Hess, *Mafia and Mafiosi: The Structure of Power* (Lexington, MA, 1973).

12 Arthur Griffiths, *The History and Romance of Crime: Italian Prisons* (London, c. 1920), p. 261.

13 Dickie, *Blood Brotherhoods*, p. 42.

14 Ibid., p. 266.

15 Paul Lunde, *Organized Crime: An Inside Guide to the World's Most Successful Industry* (New York, 2004), p. 74.

16 Behan, *See Naples and Die*; Dickie, *Blood Brotherhoods*.

17 David Leon Chandler, in *Brothers in Blood: The Rise of the Criminal Brotherhoods* (New York, 1975), p. 14.

18 Train, *Courts, Criminals and Camorra*, p. 147.

19 Pasquale Peluso, 'The Roots of the Organized Criminal Underworld in Campania', *Sociology and Anthropology*, I (2013), p. 118, offered another hypothesis: that *camorra* came from a Spanish term that denoted Spanish boys who worked for the aristocratic boss of the era.

20 Dickie, *Blood Brotherhoods*, p. 73.

21 Behan, *See Naples and Die*, p. 17.

22 Peluso, 'The Roots of the Organized Criminal World in Campania', p. 121.

23 Griffiths, *Italian Prisons*, p. 262.

24 James Fentress, *Rebels and Mafiosi: Death in a Sicilian Landscape* (Ithaca, NY, 2000), p. 157; Peluso, 'The Roots of the Organized Criminal World in Campania', p. 55.

25 Antonio Nicolò, *Narrative of Ten Years Imprisonment in the Dungeons of Naples* (London, 1861).

26 Norman Johnston, *Forms of Constraint* (Urbana, IL, 2000).

27 Nicolò, *Ten Years in the Dungeons*, pp. 52–3.

28 Ibid., pp. 72–4.

29 Ibid., pp. 52–4

30 Dickie, *Blood Brotherhoods*, p. 38.

31 A poignard is best described as a slender dagger with two sharp edges used for stabbing and piercing.

32 Nicolò, *Ten Years in the Dungeons*, p. 54.

33 Ibid., p. 75.

34 Ibid., p. 94.

35 Ibid., pp. 94–5.

36 Dickie, *Blood Brotherhoods*, p. 49.

37 Quoted in Francesca De Rosa, 'The Vicaria Prison of Naples', in *Antonio Serra and the Economics of Good Government*, ed. Sophus Reinhart and Rosario Patalano (New York, 2016), p. 25.

38 See Hugh Chisholm, ed., 'Marc Monnier', *Encyclopaedia Britannica* (Cambridge, 1911), vol. XVIII.

39 Ibid., pp. 263–4.

40 Behan, *See Naples and Die*, p. 23.

41 Quoted in Dickie, *Blood Brotherhoods*, p. 35.

42 Luigi Agnello, 'Castromediano, Sigismondo', Biographical Dictionary of Italians, XXII (1979), www.trecanni.it, accessed 31 May 2018.

43 Dickie, *Blood Brotherhoods*, p. 58.

44 Quoted ibid., p. 37.

45 Ibid., p. 47.

46 Ibid., p. 37.

47 Ibid., p. 188.

48 Ibid.

49 Ibid., p. 189.

50 Griffiths, *Italian Prisons*, p. 264.

51 Train, *Courts, Criminals and Camorra*, p. 150.

52 Train asserted that the diary was written by a Tobia Basile, aka Scarpia Leggio. After an extensive search for an alternate source on this character the author came up empty, thus I will refer to him as the 'Camorra member'.

53 Train, *Courts, Criminals and Camorra*, p. 151.

54 Ibid., p. 155.

55 Ibid., p. 170.

56 Griffiths, *Italian Prisons*, p. 266.

57 Ibid., p. 267.

58 Ibid.

59 Ibid.

60 Ibid., pp. 268–70.

61 Behan, *See Naples and Die*, p. 74.

62 Peluso, 'The Roots of the Organized Criminal World in Campania', p. 122.

63 Behan, *See Naples and Die*.

64 Ibid., p. 75.

65 Peluso, 'The Roots of the Organized Criminal World in Campania'.

66 Behan, *See Naples and Die*.

67 Ibid., p. 139.

68 Ibid., p. 137.

69 William Watkinson, 'Italian Camorra Mafia Accused of Rigging State Prison Guard Jobs Exam to Infiltrate Penal System', https://news.sky. com, 25 May 2016.

70 'In Naples, the Hit-men Are Children', *The Economist*, 22 June 2017; Felia Allum, 'Young Guns Take Charge of European Mafia Clans – with Deadly Results', *The Conversation*, 23 March 2017.

71 Watkinson, 'Italian Camorra Mafia'.

72 Ernesto Savona, 'The Businesses of Italian Mafias', *European Journal of Criminal Policy Research*, XXI/2 (2015), p. 228.

73 Alessandra Stanley, 'Where Hit Men Better Mean It When They Say "Yes Ma'am"', *New York Times*, 11 January 2001.

## 3 'THIEVES WITH A CODE OF HONOUR': LORDS OF THE RUSSIAN GULAG SYSTEM

1 Mark Galeotti, *The Vory: Russia's Super Mafia* (New Haven, CT, 2018), p. 33; Federico Varese, 'The Society of the Vory-V-Zakone, 1930s–1950s', in *Russian and Post-Soviet Organized Crime*, ed. Mark Galeotti (Burlington, VT, 2002), p. 8.

2 Email communication with author Joe Serio, 7 February 2019.

3 GULAG is an acronym of *Glavnoe Upravlenie Lagerie*, which translated from Russian means 'Main Camp Administration'. According to D. M. Thomas, the biographer of noted political prisoner Alexander Solzhenitsyn, it appears that the author of *The Gulag Archipelago*, first translated into English in 1974, 'was the first to use the word [Gulag] as an independent noun'. See D. M. Thomas, *Alexander Solzhenitsyn: A Century in His Life* (New York, 1998).

4 Federico Varese, *The Russian Mafia: Private Protection in a New Market Economy* (Oxford, 2001); Anne Applebaum, *Gulag: A History* (New York, 2003).

5 Varese, 'The Society of the Vory-V-Zakone', p. 15.

6 Anne Applebaum, *Gulag Voices: An Anthology* (New Haven, CT, 2011), p. x.

7 Fyodor Dostoevsky, *The House of the Dead* (New York, Grove Press edn), p. 8.

8 Varese, 'The Society of the Vory-V-Zakone', p. 16.

9 Galeotti, *The Vory*, p. 32.

10 A. K. Rozhnovsky, '"The Dead Man"': In Prison, They Called Him by a Nickname', *Caucasus*, XL (13 February 1882).

11 Serguei Cheloukhine and M. R. Haberfeld, *Russian Organized Corruption Networks and Their International Trajectories* (New York, 2011), p. 26.

12 Ibid.

13 Ibid., pp. 26–7.

14 Ibid., p. 29.

15 Applebaum, *Gulag: A History*.

16 Applebaum, *Gulag Voices*, pp. viii–ix.

17 Ibid., p. ix.

18 Communication with Joe Serio, 7 February 2019.

19 Applebaum, *Gulag: A History*.

20 Ibid., p. 282; Galeotti, *The Vory*, p. 47; Varese, 'The Society of the Vory-V-Zakone', p. 8.

21 Yuri Glazov, 'Thieves in the USSR – A Social Phenomenon', in *Russian and Post-Soviet Organized Crime*, ed. Mark Galeotti (Burlington, VT, 2002).

22 Ibid., p. 36.

23 Galeotti, *The Vory*, p. 64.

24 Ibid.

25 Varese, *The Russian Mafia*, p. 10.

26 Ibid., pp. 145–6.

27 Joseph D. Serio, *Investigating the Russian Mafia* (Durham, NC, 2008), p. 152.

28 Varese, *The Russian Mafia*, p. 150.

29 Serio, *Investigating the Russian Mafia*, pp. 157–8.

30 Ibid.

31 Cited in Galeotti, *The Vory*, p. 62.

32 Varese, 'The Society of the Vory-V-Zakone', p. 9.

33 Ibid., p. 12.

34 Applebaum, *Gulag*, p. 290.

35  Varese, 'The Society of the Vory-V-Zakone', p. 18.

36  Serio, *Investigating the Russian Mafia*, p. 165.

37  Meyer Galler and Harlan E. Marquess, compilers, *Soviet Prison Speech: A Survivor's Glossary* (Madison, WI, 1972), p. 23. The co-compiler of this book spent a decade in prison camps between 1942 and 1952. The authors suggest that after the publication of Alexander Solzhenitsyn's *One Day in the Life of Ivan Denisovich* in 1962, it was recognized that an aid, such as this book, was needed to explain the special prison argot that dots the pages of the book.

38  Ibid.

39  Ibid., p. 33.

40  Galeotti, *The Vory*, p. 32.

41  Ibid., p. 66.

42  Serio, *Investigating the Russian Mafia*, p. 162.

43  Ibid., pp. 162–3.

44  Ibid., p. 163; Galeotti, *The Vory*, pp. 43–6.

45  Applebaum, *Gulag*, p. 287.

46  Galeotti, *The Vory*, p. 51.

47  Glazov, 'Thieves in the USSR', p. 42.

48  Applebaum, *Gulag*, p. 282.

49  Ibid., p. 283.

50  Galeotti, *The Vory*, p. 54.

51  Ibid., pp. 58–60.

52  Ibid., p. 50.

53  Ibid., pp. 54–5.

54  Ibid., p. 56.

55  Quoted ibid.

56  Ibid., p. 57.

57  Ibid., p. 51.

58  Varese, 'The Society of the Vory-V-Zakone'.

59  Real name Lev Emmanvilovich Razgon (1908–1999). He was detained for his work as a human-rights activist.

60  Alexander Dolgun with Patrick Watson, *Alexander Dolgun: An American Who Survived the Gulag* (New York, 1975).

61  Applebaum, *Gulag*, p. 283.

62  Alexander Kupatadze, *Organized Crime, Political Transitions and State Formation in Post-Soviet Eurasia* (New York, 2012), pp. 54–5.

63  Ibid.

64  Serio, *Investigating the Russian Mafia*; Stephen Handelman, *Comrade Criminal: The Theft of the Second Russian Revolution* (New York, 1995), p. 34.

65 Kupatadze, *Organized Crime*.

66 Galeotti, *The Vory*, pp. 119–20.

67 Svetlana Stephenson, *Gangs of Russia: From the Streets to the Corridors of Power* (Ithaca, NY, 2015), p. 182.

68 Ibid., p. 186.

69 Varese, 'The Society of the Vory-V-Zakone', p. 18.

70 Ibid., pp. 17–18.

71 Stephenson, *Gangs of Russia*, p. 184.

72 Ibid.

73 Serio, *Investigating the Russian Mafia*, p. 165.

74 Translated from *Dictionary: Prison, Camp, Blatnoi, Jargon* (Speech and Graphic Portraits of Soviet Prison), 1992. Compiled by Dantsik Sergeyevich Baldaev, Vladimir Kuz'mich Belko and Igor Mikhailovich Isupov, online at 'Russian Organised Crime', https://fas.org, accessed 21 May 2020.

## 4 SOUTH AFRICA'S NUMBER GANGS

1 Frederic Le Marcis, 'Everyday Prison Governance in Abidjan, Ivory Coast', *Prison Service Journal*, CCXII (March 2014), pp. 11–15.

2 Charles Van Onselen, *The Small Matter of a Horse: The Life of 'Nongoloza' Mathebula, 1867–1948* (Johannesburg, 1984), p. 3.

3 Nicholas Haysom, *Towards an Understanding of Prison Gangs* (Cape Town, 1981); Dirk Van Zyl Smit, *South African Prison Law and Practice* (Durban, 1992).

4 Charles Van Onselen, *Studies in the Social and Economic History of the Witwatersrand, 1886–1914*, vol. II: *New Nineveh* (New York, 1982), p. 171. Hereafter cited as *New Nineveh*.

5 S. Marks and R. Rathbone, eds, *Industrialization and Social Change in South Africa: African Class Formation, 1870–1930* (London, 1982).

6 Jonathan Morgan and Sipho Madini, *White Paper, White Ink* (Johannesburg, 2014), p. 32.

7 Lukas Muntingh and Chris Tapscott, 'HIV/AIDS and the Prison System', in *HIV/AIDS in South Africa 25 Years on: A Psychological Perspective*, ed. Roul Rohelder, Leslie Swartz and Seth C. Kalichman (New York, 2009), pp. 205–322.

8 Skye Forrester, 'Inside South Africa's Brutal Prisons: "If I Didn't Join a Gang I'd Have Been Raped"', *International Business Times*, 26 October 2017.

9  Ibid.

10 Jonny Steinberg, *Nongoloza's Children: Western Cape Prison Gangs during and after Apartheid*, Centre for the Study of Violence and Reconciliation, www.csvr.org, 2004, p. 21.

11 Van Onselen, *The Small Matter of a Horse*, p. 2.

12 The origin date depends on who his relaying the historiography of the gang, with unsubstantiated accounts tracing it as far back as 1812.

13 In 2010 one longtime prison gang researcher, Heather Parker Lewis, asserted that the birth name of Nongoloza was Mzozephi, which means 'which genealogical house do you come from?' Apparently, this name is not used or recognized by The Number gangs. Heather Parker Lewis, *God's Gangsters? The Number Gangs in South African Prisons* (Cape Town, 2010), p. 156. What is known about Nongoloza is mostly taken from his life story told to a warder in 1912, who transcribed it; it was published in the Director of Prison's Annual Report. It served as a primary resource for the Van Onselen book.

14 Van Onselen, *The Small Matter of a Horse*, p. 10.

15 Ibid., pp. 5–18.

16 Also known as The Regiment of Gaolbirds, People of the Stone, and of course Nongoloza or Ninevites. See Van Onselen, *New Nineveh*, p. 171.

17 Van Onselen, *The Small Matter of a Horse*, p. 14.

18 Ibid., pp. 14–15. See also Gary Kynoch, 'Of Compounds and Cellblocks: The Foundations of Violence in Johannesburg, 1890s–1950s', *Journal of South African Studies*, XXXVII (2011).

19 Van Onselen, *New Nineveh*, p. 177.

20 Van Onselen, *The Small Matter of a Horse*, p. 18.

21 Van Onselen, *New Nineveh*, p. 184. The Second Boer War pitted the British Empire against the two Boer states of The South African Republic and the Orange Free State. It is also known as the Boer War, South African War and Anglo-Boer War.

22 Quoted in Morgan and Madini, *White Paper, White Ink*, p. 64, p. 88.

23 Jonny Steinberg, *The Number One: One Man's Search for Identity in the Cape Underworld and Prison Gangs* (Johannesburg, 2008), p. xv.

24 Van Onselen, *New Nineveh*, p. 182.

25 Sarah Lettie Nel, 'A Critical Analysis of Gangsterism in South African Correctional Centres: The Case of Barberton Management Area', unpublished dissertation, University of South Africa, February 2017, p. 23.

26 Lewis, *God's Gangsters?*, p. 39.

27 Ibid., p. 24; W. J. Schurink, 'The World of the *Wetslaners*: An Analysis of Some Organizational Features in South African Prisons', *Acta Criminologica*, II (1989), pp. 69–70.

28 Van Onselen, *New Nineveh*, p. 187.

29 Steinberg, *The Number*; Haysom, *Towards an Understanding*, p. 2.

30 Lewis, *God's Gangsters?*, p. 19.

31 Robben Island, Dutch for Seal Island, is now closed and was declared a World Heritage Site in 1999. It was used as a place of detention beginning in the 1600s. It is a popular tourist destination and remains a symbol of resistance to the apartheid regime. For more on the prison see Fran Buntman, *Robben Island and Prisoner Resistance to Apartheid* (Cambridge, 2003); D. M. Zwelonke, *Robben Island* (London, 1973); and Florence Bernault, 'The Politics of Enclosure in Colonial and Post-colonial Africa', in *A History of Prison Confinement in Africa* (Portsmouth, NH, 2003), pp. 1–53.

32 Van Onselen, *New Nineveh*, p. 183.

33 Ibid., p. 184.

34 Ibid., p. 192.

35 Ibid.

36 Ibid., p. 193.

37 Nel, 'A Critical Analysis of Gangsterism', p. 68.

38 Marie Rosenkrantz Lindegaard and Sasha Gear, 'Violence Makes Safe in South African Prisons: Prison Gangs, Violent Acts, and Victimization among Inmates', *Focaal – Journal of Global and Historical Anthropology*, LXVIII (2014).

39 Lewis, *God's Gangsters?*, p. 156.

40 Lindegaard and Gear, 'Violence Makes Safe'.

41 Steinberg, *The Number*.

42 Ibid., p. 143.

43 Ibid., pp. 150–51.

44 Ibid; Quoted in Nel, 'Violence Makes Safe', p. 60.

45 Ibid., pp. 110–11.

46 Ibid., p. 30.

47 Lewis, *God's Gangsters?*, p. 152. The term is used by the 26s for prison language and is also considered the language developed by the miners.

48 Mark Shaw, *Hitmen for Hire: Exposing South Africa's Underworld* (Johannesburg, 2017), p. 47.

49 Ibid., p. 49.

50 Ibid., p. 53.

51 Born in 1868, a year after Nongoloza, his real name was Joseph Lis; he assumed the new name in New York City some time in 1891.

52 Charles Van Onselen, *Studies in the Social and Economic History of the Witwatersrand, 1886–1914*, vol. I: *New Babylon* (New York, 1982), p. 24; Van Onselen, *The Fox and the Flies: The Secret Life of a Grotesque Master Criminal* (New York, 2007), p. 179.

53 Lewis, *God's Gangsters?*, p. 6.

54 Ibid., p. 71.

55 Ibid., p. 12.

56 Morgan and Madini, *White Paper, White Ink*, p. 30.

57 Lewis, *God's Gangsters?*, p. 82

58 Ibid., pp. 82–3.

59 Haysom, *Towards an Understanding.*

60 Lewis, *God's Gangsters?*, p. 81.

61 Ibid., pp. 81–2.

62 Schurink, 'The World of the *Wetslaners*', pp. 60–70.

63 'Numbers Gangs' Original Fighting General', *Cape Times*, 24 August 2016.

64 Steinberg, *The Number*, p. 68.

65 Haysom, *Towards an Understanding.*

66 Lindegaard and Gear, 'Violence Makes Safe', p. 40.

67 Ibid., p. 42.

68 Quoted ibid., p. 42.

69 Ibid., p. 43.

70 Ibid., p. 46.

71 Lewis, *God's Gangsters?*, p. 72.

72 Steinberg, *The Number*, p. 7.

73 According to Lewis, *God's Gangsters?*, p. 152, *die draad* is the 'Wireless Operator', selected for his incredible institutional memory, who can remember everything said at meetings. He usually accompanies the *glas* on his peregrinations in the prison.

74 Steinberg, *The Number.*

75 Morgan and Madini, *White Paper, White Ink*, pp. 100–106.

76 Steinberg, *Nongoloza's Children*, pp. 37–8.

77 'South African Gangs Use AIDS Rape as Punishment', *Reuters*, https://rense.com, 2 November 2002.

78 Fran Lisa Buntman, *Robben Island and Prisoner Resistance to Apartheid* (Cambridge, 2003), p. 14.

79 Steinberg, *The Number*, p. 224.

80 Moses Dlamini, *Hell-hole, Robben Island: Reminiscences of a Political Prisoner* (Nottingham, 1984), p. 165.

81 Buntman, *Robben Island*, p. 41.

82 Dlamini, *Hell-hole*, pp. 38–9.

83 Ibid., p. 73.

84 Ibid., p. 111.

85 Ibid.

86 Ibid., p. 128.

87 Quoted ibid., p. 133.

88 Ibid., p. 157.

89 Steinberg, *Nongoloza's Children*, pp. 43–4. The nucleus of Steinberg's book, *The Number*, comprises much of the material in *Nongoloza's Children*.

90 Quoted ibid., p. 42.

91 Quoted ibid.

92 Ibid., pp. 42–4.

93 Ibid., p. 21.

94 Ibid., p. 20.

95 Lewis, *God's Gangsters?*, p. 98.

96 Steffen Jensen, *Gangs, Politics and Dignity in Cape Town* (Oxford, 2008), p. 82.

97 Ibid.

98 Morgan and Madini, *White Paper, White Ink*, p. 135.

99 Steinberg, *The Number*, p. 72.

100 Ibid., p. 124.

101 Ibid., p. 72.

102 Ibid., pp. 72–3.

103 Ibid.

104 Nel, *A Critical Analysis*, p. 66.

105 Ibid., pp. 67–8.

106 Quoted in Shaw, *Hitmen for Hire*, p. 120.

107 Steinberg, *Nongoloza's Children*, pp. 45–6.

108 Ibid., p. 86.

109 Ibid., p. 73.

110 Nel, *A Critical Analysis*, p. xviii, p. 61.

111 Shaw, *Hitmen for Hire*, p. 113.

112 Mike Cohen, 'The Cape of Bad Dope', www.independent.co.uk, 19 September 2013.

113 Nel, *A Critical Analysis*.

114 Ibid., p. 65.

115 Sasha Gear and Kindiza Ngubeni, *Daai Ding: Sex, Sexual Violence and Coercion in Men's Prisons*, Centre for the Study of Violence and Reconciliation, www.csvr.org, 2002.

116 Nel, *A Critical Analysis*, p. 65.

117 Werner Menges, 'Judgement Gives Glimpse of Prison Gang Culture', *The Namibian*, 30 June 2008.

118 Ibid.

119 Ibid.; 'Salute Forces Discussion about Prison Life', *Windhoek Observer*, 24 November 2017.

120 Caryn Dolley, 'New Plan to Smash Prison Gangs', *Weekend Argus*, 6 June 2015.

121 Thomas Marree, 'Meet the 28s General Who Left the Number and Lived to Tell the Tale through Film', www.dailymaverick.co.za, 13 March 2018.

122 Azarrah Abdul Karrim and Sumeya Gasa, 'Gang versus Gang', *City Press* (Johannesburg), 29 October 2017.

123 Lewis, *God's Gangsters?*, p. 15.

124 Ibid., p. 11.

125 Ibid.

126 Quoted in Steve Robson and Sam Webb, 'Oscar Pistorious Will Return to Notorious Prison Filled with South Africa's Most Violent Criminals After Six-year Sentence', www.mirror.co.uk, 6 July 2016.

## 5 OCEANIA'S PRISON GANGS: AUSTRALIA AND NEW ZEALAND

1 'The Kiwi Model', *The Economist*, 1 December 2018, p. 54.

2 James Phelps, *Australia's Hardest Prison: Inside the Walls of Long Bay Jail* (North Sydney, 2016), p. 293.

3 Ibid., p. 296.

4 Ibid.

5 Ibid., p. 298.

6 Ibid.

7 Nino Bucci, 'Bikies and Killer Unite in Prison', *Sydney Morning Herald*, 6 November 2013.

8 The Comanchero Motorcycle Club was founded in the late 1960s in Sydney Australia by a Scottish immigrant named William George 'Jock' Ross. The Mongols, Bandidos and Hells Angels all originated in the United States. They spread into Australia in the 1980s,

either patching over into other OMGs, subsuming smaller clubs or just operating under their own banners thanks to the growing bikie culture there. See also Bill Hayes, *The One-percenter Encyclopedia* (Minneapolis, MN, 2011).

9 'More Bikies in Jail Creating Dangerous Prisons in South Australia', www.abc.net.au, 27 July 2017; Nino Bucci, 'Bikies and Killers Unite in Prison', www.smh.com.au, 6 November 2013.

10 Jonathan Pearlman, 'Australia Creates "Bikies Only" Prison to Deal with Warring Motorbike Gangs', www.telegraph.co.uk/worldnews, 15 October 2013.

11 Phelps, *Australia's Hardest Prison*, p. 291–2.

12 The Nomads has numerous members of Middle Eastern descent.

13 Based in Sydney, Australia, Notorious was established in 2007 by former Nomads members whose branch had recently disbanded. According to Hayes, *The One-percenter Encyclopedia*, p. 158, the gang is kind of a hotch-potch of gangsters. Most ride motorcycles, while others prefer prowling by foot. Their patch features a 'turbaned skull brandishing twin pistols with "Original Gangster" beneath it, with the motto "Only the dead see the end of war"'.

14 Chris Masters, 'Does Locking Up Radicals Breed More of Them?', *Daily Telegraph*, 19 February 2010.

15 Kesha West, 'Hells Angels Bikies Join with Victorian Jail Gang Prisoners of War Despite Moves to Combat Gang Violence', *The World Today*, 7 November 2013.

16 Phelps, *Australia's Hardest Prison*, p. 293.

17 Ibid.

18 Masters, 'Does Locking Up Radicals Breed More of Them?'; Chris Masters, 'Middle Eastern Crime Connections', *Daily Telegraph*, 8 April 2010.

19 Anthony Dowsley and Ryan Tennison, 'Prison in Turmoil as Gangs Struggle', *Melbourne Herald*, 9 April 2017.

20 Masters, 'Does Locking Up Radicals Breed More of Them?'.

21 Candace Sutton, 'Is Australia's Most Dangerous Gangster Bassam Hamzy Still in Control?', *National News*, 13 August 2013.

22 Masters, 'Middle Eastern Crime Connections'.

23 James Phelps, *Australia's Most Murderous Prison: Behind the Walls of Goulburn Jail* (Sydney, 2016), p. 138.

24 Ibid., p. 137.

25 Ibid., p. 139.

26 Ibid., pp. 140–41.

27 Callum Wood, 'Radical Australian Prisons', *The Trumpet*, 8 June 2016; Masters, 'Middle Eastern Crime Connections'.

28 Masters, 'Does Locking Up Radicals Breed More of Them?'.

29 Phelps, *Australia's Most Dangerous Prison,* 2016, pp. 60–61.

30 Lauren McMah and Megan Palin, 'Jailhouse Justice: A Look at Inmate Society in Australian Jails', www.news.com.au/lifestyle, 13 February 2016.

31 Phelps, *Australia's Hardest Prison*, p. 296.

32 While Australian prisons were busy segregating inmates, in 2005 racial segregation was abolished in California and Texas, home to the USA's two largest prison systems. This was only after the U.S. Supreme Court labelled the practice as racist and of 'limited benefit'. However, in California, segregation could be used for sixty days on an ad hoc basis when an inmate was a gang member or displayed animosity towards other racial groups.

33 Simone Ubaldi, 'The Making of "Chopper" Read', www.themonthly.com.au, November 2013.

34 Brendan Nicholson, 'Painters and Dockers Brutality Prompted Search for New Way to Fight Crime', *The Australian*, 2 January 2012. Organized crime has long maintained a presence on Australian docks. Over the years dozens of murders and violent attacks have been linked to the Federated Ship Painters and Dockers Union. By some accounts their position on the waterfront provided ample opportunity to import drugs and firearms.

35 Garth Cartwright, 'Mark "Chopper" Read Obituary', www.theguardian.com, 9 October 2013.

36 Bana would also be featured in the 2017 film *The Forgiven*, which offers the best film portrait of the South African Number prison gangs.

37 'New Zealand Has More Gangsters than Soldiers', www.economist.com, 8 February 2018.

38 Toby Manhire, 'Unlocking Maori Identity: Keeping New Zealand's Indigenous People Out of Jail', *The Guardian*, 14 August 2015.

39 Rebecca Kesby, 'New Zealand Gangs: The Mongrel Mob and Other Urban Outlaws', BBC *World*, 26 September 2012, at www.news.bbc.com.

40 Jim Rose, 'Extra Prisoners Are Nearly All Gang Members – That's Hardly a Crisis', *Dominion Post*, 29 May 2018.

41 Rebecca Kesby, 'New Zealand Gangs'.

42 Jarrod Gilbert, *Patched: The History of Gangs in New Zealand* (Auckland, 2016), p. 37.

43 John Meek, 'Gangs in New Zealand Prisons', *Australia and New Zealand Journal of Criminology*, xxv (1992), p. 255.

44 Ibid., p. 258.

45 Ibid.

46 Ibid., p. 259. In 2005 the prison was closed and turned into a bed and breakfast hostel.

47 Ibid., p. 91.

48 Ibid., pp. 90–91.

49 Quoted ibid.

50 Ibid.; 'Why New Zealand Has So Many Gang Members', www.economist.com, 14 February 2018.

51 Tuhoe Bruno Isaac and Bradford Haami, *True Red: The Life of an Ex-mongrel Mob Gang Leader* (self-published, 2007), p. 7.

52 Greg Newbold, *The Big Huey* (Auckland, 1982), pp. 220–21.

53 Gilbert, *Patched*, pp. 42–3.

54 Isaac and Haami, *True Red*, pp. 4–5.

55 Ibid., p. 10.

56 Ibid., pp. 51–2.

57 Ibid.

58 Ibid., p. 53.

59 Ibid., pp. 53, 73.

60 Ibid.

61 Greg Newbold and Rawiri Taonui, 'Gangs', Te Ara, *The Encyclopedia of New Zealand*, https://teara.govt.nz/en/gangs/print, 5 May 2011.

62 Gilbert, *Patched*, p. 42.

63 During his stint as prime minister between 1975 and 1984, Robert Muldoon 'had an unusual relationship with gangs. He believed in engaging with gangs through government-subsidized work schemes to keep people from a life in crime'. It is up for debate whether this strategy reduced gang offending and antisocial behaviour. But apparently the profits gleaned from them certainly enriched certain gangs, and made them more enticing to prospects. Negative publicity put a damper on this project in January 1987. However, the Black Power gang was well represented, performing a *haka* in his honour at Muldoon's funeral in 1992.

64 Gilbert, *Patched*, p. 63.

65 Quoted in Kesby, 'New Zealand Gangs'.

66 Dennis O'Reilly, 'Werewolf: Looking after Our Patch', *Scoop Independent News*, 19 November 2009.

67 This culture has been well documented by Greg Newbold, who spent two years there in the late 1970s and later wrote a master's-thesis field study of it and a popular account of his time in prison. See Greg Newbold, *The Big Huey* (Auckland, 1982).

68 Greg Newbold, *Punishment and Politics: The Maximum Security Prison in New Zealand* (Auckland, 1989), p. 288.

69 Quoted in Meek, 'Gangs in New Zealand Prisons', p. 262.

70 Ibid., p. 263.

71 Ibid., p. 261.

72 Newbold, *Punishment and Politics*, p. 289.

73 Quoted ibid., p. 289.

74 Ibid., p. 290.

75 Ibid., p. 264.

76 Ibid., pp. 265–6.

77 Gilbert, *Patched*, p. 252.

78 Ibid., pp. 252–4. Mike Tyson got his tattoo in 2003.

79 Kirsty Johnston, 'LA-style Gangs Fuel Problems in New Zealand Prisons', www.stuff.co.nz, 9 June 2013.

80 Ibid.

81 Quoted ibid.

82 'The Kiwi Model', p. 54.

83 Manhire, 'Unlocking Maori Identity'.

## 6 ASIAN PRISON GANGS

1 Michael Bachelard, 'The Dark Side of the Sun', *Sydney Morning Herald*, 9 August 2014. These former royal families were disenfranchised when Indonesia became a republic in 1950, but their descendants remain influential in local politics.

2 'This Is a Gang Restaurant Run by the Laskar Bali Gang', www.tripadvisor.com, 11 November 2018.

3 Kathryn Bonella, *Hotel K: The Shocking Inside Story of Bali's Most Notorious Jail* (Sydney, 2012).

4 Cindy Wockner and Komang Erviani, 'Deadly Gang Riot Breaks Out at Bali's Kerobokan Prison Where Australians are Held', www.news.com. au, 18 December 2015.

5 Bonella, *Hotel K*, p. 109.

6 Quoted ibid.

7 Ibid., p. 137.

8 Quoted ibid., pp. 184–5.
9 Ibid., p. 192.
10 Ibid., p. 196.
11 Clarke R. Jones, Raymund E. Narag and Resurrecion S. Morales, 'Philippine Prison Gangs: Control or Chaos?', *RegNet Working paper*, LXXI (Regulatory Institutions Network, 2015), p. 7.
12 The moniker Sigue Sigue Sputnik was supposedly adopted on the day in 1969 when man first stepped on the Moon; hence their fondness for the spaceship symbol.
13 Sou Lee and Raymund E. Narag, 'Fanning the Flames: Understanding Gang Involvement among Philippine Prisoners', *International Journal of Offender Therapy and Comparative Criminology*, LXIII/3 (2019), https://doi.org/10.1177/0306624X18798225, 5 September 2018.
14 Aurora Alemendral, 'Where 518 Inmates Sleep in Space for 170, and Gangs Hold it Together', *New York Times*, 7 January 2019; 'Highest to Lowest – Occupancy Level (based on official capacity)', *World Prison Brief*, www.prisonstudies.org, accessed February 2020.
15 Clarke R. Jones and Raymund E. Narag, 'Why Prison Gangs Aren't All Bad', https://edition.cnn.com, 11 December 2014, claims that these gangs first appeared as early as the late 1940s.
16 Filomin Candaliza-Guttierez, 'Pangkat: Inmate Gangs at the New Bilibid Maximum Security Compound', *Philippine Sociological Review*, CX (2012), p. 210.
17 Ibid., p. 211.
18 Quoted ibid., p. 210.
19 Ven J. Tesoro, 'Prison Gangs: A Discussion, Organized Crime in the Philippines: Prison Gangs in Particular', www.philippineprisons.wordpress.com, 7 July 2011.
20 Ibid.
21 Ibid.
22 Ibid.
23 *Pangkat* is a Filipino word that refers to a group bound by common experience and interests and by the pledge 'to protect and contribute to the group' (Candaliza-Guttierez, 'Pangkat: Inmate Gangs', p. 199).
24 Ibid., p. 193.
25 Lee and Narag, 'Fanning the Flames', p. 4.
26 Raymund E. Narag and Sou Lee, 'Putting Out Fires: Understanding the Developmental Nature and Roles of Inmate Gangs in the Philippines Overcrowded Jails', *International Journal of Offender Therapy and*

*Comparative Criminology*, LXII/11 (2018), https://doi.org, 3 December 2017.

27 Ibid.

28 Quoted in Lee and Narag, 'Fanning the Flames', p. 12.

29 Quoted in Narag and Lee, 'Putting Out Fires'.

30 Ibid.

31 Raymund E. Narag, *Freedom and Death inside the Jail: A Look into the Condition of the Quezon City Jail* (Manila, 2005), p. 148.

32 Ibid., p. 149.

33 Clarke R. Jones and Resurrecion S. Morales, 'Integration versus Segregation: A Preliminary Examination of Philippines Correctional Facilities For De-radicalization', *Studies in Conflict and Terrorism*, XXXV/3 (2012), pp. 211–28.

34 Narag and Lee, 'Putting Out Fires', p. 17.

35 Narag, *Freedom and Death inside the Jail*, pp. 149–50.

36 Narag and Lee, 'Putting Out Fires'.

37 Ibid., p. 80.

38 Ibid., p. 83.

39 Quoted in Narag and Lee, 'Putting Out Fires'.

40 Ibid., pp. 13–14.

41 Ibid.

42 Narag, *Freedom and Death Inside the Jail*, p. 96.

43 Alemendral, 'Where 518 Inmates Sleep'.

44 Ibid.

45 Ibid., p. 100.

46 Narag, *Freedom and Death Inside the Jail*, p. 101.

47 Ibid.

48 Ibid., p. 102.

49 Candaliza-Guttierez, 'Pangkat: Inmate Gangs', p. 203.

50 Filomin Candaliza-Guttierrez, 'Pangkat: Inmate Gangs at the New Bilibid Prison Maximum Security Compound', *Philippine Sociological Review*, LX (2012), p. 195.

51 Ibid.

52 Sophia Dedace, 'New Prison Chief Vows to Stamp Out Crimes in Bilibid', *GMA News*, 28 July 2011; Candaliza-Guttierez, 'Pangkat: Inmate Gangs'.

53 Ruth Cabal, 'Gangs Roles Unique to Philippine Prison System', CNN Philippines, https://cnn.philippines.com, 15 October 2016.

54 Candaliza-Guttierez, 'Pangkat: Inmate Gangs', pp. 203–4.

55 Jones and Narag, 'Why Prison Gangs Aren't All Bad'.

56 Candaliza-Guttierez, 'Pangkat: Inmate Gangs', p. 203.

57 Ibid.

58 Ibid.

59 Quoted ibid., p. 205.

60 Ibid.

61 Jones, Narag, Morales, 'Philippine Prison Gangs', p. 11.

62 Ibid.

63 Lee and Narag, 'Fanning the Flames'.

64 Jones, Narag, Morales, 'Philippine Prison Gangs', p. 11.

65 Ibid., p. 11.

66 Candaliza-Guttierez, 'Pangkat: Inmate Gangs', p. 198.

67 Lee and Narag, 'Fanning the Flames'.

68 Ibid., p. 13.

69 Ibid.

70 Narag, *Freedom and Death inside the Jail*, p. 150.

71 Evan McKirdy, 'Life inside the Philippines' Most Overcrowded Jail', www.cnn.com, 23 August 2016.

72 Narag, *Freedom and Death inside the Jail*, pp. 82–3.

73 Candaliza-Guttierez, 'Pangkat', p. 205.

74 Narag, *Freedom and Death inside the Jail*.

75 Ibid.

76 Ibid., p. 85.

77 Ibid., p. 105.

78 Ibid.

79 Candaliza-Guttierez, 'Pangkat: Inmate Gangs', p. 211.

80 Ibid., pp. xviii, 198.

81 Ibid., p. 211.

82 Norman Johnston, *Forms of Constraint: A History of Prison Architecture* (Urbana, IL, 2000), p. 101.

83 Mir Mehraj-Ud-Din, *Crime and Criminal Justice System in India* (New Delhi, 1984), p. 175.

84 Ibid., pp. 176–8.

85 The Dawood Gang is led by Dawood Ibrahim, considered South Asia's Al Capone. In the 1980s and '90s he was the undisputed crime boss of the Mumbai underworld, directing a billion-dollar vice empire. The nucleus of his so-called 'D' Company gang was drawn from the minority Muslim population of Mumbai. He is distinct from other crime bosses for his participation in both terrorist and organized crime activities. As of 2016 he was taking refuge in Pakistan.

86  Raj Shekhar, 'No Tattoos in Tihar but the Gangs Inside Are as Dangerous as the Mexican Prisons', originally published in *Times of India*, 9 June 2015.

87  Sarah Hafeez, 'Increase in Gang Formations, Use of Cellphones in Tihar: Director General of Prisons', *Indian Express*, 9 July 2015. According to security officers, a large portion of the phones are thrown in from outside.

88  Shekhar, 'No Tattoos', 9 June 2015.

89  Ibid.

90  Ibid.

91  Kiran Bedi, *It's Always Possible: Transforming One of the Largest Prisons in the World* (Briar Hill, Vic., 1999), p. 124.

92  Lydia Polgreen, 'Rehabilitation Comes to a Prison and to Its Inmates', *New York Times*, 18 July 2011.

93  Abhishek Behi, 'Gang Fight in Bhondsi Jail, Three Officials among Six Injured; 22 Mobile Phones Recovered', *Hindustan Times*, 7 February 2018.

94  Gadoli had been killed outside prison by Gurgaon police in a Mumbai hotel in 2016.

95  Sanjay Yadav, 'Gangster Mahal Moved to Tihar, but Gang War Threat Still Real in Bhondsi', *Times of India*, 20 July 2017.

96  Vij-Aurora, 'Right to Justice Bill: Helplessness, Psychological Disorders Torture Indian Prisoners', *India Today*, 24 June 2011.

97  Sandeep Unnithan and Kiran Tare, 'Abu Salem and Arun Gawli Live Life on Their Own Terms in Jail', *India Today*, 11 July 2012.

98  Quoted in Sunetra Choudhury, *Behind Bars: Prison Tales of India's Most Famous* (New Delhi, 2017).

99  Ibid.

100  'Bladebaaz Gangs Operate with the Help of Certain Officials', http://royalespot.blogspot.com, 2 May 2008.

101  He comes from the Jansi tribe of Delhi, noted for bootlegging, drug running and thieving. In 2008 his entire family was behind bars, including mother, uncle and brothers.

102  Solanki is related to a Delhi politician and has a long rap sheet, mostly for extortion and crimes of violence. He reportedly served as an enforcer for Dhoti. When he is not locked up, he has a small business in Palam Village.

103  Vishwas Kumar, 'Bladebaaz Gangs Are Tihar's Fearsome Extortionists', *Tihar Jail Special*, 17 March 2008.

104  Pratik Kumar and Vishnu Sukumaran, 'Gang Rivalries Thrive inside Tihar Jail Too', *Deccan Herald*, 5 April 2015.

105  Kumar, 'Bladebaaz Gangs', 17 March 2008.

106 Choudhury, *Behind Bars*, p. 250.

107 Ibid., pp. 249–50.

108 On the other side of Bangkok is the Central Women's Correctional Institution, known as the Bangkok Hilton. It has been chronicled in television series and films, including a 1989 Australian series, *Bangkok Hilton*, featuring Nicole Kidman.

109 Warissara Sirisutthidacha and Dittita Titiampruk, 'Patterns of Inmate Subculture: A Qualitative Study of Thai Inmates', *International Journal of Criminal Justice Sciences*, IX (2014), p. 101. The authors state up front that their examination of five Thai prisons is 'not generalizable to other units, settings and times'. However, it is the most detailed account of Thai prison gangs to date.

110 Ibid., p. 102.

111 Ibid.

112 Ibid., p. 103.

113 Ibid., p. 104.

114 Ibid.

115 Ibid., quoted on p. 105.

116 Quoted in 'Inmates Create Biggest Drug Network', www.bangkokpost.com, 24 April 2012.

117 'Drugs Suspect Linked to Prison Gang Arrested', www.bangkokpost.com, 8 July 2014.

118 Matt Blake, 'Drugs, Disease and Dead Bodies: How I Survived a Thai Prison', www.shortlist.com, 17 July 2017.

119 Sirisutthidacha and Titiampruk, 'Patterns of Inmate Subculture', quoted p. 106.

120 Ibid.

121 Ibid., pp. 112–13.

122 Ibid., p. 119.

123 Narayanan Ganapathy, '"Us" and "Them": Ethnic Minority Gangs in Singapore Prisons', *Journal of Contemporary Criminal Justice*, XXXII (2016), p. 270. Research included interviews with eight Sara Jumbo members, eleven from Omega and ten CSS in both free and prison society between 2004 and 2010.

124 Ibid., p. 273.

125 Ibid., pp. 273–4.

126 Kamaludeen Mohamed Nasir, 'Protected Sites: Reconceptualizing Secret Societies in Colonial and Postcolonial Singapore', *Journal of Historical Sociology*, XXIX (2014).

127 Ibid.

128 Ganapathy, '"Us" and "Them"', p. 265.

129 Nafis Muhamad Hanif, 'Prison in Society, Society in Prison: Analysing OMEGA's Racially Structured Realities Within and Beyond', Unpublished thesis, National University of Singapore, 2008, p. 127, note 7.

130 Ibid., p. 127, note 3.

131 Ibid., p. 128, note 10.

132 Ibid., note 11.

133 Zul Othman, 'Some Gang Ties Continue in Prison', www.asiaone.com, 26 October 2012.

134 Quoted in Ganapathy, '"Us" and "Them"', p. 276.

135 Quoted in Ganapathy, p. 275.

136 Quoted ibid., pp. 273–6.

137 Ibid., p. 280.

138 Ibid., p. 275.

139 Ibid., p. 278.

140 Ibid.

141 Hanif, 'Prison in Society', p. 107.

142 Quoted ibid., pp. 108–10.

143 Ibid., quoted p. 112.

144 Ibid., pp. 8–9.

145 Ibid., quoted pp. 8–9.

146 Ganapathy, '"Us" and "Them"', p. 279.

## 7 PRISON GANGS OF EUROPE

1 David Skarbek and Courtney Michaluk, 'To End Prison Gangs, It's Time to Break Up the Largest Prisons', www.politico.com, p. 5.

2 Bill Hayes, *The One-percenter Encyclopedia: The World of Outlaw Motorcycle Clubs from Abyss Ghosts to Zombie Elite* (Minneapolis, MN, 2011), p. 18.

3 'Swedish Bikers Lay Leader to Rest', http://news.bbc.co.uk, 17 July 1998.

4 The term 'grypsmen' comes from the word *gryps*, denoting a secret message delivered within or smuggled outside of prison. Grypsmen communicate frequently with gryps and maintain efficient delivery channels. Marek M. Kaminski, *Games Prisoners Play: The Tragicomic Worlds of Polish Prisons* (Princeton, NJ, 2004), p. 197, note 7.

5 Ibid., pp. 202–3, note 9, note 16; See also Marek M. Kaminski and Don C. Gibbons, 'Games Prisoners Play: Allocation of Social Roles in a Total Institution', *Rationality and Society*, xv (1994), pp. 188–218.

6 Kaminski, *Games Prisoners Play*, p. 34.

7 Ibid., p. 35.

8 Lukasz Zarzycki, 'Socio-lingual Phenomenon of the Anti-Language of Polish and American Prison Inmates', *Crossroads: A Journal of English Studies*, iv (2015), p. 11.

9 Kaminski, *Games Prisoners Play*, p. 106.

10 Ibid., p. 125.

11 If the reader will recall, in Chapter Two a similar process takes place in South African prisons; when a new inmate arrives, he is asked, 'What is your number?' There is a protocol in place directing how a newbie should be treated according to his initial answer.

12 Kaminski, *Games Prisoners Play*, pp. 16–17.

13 Ibid., p. 18.

14 Ibid., p. 39.

15 Ibid., p. 46.

16 Ibid., p. 56.

17 Ibid., p. 64.

18 Ibid., p. 67.

19 Ibid., p. 119.

20 Benjamin Lessing, 'The Danger of Dungeons: Prison Gangs and Incarcerated Militant Groups', in *Small Arms Survey 2010: Gangs, Groups, and Guns* (Cambridge, 2010), p. 165.

21 Ibid.

22 Greg Hannah, Lindsay Clutterbuck, Jennifer Rubin, *Radicalization or Rehabilitation: Understanding the Challenges of Extremist and Radicalized Prisoners* (Santa Monica, ca, 2008), pp. 22–3.

23 Ibid.

24 Ibid., p. ix.

25 Ibid., pp. 22–3.

26 Elizabeth Mulcahy, Shannon Merrington and Peter Bell, 'The Radicalisation of Prison Inmates: Exploring Recruitment, Religion and Prisoner Vulnerability', *Journal of Human Security*, ix (2013), pp. 4–14.

27 Ibid.

28 Graeme Wood, 'How Gangs Took Over Prisons', *The Atlantic*, October 2014; Similarly, David Skarbek, *The Social Order of the Underworld*

(Oxford, 2014), p. 66, states 'prison gangs rarely operate in U.K. prisons, and when they do, they are significantly less powerful, permanent, or influential than those in the United States.'

29 George W. Knox, Gregg W. Etter and Carter F. Smith, *Gangs and Organized Crime* (New York, 2019), pp. 141–2.

30 J. Wood, 'Gang Activity in English Prisons: The Prisoner's Perspective', *Psychology, Crime and Law*, XII (2006), pp. 605–17.

31 Skarbek, *The Social Order*, p. 66.

32 Nicola Bartlett, 'Inside HMP Birmingham, the G4S-run Jail Where the Inmates Have Taken Over', *The Mirror*, 20 August 2018.

33 Thea Jacobs and Tom Wells, 'Drug Battle: Eight Gangs in Fight to Run the Drugs Trade in Britain's Most Dangerous Prison, HMP Birmingham', *The Sun*, 26 August 2018.

34 Mike Lockley, 'Ex-prisoner Who Was Violent Gang Member Reveals All', *Midlands News*, 14 April 2018.

35 Ben Gelblum, 'Gang Films Themselves Attacking Prisoner at Scandal-hit HMP Birmingham', *The London Economic*, 8 July 2019.

36 Quoted in Coretta Phillips, *The Multicultural Prison: Ethnicity, Masculinity, and Social Relations among Prisoners* (Oxford, 2012), pp. 137–8.

37 Emily Setty with Rachel Sturrock and Elizabeth Simes, *Gangs in Prison: The Nature and Impact of Gang Involvement among Prisoners*, https://cdn.catch-22.org.uk, October 2014.

38 Quoted in Phillips, *The Multicultural Prison*, p. 136.

39 Ibid., p. 140.

40 Ibid., p. 141.

41 Ibid., p. 142.

42 Nick Harley, 'UK Muslim Prison Gangs Dubbed the "Brotherhood" Fuel Radicalisation Fears', *The National*, 11 June 2019.

43 Ibid.

44 Beverly Powis, Louise Dixon and Jessica Woodhams, *Exploring the Nature of Muslim Groups and Related Gang Activity in Three High Security Prisons: Findings from Qualitative Research*, Ministry of Justice Analytical Series, 2019.

45 Ibid.

46 Ibid.

47 Ibid.

48 Quoted ibid.

49 Ibid.

50  Ibid.

51  Ibid.

52  Beghal trained under Osama bin Laden, and in 2001 was convicted of plotting to bomb the American Embassy in Paris. Although he was kept in isolation, crowded prison conditions made it impossible to completely segregate him from other prisoners.

53  Quoted in Dina Temple-Raston, 'French Prisons Prove to Be Effective Incubators for Islamic Extremism', NPR, 22 January 2015.

54  Ibid.

55  Tom Burgis, 'The Making of a French Jihadi', *Financial Times*, 26 January 2015.

56  R. Bruce, 'For ISIS, Prisons Have Become Terror Incubators', *Arab Weekly*, 15 January 2017.

57  Kieran McEvoy, *Paramilitary Imprisonment in Northern Ireland: Resistance, Management, and Release* (Oxford, 2001), p. 126.

58  Conor Gallagher, 'Ireland's Prison Gangs', *Irish Times*, 15 September 2018.

59  Named for being built in the shape of an H.

60  Michelle Butler, Gavin Slade and Camila Nunes Dias, 'Self-governing Prisons: Prison Gangs in an International Perspective', *Trends in Organized Crime*, 30 March 2018.

61  Chris Ryder, *Inside the Maze: The Untold Story of the Northern Ireland Prison Service* (London, 2000).

62  It was the same design as that used in the United States, in the rebuilding of Louisiana's Angola Penitentiary in 1955.

63  James Challis, *The Northern Ireland Prison Service, 1920–90* (Belfast, 1999); Ryder, *Inside the Maze*; Donovan Wylie, ed., *The Maze* (London, 2004).

64  Butler et al., 'Self-governing Prisons'; See also Sean McConville, *A History of English Prison Administration, 1750–1977*, vol. 1 (London, 1981).

65  Lessing, 'The Danger of Dungeons'.

66  McEvoy, *Paramilitary Imprisonment*, p. 131.

67  Ibid., p. 127.

68  Ibid., p. 127, note 37.

69  Quoted in Ciaran Barnes, 'Maghaberry Race Wars', *Northern Ireland's Sun Life*, 21 September 2015.

70  Ibid.

71  'Gangs Operate International Empires from Inside Irish Prison', www.bignewsnetwork.com, 20 April 2018.

72 Tim Carey, *Mountjoy Prison: The Story of a Prison* (Cork, 2000), p. 224.

73 Niall O'Connor, 'Gang Feuds in Mountjoy Prison Are Stretching Officers to Breaking Point', *Irish Mirror,* 19 April 2018.

74 Ibid.

75 Conor Gallagher, 'Ireland's Prison Gangs: You Hear a Scream and Suddenly a Fella's Pumping Blood', *Irish Times*, 15 September 2018.

76 Ibid.

77 McEvoy, *Paramilitary Imprisonment*, p. 128.

78 Ibid.

79 Phillips, *The Multicultural Prison*, pp. 138–9.

80 'Maghaberry Prison "Most Dangerous" in the UK', *Belfast Telegraph*, 5 November 2015.

81 Brian Hutton, 'Gang Feuds and Staff Shortages Blamed for Prison Assaults', *The Irish Times*, 19 July 2019.

82 Mia Harris, 'Are There Muslim Gangs in Prison', www.russellwebster. com/miah, 5 July 2019.

83 Rebecca Flood, 'Yorkshire Ripper Turns to Islam after Muslim Gangs Offer Mass Murderer Jail Protection', *Express*, 4 September 2016. Despite this headline, a more accurate description of Peter Sutcliffe would be serial killer, rather than mass murderer.

84 Holly Christodoulou, 'Yorkshire Snipper', www.thesun.co.uk, 2 October 2016.

85 Joshua Nevett, 'Millie Dowler Killer Levi Bellfield "Joined Biggest Muslim Jail Gang to Impress Terrorists"', www.dailystar.co.uk, 21 March 2018.

86 Ibid.

## 8 PRISON GANGS OF NORTH AMERICA

1 As early as 1983, a book by Charles Stastny and Gabrielle Tyrnauer, *Who Rules the Joint? The Changing Political Culture of Maximum Security Prisons in America* (Lexington, MA), gave rise to the specious claim that the Gypsy Jokers was the first documented prison gang. After the publication of George M. Camp and Camille G. Camp, *Prison Gangs: Their Extent, Nature, and Impact on Prisons* (Washington, DC, 1985), p. 20, it became pro forma for any historical research on prison gangs in America to assert either of the aforementioned two studies as the main evidence for this claim. However, these authors/researchers should probably be given some slack for this claim, since they were relative pioneers in modern prison gang research. Less forgivable is the fact

that, until 2016, this claim has not even been challenged by the increasing number of prison gang-scholars and researchers. It should not be overlooked that this was among the earliest works on prison gangs. That said, there is no evidence that the Gypsy Jokers was 'the first known prison gang in the United States', nor a prison gang at all.

2 Carter F. Smith, 'When Is a Prison Gang Not a Prison Gang: A Focused Review of Prison Gang Literature', *Journal of Gang Research*, XXIII (2016), pp. 41–52.

3 Bill Hayes, *The One-percenter Encyclopedia: The World of the Outlaw Motorcycle Clubs from Abyss Ghosts to Zombies Elite* (Minneapolis, MN, 2011), p. 93. According to Hayes, the Gypsy Jokers motorcycle club was established on 1 April 1956 in San Francisco before expanding into the Pacific Northwest in 1967, where they appeared on the radar of law enforcement in Oregon and Washington.

4 'Penologists Back Wickersham Data', *New York Times*, 23 October 1931, p. 17.

5 The research director was Harry M. Shulman. He ended his interview with the reporter by explaining, 'Most of what I told you is information that came to me and my workers from the 1,000 prisoners we interviewed. It had little to do with our clinical survey.'

6 'Prison Gang Chiefs Served by Valets', *New York Times*, 25 January 1934, p. 1.

7 Ibid., pp. 1, 3.

8 Ibid., p. 3.

9 'Welfare Island Raid Bares Gangster Rule over Prison: Weapons, Narcotics Found', *New York Times*, 25 January 1934, pp. 1, 3.

10 Ibid.

11 'Prison Gangs Face a Federal Inquiry; Clean-up Presses', *New York Times*, 26 January 1934, p. 1.

12 The Purple Gang was active between the 1910s and the 1940s. Originally a loose confederation of independent criminals, the gang was prominent during the bloodletting of the Prohibition era. At their apogee the gang was supplying Chicago's Al Capone mob with whisky. Most of its early members were sons of recent Jewish immigrants from Eastern Europe. See also Paul R. Kavieff, *Purple Gang: Organized Crime in Detroit, 1910–1945* (New York, 2000).

13 Judy Gail Krasnow, *Jacktown: History and Hard Times at Michigan's First State Prison* (Charleston, SC, 2017), p. 106.

14 Joseph F. Spillane, *Coxsackie: The Life and Death of Prison Reform* (Baltimore, MD, 2014), pp. 75–6.

15 Ibid., pp. 163–4; See also Mwlina Imiri Abudadika (Sonny Carson), *The Education of Sonny Carson* (New York, 1972), pp. 50–51. Carson changed his name when he converted to Islam.

16 Ibid.

17 Benjamin Lessing, 'The Danger of Dungeons: Prison Gangs and Incarcerated Militant Groups', in *Small Arms Survey 2010: Gangs, Groups and Guns* (Cambridge, 2010), pp. 160–62.

18 James B. Jacobs, *Stateville: The Penitentiary in Mass Society* (Chicago, IL, 1978), p. 48.

19 Freedom of Information Act (FOIA), 'Mexican Mafia', 7 December 1973, p. 18.

20 Anti-Defamation League (ADL), *Dangerous Convictions: An Introduction to Extremist Activities in Prison* (New York, 2006), p. 10.

21 David Grann, 'The Brand: How the Aryan Brotherhood Became the Most Murderous Prison Gang in America', *New Yorker*, 16 and 23 February 2004.

22 'David Arenberg Reflects on Being Jewish in State Prison', www.quora.com, 12 March 2013.

23 'How Do Mixed-race Prisoners Decide Which Prison Gangs to Join?', www.quora.com, 2016.

24 Ibid.

25 Arenberg, 'David Arenberg Reflects on Being Jewish in State Prison'.

26 Quoted in Rebecca Trammell, 'Values, Rules, and Keeping the Peace: How Men Describe Order and Inmate Code in California Prisons', *Deviant Behavior*, xxx (2009), p. 756.

27 Bill Valentine, *Gangs and Their Tattoos: Identifying Gangbangers on the Street and in Prison* (Boulder, CO, 2000), pp. 100, 111.

28 Ibid.

29 Tony Rafael, *The Mexican Mafia* (New York, 2007), p. 274. Today DVI is a minimum-security prison and reception centre for incoming prisoners. It is just one of several facilities in the California Department of Corrections (CDC) where new convicts are evaluated and processed to determine medical and mental conditions and propensity for violence.

30 Chris Blatchford, *The Black Hand: The Bloody Rise and Redemption of 'Boxer' Enriquez, a Mexican Mob Killer* (New York, 2008), p. 4.

31 William Dunn, *The Gangs of Los Angeles* (New York, 2007), p. 128; Rafael, *Mexican Mafia*, p. 274.

32 Dunn, *Gangs of Los Angeles*, p. 129.

33 David G. Curry, Scott H. Decker and David Pyrooz, *Confronting Gangs: Crime and Community* (New York, 2014), p. 160.

34 According to Trammell, 'Values, Rules, and Keeping the Peace', p. 759, 'the term shot-caller was originally used by members of the Mexican Mafia'. More recently, the term 'key holder' has been adopted in its place by most prison and street gangs.

35 Rafael, *Mexican Mafia*, pp. 274–5.

36 Ibid., p. 276.

37 Ibid., p. 273; Ramon Mendoza and Rene Enriquez, *The Mexican Mafia Encyclopedia* (Santa Ana, CA, 2012), p. 11.

38 Ibid., p. 13.

39 Ibid., p. 274.

40 Rafael, *Mexican Mafia*, p. 277.

41 Ibid.

42 Ibid.

43 Blatchford, *Black Hand*, p. 4.

44 Ibid., p. 7; Dunn, *Gangs of Los Angeles*, claims he was Hungarian. Richard Valdemar, 'History of the Mexican Mafia Prison Gang', www.policemag.com, 25 July 2007.

45 John Hammarly, 'Inside the Mexican Mafia', *New West*, 19 December 1977, p. 70.

46 Dunn, *Gangs of Los Angeles*, p. 131.

47 Al Valdez, 'The Origins of Southern California Latino Gangs', in *Maras: Gang Violence and Security in Central America*, ed. Thomas Bruneau, Lucia Dammert and Elizabeth Skinner (Austin, TX, 2011), p. 28.

48 Ibid.

49 Ibid.

50 Ibid., p. 29.

51 Ibid.

52 Keramet Reiter, *23/7: Pelican Bay Prison and the Rise of Long-term Solitary Confinement* (New Haven, CT, 2016), p. 148.

53 Quoted ibid.

54 Blatchford, *Black Hand*; see Al Valdez and Rene Enriquez, *Urban Street Terrorism: The Mexican Mafia and the Sureños* (Santa Ana, CA, 2011), and Ramon Mendoza and Rene Enriquez, *The Mexican Mafia Encyclopedia* (Santa Ana, CA, 2012).

55 FOIA.

56 Teletype to FBI director, 18 May 1974, SF 157-5274, p. 1, FOIA; see also FOIA 1971.

57 FOIA, 'Mexican Mafia', 7 December 1973, p. 19.

58 Blatchford, *Black Hand*; Rafael, *Mexican Mafia*.

59  FOIA, 'Mexican Mafia', 7 December 1973. Declassified 13 August 1999.

60  Ibid., Enclosure 157-31171-1.

61  Ibid.

62  U.S. Department of Justice, 'The Mexican Mafia', FBI, Freedom of
    Information Act, 8 July 1974 correspondence, Enclosure 157-31171-2. See
    also Teletype to Director, 18 May 1974, SF Office, 157-5274.

63  Venceremos Organization is 'composed of third world and white
    revolutionaries operating in the SF Peninsula area. Publicly stated goal
    was to build a united front against the imperialist U.S. leading to the
    overthrow of the U.S. government by force and urban guerrilla struggles.'
    FOIA, 'Mexican Mafia', p. 2.

64  'Mexican Mafia', 8 July 1974, Director Kelly to Secret Service.

65  Rafael, *Mexican Mafia*, p. 3.

66  Quoted ibid.

67  Jesse Katz, 'Don't Underestimate These People', *Houston Chronicle*,
    13 June 1993, p. 8A.

68  Some of the introductory material in the film was drawn from
    Beatrice Griffith, *American Me* (New York, 1948). This book covered
    the migration of Mexicans to America and introduced readers to
    life in the Mexican-American southwest. According to the Mexican
    Mafia chroniclers and former members Ramon Mendoza and Rene
    Enriquez, the book was originally published in *Seventeen Magazine*
    and won the Houghton Mifflin Literary Fellowship for non-fiction in
    1945. See Mendoza and Enriquez, *The Mexican Mafia Encyclopedia*,
    p. 197.

69  Katz, 'Don't Underestimate These People'.

70  Congress created RICO in 1970, as part of the Organized Crime Control
    Act. It revolutionized the crusade against organized crime groups.

71  Julia Reynolds, *Blood in the Fields: Ten Years inside California's Nuestra
    Familia Gang* (Chicago, IL, 2014).

72  Bill Valentine, *Gangs and Their Tattoos* (Boulder, CO, 2000).

73  David Skarbek, *The Social Order of the Underworld: How Prison Gangs
    Govern the American Penal System* (New York, 2014), p. 89.

74  Valentine, *Gangs and Their Tattoos*.

75  Mike Tapia, 'Barrio Criminal Networks and Prison Gang Formation in
    Texas', *Journal of Gang Research* (Summer 2018), p. 109.

76  Ibid., pp. 110–11.

77  Ibid., p. 111.

78  Ibid., p. 112.

79 FBI, San Angelo, 'Texas Gang Member Sentenced to 20 Years in Federal Prison Without Parole', U.S. Attorney's Office, 17 September 2009, https://archives.fbi.gov.

80 Grann, 'The Brand'.

81 David Holthouse, 'Smashing the Shamrock', *Intelligence Report*, Southern Poverty Law Center, Autumn 2005.

82 The shamrock originated with an early founder who was obviously proud to be Irish. The tattoo was allowed only after performing a successful first mission.

83 Grann, 'The Brand'.

84 David Holthouse, 'Inside the Brotherhood', *Intelligence Report*, Southern Poverty Law Center, Winter 2012.

85 Dane Schiller, 'Feds Target Aryan Gang', *Houston Chronicle*, 26 November 2012, pp. A1, A6.

86 This victim survived the attack with only scars and skin grafts. Trouble apparently followed him; he was killed months after getting out of state prison for meth charges.

87 Dane Schiller, 'Blowtorch Attacks Send 2 Aryans to Prison', *Houston Chronicle*, 10 October 2014, p. B2.

88 Grann, 'The Brand', p. 158.

89 Ibid., p. 165.

90 Reiter, 23/7, p. 13.

91 Holthouse, 'Inside the Brotherhood'.

92 Ibid., p. 10.

93 Gillian Flaccus, 'White Supremacists Could Get Death in Prison Gang War Trial', *Houston Chronicle*, 15 March 2006, p. A7.

94 Ibid.

95 Dane Schiller, 'Aryan Brothers: Resume Is Required to Join This Prison Gang', *Houston Chronicle*, 7 September 2012, pp. A1, A17.

96 Reiter, 23/7, p. 16.

97 Schiller, 'Feds Target Aryan Gang', pp. A1, A6.

98 Schiller, 'Aryan Brothers: Resume Is Required', pp. A1, A17.

99 Ibid.

100 Ibid.

101 'Nazi Low Riders', Anti-Defamation League, www.adl.org, accessed 21 May 2020.

102 Ibid.

103 Ibid.

104 Ibid.

105 Ibid.

106 Charles Montaldo, 'The Aryan Warriors: Profile of the Aryan Warriors Prison Gang', www.thoughtco.com, 27 January 2019.

107 Ibid.

108 Valentine, *Gangs and Their Tattoos*; Bill Valentine, *Gang Intelligence Manual: Identifying and Understanding Modern-day Violent Gangs in the United States* (Boulder, CO, 1995).

109 Gary Hunter, 'Aryan Warriors Prison Gang Prosecuted in Nevada', *Prison Legal News*, August 2010.

110 Seth Ferranti, 'This Is What It's Like to Belong to a Prison in the Deep South', 17 June 2015.

111 Ibid.

112 Joseph T. Hallinan, *Going Up the River: Travels in a Prison Nation* (New York, 2001), p. 25.

113 Reiter, *23/7*, p. 39.

114 Ibid., p. 3.

115 Valentine, *Gangs and Their Tattoos*.

116 Quoted in Skarbek, *Social Order of the Underworld*, p. 55.

117 Ibid.

118 National Gang Crime Research Center Report, 2006, www.ngrc.com/introcha.html.

119 In 1983 the Kumi Africa Nation, or 415, broke off from the BGF. The 415 refers to the San Francisco Bay area code. Kumi is a Swahili word meaning ten, or the equivalent of 4+1+5. Only inmates and ex-inmates are permitted to identify as Kumi, or 415s. The BGF and Kumi share intelligence and are known to honour each other's hit lists. Meanwhile, the 415 seeks to spread to other western states. See Bill Valentine, *Gangs and Their Tattoos*, pp. 17–20.

120 Juliet Linderman, 'Gang Leader of a Notorious Baltimore Jail Has Become Prosecutors' Greatest Snitch', *Houston Chronicle*, 4 December 2014, p. A2.

121 Ibid.

122 Ibid.

123 Matt O'Connor, 'Ex-member Tells of Gang's Jail Rules', *Chicago Tribune*, 6 February 1996.

124 Jeremy Gorner, 'Police Blame "Gangster Disciples" for Chicago's Soaring Homicide Rate', *Business Insider*, 3 October 2012.

125 Ibid.

126 Mary Ann Mowatt and Adam K. Matz, 'Native American Involvement in Gangs', *Perspectives* (Summer 2014), p. 38.

127 Paul Chaat Smith and Robert Allen Warrior, *Like a Hurricane: The Indian Movement from Alcatraz to Wounded Knee* (New York, 1996), pp. 127–8.

128 Ibid., p. 128.

129 Christopher M. Grant, *Native American Involvement in the Gang Subculture: Current Trends and Dynamics* (Washington, DC, 2013), p. 19.

130 Ibid., p. 24.

131 Ibid., p. 23.

132 'Directions: Keynotes of the Arizona Department of Corrections', June 2001, https://azmemory.azlibrary.gov/digital/api/collection/statepubs/id/17598/download.

133 Ibid.

134 Ibid., p. 24.

135 Arizona Department of Corrections, 'Warrior Society', https://corrections.az.gov.

136 Members are mainly from the Apache and Navajo tribes. The largest concentration of them are housed at the Arizona State Prison Complex in Winslow.

137 Christian Richardson, 'American Indian Prison Gang Certified as a Security Threat', *Arizona Daily Star*, 7 July 2001, p. B1.

138 Christian Richardson, 'American Indian Prison Gang Certified as a Security Threat', *Arizona Daily Star,* 7 July 2001, p. B1.

139 'Police Arrest Native Mob Leader', *Duluth News Tribune*, 3 February 2012.

140 'Interview with a Marked Man', *Al Jazeera America*, http://projects.aljazeera.com, 22 January 2015.

141 Helen Barrett, 'Tattoos Tell Tales', *Indian Country News*, 8 October 2008.

142 U.S. Department of Justice, 'Three Individuals Sentenced on Methamphetamine Distribution, Conspiracy, and Assault Charges', www.justice.gov, 1 June 2017; see also Tesina Jackson, 'Local Gang Leader Jailed for Drug Trafficking', *Tahlequah Daily Press*, 2 June 2017.

143 Arizona Department of Corrections, 'Dine Pride', https://corrections.az.gov.

144 Anti-Defamation League, 2006, p. 11.

145 Ibid., pp. 11–12.

146 Kathleen Harris, 'Diverse Mix of Gangs a Growing Security Challenge for Federal Prisons', www.cbc.ca, 25 March 2018.

147 Ibid.

148 'The Decline of Traditional Prison Gangs', http://prisonoffenders.com.

149 Ibid.

150 Texas Department of Public Safety, 'Texas Gang Threat Assessment', Austin, TX, www.dps.texas.gov, August 2015, p. 35.

151 Mike Glenn, 'Gang Membership Growing in Texas', *Houston Chronicle*, 18 April 2014.

152 Ibid.


## 9 PRISON GANGS OF LATIN AMERICA

1 Sacha Darke and Chris Garces, 'Surviving the New Mass Carceral Zone', *Prison Service Journal*, CCXXIX (2017), p. 2.

2 Ioan Grillo, *Gangster Warlords: Drug Dollars, Killing Fields and the New Politics of Latin America* (London, 2016), p. 49.

3 Steven Dudley and James Bargent, 'The Prison Dilemma: Latin America's Incubators of Organized Crime', www.insightcrime.org, 19 January 2017.

4 Deborah T. Levenson, *Adios Nino: The Gangs of Guatemala City and the Politics of Death* (Durham, NC, 2013), p. 110.

5 Grillo, *Gangster Warlords*, p. 53.

6 Geoffrey Ramsey, '"At Least 10" Gangs in Bolivia are Run from Prison: Police', www.insightcrime.org, 24 October 2012.

7 Geoffrey Ramsey, 'Overcrowding Allows Bolivia's Prison Gangs to Flourish', www.insightcrime.org, 20 January 2012.

8 Marguerite Cawley, 'Ecuador Jails Swell with Pre-trial Detentions, Cocaine Trafficking', www.insightcrime.org, 12 December 2013.

9 Parker Asmann, 'Ecuador Sends in Troops amid Troubling Prison Gang Violence', www.insightcrime.org, 16 May 2019.

10 'Murder in Brazil: Dying Young', *The Economist*, 26 January 2019, p. 30.

11 Sacha Darke, 'Inmate Governance in Brazilian Prisons', *The Howard Journal of Criminal Justice*, LII (2013), p. 282.

12 Sacha Darke, 'Who Is Really in Control of Brazil's Prisons', www.insight-crime.org, 7 February 2017.

13 Grillo, *Gangster Warlords*, p. 52.

14 Ibid., p. 63.

15 Ibid.

16 Roberta Novis, *Hard Times: Exploring the Complex Structures and Activities of Brazilian Prison Gangs* (London, 2013), p. 22.

17 Ibid.

18 Grillo, *Gangster Warlords*, p. 42.

19 Ibid.

20 Ibid., p. 69.

21 Ibid., p. 93.

22 Ibid., p. 92.

23 Benjamin Lessing, 'Brazil's Prison Massacres Are a Frightening Window into Gang Warfare', *Washington Post*, 17 January 2017.

24 Novis, *Hard Times*, p. 139.

25 Quoted ibid., p. 142.

26 Ibid., p. 126.

27 Quoted ibid., p. 159.

28 Ibid., p. 145.

29 Camila Nunes Dias, 'Organized Crime in Brazilian Prisons: The Example of the PCC', *International Journal of Criminology and Sociology*, II (2013), p. 404; Novis, *Hard Times*, p. 148.

30 Quoted in Novis, *Hard Times*, p. 128.

31 Ibid., pp. 138–9.

32 Quoted ibid.

33 Ibid., p. 145.

34 Built in the 1920s as a model prison housing 1,200 inmates, by the 1990s it contained more than 8,000, making it Latin America's largest prison.

35 Karina Biondi, *Sharing This Walk: An Ethnography of Prison Life and the PCC in Brazil*, ed. and trans. John F. Collins (Chapel Hill, NC, 2016), p. 35.

36 Ignacio Cano, 'Violence and Organized Crime in Brazil: The Case of Militias in Rio de Janeiro', in *Transnational Organized Crime: Analyses of a Global Challenge to Democracy*, ed. Heinrich-Boll-Siftung and Regine Schonenberg, (New York City, 2013), pp. 179–88.

37 Biondi, *Sharing This Walk*.

38 Ibid., pp. 36–7.

39 William Langewiesche, 'City of Fear', *Vanity Fair*, April 2007.

40 Luis Esteban Manrique, 'A Parallel Power: Organized Crime in Latin America', Real Instituto Elcano, Madrid, http://realinstitutoelcano.org, 2006.

41 'First Command of the Capital: Prison Gang Profile', http://inside-prison.com, 2006.

42 Biondi, *Sharing This Walk*, p. 60.

43 Andrew Downie, 'Brazil Gang Takes on State', *Christian Science Monitor*, 16 May 2006, p. 2.

44 Stephanie Hanson, 'Brazil's Most Powerful Gang', www.cfr.org/publication/11542, n. d., p. 5.

45  Kyra Gurney, 'Police Documents Reveal "Hezbollah Ties" to Brazil's PCC', www.insightcrime.org, 10 November 2014.

46  Elyssa Pachico, 'Brazil's PCC Gang Worked with Italian Mafia', www.insightcrime.org, 4 November 2014.

47  Charles Parkinson, 'Paraguay Captures Members of Brazil's PCC', www.insightcrime.org, 1 November 2013.

48  Michael Lohmuller, 'PCC Faction Linked to Spate of Armed Robberies in Paraguay', www.insightcrime.org, 15 April 2015.

49  Kyra Gurney, 'Brazil's PCC, Mimicking the Country, Shifts towards China', www.insightcrime.org, 19 January 2015.

50  Hanson, 'Brazil's Most Powerful Gang', p. 3.

51  Biondi, *Sharing This Walk*, p. 55.

52  Ibid.

53  Ibid.

54  Ibid., p. 82.

55  Chris Dalby, 'Brazil Prisons Become Battlegrounds for Familia do Norte Civil War', www.insightcrime.org, 29 May 2019.

56  Ibid.

57  Parker Asmann, 'Turf Dispute Breaks North Brazil Gang Pact, Opening Door for PCC', www.insightcrime.org, 15 May 2018.

58  Dalby, 'Brazil Prisons'.

59  Marina Lopes, 'Prison Members in Brazil Stabbed to Death in Front of Visiting Family Members: At Least 55 Dead', *Washington Post*, 28 May 2019.

60  Dalby, 'Brazil Prisons'.

61  Manuel A. Gomez, 'Pran Justice: Social Order, Dispute Processing, and Adjudication in the Venezuelan Prison Subculture', 8 UC *Irvine L. Rev.*, CLXXXIII (2018), p. 185.

62  Ibid.

63  Jason Mitchell, 'In Chaotic Venezuela, Life Is Better in Prison', www.spectator.com.au, February 2018.

64  Gomez, 'Pran Justice', p. 188.

65  Ibid., p. 195.

66  Ibid.

67  Ibid., pp. 196–7.

68  Ibid.

69  Ibid., p. 198.

70  Ibid.

71  'The Devolution of State Power, "The Pranes"', www.insightcrime.org, 23 April 2019.

72 Gomez, 'Pran Justice', p. 199.

73 Ibid.

74 Ibid., p. 200.

75 There is a parallel here to the developing states of early modern Europe. Most were insecure in their early years and freely used horrific public punishments to demonstrate that serious crimes were not just against the law but a threat to state power as well. The punishment of hanging, drawing and quartering in England or breaking on the wheel in continental Europe are prime examples.

76 Gomez, 'Pran Justice', pp. 203–4.

77 Ibid.

78 Ibid., p. 197.

79 Ibid., p. 200.

80 Ibid., p. 201.

81 Ibid., p. 202.

82 'Prison Mafia in Venezuela Is Not Just the Pranes': Carlos Nieto [Palma]', Venezuelan Investigative Unit, www.insightcrime.org, 30 April 2019.

83 'The Devolution of State Power'.

84 Ibid.

85 Ibid.

86 Ibid.

87 Ibid.

88 'Prison Mafia in Venezuela'; 'The Devolution of State Power'.

89 Quoted in Mitchell, 'In Chaotic Venezuela'.

90 Armin Rosen, 'This Man Was the "Steve Jobs" of Venezuelan Prison Gang Lords', *Business Insider*, 28 January 2016.

91 Simon Romero, 'When Prisoners Can Do Anything, Except Leave', *New York Times*, 3 June 2011.

92 Rosen, 'This Man Was the "Steve Jobs"'.

93 Grillo, *Gangster Warlords*, p. 188.

94 José Miguel Cruz, 'Government Suppression and the Dark Side of Gang Suppression in Central America', in *Maras: Gang Violence and Security in Central America*, ed. Thomas Bruneau, Lucia Dammert and Elizabeth Skinner (Austin, TX, 2011), p. 155.

95 Benjamin Lessing, 'Study Shows Prison Gangs Rule Much More than Penitentiaries', www.insightcrime.org, 30 September 2016; Tom Wainwright, *Narconomics: How to Run a Drug Cartel* (New York, 2016), p. 42.

96 Grillo, *Gangster Warlords*, p. 200.

97 Thomas Bruneau, *Maras: Gang Violence and Security in Central America* (Austin, TX, 2011), p. 3.

98 In the modern era, cholo is informal Spanish slang designating a certain type of tough street-wise appearance adopted by the Mexican American gang subculture. It has been adopted by many Central American gang members as well. Often the buzzed short hair cuts are accompanied by loose-fitting khaki pants or shirts, white knee-high shorts and white tank top undershirt (wife beater), finished off with a button front shirt, commonly plaid or flannel. This sartorial look has been adopted by the fashion industry to a certain extent and is considered a symbol of ethnic pride to many.

99 Grillo, *Gangster Warlords*, p. 200.

100 Ibid., p. 201; Bruneau, *Maras*, p. 3.

101 California's Hispanic prison gangs are distinguished by their affiliation with either northern California (*Norteños*) street gangs or the southern gangs. More detail can be found in the Chapter Eight.

102 Grillo, *Gangster Warlords*, p. 201.

103 Ibid., p. 204.

104 Steven Dudley and Juan José Martinez D'Aubuisson, 'El Salvador's Prisons and the Battle for the MS13's Soul', www.insightcrime.org, 16 February 2017.

105 Ibid.

106 Ibid.

107 Lessing, 'Study Shows Prison Gangs Rule', p. 5.

108 Sonia Nazario, 'Pay or Die', *New York Times Sunday Review*, 28 July 2019, pp. 1, 6–7.

109 Dudley and D'Aubuisson, 'El Salvador's Prisons', 16 February 2017.

110 Ibid.

111 'Dealing with the Devil', *The Economist*, 8 February 2014, p. 16.

112 'Rivers of Blood', *The Economist*, 10 October 2015, p. 35.

113 Dudley and D'Aubuisson, 'El Salvador's Prisons and the Battle for the MS13's Soul'.

114 Ibid.

115 Jon Horne Carter, 'Gothic Sovereignty: Gangs and Criminal Community in a Honduran Prison', *South Atlantic Quarterly*, CXIII (2014), pp. 475–502.

116 Juan José Martinez D'Aubuisson and Steven Dudley, 'Where Chaos Reigns inside San Pedro Sula Prison', www.insightcrime.org, 2 February 2017.

117 Quoted ibid.

118 Ibid.

119 Ibid.

120 Jon Carter, 'Mass Incarceration, Co-governance, and Prison Reform in Honduras', NACL Report on the Americas, XLIX (2017), pp. 354–9.

121 Sandrine McDuff, 'El Salvador Inmates Defy Phone Ban with Toilet Paper, Toothpaste', www.insightcrime.org, 15 July 2019.

122 Ibid.

123 Levenson, *Adios Nino*, p. 111.

124 Ibid., p. 112.

125 Ibid., pp. 112–13.

126 Ibid.

127 Ibid., p. 115.

128 Ibid.

129 The Kaibil is an elite group of soldiers, named after a legendary indigenous leader who fought the Spanish conquistadors.

130 Juan José Martinez d'Aubuisson and Steven Dudley, 'Reign of the Kaibil: Guatemala's Prisons under Lima', www.insightcrime.org, 26 January 2017.

131 Quoted ibid.

132 Ibid.

133 Ibid.

134 Ibid., p. 11. Many gang members were from southern California, where it was not uncommon for gangs to agree to 'prison pacts'. 'They call them "southern pacts" or "southern blood" (*Correr el sur*).' The gangs were also 'part of the same umbrella organization known as the Surenos, giving them some common ground. After the accord, the gangs obtained knives, grenades and munitions, and waited.'

135 D'Aubuisson and Dudley, 'Reign of the Kaibil', p. 17.

136 Ibid.

137 LaVerle Berry, Glenn E. Curtis, John N. Gibbs, Rex A. Hudson, Tara Karacan, Nina Kollars and Ramon Miro, 'Nations Hospitable to Organized Crime and Terrorism' (Washington DC, 2003), p. 134.

138 'Barrio Azteca', www.insightcrime.org, 9 July 2018; See also Mike Tapia, *Gangs of the El Paso-Juarez Borderland* (Albuquerque, NM, 2019), pp. 108–111.

139 Ibid.

140 'Six in 10 Prisons "Self-governed" by Gangs', www.telegraph.co.uk, 25 September 2012.

141 'Barrio Azteca Leader Extradited from Mexico to United States to Face Charges Related to the U.S. Consulate Murders in Juarez, Mexico', www.

justice.gov, 29 June 2012; 'Barrio Azteca Leader Sentenced to Life in Prison and Two Barrio Azteca Soldiers Sentenced to 20 and 30 Years in Prison', www.fbi.gov, 30 June 2012.

142 Jo Tuckman, 'At Least 20 Dead in Mexican Prison Riot', *The Guardian*, 4 March 2009; Dudley Althaus, 'Rival Gangs in Juarez Prison Clash, leaving 20 Convicts Dead: 200 Police Needed to Gain Prison Control', *Houston Chronicle*, 5 March 2009.

143 Damien Cave, 'Even Violent Drug Cartels Fear God', *New York Times Magazine*, 20 April 2013.

144 James Bargent, 'Mexico Prison Massacre Linked to Zetas Takeover Allegations', www.insightcrime.org, 11 October 2017.

145 James Babcock, 'Zetas Drug Gang Used Mexican Prison as Extermination Camp to Kidnap and Kill 150', *The Telegraph*, 6 June 2016.

146 Maria Verza, 'Report Details Zetas Total Control over Mexican Prison', www.apnews.com, 21 November 2017.

147 Ibid.

148 Patricia Davila, 'The Yolk of Los Zetas' in Coahuila', *Borderland Beat*, 23 November 2017.

149 Darke and Garces, 'Surviving the New Mass Carceral Zone'.

## EPILOGUE

1 Benjamin Lessing, 'The Danger of Dungeons: Prison Gangs and Incarcerated Militant Groups', in *Small Arms Survey* (Cambridge, 2010), p. 159.

2 Clarke R. Jones and Raymund E. Narag, 'Why Prisons Aren't All Bad', www.cnn.com, 11 December 2014.

3 John Dickie, *Blood Brotherhoods: The Rise of the Italian Mafia* (London, 2011), p. 35

4 Ioan Grillo, *Gangster Warlords: Drug Dollars, Killing Fields and the New Politics of Latin America* (London 2016), p. 69.

5 Joe Miguel Cruz, 'Government Responses and the Dark Side of Gang Suppression in Central America', in *Maras: Gang Violence and Security in Central America*, ed. Thomas Bruneau, Lucia Dammert and Elizabeth Skinner (Austin, tx, 2011), p. 155.

6 Lessing, 'The Danger of Dungeons', pp. 160–62.

7 Cited in Rebecca Trammel, 'Values Rules, and Keeping the Peace: How Men Describe Order and the Inmate Code in California Prisons', *Deviant Behavior*, xxx (2009), p. 756.

8 Heather Parker Lewis, *God's Gangsters? The Number Gangs in South African Prisons* (Cape Town, 2010), p. 15.

9 Kathryn Bonella, *Hotel K: The Shocking Inside Story of Bali's Most Notorious Jail* (Sydney, 2012), p. 109.

10 Simon Tisdall, 'About 41% of the World's People Are Under 24. And They're Angry . . ', www.theguardian.com, 26 October 2019.

# SELECT BIBLIOGRAPHY

Allum, Felia, 'Young Guns Take Charge of European Mafia Clans – with Deadly Results', *The Conversation*, 23 March 2017

Applebaum, Anne, *Gulag: A History* (New York, 2003)

—, *Gulag Voices: An Anthology* (New Haven, CT, 2011)

Baldaev, Dantsik Sergeyevic, Vladimir Kuz'mich Belko and Igor Mikhailovich Isupov (compilers and translators), *Dictionary: Prison, Camp, Blatnoi, Jargon* (Speech and Graphic Portraits of Soviet Prison), n.d.

'Brazil's Mighty Prison Gangs', *BBC News*, www.news.bbc.co.uk, 15 May 2006

Bedi, Kiran, *It's Always Possible: Transforming One of the Largest Prisons in the World* (Briar Hill, Vic., 1999)

Behan, Tom, *See Naples and Die: The Camorra and Organised Crime* (London, 2002)

Behi, Abhishek, 'Gang Fight in Bhondsi Jail, Three Officials among Six Injured; 22 Mobile Phones Recovered', *Hindustan Times*, 7 February 2018

Bhutta, Mazhar Hussain, and Muhammad Siddique Akbar, 'Situation of Prisons in India and Pakistan: Shared Legacy, Same Challenges', *South Asian Studies*, XXVII/1 (2012), pp. 171–81

Biondi, Karina, *Sharing This Walk: An Ethnography of Prison Life and the PCC in Brazil*, ed. and trans. John F. Collins (Chapel Hill, NC, 2016)

Blatchford, Chris, *The Black Hand: The Bloody Rise and Redemption of 'Boxer' Enriquez, A Mexican Mob Killer* (New York, 2008)

Bronson, Eric, 'Medium Security Prisons and Inmate Subcultures: The "Normal Prison"', *Southwest Journal of Criminal Justice*, III/2 (2006), pp. 61–86

Bruneau, Thomas, Lucia Dammert and Elizabeth Skinner, eds, *Maras: Gang Violence and Security in Central America* (Austin, TX, 2011)

Bucci, Nino, 'Bikies and Killer Unite in Prison', *Sydney Morning Herald*, www.smh.com.au, 6 November 2013

Buentello, Salvador, Robert S. Fong and Ronald E. Vogel, 'Prison Gang Development: A Theoretical Model', *Prison Journal*, LXXI/2 (1991), pp. 3–14

Buntman, Lisa, *Robben Island and Prisoner Resistance to Apartheid* (Cambridge, 2003)

Butler, Michelle, Gavin Slade and Camila Nunes Dias, 'Self-governing Prisons: Prison Gangs in an International Perspective', *Trends in Organized Crime*, 30 March 2018

Cabal, Ruth, 'Gang Roles Unique to Philippines Prison System', CNN *Philippines*, 15 October 2016

Camp, George M., and Camille Graham Camp, *Prison Gangs: Their Extent, Nature, and Impact on Prisons* (South Salem, NY, 1985)

Caracciolo, Artur (Words by), 'Ten Years in Jail with the 28s', Cape Chamelon, www.capechameleon.co.za, 11 April 2016

Cheloukhine, Serguei, and M. R. Haberfeld, *Russian Organized Corruption Networks and their International Trajectories* (New York, 2011)

Chisholm, Hugh, ed., 'Marc Monnier', *Encyclopaedia Britannica* (Cambridge, 1911)

Choudhury, Sunetra, *Behind Bars: Prison Tales of India's Most Famous* (New Delhi, 2017)

Christianson, Scott, *With Liberty for Some* (Boston, MA, 1998)

—, *Notorious Prisons: An Inside Look at the World's Most Feared Institutions* (Guilford, CT, 2004)

Clemmer, Donald, *The Prison Community* (Boston, 1940)

Cohen, Mike, 'The Cape of Bad Dope', *The Independent*, www.independent.co.uk, 19 September 2013

Cruz, Joe Miguel, 'Government Responses and the Dark Side of Gang Suppression in Central America', in *Maras: Gang Violence and Security in Central America*, ed. Thomas Bruneau, Lucia Dammert and Elizabeth Skinner (Austin, TX, 2011), pp. 137–57

Cummins, Eric, *The Rise and Fall of California's Radical Prison Movement* (Stanford, CA, 1994)

Currie, Cathy, *Art in Prison: An Evaluation of a New Zealand Prison Programme* (Wellington, 1989)

Curry, G. David, Scott H. Decker and David C. Pyrooz, *Confronting Gangs: Crime and Community* (New York, 2014)

Darke, Sacha, 'Inmate Governance in Brazilian Prisons', *Howard Journal of Crime and Justice*, LII/3 (July 2013), pp. 272–84

—, and Maria Lucia Karam, 'Latin American Prisons', in *Handbook on Prisons*, ed. Y. Jewkes, B. Crewe and J. Bennett (Abingdon, 2014), pp. 460–74

Davidson, R. Theodore, *Chicano Prisoners: The Key to San Quentin* (New York, 1974)

De Rosa, Francesca, 'The Vicaria Prison of Naples', in *Antonio Serra and the Economics of Good Government*, ed. Sophus Reinhart and Rosario Patalano (New York, 2016)

Decker, Scott, and David Pyrooz, 'The Real Gangbanging is in Prison', in *The Oxford Handbook of Prisons and Imprisonments*, ed. J. Wooldredge and P. Smith (New York, 2015), pp. 143–62

Dedace, Sophia, 'New Prison Chief Vows to Stamp Out Crimes in Bilibid', GMA *News*, www.gmanetwork.com, 28 July 2011

Dermota, Ken, 'Snow Fall', *The Atlantic* (July–August 2007), pp. 24–5

Dickie, John, *Blood Brotherhoods: The Rise of the Italian Mafias* (London, 2011)

Dioquino, Jessica, 'Gang Culture Part of a Long-standing System in Bilibid', *GMA News*, www.gmanetwork.com, 18 December 2014

Dizon, David, 'Gangs of Bilibid: Managing Prisons in PH', *ABS-CBN News*, http://news.abs-cbn.com, 10 June 2011

Dlamini, Moses, *Hell-hole, Robben Island: Reminiscences of a Political Prisoner* (Nottingham, 1984)

Dolley, Caryn, 'New Plan to Smash Prison Gangs', *Weekend Argus*, 6 June 2015

Dostoevsky, Fyodor, *The House of the Dead* (New York, n.d.)

Downie, Andrew, 'Brazil Gang Takes on State', *Christian Science Monitor*, 16 May 2006

Dunn, William, *The Gangs of Los Angeles* (Lincoln, NE, 2007)

—, 'A Journey into Hell', *The Economist*, 22 September 2012, pp. 44–6

—, 'In Naples, the Hit-men are Children', *The Economist*, 22 June 2017

FBI, Freedom of Information Act (FOIA), 'Mexican Mafia', 7 December 1973

Fentress, James, *Rebels and Mafiosi: Death in an Italian Landscape* (Ithaca, NY, 2000)

Findlay, Mark, Stephen Odgers and Stanley Yeo, *Australian Criminal Justice* (New York, 1994)

Forrester, Skye, 'Inside South Africa's Brutal Prisons: 'If I Didn't Join Gang I'd Have Been Raped'', *International Business Times*, www.ibtimes.co.uk, 13 April 2016

Foucault, Michel, *Discipline and Punish: The Birth of the Prison* (Harmondsworth, 1977)

Galeotti, Mark, 'The Russian 'Mafiya': Consolidation and Globalization', in *Global Crime Today: The Changing Face of OC*, ed. Mark Galeotti (London, 2005), pp. 54–69

—, *The Vory: Russia's Super Mafia* (New Haven, CT, 2018)

Galler, Meyer, and Harlan E. Marquess, *Soviet Prison Speech: A Survivor's Glossary* (Madison, WI, 1972)

Gambetta, Diego, *Codes of the Underworld: How Criminals Communicate* (Princeton, NJ, 2009)

Ganapathy, Narayanan, ''Us' and 'Them', Ethnic Minority Gangs in Singapore Prisons', *Journal of Contemporary Criminal Justice*, XXXII/3 (2016), pp. 264–84

'Gangs and Violence', in Prison Conditions in South Africa', Human Rights Watch, www.hrw.org, 1994

Garces, C., T. Martin and S. Darke, 'Informal Prison Dynamics in Africa and Latin America', *Criminal Justice Matters*, XCI/1 (2013), pp. 26–7

Gear, Sasha, and Kindiza Ngubeni, *Daai Ding: Sex, Sexual Violence and Coercion in Men's Prisons* (Johannesburg, 2002)

Gilbert, Jarrod, *Patched: The History of Gangs in New Zealand* (Auckland, 2016)

Gilinskiy, Yakov, and Yakov Kostjukovsky, 'From Thievish Artel to Criminal Corporation: The History of Organised Crime in Russia', in *Organised*

*Crime in Europe*, ed. Cyrille Fijnaut and Letizia Paoli (Dordrecht, 2004), pp. 181–202

Glazov, Yuri, 'Thieves in the USSR – A Social Phenomenon', in *Russian and Post-Soviet Organized Crime*, ed. Mark Galeotti (Burlington, 2002)

Goffman, Erving, 'On the Characteristics of Total Institutions: The Inmate World', in *The Prison: Studies in Institutional Organization and Change*, ed. Donald R. Cressey (New York, 1961), pp. 15–67

Gomez, Manuel A., 'Pran Justice: Social Order, Dispute Processing, and Adjudication in the Venezuelan Prison Subculture', *UC Irvine Law Review*, VIII/2 (March 2018), pp. 183–206

Grann, David, 'The Brand: How the Aryan Brotherhood became the Most Murderous Prison Gang in America', *New Yorker* (16 February 2004), pp. 157–71

Griffiths, Major Arthur, *Italian Prisons* (London, c. 1920)

—, *Russian Prisons* (London, c. 1920)

Grillo, Ioan, *Gangster Warlords: Drug Dollars, Killing Fields and the New Politics of Latin America* (London, 2016)

Gutierrez, Filomin Candaliza, 'Pangkat: Inmate Gangs at the New Bilibid Maximum Security Compound', *Philippine Sociological Review*, LX (2012), pp. 193–237

Hafeez, Sarah, 'Increase in Gang Formations, Use of Cellphones in Tihar: D-G of Prisons', *Indian Express*, 9 July 2015

Hagedorn, John M., 'The Global Impact of Gangs', *Journal of Contemporary Criminal Justice*, XXI/2 (2005), pp. 153–69

—, 'Gangs in Late Modernity', in *Gangs in the Global City: Alternatives to Traditional Criminology* (Urbana and Chicago, IL, 2007), pp. 295–319

Hallinan, Joseph T., *Going Up the River: Travels in a Prison Nation* (New York, 2001)

Handelman, Stephen, *Comrade Criminal: Russia's New Mafia* (New Haven, CT, 1995)

Hanif, Nafiz Muhamad, Prison in Society, Society in Prison: Analysing OMEGA's Racially Structured Realties Within and Beyond, unpublished thesis, National University of Singapore, 2008.

Hanson, Stephanie, 'Brazil's Powerful Prison Gang', Council on Foreign Relations, www.cfr.org, n.d.

Haysom, Nicholas, *Towards an Understanding of Prison Gangs* (Cape Town, 1981)

Hazlehurst, Kayleen, and Cameron Hazlehurst, *Gangs and Youth Subcultures: International Explorations* (New Brunswick, NJ, 1998)

Hess, Henner, *Mafia and Mafiosi: The Structure of Power* (Lexington, MA, 1973)

Houston, J., and J. Prinsloo, 'Prison Gangs in South Africa: A Comparative Analysis', *Journal of Gang Research*, V/3 (Spring 1998), pp. 41–52

'How Australia's Highest-security Prisoner Exerts Power over Brutal Gang', ABC News, www.abc.net.au, 3 July 2013

'First Command of the Capital: Prison Gang Profile', Inside Prison, www.insideprison.com (2006)

Irwin, John, *The Felon* (Englewood Cliffs, NJ, 1970)

—, *Prisons in Turmoil* (Boston, MA, 1980)

—, and Donald R. Cressey, 'Thieves, Convicts and the Inmate Culture', *Social Problems*, x/2 (October 1962), pp. 142–55

Isaac, Tuhoe, and Bradford Haami, *True Red: The Life of an Ex-mongrel Mob Gang Leader* (self-published, 2007)

Isaacs, Sedick, *Surviving in the Apartheid Prison: Robben Island, Flash Backs of an Earlier Life* (self-published, 2010)

Jacobs, James B., 'Street Gangs Behind Bars', *Social Problems*, XXI/3 (January 1974), pp. 395–409

—, *Stateville: The Penitentiary in Mass Society* (Chicago, IL, 1977)

Jensen, Steffen, *Gangs, Politics and Dignity in Cape Town* (Oxford, 2008)

Jeppie, S., 'Leadership and Loyalties: The Inmates of Nineteenth-century Cape Town, SAF', *Journal of Religion in Africa*, XXVI/2 (1996), pp. 139–62

Johnston, Kirsty, 'LA-Style Gangs Fuel Problems in NZ Prisons', *Stuff*, www.stuff.co.nz, 9 June 2013

Johnston, Norman, *Forms of Constraint: A History of Prison Architecture* (Urbana and Chicago, IL, 2000)

Jones, Clarke R., and Resurrecion S. Morales, 'Integration versus Segregation: A Preliminary Examination of Philippine Correctional Facilities for De-radicalization', *Studies in Conflict and Terrorism*, XXXV/3 (2012), pp. 211–28

—, 'Prison Gangs and Prison Governance in the Philippines', *Griffith Asia Quarterly*, II/1 (2014), pp. 57–74

Jones, Clarke R., Raymund E. Narag and Resurrecion S. Morales, 'Philippine Prison Gangs: Control or Chaos?', *RegNet Working Paper*, 71, Regulatory Institutions Network, 2015

Kaminski, Marek M., *Games Prisoners Play: The Tragicomic Worlds of Polish Prison* (Princeton, NJ, 2004)

Kane, Frank, *In the Shadow of Papillon: Seven Years of Hell in Venezuela's Prison System* (Edinburgh, 2011)

Kesby, Rebecca, 'New Zealand Gangs: The Mongrel Mob and Other Urban Outlaws', *BBC World*, www.bbc.co.uk, 26 September 2012

King, Jennifer, and Parthena Stavropoulos, 'Obituary: Mark 'Chopper' Read, Notorious Gangster and Children's Author, Dies Aged 58', *ABC News*, www.abc.net.au, 19 September 2014

Kizny, Tomasz, *GULAG: Life and Death Inside the Soviet Concentration Camps* (Buffalo, NY, 2004)

Knaus, Christopher, and Noor Gilliani, '"There's a lot of Repenting": Why Australian Prisoners Are Converting to Islam', *The Guardian*, www.theguardian.com, 5 January 2018

Knox, George W., 'The Problem of Gangs and Security Threat Groups (STG's) in American Prisons and Jails Today: Recent Findings from the 2012 NGRC National Gang/STG Survey', National Gang Research Survey, www.ngrc.com (2012)

Kupatadze, Alexander, *Organized Crime, Political Transitions and State Formation in Post-Soviet Eurasia* (London, 2012)

—, 'Prisons, Politics and Organized Crime: The Case of Kyrgyzstan', *Trends in Organized Crime*, XVII/3 (2014), pp. 141–60

Kynoch, Gary, 'From the Ninevites to the Hard Livings Gang: Township Gangsters and Urban Violence in Twentieth-century SAF', *African Studies*, LVIII/1 (1999), pp. 55–85

—, 'Of Compounds and Cellblocks: The Foundations of Violence in Johannesburg, 1890s–1950s', *Journal of Southern African Studies*, XXXVII/3 (2011), pp. 463–77

Langewiesche, William, 'City of Fear', *Vanity Fair* (April 2007), pp. 158–77

Lessing, Benjamin, 'The Danger of Dungeons: Prison Gangs and Incarcerated Militant Groups', *Small Arms Survey* (January 2010), pp. 157–83

—, 'How to Build a Criminal from Behind Bars: Prison Gangs and Projection of Power' Institute for the Study of Labor, 5 May 2014(?)

—, *Inside Out: The Challenge of Prison-based Criminal Organizations* (Washington, DC, 2016)

—, *Making Peace in Drug Wars: Crackdowns and Cartels in Latin America* (Cambridge, 2018)

Levenson, Deborah T., *Adios Nino: The Gangs of Guatemala City and the Politics of Death* (Durham, NC, 2013)

Lewis, Heather Parker, *God's Gangsters? The Number Gangs in South African Prisons* (Cape Town, 2010)

Lindegaard, Marie Rosenkrantz, and Sasha Gear, 'Violence makes Safe in South African Prisons: Prison Gangs, Violent Acts, and Victimization Among Inmates', *Focaal: Journal of Global and Historical Anthropology*, 68 (2014), pp. 33–54

Lotter, J. M., 'Prison Gangs in South Africa: A Description', *South African Journal of Sociology*, XVIIII/2 (1988), pp. 67–75

Lupo, Salvador, *History of the Mafia* (New York City, 2009)

McEvoy, Kieran, *Paramilitary Imprisonment in Northern Ireland: Resistance, Management, and Release* (Oxford, 2001)

McKinney, Wilson, *Fred Carrasco: The Heroin Merchant* (Austin, TX, 1975)

McMah, Lauren, and Megan Palin, 'Jailhouse Justice: A Look at Inmate Society in Australian Jails', www.news.com.au, 13 February 2016

MacNeil, Donald, *Journey to Hell: Inside the World's Most Violent Prison System* (Preston, 2006)

Manhire, Toby, 'Unlocking Maori Identity: Keeping New Zealand's Indigenous People Out of Jail', *The Guardian*, www.theguardian.com, 14 August 2015

Manrique, Luis Esteban G., 'A Parallel Power: Organized Crime in Latin America', Real Instituto Elcano, Madrid, http://realinstitutoelcano.org, 28 September 2006

Maree, Thomas, 'Meet the 28s General who left the Number and Lived to Tell the Tale through Film', *Daily Maverick*, www.dailymaverick.co.za, 13 March 2018

*S. v. Masaku* 1985 3 SA 908 (A); *S. v. Magubane* 1987 2 SA 663 (A) reaching the South African court system as a result of murders committed in prison confirm that gang members may be instructed to kill other prisoners. In such cases, the fact of gang membership may be regarded as extenuating circumstances.

Meek, John, 'Gangs in New Zealand Prisons', *Australia and New Zealand Journal of Criminology* (December 1992), pp. 255–77

Mehraj-ud-Din, Mir, *Crime and Criminal Justice System in India* (New Delhi, 1984)

Mendoza, John 'Boxer', *Nuestra Familia: A Broken Paradigm* (San Bernardino, CA, 2014)

Mendoza, Ramon, *Mexican Mafia: The Gang of Gangs, The Life of Ramon 'Mundo' Mendoza* (Santa Ana, CA, 2011)

—, and Rene Enriquez, *The Mexican Mafia Encyclopedia* (Santa Ana, CA, 2012)

Merueñas, Mark D., '"Sputnik," "Bahala Na" Gang members Share Cells with Maguindanao Massacre Detainees', *GMA News*, www.gmanews.com, 19 June 2011

Mirande, Alfredo, *Gringo Justice* (South Bend, IN, 1987)

Mitchell, Meghan M., Chantal Fahmy, David C. Pyrooz and Scott C. Decker, 'Criminal Crews, Codes, and Contexts: Differences and Similarities across the Code of the Street, Convict Code, Street Gangs, and Prison Gangs', *Deviant Behavior*, XXXVIII/10 (2017), pp. 1197–222

Montgomery, Reid H., and Gordon A. Crews, *A History of Correctional Violence: An Examination of Reported Causes of Riots and Disturbances* (Lanham, MD, 1998)

Morales, Gabriel C., *La Familia – The Family: Prison Gangs in America* (Des Moines, WA, 2008)

'More Bikies in Jail Creating Dangerous Prisons in South Australia', *ABC News*, www.abc.net.au, 28 July 2017

Morgan, Jonathan, and Sipho Madini, *White Paper, White Ink* (Johannesburg, 2014)

Morrill, Robert, *The Mexican Mafia, La Eme: The Story* (San Antonio, TX, 2007)

Narag, Raymund E., *Freedom and Death Inside the Jail: A Look into the Condition of the Quezon City Jail* (Manila, 2005)

—, and Sou Lee, 'Putting Out Fires: Understanding the Developmental Roles of Inmate Gangs in the Philippine Overcrowded Jails', *International Journal of Offender Therapy and Comparative Criminology*, 3 December 2017

Nasir, Kamaludeen Mohamed, 'Protected Sites: Reconceptualising Secret Societies in Colonial and Postcolonial Singapore', *Journal of Historical Sociology*, XXVIIII/2 (August 2014)

Nel, Sarah Lettie, 'A Critical Analysis of Gangsterism in South African Correctional Centres: The Case of Barberton Management Area', unpublished dissertation, University of South Africa, February 2017

'New Zealand Gangs Recruiting Bigger Number than the Army', *New Zealand Herald*, 12 February 2018

Newbold, Greg, *The Big Huey* (Auckland, 1982)

—, and Rawiri Taonui, '"Gangs", Te Ara', *Encyclopedia of New Zealand*, www.teara.govt.nz, 5 May 2011

—, —, *Punishment and Politics: The Maximum Security Prison in New Zealand* (Auckland, 1989)

Niehaus, Isak, 'Renegotiating Masculinity in the South African Lowveld: Narratives of Male-male Sex in Labour Compounds and Prisons, *African Studies*, LXI/1, pp. 77–97.

Novis, Roberta, 'Hard Times: Exploring the Complex Structures and Activities of Brazilian Prison Gangs', PhD Thesis, London School of Economics, September 2013

O'Ballance, Edgar, *Terror in Ireland* (Novato, CA, 1981)

Olenik, A. N., and A. Touraine, *Organized Crime, Prison and Post-Soviet Societies* (Farnham, 2003)

O'Reilly, Dennis, 'Looking After Our Patch', *Werewolf*, www.werewolf.co.nz, 3 September 2009

Pearlman, Jonathan, 'Australia Creates "Bikies-only" Prison to Deal with Warring Motorbike Gangs', *The Telegraph*, www.telegraph.co.uk, 15 October 2013

Peluso, Pasquale, 'The Roots of the Organized Criminal Underworld in Campania', *Sociology and Anthropology*, 1/2 (2013), pp. 118–34

Phelps, James, *Australia's Hardest Prison: Inside the Walls of Long Bay Jail* (North Sydney, 2016)

—, *Australia's Most Dangerous Prison: Behind the Walls of Goulburn Jail* (Sydney, 2016)

Phillips, Coretta, *The Multicultural Prison: Ethnicity, Masculinity, and Social Relations among Prisoners* (Oxford, 2012)

Pinnock, Don, *The Brotherhoods: Street Gangs and State Control in Cape Town* (Cape Town, 1983)

—, *Gang Town* (Cape Town, 2016)

Pohl, J. Otto, *The Stalinist Penal System* (Jefferson, NC, 1997)

Polgreen, Lydia, 'Rehabilitation Comes to a Prison and to Its Inmates', *New York Times*, 18 July 2011

Powis, Beverly, Louise Dixon and Jessica Woodhams, *Exploring the Nature of Muslim Groups and Related Gang Activity in Three High Security Prisons: Findings from Qualitative Research* (London, 2019)

Price, Thorton W. III, *Murder Unpunished: How the Aryan Brotherhood Murdered Waymond Small and Got Away with It* (Tucson, AZ, 2005)

Pyrooz, David C., and Scott H. Decker, *Competing for Control: Gangs and the Social Order of Prisons* (Cambridge, 2019)

Rafael, Tony, *The Mexican Mafia* (New York, 2007)

Reed, Daniel, *Beloved Country: South Africa's Silent Wars* (Oxford, 1994)

Reid, Tony, 'Paremoremo – the Prison that Drives Men Mad', *New Zealand Times*, 12 May 1985

Reynolds, Julia, *Blood in the Fields: Ten Years inside California's Nuestra Familia Gang* (Chicago, IL, 2014)

Rose, Jim, 'Extra Prisoners Are Nearly All Gang Members – that's Hardly a Crisis', *Dominion Post*, 29 May 2018

Roth, M. Garrett, and David Skarbek, 'Prison Gangs and the Community Responsibility System', *Review of Behavioral Economics*, 1/3 (2014), pp. 223–43

Roth, Mitchel P., *Prisons and Prison Systems: A Global Encyclopedia*
(Westport, CT, 2006)
—, *Global Organized Crime: A 21st Century Approach* (London, 2017)
Rozhnovsky, A. K., '"The Dead Man": In Prison, They Call Him by a
Nickname,' in *The Dostoevsky Archive: Firsthand Accounts of the
Novelist from Contemporaries' Memoirs and Rare Periodicals*, ed. Peter
Sekerin (Jefferson, NC, 1997), pp. 36–7
Ruddell, R., and S. Gottschall, 'Are All Gangs Equal Security Risks? An
Investigation of Gang Types and Prison Misconduct', *American Journal
of Criminal Justice*, XXXVI/3 (2011), pp. 265–79
Salvatore, Ricardo D., and Carlos Aguirre, eds, *The Birth of the Penitentiary
in Latin America: Essays on Criminology, Prison Reform, and Social
Control, 1830–1940* (Austin, TX, 1996)
Schrag, Clarence C., 'Leadership among Prison Inmates', *American
Sociological Review*, 19 February 1954
Schurink, W. J., 'The World of the *Wetslaners*: An Analysis of Some
Organizational Features in South African Prisons', *Acta criminologica*,
II/2 (1989), pp. 60–70
Sekerin, Peter, ed., *The Dostoevsky Archive: Firsthand Accounts of the
Novelist from Contemporaries' Memoirs and Rare Periodicals* (Jefferson,
NC, 1997)
Serio, Joseph D., *Investigating the Russian Mafia* (Durham, NC, 2008)
—, and Vyacheslav Razinkin, 'Thieves Professing the Code: The Traditional
Role of Vory v Zakone in Russia's Criminal World and Adaptations to
a New Social Reality', *Low Intensity Conflict and Law Enforcement*, IV/1
(Summer 1995), pp. 72–88
Shaw, Mark, *Hitmen for Hire: Exposing South Africa's Underworld*
(Johannesburg, 2017)
Shekhar, Raj, 'No Tattoos in Tihar but Gangs Inside are as Dangerous as the
Mexican Prisons,' *Time of India*, 9 June 2015
Silvester, John, 'Prison Gangs Flex Their Muscle Inside and Outside Jail', *The
Age*, www.theage.com.au, 28 April 2017
Sirisutthidacha, Warissara, and Dittita Titampruk, 'Patterns of Inmate
Subculture: A Qualitative Study of Thai Inmates', *International Journal
of Criminal Justice Sciences*, IX/1 (June 2014), pp. 94–109
Skarbek, David, 'Covenants without the Sword? Comparing Prison Self-
governance Globally', *American Political Science Review*, CX/4 (2016), pp.
845–62
—, 'Governance and Prison Gangs', *American Political Science Review*, CV/4
(November 2011), pp. 702–16
—, *The Social Order of the Underworld: How Prison Gangs Govern the
American Penal System* (New York, 2014)
—, and Courtney Michaluk, 'To End Prison Gangs, It's Time to Break Up
the Largest Prisons', *Politico*, www.politico.com, 13 May 2015
—, and D. Freire, 'Prison Gangs,' in *Routledge Handbook of Corrections in
the United States*, ed. O. H. Griffin and V. H. Woodard (Abingdon, 2017),
pp. 399–409

Slabbert, M., and J. H. van Rooyen, *Some Implications of Tattooing In and Outside Prison*, Institute of Criminology, University of Cape Town, 1978

Slade, Gavin, *Reorganizing Crime: Mafia and Anti-mafia in Post-Soviet Georgia* (New York, 2011)

Small Arms Survey 2010: Gangs, Groups, and Guns (Cambridge, 2010)

Smit, Van Zyl, *Prison Law and Practice* (Johannesburg, 1992), pp. 48–50

Sou, Lee, and Raymund E. Narag, 'Fanning the Flames: Understanding Gang Involvement Among Philippine Prisoners,' *International Journal of Offender Therapy and Comparative Criminology*, 5 September 2018

Spillane, Joseph F., *Coxsackie: The Life and Death of Prison Reform* (Baltimore, MD, 2014)

Steinberg, Jonny, *Nongoloza's Children: Western Cape Prison Gangs: During and After Apartheid*, Centre for the Study of Violence and Reconciliation, www.csvr.org.za (1994)

—, *The Number: One Man's Search for Identity in the Cape Underworld and Prison Gangs* (Johannesburg, 2008)

Stephenson, Svetlana, *Gangs of Russia: From the Streets to the Corridors of Power* (Ithaca, NY, 2015)

Suttner, Raymond, *Inside Apartheid's Prison: Notes and Letter of Struggle* (Melbourne, 2001)

Sykes, Gresham, *The Society of Captives: A Study of Maximum Security Prison* (Princeton, NJ, 1958)

—, and S. L. Messenger, 'The Inmate Social System', in *Theoretical Studies in Social Organization of the Prison*, ed. Richard Cloward, Donald Cressey and G. H. Grosser (New York, 1960), pp. 5–19

Tesoro, Ven J., 'Prison Gangs: A Discussion', in *Organized Crime in the Philippines: Prison Gangs in Particular*, 7 July 2011

Thomas, D. M., *Alexander Solzhenitsyn: A Century in His Life* (New York, 1998)

Thomas, J. E., and Alex Stewart, *Imprisonment in Western Australia: Evolution, Theory and Practice* (Nedlands, Australia, 1978)

Tops, Pieter, and Ronald van der Wal, 'Exploration of Organised Crime and "Undermining" in Sweden', www.kennisopenbaarbestuur.nl

Train, Arthur, *Courts, Criminals and the Camorra* (New York, 1912)

Trammell, Rebecca, 'Values, Rules, and Keeping the Peace: How Men describe Order and the Inmate Code in California Prisons', *Deviant Behavior*, xxx/8 (2009), pp. 746–71

Trulson, Chad, and James W. Marquart, *First Available Cell* (Austin, TX, 2009)

'Two Inmates Dead, over a Dozen Injured in Gang War in Delhi's Tihar Jail', NDTV, www.ndtv.com, 8 October 2015

United Nations Office on Drugs and Crime, *Handbook on the Management of Violent Extremist Prisoners and the Prevention of Radicalization to Violence in Prisons* (New York, 2016)

Useem, Bert, and Peter Kimball, *States of Siege: U.S. Prison Riots, 1971–1986* (New York, 1989)

Valdez, Al, *Urban Street Terrorism: The Mexican Mafia and the Surenos* (Santa Ana, CA, 2011)

Valentine, Bill, *Gang Intelligence Manual: Identifying and Understanding Modern-day Violent Gangs in the United States* (Boulder, CO, 1995)

—, *Gangs and Their Tattoos: Identifying Gangbangers on the Street and in Prison* (Boulder, CO, 2000)

Van Onselen, Charles, *Studies in the Social and Economic History of the Witwatersrand, 1886–1914*, vol. I: *New Babylon* (New York, 1982)

—, *Studies in the Social and Economic History of the Witwatersrand, 1886–1914*, vol. II: *New Nineveh* (New York, 1982)

—, *The Small Matter of a Horse: The Life of 'Nongoloza' Mathebula, 1867–1948* (Johannesburg, 1984)

—, *The Fox and the Flies: The Secret Life of a Grotesque Master Criminal* (New York, 2007)

Van Zyl Smit, Dirk, *South African Prison Law and Practice* (Durban, 1992)

Varese, Federico, *The Russian Mafia: Private Protection in a New Market Economy* (New York, 2001)

—, 'The Society of the Vory-V-Zakone, 1930s–1950s', in *Russian and Post-Soviet Organized Crime*, ed. Mark Galeotti (Burlington, IN, 2002), pp. 7–30.

Vij-Aurora, Bhavna, 'Right to Justice Bill: Helplessness, Psychological Disorders Torture Indian Prisoners', *India Today*, 24 June 2011

Von Lampe, Klaus, *Organized Crime: Analyzing Illegal Activities, Criminal Structures, and Extra-legal Governance* (Los Angeles, CA, 2016)

Wainwright, Tom, *Narconomics: How to Run a Drug Cartel* (New York, 2016)

Ward, T. W., *Gangsters without Borders: An Ethnography of a Salvadoran Street Gang* (New York, 2013)

Watkinson, William, 'Italian Camorra Mafia Accused of Rigging State Prison Guard Jobs to Infiltrate Penal System', SKY *News*, 23 May 2016

'Why New Zealand Has So Many Gang Members', *The Economist*, www.economist.com, 14 February 2018

'Why Prison Gangs Aren't All Bad', CNN, www.cnn.com, 11 December 2015

Winter, Pahmi, 'Pulling the Teams Out of the Dark Room: The Politicization of the Mongrel Mob', in *Gangs and Youth Subcultures: International Explorations*, ed. Kayleen Hazlehurst and Cameron Hazlehurst (New Brunswick, NJ, 1998), pp. 245–66

Winterdyk, John, and Rick Ruddell, 'Managing Prison Gangs: Results from a Survey of U.S. Prison Systems', *Journal of Criminal Justice*, XXXVIII/4 (2010), pp. 730–36

Wolf, Sonja, 'Street Gangs of El Salvador', in *Maras: Gang Violence and Security in Central America*, ed. Thomas Bruneau, Lucia Dammert and Elizabeth Skinner (Austin, TX, 2011), pp. 43–69

Wood, Callum, 'Radical Australian Prisons', *The Trumpet*, www.thetrumpet. com, 8 June 2016

Wood, Graeme, 'How Gangs Took Over Prisons', *The Atlantic*, www. theatalantic.com (October 2014)

Wood, J. L., 'Gang Activity in English Prisons: The Prisoners' Perspective', *Psychology Crime and Law*, XII/6 (2006), pp. 605–17

Yap, D. J., '10 Gangs Hold Key to the Good Life in Prison', *Inquirer News*, http://newsinfo.inquirer.net, 10 June 2011

# ACKNOWLEDGEMENTS

This book has had a very long gestation period and thankfully Reaktion Books has been nothing but patient waiting for this baby to arrive. First of all, I want to thank publisher Michael Leaman for his support of this project. You couldn't ask for a more communicative publisher. Managing editor Martha Jay and editor Phoebe Colley made sure I was in step with the book's production schedule. This richly illustrated book is a testament to the hard work of Alex Ciobanu, assistant to the publisher. Alex played an enormous role in selecting photos and getting photo permissions. The diligent proofreading of Ann Kay caught numerous authorial faux pas and literary infelicities. Thanks to art director Simon McFadden for his eye for marketing. Finally, several of my colleagues have read parts of the manuscript and have offered excellent suggestions that have made this a better book than it would otherwise have been. Recommendations by Russian mafia expert Dr Joe Serio made sure my chapter on the Russian gulag was historically and culturally accurate. Dr Chad Trulson at the University of North Texas, my go-to Texas prison expert, offered valuable advice and was highly supportive as I tortured him with each chapter. Finally, this book was made so much better thanks to my multilingual wife, Ines Papandrea, who has suffered through my many book projects and provided unparalleled proofreading on each one. She has read every single word, page and chapter as they were written, offering critical advice at every step of the project.

# PHOTO ACKNOWLEDGEMENTS

The author and publishers wish to express their thanks to the below sources of illustrative material and/or permission to reproduce it:

Photo Enzo Abramo/Pixabay: p. 40; photo Ajay Sood Travelure/www.travelure.in: pp. 172–3; photo Andressa Anholete/AFP via Getty Images: p. 290; photos Arizona Department of Corrections, Phoenix: p. 278; photo Noel Celis/AFP via Getty Images: p. 166; City Government of Muntinlupa: p. 14; photo Leonel Cruz/AFP via Getty Images: p. 323; photo courtesy Diario *La Hora*, Guatemala: p. 326; photos El Paso County Sheriff's Department, Corrections Gang Unit/Gang Intelligence Unit of the West Texas HIDTA: p. 333; photos Federal Bureau of Investigation (FBI), U.S. Department of Justice: pp. 22, 255, 281, 315, 316–17; photo Marcel Gnauk/Pixabay: p. 149; from George Kennan, *Siberia and the Exile System*, vol. II (New York, 1891), photo courtesy Robarts Library, University of Toronto: p. 54; Library of Congress, Prints and Photographs Division, Washington, DC: pp. 6, 30, 55, 56, 58; from Cesare Lombroso, *L'homme criminel: Atlas*, 2nd edn (Paris, 1895), photo courtesy Getty Research Institute, Los Angeles: pp. 44–5; photo Steve Lovegrove/Shutterstock.com: p. 187; photo Marty Melville/Getty Images: p. 143; National Library of Ireland, Dublin: p. 220; © Lee-Ann Olwage, reproduced with permission: p. 89; photo courtesy Periódico *Claridad*/Periódico de la Nación Puertorriqueña, Inc.: p. 338; Public Record Office of Northern Ireland (PRONI), Belfast: p. 214; photo Mitchel P. Roth: p. 27; © Jono Rotman, reproduced with permission: p. 135; photo Dean Sewell/Sydney Morning Herald/Fairfax Media via Getty Images: p. 122; photo Bhawan Singh/India Today Group via Getty Images: p. 175; photo Stringer/AFP via Getty Images: p. 151; © Mikhael Subotzky, courtesy Goodman Gallery: pp. 78–9; photo Texas District and County Attorneys Association (TDCAA), Austin: p. 263; photo U.S. Customs and Border Protection: p. 243; photo U.S. Geological Survey (USGS), Department of the Interior: p. 336; photos U.S. Immigration and Customs Enforcement: p. 313; photos Virginia Department of Corrections, Richmond: p. 258; photo Mark A. Wilson: p. 217.

# INDEX